*Published under the auspices of
the Center for Japanese Studies
University of California, Berkeley*

The Self-Made Man
in Meiji Japanese Thought

The Self-Made Man in Meiji Japanese Thought

from Samurai to Salary Man

EARL H. KINMONTH

UNIVERSITY OF CALIFORNIA PRESS
Berkeley · Los Angeles · London

University of California Press
Berkeley and Los Angeles, California

University of California Press, Ltd.
London, England

© 1981 by
The Regents of the University of California

Printed in the United States of America

1 2 3 4 5 6 7 8 9

Library of Congress Cataloging in Publication Data

Kinmonth, Earl H   1946–
 The self-made man in Meiji Japanese thought.

 Revision of thesis, University of Wisconsin—Madison, 1974.
  Bibliography: p.
  Includes index.
  1. Men—Japan. 2. Men —Japan—Psychology.
 3. Achievement motivation. 4. Occupational mobility—Japan. 5. Middle classes—Japan—History.
 6. Success. I. Title.
 HQ1090.7.J3K56   1981   305.5'5'0952   80-17984
 ISBN 0-520-04159-3

for Hosoda Tamako

Contents

Acknowledgments		ix
Introduction		1
1	Self-Help: Victorian, Confucian, Samurai	9
2	Study for Wealth and Honor	44
3	Political Youth	81
4	The Stabilized Social Order	117
5	Success!	153
6	Anguished Youth	206
7	New Ethics for a New Generation	241
8	Afterward: The Sarariiman (Salary Man)	277
	Conclusion: The Self-Made Man and the Japanese Sense of Self	326
Appendix: *Eisai shinshi* Contributors and Contributions		353
Bibliography		357
Index		373

Acknowledgments

This book is a substantial revision of my doctoral dissertation "The Self-Made Man in Meiji Japanese Thought," the result of three years (1971–1974) of research conducted in Japan. Among the many Japanese to whom I owe a great debt of gratitude, Professor Sumiya Mikio, my advisor at Tokyo University, must be thanked first. His writings provided some of the first direction for my dissertation, and during my stay in Japan, Professor Sumiya gave freely of his time, reading and commenting on my first drafts, lending materials, and aiding my research in ways too numerous to mention. Mrs. Uchida, his research assistant, also made great and gracious efforts on my behalf.

Various other Japanese scholars shared with me their ideas concerning Japanese conceptions of self-advancement, including Mita Munesuke of Tokyo University, Okawada Tsunetada of Kokugakuin University, and Funahashi Naomichi of Hōsei University. I am most appreciative of their willingness to discuss their ideas with me. On an even more fundamental level, I must thank the staff of the Inter-University ("Stanford") Center for Japanese Language Studies in Tokyo for helping to cushion the many frustrations and aggravations involved in setting up housekeeping and research in Japan and for their heroic efforts in helping me toward a useful command of the Japanese language. The staff of the Meiji Newspaper and Magazine Archive (Meiji Shinbun Zasshi Bunko) at Tokyo University was most helpful in finding materials for me and in providing introductions to other collections. Revision of the original manuscript de-

ACKNOWLEDGMENTS

pended on the sources and assistance provided by the East Asiatic Library, University of California, Berkeley.

In the United States my deepest debt is to Professor Harry Harootunian of the University of Chicago. This essay was begun under Professor Harootunian, and his continued interest and comments through numerous revisions have helped to give such direction as it possesses, although I must take responsibility for any confusion that remains. Professor John Dower of the University of Wisconsin, Madison, gave invaluable assistance at the dissertation stage. Both Professor Harootunian and Professor Dower have provided aid and advice in other areas, for which no amount of thanks is adequate.

Professor Solomon B. Levine and Professor Maurice Meisner of the University of Wisconsin, Madison, must be thanked for their efforts on my behalf as a graduate student and for stimulating my interest in areas outside of Japanese history, leading me to a knowledge that broadened my perspective on the Japanese self-made man. Professors Robert J. Smith at Cornell, Jay Rubin at the University of Washington, Henry Dewitt Smith, II, at the University of California, Santa Barbara, and Peter Duus at Stanford University have aided me by reading and commenting on all or part of this manuscript. Professor K. C. Liu at the University of California, Davis, provided gracious and expert counsel on Chinese language usage, and students Tani Barlow and Mari Mayeda asked many thoughtful questions that helped me to clarify my own thinking and expression during the course of revision. In the five-year progress of this book from dissertation to final manuscript, the continued and patient interest of Philip Lilienthal of the University of California Press was an invaluable and appreciated incentive, and the efforts of Phyllis Killen and Gladys Castor of the Press have done much to make the manuscript into a book.

As is perhaps appropriate to a study of the self-made man, no grants deserving or requiring acknowledgment were received. In this context Professors Leonard Weiss and Jeffrey Williamson of the University of Wisconsin, Madison, are warmly thanked for employment opportunities they extended to me as a graduate student. Without that employment and the training in computer programming it provided for subsequent employment, this study could not have been financed.

ACKNOWLEDGMENTS

Finally, Professor Takeuchi Yō of Kansai University deserves a special note of thanks. Perhaps the only Japanese scholar now working seriously on the subject matter of this book, Professor Takeuchi was unknown to me until the final draft of this text was being typed. In a short period of time, he has become a most generous, thoughtful, and valuable critic, sharing materials and giving the final draft the sort of reading that only a Japanese scholar familiar with the subject and sources could. While I must take full responsibility for the errors of fact and interpretation that remain, Professor Takeuchi has helped me to reduce their number substantially.

The Association for Asian Studies has permitted the use of material which originally appeared as "Fukuzawa Reconsidered: *Gakumon no susume* and Its Audience," *Journal of Asian Studies* 37:4 (August 1978): 677–696. Portions of "Nakamura Keiu and Samuel Smiles: A Victorian Confucian and a Confucian," *American Historical Review* 85 (June 1980): 535–556, are used with permission of the American Historical Association.

My wife Yoshiko assisted in the romanization of the notes and the bibliography. This book is dedicated to the memory of her mother who graciously suffered through the years of its writing but who did not live to see its completion.

Earl H. Kinmonth
University of California, Davis
January 1980

Introduction

Japan today is known as a nation of achievers, even overachievers, whose competitive instincts and desires to be number one rival or exceed those traditionally attributed to Americans. Perhaps no feature of contemporary Japanese society has attracted as much attention abroad as its series of "examination hells" (*shiken jigoku*) that determine admission to elite schools and the future prospects of young men who would rise in the world as employees (salary men) in prestigious companies and government agencies. This pattern of competition is not, however, a recent development. It existed before World War II and may be traced to institutions that first became significant during the Meiji era (1868–1912) and to even earlier ideals. The white-collar worker, or salary man (*sarariiman*), of today, his ethos, and the institutions in which he works and acquires his status, are the product of nineteenth-century developments.

Beginning with an analysis of *Self-Help* by Samuel Smiles and its popularity among samurai in the 1870s, this book describes the changes that occurred as the ideal of self-advancement through education and salaried employment spread from its samurai origins to the general populace in the next fifty years. This is a study in part in intellectual history, not in the conventional sense, which usually involves the study of a discrete individual, but in describing the evolution of a system which all members of the Japanese intelligentsia have experienced and in describing an ethos to which they had to subscribe in order to obtain their education and subsequent employment. The thought described here was part of would-be elite and not of popular culture. The ethos that appears in it belonged not to the Japanese as a whole but to those young men who sought to become the political, business, and intellectual leaders of modern Japan. This is the story of the emergence of Japan's "new middle class" and the struggles and sacrifices made by those young men who sought to become members of this ever expanding group.

The sources used in this study range in time from seventeenth-century samurai family codes to guides for unemployed college and university graduates of the 1930s. By type and authorship they range from tracts and comments by some of the most noted intellectuals of the Meiji period to anonymous advertisements and cartoons in mass circulation magazines and newspapers. Schoolboy compositions and letters to advice columns, mostly by young men who are otherwise unknown, give a unique aspirant's view of the quest for self-advancement and the changing competitive environment. Most attention is given to a variety of journals and periodicals written for, and sometimes written by, young men who sought to raise themselves in the world.

The choice of sources reflects a belief that to trace out the historical development of Japanese thinking about self-advancement, it is best to examine writings by and for those seeking to advance. Previous scholarship touching on Japanese thought about personal achievement and advancement has, for the most part, relied on materials such as biography and autobiography or on formulas assembled by intellectuals and religious thinkers. Neither corpus of literature is satisfactory in this context. Biography and autobiography are inherently the products of a period later than the one they nominally describe, and in Japan the biography of anyone who has risen to any prominence from obscure origins is almost invariably hagiography. All types of biography exist only for those who have succeeded in fairly large measure and not for the majority who try and fail or who achieve only a limited rise in the world. Intellectual and religious thinkers may or may not be in touch with popular sentiment. Even when a thinker can be demonstrated to have been popular and widely read, there is still no a priori reason to assume that followers accepted or understood the various ideas he put forward in the proportion or form he himself intended.

The original motivation for this study was the failure of scholarship based on the types of sources criticized above to account for

INTRODUCTION

certain long-known bits of data that seemed to bear on the achievement orientation of Japanese. Among the challenging claims made concerning striving in Japan was the assertion that Meiji-era entrepreneurs had been motivated by a concern for community benefit rather than individual profit. Closely related to this assertion was the idea that there existed a contrasting Western, or at least Anglo-American, tradition of thinking and writing about advancement and achievement that was centered on individual competition and was concerned solely with the maximization of individual profit, unlike Japanese traditions that stressed harmony, group effort, and communal benefit.[1]

Given that such classic Anglo-American works on self-advancement as *Self-Help* by Samuel Smiles and *Pushing to the Front* by Orison Swett Marden had both been best sellers in Meiji Japan, it seemed that the distinction made between Anglo-American and Japanese traditions had, at the very least, to be overdrawn. Otherwise these works would have been incomprehensible to Japanese or greeted with extreme hostility. The failure of Meiji observers to describe contemporary entrepreneurs as anything but profit-motivated raised the issue of when they had first begun to appear community-centered and to whom, if they had not so appeared to their contemporaries, those in a position to observe their activities most thoroughly. Resolution of the apparent contradiction between the picture of Japanese striving that is found in scholarship published in the United States in the 1950s and 1960s and that appearing in the raw data of Japanese history was the first goal of this study.

The issue of community-centered versus profit-centered entrepreneurs soon turned out to be a problem in American political history rather than in the economic or social history of Japan. The community-centered entrepreneur existed only in the biographies, autobiographies, and hagiographies written during the 1920s and 1930s when Japanese businessmen were coming under attack from all

---

1. Among the works that generated the first problems explored in this study, the following were especially important: Gustav Ranis, "The Community Centered Entrepreneur in Japanese Development," *Explorations in Entrepreneurial History* 8:2 (December 1955): 80–98; Johannes Hirschmeier, *The Origins of Entrepreneurship in Meiji Japan* (Harvard University Press, 1964); Byron K. Marshall, *Capitalism and Nationalism in Prewar Japan* (Stanford University Press, 1967); James Abegglen, *The Japanese Factory* (Free Press, 1958); and Robert N. Bellah, *Tokugawa Religion. The Values of Pre-Industrial Japan* (Free Press, 1957).

sides, especially the radical right. That this image had gained currency in the United States was to be explained in terms of Cold War politics. Scholars operating in the United States were looking for a nonsocialist model of modernization for late-developing countries. Japan and the community-centered entrepreneur fit neatly into this need by being both nonsocialist and apparently more benevolent than Anglo-American laissez faire types.[2] This study has been carried out on the assumption that unless hard evidence to the contrary exists, aspirants to self-advancement in Japan can be assumed to have been motivated by self-interest (or a functional equivalent), their statements to the contrary notwithstanding.

The dichotomy drawn between Anglo-American and Japanese traditions also soon proved to be an issue of limited potential for further research. A review of the extensive body of scholarship on Anglo-American writing concerning self-advancement revealed that there were actually a number of different modes of thought concerning the subject, some that fitted the individualistic profit-maximizer model, and a great many more that did not.[3] The same research made clear that the components of writing on self-advancement are determined less by national culture than by the class (or stratum) producing the literature, the stage and type of economic development, and the objective possibilities for advancement faced by the writers of or the audience for such literature. No attempt at comparing Japanese or Western writing or values has been made here because it is believed that nations are aggregations too large to be meaningful. If the nation is significant in this context, it is in terms of the relative strength of a

---

2. The community-centered entrepreneur and the related emphasis on the role of samurai in early Meiji economic development has been devastatingly challenged by Kozo Yamamura in a variety of writings, including *A Study of Samurai Income and Entrepreneurship* (Harvard University Press, 1974) and "A Re-Examination of Entrepreneurship in Meiji Japan (1868–1912)," *Economic History Review* 21:1 (1968): 144–158. While engaging in this debunking, Yamamura has not, however, dealt with the reasons that allowed the idea to be taken seriously in the first place. The overall context of American research on modernization has been addressed most extensively in John W. Dower, "E. H. Norman and the Uses of History," pp. 3–102 in E. Herbert Norman, *Origins of the Modern Japanese State*, ed. John W. Dower (Pantheon, 1975).

3. Among the most important works providing background on the Anglo-American tradition are the following: Reinhard Bendix, *Work and Authority in Industry* (Harper Torchbooks, 1963); John G. Cawelti, *Apostles of the Self-Made Man* (University of Chicago Press, 1965); Irwin G. Wyllie, *The Self-Made Man in America* (Rutgers University Press, 1954); and Richard M. Huber, *The American Idea of Success* (McGraw-Hill, 1971).

given concept of self-advancement compared with other competing concepts. Specific Anglo-American works popular in Japan are, however, carefully analyzed both in terms of what their reception says about Japanese thought and in terms of seeing previously obscured aspects of all too familiar writing by borrowing the eyes of readers who find this material new and exciting.

Just as the problems addressed by this study changed during the course of research, so too did the range of thought to be covered undergo redefinition. Originally this was to have been a survey that would deal with all varieties of Japanese writing on self-advancement during the Meiji era, comparing and contrasting within Japanese culture. The volume of identifiable writing quickly proved forbidding, and the task of tracking it down still more so, since much of it was not the sort of thing research libraries collected or individuals saved over the years. The study was then focused on just one type of self-advancement, that which was achieved through the acquisition of secondary and higher education followed by salaried employment in government, corporate, or academic bureaucracies. Materials for the study were restricted to those written for young men from the period when they first thought of secondary education through their first years of employment (or unemployment, as was frequently the case). It is this audience of possessors and would-be possessors of secondary and higher education that constitute the youth (*seinen*) referred to throughout the following pages.

The readers of the literature on self-advancement used as sources here were not all Japanese nor even a large fraction of all males. This study cannot be taken as descriptive of *Japanese* ideas about self-advancement. It touches only lightly, and then primarily for contrast, the concepts of self-advancement held by peasants, merchants, and those owning what Japanese call small and medium enterprises (*chūshō kigyō*). At the beginning of the Meiji era, those oriented to the academic-bureaucratic concept of advancement were distinctly a minority, even of young males. The literature utilized and described here must be thought of not as "popular culture" but as elite or would-be elite culture. It was not even characteristic of urban culture in general, for Japan had (and still has) two major urban centers with rather different orientations. The literature here all belonged to the Kantō (Tokyo) and says little about what Japanese in the Kansai (Kobe-Osaka-Kyoto) thought about self-advancement. Nevertheless, while those covered by this study were initially a small fraction of the Japanese people, their importance was considerably greater than their numbers. They became the academic, managerial, journalistic, and intellectual elite of modern Japan, and their strategic position resulted in the spread of their ethos to an ever larger portion of the Japanese people.

Even this much more narrowly focused study proved to be a wide-ranging project because Japanese scholars have written little in areas of interest, and with rare exceptions the scholarship is both hostile and poorly researched. There is nothing in Japanese comparable in quality or comprehensiveness to the work of Wyllie, Cawelti, Huber, Bendix, and others who have written about the Anglo-American case. Three or four articles, each covering a decade or less and restricted to one type of literature or even one single source, constitute the total of *well-researched* Japanese writing on self-advancement and the institutions that contain it.[4]

One cause for the neglect of this subject is the predominantly Marxist academic tradition in Japan. Because the literature of self-advancement is written by and for what might be styled the lower middle class, it is associated with a suspect and amorphous element of the class structure. Where it is not ignored, this literature and its associated competitive ethos offends humanitarian sensibilities. Some writers have been openly hostile and concerned with the allegedly pathological consequences of the quest for self-advancement in Japan. One monograph on the subject borrows the metaphor of cannibalism from "Diary of a Madman" by Chinese author Lu Hsun and applies it to Japanese concepts of advancement.[5] Another has styled the producers of one type of self-advancement literature as "merchants of death."[6] The noted intellectual historian Maruyama

4. The key word here is "well-researched." There is much writing, but most of it is impressionistic. The Japanese research without which this study could not have been done includes the following: Maeda Ai, "Meiji risshin shusse shugi no keifu," *Bungaku* 33:4 (April 1965): 10–21; Mita Munesuke, "'Risshin shusse shugi' no kōzō," in *Gendai Nihon no shinjō to ronri* (Chikuma shobō, 1971), pp. 185–215; Oka Yoshitake, "Nichiro sensō go ni okeru atarashii sedai no seichō," *Shisō*, no. 512 (February 1967): 1–13 [137–149], and no. 513 (March 1967): 89–104 [361–376]; and Okawada Tsunetada, "Seinen ron to sedai ron," *Shisō*, no. 514 (April 1964): 37–57. A sampling of the more typical impressionistic treatments is to be found in Kadowaki Atsushi, ed., "Risshin shusse," *Gendai no esupuri*, no. 118 (May 1977).

5. Ogawa Tarō, *Risshin shusse shugi no kyōiku* (Reimei shobō, 1968).

6. Shinbori Michiya, *Gakureki: jitsuryoku shugi o habamu mono* (Daiyamondo sha, 1966), p. 100.

INTRODUCTION

Masao has described the success ethic in prewar Japan as joining with nationalism to lead Japan into decay and fascism.[7]

Marxist or humanitarian thought is not, however, sufficient to explain the neglect or the hostility. Elitism, which coexists with the two more noble strains of thought, is a major factor. The situation in Japan would appear to be similar to Europe, where scholars have also done little with the lower middle class, its literature, and its ethos. As one observer of this pattern in European scholarship has observed, so too of Japan: "Could it be that social scientists are hesitant to expose the aspirations, life-style, and world view of the social class in which so many of them originate and from which they seek to escape?"[8]

This hostility and neglect mean that any attempt to study the subject of self-advancement literature in Japan meets with problems not faced in research on other subjects. Indifference and an inability to understand why anyone would want to study this literature represent the modal responses of scholars approached concerning the subject. More important, there is relatively little scholarship to be drawn on for any such study. The few well-researched articles have been invaluable, but even with them large areas have been left uncovered and beyond the reach of a foreign researcher. Inspirational biography and fiction had to be excluded from any consideration because of the volume of material and the absence of prior research concerning these two popular components of the literature on self-advancement.

At least three areas essential to the subject under consideration have been studied either not at all or without sufficient rigor to allow reliance on the published research. No work has been done on samurai aspirations during the Tokugawa period or on any literature that may have addressed itself to their desires.[9] The prewar examination system for secondary and higher education has received only the most casual, fragmentary, and impressionistic treatments. White-

7. Maruyama Masao, *Thought and Behavior in Modern Japanese Politics*, ed. by Ivan Morris (Oxford University Press, 1969), p. 7.

8. Arno J. Mayer, "The Lower Middle Class as a Historical Problem," *Journal of Modern History* 47:3 (1975): 409. The failure of European writers and specialists on Europe to treat with the literature corresponding to that discussed here prevented the inclusion of an originally intended section comparing European and Japanese writing for would-be white-collar employees.

9. Some research has been done on the idea of meritocracy during the Tokugawa period, but while this is a reflection of samurai aspirations, such writing is several

collar workers, their life-style, employment, and compensation, have been given only journalistic coverage, and standard histories of the labor and social movements virtually ignore their existence, as do major statistical series. These areas are deserving of much more intensive study, and the work presented here must be regarded as only a meager fraction of what can and should be done.

If the weaknesses of the present study arouse others to further research and rebuttal, I shall be delighted. A *thoroughly researched* challenge to or expansion on what has been done here would benefit scholars on both sides of the Pacific. Such a study would help to wean American students of Japanese thought from their dependency on *denki* (biography) and *zenshū* (collected works) that gives a steady flow of detailed histories about dull people or those who are dulled by the genre. Those Japanese writers who are bound by the chains of nineteenth-century Marxism and concern with the prewar "imperial system" (*tennōsei*), producing a seemingly endless succession of jargon-ridden books plowing and replowing the same material to the point of mind-numbing dullness, might find some new issues to explore and possibly even some new answers to the question of who supported militarism and why. Those who adhere to folklorist impressionism and make gross generalizations and formulate cosmic theories about the alleged differences between Japan and "the West," citing only trivial anecdotes and isolated personal experiences as evidence, might find that there are indeed differences and techniques to identify them, but their nature and magnitude are not necessarily what many Japanese would like to believe.

---

steps removed from the lives of ordinary samurai. See Thomas C. Smith, "'Merit' as Ideology in Tokugawa Japan," pp. 71–90 in *Aspects of Social Change in Modern Japan*, ed. Ronald P. Dore (Princeton University Press, 1967), and Ronald P. Dore, *Education in Tokugawa Japan* (Routledge and Kegan Paul, 1965).

Self-Help: Victorian, Confucian, Samurai | 1

In early 1868 (Meiji 1), shortly after they had toppled the former regime, the leaders of the new Meiji government issued a proclamation known as the Charter Oath. One provision of this oath stated, "The common people, no less than the civil and military officials, shall each be allowed to pursue [their] own calling[s] so that there shall be no discontent."[1] This implied that the new Meiji government was dedicated to the dismantling of the social structure of the former regime, which had been based largely on hereditary succession enforced by legal restraints and supported by ideologues who advised that, since wealth and honor were fixed by heaven, the individual ought not to seek to alter his status.[2] Nevertheless despite this implied commitment to reform, restrictions on personal activities, especially as they applied to the members of the samurai class, were carried over with little change from the preceding regime.[3] The

1. This translation is from Ryusaku Tsunoda, Wm. Theodore de Bary, and Donald Keene, eds., *Sources of Japanese Tradition* (Columbia University Press, 1964), vol. 2, p. 137.

2. The theme that heaven assigns wealth and honor (rank) at birth and that it therefore cannot be changed by human effort is found throughout Tokugawa writing. For examples that had wide circulation, see *Rikuyu engi tai-i*, in *Kyōjun*, vol. 5 in *Nihon kyōkasho taikei* (Kōdansha, 1969), p. 421, and Kaibara Ekiken, "Rakujun," in *Kaibara Ekiken*, vol. 14 of *Nihon no meicho*, ed. Matsuda Michio (Chūō kōron sha, 1969), p. 251, and "Yamato zokujun," ibid., p. 123.

3. The term *samurai* is used here with full knowledge that it was neither a term commonly used during the period under discussion nor a term that stood for a well-defined social category. For a cogent discussion of the problems involved in describing the Tokugawa class structure and defining the limits of the warrior class, see W. G. Beasley, *The Meiji Restoration* (Stanford University Press, 1972), pp. 22–34.

THE SELF-MADE MAN IN MEIJI JAPANESE THOUGHT

samurai continued to receive their hereditary stipends and to move about wearing the two swords that were the symbols of their membership in a hereditary ruling class.

In the face of this apparent continuity between the Tokugawa regime and its successors, there was one early indication that Meiji Japan was not to be simply Tokugawa Japan with a new set of leaders in political control. In early 1871 (Meiji 4) many members of the samurai class, especially government officials and educators, were lining up—even camping out overnight—to buy copies of a work that from its famous first line, "Heaven helps those who help themselves," was an attack on hereditary wealth and power.[4] This book was *Saikoku risshi hen*, a rendering by Nakamura Keiu (Masanao) of *Self-Help* by the English author Samuel Smiles.

This introduction was only the beginning of the popularity of *Self-Help* and *Saikoku risshi hen*. Reprints of the latter were still commercially viable as late as 1921 (Taishō 10), and new translations of the former were produced as late as 1938 (Shōwa 13).[5] Nevertheless, it is with the first decades of the Meiji era that the works are most intimately associated. Late Meiji writers who grew up with *Saikoku risshi hen* declared that it was "almost beyond imagination" to understand the impact of *Self-Help* on early Meiji youth or that it and *Character* (also by Smiles and translated by Nakamura) "had a greater influence over young men in the early [1870s] than any other book of the day."[6] To enumerate those Meiji figures who used *Saikoku risshi hen* in their own writings, praised it, or cited its influence on their lives would be to list the Meiji intellectual, aca-

---

4. That the readership was largely samurai is suggested by the language and style of *Saikoku risshi hen* (discussed below) and by various recollections. For example, Ishii Tamaji states that the initial readers of *Saikoku risshi hen* were officials and educators, a largely samurai group. Ishii Tamaji, *Nakamura Masanao den* (Seikō zasshi sha, 1907), pp. 10–11. One G. Takeda reported to Samuel Smiles that "almost all the high class of our fellow countrymen know what *Self-Help* is." Quoted in Samuel Smiles, *The Autobiography of Samuel Smiles, LL.D.*, ed. Thomas Mackay (E. P. Dutton, 1905), p. 230.

5. For the publication history of *Saikoku risshi hen* and derivatives, see Sangu Makoto, "'Saikoku risshi hen' oyobi sono ruisho ni tsuite," *Gakutō* 43:2 (February 1939): 20–25, and 43:3 (March 1939): 15–16.

6. See Yone Noguchi, "A True Founder of Empire," *Japan Times* (March 9, 1907), reproduced in Ishii, *Nakamura Masanao den*. See also Ukita Kazutami, "Educationalists of the Past and Their Share in the Modernization of Japan," in *Fifty Years of New Japan*, ed. Ōkuma Shigenobu (Dutton, 1909), vol. 2, p. 156.

demic, and journalistic world.[7] Not only did early Meiji Japanese read *Saikoku risshi hen*, they attended plays based on its stories, studied it as a textbook, and were treated to a variety of imitations and derivative works that to varying degrees held to the same ideas as the original.[8] Commonly, and quite correctly, *Saikoku risshi hen* is described as one of the "holy books" (*seisho*) of the Meiji era.

The first step in analyzing the popularity of *Self-Help* and *Saikoku risshi hen* in Japan must necessarily be an explication of the ideas in *Self-Help* and the motivation behind those ideas. This necessity arises because *Self-Help* is no longer popular and few readers can be expected to be familiar with it. Even more important, Anglo-American writing on personal advancement has changed radically since Smiles's day. The contemporary reader who has only been exposed to such later efforts as Norman Vincent Peale and his *Power of Positive Thinking*, or even worse, Robert J. Ringer and his *Looking Out for No. 1*, is likely to have a seriously distorted view of what a Victorian writer on self-culture might have to say. A second danger involves the possibility of confusing Smiles's ideas with those of roughly contemporary authors such as Horatio Alger who in fact preached a very different message. Fortunately, Smiles was an important and popular author whose ideas were an essential part of nineteenth-century Anglo-American history and well worth examining in detail. Once what Smiles had to say and why he said it is properly determined, his work becomes not only something of a bench mark and reference for examining what early Meiji Japanese did with *Self-Help* but also a standard by which subsequent changes in the Anglo-American tradition, particularly those works that were later introduced into Meiji Japan, may be set in proper historical perspective.[9]

    7. Such lists may be found in Mihashi Takeo, *Meiji zenki shisō shi bunken* (Meijidō shoten, 1976), pp. 80–86, and "Meishi sentaku no 'Hinsei shūyōsho,'" *Seikō* 3:1 (January 1, 1904): 9–18.
    8. For a listing of various editions of *Saikoku risshi hen* as an ethics text, see Torii Miwako, *Meiji ikō kyōkasho sōgō mokuroku I shōgakkō hen* (Komiya shoten, 1967), p. 18. Concerning plays based on *Saikoku risshi hen*, see Yanagida Izumi, *Meiji shoki honyaku bungaku no kenkyū*, vol. 5 of *Meiji bungaku kenkyū* (Shunjū sha, 1961), p. 169.
    9. The situation with Smiles and *Self-Help* is somewhat similar to that observed by Benjamin Schwartz in his work on Yen Fu and his translations of Herbert Spencer.

In saying that *Self-Help* may be used as a bench mark, the intention is not to imply that the work is in any way representative of *the* Western tradition of thinking about the self-made man. There is *no* such tradition. Even when the West is defined as Anglo-America and the period of consideration is limited to the mid-nineteenth century, there still remain too many diverse modes of writing about personal advancement to allow speaking of "the" tradition. Nevertheless, *Self-Help* can fulfill the bench-mark function because it was a major work in one of the more important genres of writing on the subject, the genre scholars of writing on personal advancement have designated "the character ethic."[10]

In the character ethic, accomplishment and advancement were

"I suspect it is not simply the obsolescence and mediocrity of his thought which explains the fact we no longer read his books. His synthesis may be a compendium of commonplace and typical nineteenth century views, but many of these views still form part of the unstated creed of our age. In part, it is because so many of his notions are so widely accepted that they seem commonplace." See Benjamin Schwartz, *In Search of Wealth and Power* (Harvard University Press, 1964), p. 47. These ideas were not quite so commonplace for Yen Fu, nor as it turns out, were Smiles's ideas completely commonplace in Japan despite considerable precedents.

More important, because *some* of the ideas of thinkers such as Smiles and Spencer are now commonplace, imagined familiarity breeds contempt. This was brought home to me in countless personal encounters during the writing of this book. Among academics, both in Japan and in the United States, mere mention of the name Samuel Smiles usually brought snickers of imagined recognition and some statement that indicated that the respondent thought Smiles a crass apologist for materialism, a Victorian Babbitt or a Norman Vincent Peale, an English Horatio Alger, etc., etc. Several such views of Smiles have even found their way into print. Marleigh Ryan in her study of Futabatei Shimei writes, "Sycophantic, opportunistic, materialistic, Noboru is the very antithesis of the Confucian gentleman. He has learned well the lessons taught by such monuments to success as Samuel Smiles's *Self-Help*." Marleigh Grayer Ryan, *Japan's First Modern Novel: Ukigumo of Futabatei Shimei* (Columbia University Press, 1967), p. 171. Thomas P. Rohlen in describing a bank's efforts at indoctrination of its employees writes of "the themes of 'spiritual' strength and the psychology of accomplishment (reminiscent of Samuel Smiles and Norman Vincent Peale." Thomas P. Rohlen, *For Harmony and Strength: Japanese White-Collar Organization in Anthropological Perspective* (University of California Press, 1974), p. 202. Such misreading of Smiles is not confined to Japanologists. Travers notes similarly incorrect evaluations in European writing. See Timothy H. E. Travers, "Samuel Smiles and the Victorian Work Ethic," (Ph.D. dissertation, Yale University, 1970), pp. 210–211.

10. For a comparison of later American writing with the "character ethic," see Richard M. Huber, *The American Idea of Success* (McGraw-Hill, 1971), pp. 160 ff. Note that within the "character ethic" there is considerable variation; the explanation given below is most applicable to Smiles.

the products primarily of individual virtues of character: hard work, diligence, frugality, perseverance, attention to detail, and so forth. Developing these virtues was a task for the individual himself, and they and his performance were depicted as the sole factors determining achievement and advancement. The character ethic did not rely on any mechanisms outside the individual. As a noted scholar of Victorian England, Asa Briggs, has observed, "There were no fairy godmothers or fairy godfathers in Smiles assisting the thrifty hero to find money and success as there were in [Horatio] Alger's stories."[11] The character ethic, moreover, did not in fact concern itself with moneymaking or success in the first place. As typified by *Self-Help*, the character ethic defined advancement not as a publicly recognized increase in wealth and rank (success) but as the accomplishment of something that advanced modern civilization either in its material or its cultural aspects.[12] The character ethic largely ignored interpersonal relations. It did not tell you how to cultivate a "success personality" that would cause others to like and to favor you. It did not suggest, as did later American writing, that you could think your way to success or that you ought to live each day with pleasure. The character ethic emphasized rather than minimized the difficulties, especially the hard labor, involved in any type of accomplishment.[13]

Although it placed ultimate responsibility for advancement and accomplishment on the individual, the character ethic did not preclude mutual aid or cooperative groups. Nothing demonstrates this better than the genesis of *Self-Help*. It began as a series of lectures Samuel Smiles gave in 1845 to a mutual study group organized by young workmen in the city of Leeds. Smiles had lived in Leeds for a number of years, practicing medicine and editing a Radical newspaper. When he was approached by a group of young workmen "to talk to them a bit," he responded with a series of lectures entitled

---

11. Asa Briggs, *Victorian People* (Penguin Books, 1965), p. 126. For Alger in the American context, see John G. Cawelti, *Apostles of the Self-Made Man* (University of Chicago Press, 1965), pp. 101–124. A less analytical and rather gossipy biography of Alger, which is nonetheless worth reading, is Edwin P. Hoyt, *Horatio's Boys: The Life and Works of Horatio Alger, Jr.* (Chilton, 1974).

12. For a discussion of the difference between "success" and "achievement," see Karl Mannheim, *Essays on the Sociology of Knowledge*, ed. Paul Kecskemeti (Routledge and Kegan Paul, 1952), pp. 236–237.

13. Concerning the "personality ethic" and Norman Vincent Peale, see Huber, *American Idea*, pp. 316–317, and Cawelti, *Apostles*, pp. 209–218.

THE SELF-MADE MAN IN MEIJI JAPANESE THOUGHT

"The Education of the Working Classes." During a subsequent career as a secretary for several railroad companies operating in the vicinity of Leeds, Smiles continued to lecture on the subject of self-help for the working class and to embroider those lectures with ever more examples. In 1857 at a low point in his railroad career, Smiles assembled his notes and pieces of his lectures into the manuscript of *Self-Help*.[14] Initially, no publisher would accept his manuscript, and Smiles was forced to subsidize publication of it. His risk was well rewarded, however, for beginning in 1859 *Self-Help* started on a course that would see it sell some 160,000 copies in the next thirty years in England alone.[15]

There were also numerous translations of *Self-Help* into foreign languages of which Japanese was but one. During his later years Smiles was able to travel to a number of countries (but not to Japan) where *Self-Help* had been popular, receiving awards and acclaim. In Italy he was treated as visiting royalty. In England, Gladstone, George Eliot, and even Queen Victoria herself at one time or another acknowledged Smiles and praised his works.[16] After *Self-Help*, Smiles wrote four other didactic works of similar style of which three were published: *Character* (1871), *Thrift* (1875), and *Duty* (1880). All were translated into Japanese, but only *Self-Help*, through *Saikoku risshi hen*, was sufficiently popular to warrant discussion here.[17]

Anecdotal illustration was the key stylistic feature of Smiles's didactic writing. In *Self-Help* this meant nearly three-hundred different figures cited or introduced, ranging from Richard Arkwright to Francis Xavier and including such men as Benvenuto Cellini, Humphrey Davy, Isaac Newton, Granville Sharp, and James Watt. Many names were simply introduced as part of lists Smiles used to illustrate his points ("The common class of day laborers has given us . . . ," "Shoemakers have given us . . ."), but in other cases, including those mentioned above, he devoted several pages to each

---

14. Smiles, *Autobiography*, 131–134.

15. Travers reports that between 1859 and 1894, a total of 164,560 copies of *Self-Help* were sold. Travers, "Samuel Smiles," appendix F, p. 333. Smiles himself claimed that 258,000 were sold by 1905. Smiles, *Autobiography*, p. 223.

16. Briggs, *Victorian People*, p. 130. For other appreciations, see Smiles, *Autobiography*, pp. 224–231.

17. *Character* is discussed in Earl H. Kinmonth, "The Self-Made Man in Meiji Japanese Thought" (Ph.D. dissertation, University of Wisconsin, 1974), pp. 78–80.

model. Those models to whom Smiles gave the greatest attention were primarily men who had been technologically innovative manufacturers or scientists or engineers. He waxed most eloquent over all of these, especially innovative manufacturers.

Men such as these are fairly entitled to take rank as the Industrialized Heros of the civilized world. Their patient self-reliance amidst trials and difficulties, their courage and perseverance in the pursuit of worthy objects, are not less heroic of their kind than the bravery and devotion of the soldier and sailor, whose duty it is heroically to defend what these valiant leaders of industry have so heroically achieved.[18]

These were the men Smiles most admired personally and who best illustrated and embodied the virtues he wished to teach through *Self-Help*.

First among these virtues was "perseverance," which was part of the subtitle of *Self-Help*. For Smiles perseverance was the ability to carry on in the face of adversity and minimal progress. Smiles's message was that "great results can not be achieved at once; and we must be satisfied to advance in life as we walk, step by step."[19] Such an injunction by itself may be used to caution against impatience and rash expectations of advancement in a stagnant system, but Smiles was more concerned with teaching a sort of elementary "scientific method," and he went into some detail on this. His "step by step" was always in the context of progress toward some ultimate achievement, and not mere endurance. This concern with scientific achievement reflected Smiles's own interests. He was trained as a medical doctor at Edinburgh, although he practiced only sporadically. He demonstrated his interest in science and engineering in a series of biographies, beginning with one of George Stephenson in 1857. Smiles took considerable pains with these biographies, doing substantial original research and conducting extensive interviews, giving attention to both the technical accomplishments and the personal attributes of those he wrote about. There is sufficient sub-

---

18. As might be imagined, *Self-Help* is available in a large number of different editions. I have used Samuel Smiles, *Self-Help; with Illustrations of Conduct and Perseverance* (London: John Murray, 1876). This appears to be a slightly later printing of the second (revised) edition text which Nakamura used for *Saikoku risshi hen*. Hereafter this text is cited as *SH*. The quote is from *SH*, p. 93.

19. *SH*, p. 98.

stance to these works that they are still read by scholars of this period, especially his series *Lives of the Engineers*.[20]

Despite his veneration of men who had been technologically and scientifically creative, Smiles did not attribute to them extraordinary characteristics. Least of all did he attribute to them genius. Instead, he claimed that "the men who have most moved the world, have not been so much men of genius, strictly so called, as men of intense mediocre abilities and untiring perseverance."[21] Genius as it appeared in *Self-Help* was not raw intelligence but the ability to work diligently at a single goal, to combine simple principles and common knowledge together and turn them to new ends, putting together that which many had seen before but no one else had been able to use.[22] Smiles asserted that all who were at least mediocre could work what they had into achievement by intense application and perseverance. Nevertheless, Smiles did not deny talent entirely. He argued that genius and talent without hard work and similar virtues were bound to come to naught.[23] Smiles did not seek to reduce invention to a series of mechanical steps carried out by methodical mediocrities. He vividly and sympathetically described a man, Bernard Palissy, who was consumed by his experimental quest until he was reduced to smashing his last unpawned furniture to kindling in order to fuel one last experiment as neighbors and wife stood by in shocked amazement.[24] Scientific experimentation in *Self-Help* belonged to an era before the think-tank and the research institute had been invented.

Innovative industrialists and inventors embodied the virtues Smiles admired, but he located the origin of those virtues in social circumstances rather than in a certain stratum of the middle class. Smiles was the supreme champion of humble origins. In *Self-Help* he repeatedly related subsequent accomplishment to the difficulties

20. The interest in Smiles's biographies is indicated by their continued publication. See for example, Samuel Smiles, *Selections from Lives of the Engineers*, ed. Thomas Parke Hughes (MIT Press, 1966).
21. *SH*, pp. 96–97.
22. See his discussion of James Watt in *SH*, pp. 30 ff., and *SH*, chap. 5, "Helps and Opportunities—Scientific Pursuits."
23. This point is also made in terms of artistic creation. See *SH*, chap. 6, "Workers in Art."
24. *SH*, pp. 69 ff, esp. p. 74.

that individuals experienced during their formative years. Poverty acquired a special mystique in *Self-Help*:

> Indeed, so far from poverty being a misfortune, it may, by vigorous self-help be converted into a blessing; rousing a man to that struggle with the world in which, though some may purchase ease by degradation, the right-minded, and the true-hearted find strength, confidence and triumph.[25]

In some instances this assertion seems almost to be a glorification of poverty and might be read as an effort to make the poor content with their lot. Nevertheless, Smiles clearly stated that he did not expect the poor to be content but instead to aim at improvement. Most certainly he did not call for this improvement to be achieved by revolutionary means; but that he could consider dissatisfaction with one's lot in life in positive terms represented a significant change from earlier British thought.[26] Moreover, Smiles, in making such an assertion of the benefits of poverty, framed his statements in terms of "may." He did not play down the difficulties of such a rise, nor did he try to portray it as automatic. By the same token Smiles was not a blind and uncritical believer in laissez faire, though he shared many of its assumptions and vocabulary. He was particularly critical of what he called the "let alone" philosophy, which allowed food to be poisoned and cities to become dirty and crime ridden.[27]

While championing those of humble origins, Smiles did not celebrate all who had risen. The mere acquisition of fortune by a man of humble origin had no value for him. He declared, "Riches are no proof whatever of moral worth; and their glitter often serves only to draw attention to the worthlessness of their possessor, as the light of the glowworm reveals the grub."[28] He continually warned throughout *Self-Help* that the self-culture he was expounding was not to be seen just as a means to making money.[29] He professed to be disturbed that the original edition of *Self-Help* had been misinterpreted as a "eulogy of selfishness" and rewrote the work in an attempt to prevent such misinterpretation. In the preface to the revised edition (1867), he commented, "It will also be found, from the examples of

25. *SH*, p. 19.
26. Reinhard Bendix, *Work and Authority in Industry* (Harper Torch Books, 1963), p. 113.
27. Briggs, *Victorian People*, pp. 133–134.
28. *SH*, p. 310.   29. *SH*, pp. 330–332.

literary, scientific men, artists, inventors, educators, philanthropists, missionaries, and martyrs, that the duty of helping one's self in the highest sense involves the helping of one's neighbors."[30] Smiles insisted that those possessing wealth had responsibilities, and a number of those models to whom he gave more than casual attention were philanthropists or men who had engaged in social activism of one type or another.[31]

Despite his concern for the workingman and his criticism of the wealthy, Smiles did not speak *for* a rising working-class consciousness: he spoke *to* such a consciousness. Smiles was speaking for a newly risen and still rising entrepreneurial class. His condemnation of wealth, particularly the inherited variety, and his celebration of humble birth reflected the claims of first-generation wealth against established hereditary power and privilege. This may be seen in the seventh chapter of *Self-Help* where Smiles departed from his stories of men of humble origin to deal with the English peerage. Even while confirming their claims to wealth and power, he did this by noting that the English peerage, in contrast to that of other countries, had been enriched by new blood coming up from below, by men who moved upward by "the diligent exercise of qualities in many respects of an ordinary character, but potent by force of application and industry."[32] Moreover, as Smiles went on to emphasize, there were many who would certainly move down, owing to the ill effects of inherited and unearned wealth.[33] This does not mean, however, that Smiles denied titles and rank; indeed, many of his examples end in such.[34] But for Smiles only those who had earned their position and wealth through an extraordinary display of ordinary talents were justified in their position, and he stressed that these ordinary qualities are found in all men. They were the exclusive privilege of no one class, least of all the peerage.[35] The only areas in which those born to wealth generally excelled, said Smiles, were politics and literature; but even in these fields he had a good supply of men of humble origin who had achieved.

30. *SH*, p. iv.
31. See Smiles's treatment of Jonas Hanway and Granville Sharp in *SH*, pp. 245–257.
32. Bendix, *Work*, p. 112; and *SH*, p. 222.
33. *SH*, p. 203.
34. For example, see Smiles's treatment of Sir William Patty in *SH*, pp. 212–216.
35. *SH*, pp. 19–24.

By attacking the immorality of the rich, by emphasizing the humble origins of men of achievement, and by describing as ordinary the qualities needed for advancement, Smiles worked to put the new industrialists into a position of moral leadership vis-à-vis the working class. In an era of rising class consciousness among workers, Smiles was in effect saying that there really was not all that much difference between industrialists and workers. The successful industrialist had arrived where he was, not by special privileges or foul means, but by more diligent application of what was available to all. Since the gains the industrialists had made had been achieved by their own efforts in utilizing qualities and values available to the working class as well, Smiles had an argument to meet demands for legislated help for workers and for franchise extension.[36] This thrust was quite explicit in *Self-Help*. Smiles declared that "over guidance and over government" invariably render people helpless, that "the value of legislation in human advancement has usually been much overestimated," and that voting for representatives every few years could have little effect on one's life, since more of an individual's life was shaped by his own efforts than by those of the government.[37]

Nevertheless, this aspect of his thought may easily be overemphasized. The bourgeoisie Smiles sought to speak for was a rather confident class, and it would be most incorrect to see him writing in a purely defensive tone.[38] Not only was the rise of members of the working class into the bourgeoisie not to be feared, it was to be welcomed.[39] Smiles continually emphasized that the worker too might move up from dependency and impoverishment through self-help, making his gospel one of hope and not just of work.[40]

A balanced appraisal of Smiles and his writing must recognize where they stood compared with earlier and still current ideas. When Smiles wrote *Self-Help*, aristocratic and mercantilist ideas that put small value on labor and frugality were still being voiced.[41]

---

36. Bendix, *Work*, p. 112.   37. *SH*, pp. 1–3.
38. Travers sees Smiles as uncomfortable with social mobility. See Travers, "Samuel Smiles," pp. 70–71.
39. In his preface to the revised edition of *Self-Help*, Smiles cites with favor the case of a worker who had risen to become an employer. See *SH*, p. ix.
40. Bendix, *Work*, p. 111.
41. The novels of Disraeli and Lytton discussed in chapter 3 are prime examples of the persistence of aristocratic values in Victorian England. Also, see Briggs, *Victorian People*, p. 141.

Against this attitude, Smiles was quite vehement and specific in his appreciation of labor and the laboring man. When he said, "Labor is not only a necessity and a duty, but a blessing: only the idler feels it to be a curse," he was not criticizing idle poor on welfare. He was asserting the value of work as an absolute for all people of all classes and ranks. Moreover, he went so far as to assert that labor was "not inconsistent with high mental culture," again a significant upgrading of the workingman in a society of strong aristocratic values.[42] Thus, for the most part, Smiles's treatment of the workingman was most sympathetic, and while he was no radical (in a modern sense), his assertion that "there is no reason why the condition of the average workman should not be a useful, honorable, respectable and happy one"[43] represented an appreciation and a respect for workers that was far from universal in the England in which he wrote.

When *Saikoku risshi hen* first appeared as a best seller in 1871 (Meiji 4), neither the political issues nor the social classes to which *Self-Help* had been addressed existed in Japan. There was no industrial bourgeoisie, no industrial labor force, no franchise, and no parliament. The issue of legislated aid versus self-help had no meaning in Japan. What then was the appeal of *Self-Help* and *Saikoku risshi hen*? For the translator, Nakamura Keiu, the chief attraction of *Self-Help* was this assertion by Smiles: "National progress is the sum of individual industry, energy, and uprightness, as national decay is of individual idleness, selfishness, and vice."[44] The relation between individual and national character expressed here was not part of an injunction against tampering with the free play of natural forces in the marketplace, nor was it seen as an argument against legislated aid to the working class. This was part of a formula for the achievement of national prosperity, security, and world peace.

In the preface he wrote to the first chapter of *Saikoku risshi hen*, Nakamura noted that he had been asked why he did not translate a work on military affairs. Explaining that it was a mistake to believe that the strength of Western nations was based on military might alone, he argued that Western nations were strong because their people followed the way of heaven (*tendō*), they had the right of autonomy (*jishu no ken*), and they enjoyed benevolent government.

42. *SH*, p. 28.   43. *SH*, p. 294.   44. *SH*, p. 3.

As for war, Nakamura could cite no less an authority than Napoleon to the effect that virtuous conduct (*tokkō*) was ten times as important as mere military might. Smiles himself had explained that a country was weak or strong according to the character of its people. To emphasize martial virtues and military affairs would be to invite war and killing, to go against the way of heaven that sought to have all men enjoy tranquility and happiness, not to have men and nations engage in military competition. Therefore, the way to national strength and social benefit was through the cultivation of peaceful virtues: respecting the will of heaven and doing good on the basis of a true heart. This was the way for the individual, the family, the nation, and the world. If men cultivated such virtues, the light of love and the wind of benevolence would spread to the four seas; clouds of affection and the spirit of harmony would envelop the universe.[45]

The Confucian-sounding expectations pinned on *Self-Help* were not just the reflection of the intellectual background that all educated Japanese of the period shared. Nakamura Keiu had been and for all practical purposes still was a Confucian scholar in the employ of the Tokugawa house.[46] Born in 1832 into an ambitious peasant family that had purchased samurai status, Nakamura had early shown intellectual brilliance. At age ten he won a scholarship to the Shōheikō (School of Prosperous Peace), the official Confucian academy of the Tokugawa house operated by the Hayashi family. He studied at the Shōheikō between 1848 and 1853 and upon graduation served the Tokugawa in various educational posts. In 1862 at the unusually young age of twenty-nine he was appointed a full-fledged Confucian scholar at the Shōheikō. Although educated and employed within one of the more conservative academies of the period, Nakamura had early tempered his Confucian learning with a secret

---

45. Nakamura Keiu, "Jijoron dai-ichi hen jo," in *Meiji keimō shisō shū*, ed. by Ōkubo Toshiaki, vol. 3 of *Meiji bungaku zenshū* (Chikuma shobo, 1967), pp. 283–284. An alternative source for this and the other prefaces is *Meiji shisōka shū*, vol. 13 of *Nihon gendai bungaku zenshū* (Kōdansha, 1968), pp. 89–100.

46. Biographical details of Nakamura are largely from Takahashi Masao, *Nakamura Keiu* (Yoshikawa kōbunkan, 1966). In addition, the following are useful: "Nakamura Masanao," in *Kindai bungaku sōsho*, ed. Shōwa joshi daigaku kindai bungaku kenkyū-shitsu (Shōwa joshi daigaku kōyō-kai, 1956), vol. 1, pp. 406–458; Maeda Ai, "Nakamura Keiu," *Bungaku* 33:10 (October 1965): 61–71; Yanagida Izumi, *Meiji shoki no bungaku shisō I*, vol. 4 of *Meiji bungaku kenkyū* (Shunjū sha, 1965), pp. 250–261; and Jerry K. Fisher, "The Meirokusha" (Ph.D. dissertation, University of Virginia, 1974).

study of Western works hidden inside his Confucian texts. When the Tokugawa policy on foreign studies changed, this surreptitiously acquired knowledge served him well. In 1866 he was chosen to go to London to study English and to chaperon younger students sent abroad by the Tokugawa government.

The England that Nakamura confronted was a particular England. It was Great Britain and Victorian England and the England of Samuel Smiles. It was England at virtually the height of its wealth and power, and it was more than enough to overawe Nakamura, who later remarked that the Chinese text[47] he had read before going to England had not prepared him to understand how such a tiny nation, let alone one ruled by a woman, could have humbled the Middle Kingdom in war. In contrast to the Chinese view of the English as fond of liquor, extravagant, and only clever with gadgets, Nakamura came to see the English as an exceptional people. They were a nation ruled by a parliament, the members of which were all learned. The people loved heaven and revered mankind. The workers were prudent and exercised self-restraint.[48]

Less than a year after Nakamura arrived in England, the Tokugawa regime was overthrown. After some debate, he and his charges decided to return to Japan. Before leaving, Nakamura sought advice on how he might transmit to the Japanese people that spirit he had discovered in England. In answer an English friend, H. U. Freeland, presented Nakamura with a copy of *Self-Help* (revised edition). On the return trip to Japan, Nakamura, in true Confucian fashion, occupied himself with the task of memorizing *Self-Help*. After his return to Japan, Nakamura, still a loyal retainer of the Tokugawa house, dutifully followed it into exile in Shizuoka. There he returned to his profession of educator, operating the local domainal school and working on his translation of *Self-Help*, a major undertaking considering the circumstances and the brevity of his training in the English language. Despite the difficulties of rendering the ideas of a work aimed at the British working class into terms comprehensible to Japanese for whom many features of feudalism were

---

47. Nakamura specifically refers to *Hai-kuo t'u-chih* by Wei Yuan. This was a geography written between 1844 and 1852.

48. These comments were contained in an afterword appended to the first book (chapter) of *Saikoku risshi hen*. See "Sho Saikoku risshi hen go," in *Meiji keimō shisō shū*, p. 286.

more than just a memory, the first hand-printed copies of *Saikoku risshi hen* were ready early in 1871 (Meiji 4).⁴⁹

Nakamura had no sooner completed translation of *Self-Help* than he turned to rendering *On Liberty* by J. S. Mill. This appeared in 1872 (Meiji 5) under the title *Jiyū no ri* [Principle of Freedom]. It too enjoyed a most favorable reception, later becoming one of the basic ideological tracts of the so-called movement for liberty and people's rights (*jiyū minken undō*).⁵⁰ Subsequently, Nakamura turned to a translation of *Character* by Smiles. This was published in 1878 (Meiji 11) under the title *Seiyō hinkō ron* [On Western Moral Conduct]. It enjoyed a significant though lesser reception than had *Saikoku risshi hen*. His version of *Thrift*, under the title *Seiyō setsuyō ron* [On Western Frugality], was published in 1886 (Meiji 19) but went largely unnoticed.⁵¹

Translation of *Saikoku risshi hen* was only the beginning of what proved to be a long and productive career of intellectual and social-welfare activity. As early as 1868 (Meiji 1) Nakamura had demonstrated an interest in Christianity. In 1871 (Meiji 4) he wrote a famous memorial on the subject entitled "Gi taiseijin jōsho" [Memorial on the Imitation of Westerners]. In this address to the emperor, he argued that while it was now official policy to adopt Western forms, Christianity was not tolerated, let alone encouraged. Christianity was, however, the source of the spirit and essence of Western civilization, the ultimate base from which the wealth and power of Western nations was derived. To attempt to adopt Western forms without Christianity was to seek to import the fruit of Western civilization without planting in Japan the tree that bore the fruit. Nakamura urged not only the toleration of Christianity but also that the emperor himself be baptized, as a model for the Japanese people.⁵² Although he phrased his public appeal in terms of national in-

49. Details of the printing and financing of *Saikoku risshi hen* may be found in Ōkubo Toshiaki, "Nakamura Keiu no shoki yōgaku shisō to 'Saikoku risshi hen' no yakujutsu oyobi kankō," *Shien* 26:2–3 (January 1966): 67–92.

50. Takahashi, *Nakamura Keiu*, pp. 102–109.

51. References to *Seiyō hinkō ron* appear frequently in the writings of Tokutomi Iichirō (discussed in chap. 3) and others. It is not discussed here because of its similarity to *Self-Help*. For the facts of publication, see Takahashi, *Nakamura Keiu*, pp. 110–111.

52. Nakamura Keiu, "Gi taiseijin jōsho," in *Meiji keimō shisō shū*, pp. 281–282. This memorial appeared in English, Japanese, and Chinese (*kanbun*) with and with-

terest, Nakamura, who was himself baptized as a Methodist in 1874 (Meiji 7), was more attracted by the charitable and social-welfare orientation of Christianity than he was by its utility in the quest for national wealth and power. As early as 1871 (Meiji 4) he had worked with missionaries to found a "mission home" for children of mixed parentage. In 1875 (Meiji 8) he began what would prove to be a five-year campaign to establish the first modern school for the blind in Japan.

Beyond his charitable activities, Nakamura was especially interested in the education of women. He saw their proper education as essential to the achievement of his vision of a prosperous and peaceful society.[53] Insisting on equal educational opportunities for women, he was unique in using texts that called for equal rights for women in his own academy, the Dōjinsha. Appointed principal of the government-financed Tokyo Women's Normal School (Tōkyō Joshi Shihan Gakkō), Nakamura tried to make it into an organ of higher (not just vocational) education for women.[54] A founding member of the Meirokusha (Meiji Six Society), Nakamura was a prolific essayist on a number of subjects, including women's education, literature, and Chinese studies. His official positions included a professorship at the Imperial University, counselor to the Council of Elders (Genrōin), and shortly before his death, a peerage. Although the emphasis here must be on *Saikoku risshi hen* and its function to Meiji society, it is of some interest that Nakamura pursued a career that resembled those of the philanthropic models Smiles most celebrated in *Self-Help*.

On the title page of *Saikoku risshi hen*, Nakamura styled the work (in English) a "translation" of *Self-Help*.[55] By modern standards it was no such thing. It was a paraphrase and an incomplete one at

---

out the suggestion for an imperial baptism. For the background of this appeal, see Ōkubo Toshiaki, "Kaidai," in *Meiji keimō shisō shū*, pp. 448–449; Takahashi, *Nakamura Keiu*, pp. 98–99; and Kosaka Masaaki, *Japanese Thought in the Meiji Era*, trans. David Abosch (Tōyō bunko, 1958), p. 117.

53. Nakamura Keiu, "Zenryō naru haha o tsukuru setsu," in *Meiji keimō shisō shū*, pp. 300–302.

54. For this aspect of his career, see Takahashi, *Nakamura Keiu*, pp. 161–168.

55. *Saikoku risshi hen* exists in numerous editions. I have used Nakamura Masanao, *Saikoku risshi hen* (Nomura Genjirō, 1888). This text is based on the original 1871 (Meiji 4) version. Three chapters of the original version have been reproduced in

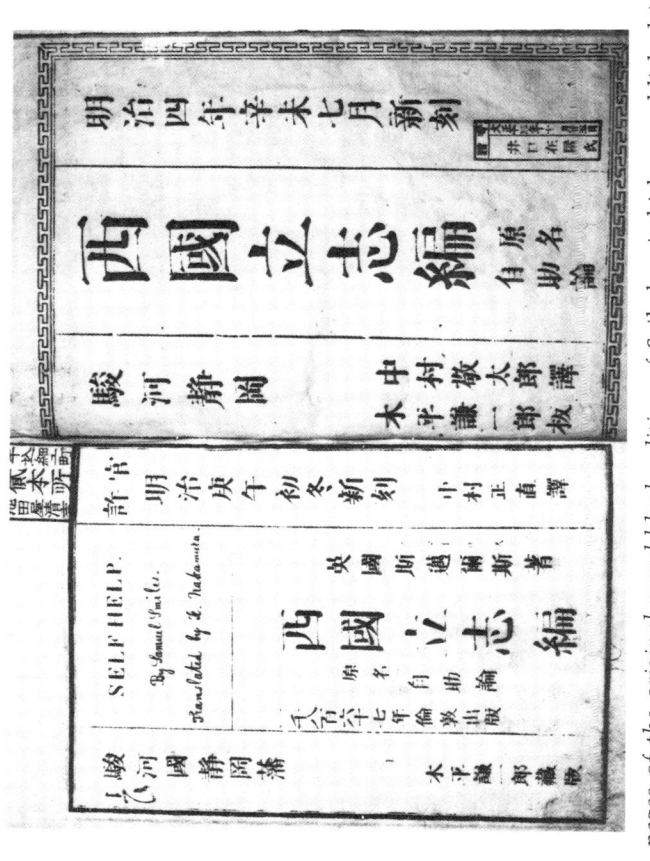

Title pages of the original wood-block edition of Saikoku risshi hen, published in 1871 (Meiji 4) in "the fief of Shizuoka" (Shizuoka han).

that. Nakamura frequently cut and occasionally expanded sections of *Self-Help*, with the net result that *Saikoku risshi hen* was at least 20 percent shorter than a full rendering would have been. His cutting and compression was most noticeable in those chapters dealing with industrial and artistic activities. His fullest renderings were directed to the ethical and moral portions of the text. The chapter on potters (3) was 6 percent of *Self-Help* but only 4 percent of *Saikoku risshi hen*. In contrast, the chapter on character (13) was 6 percent of the original but 10 percent of the translation. As a consequence, *Saikoku risshi hen* was even more of an ethical treatise than was *Self-Help*, but not absolutely. Because of a great amount of repetition in *Self-Help* and the moderate nature of the cuts, no theme disappeared entirely in the transition to *Saikoku risshi hen*. You can still learn more about pottery-making from it than most people other than would-be potters would want to know.

The interest in national prosperity and social progress expressed by Nakamura in his preface to *Saikoku risshi hen* was much in evidence in the text itself. Over and over again, Nakamura added references to national prosperity to otherwise more or less literally translated passages. When Smiles declared that "the world" was indebted to those from humbler ranks, Nakamura wrote of those who "profit the world and benefit the country." When Smiles declared that not "a single step in civilization has been made without labor," Nakamura added "in our country" to his translation. When Smiles condemned petty businessmen who thought only of profit for themselves and then asserted that "there are also businessmen of large . . . and comprehensive minds, capable of action on the very largest scale," Nakamura rendered this as "there are also those of a ministerial spirit who think of the country."[56] In making such changes, Nakamura was altering the text more than he was distorting the thought. As Timothy H. E. Travers has pointed out, Smiles was in-

---

modern printed form. Nakamura Masanao, *Saikoku risshi hen*, in *Nihon kyōkasho taikei kindai hen*, ed. Ishikawa Ken (Kōdansha, 1961), vol. 1, pp. 7–77. Because pagination in the early editions is unreliable, citations are given in the format X:Y where X is the chapter (book) and Y the arbitrary section numbers that Nakamura gave to the subdivisions of *Saikoku risshi hen*. Hereafter it is abbreviated *SKRH*.

56. *SKRH*, 1:25; 2:2, and 9:1, corresponding to *SH*, pp. 19, 27–28, and 263. Note that "ministerial spirit" does not refer to the clergy. The Japanese is *daijin no seishin*, or "the spirit of a minister of state."

tensely interested in the prosperity of England.⁵⁷ The difference was that Smiles was content to mention the nation once at the beginning of a paragraph or a chapter, and thereafter to refer to society, civilization, the world, or some other transnational beneficiary, while Nakamura never let the reader forget that the virtues or action being described had benefited the country (*hōkoku*).

A potentially more serious problem involved the lack of equivalents for many English terms, especially those pertaining to relations between individuals and the state or between individuals and society. Nakamura's Confucian vocabulary was not well prepared to deal with such terms as rights, liberty, and freedom, and at some points he resorted to parenthetical explanations and English glossings for his Chinese vocabulary. For example, he glossed *jishu jiyū* ("autonomy and freedom") as "independence."⁵⁸ Nevertheless, there is no evidence of any attempt to avoid introducing such concepts, even though they were in conflict with both Confucian and samurai values. Quite the contrary, Nakamura went out of his way to translate and explain these terms, which could just as well have been left out of *Saikoku risshi hen*. Nakamura emphasized what he called "the right of autonomy" (*jishu no ken*) held by the English people and stressed the role of parliament in both his preface and his afterword to *Saikoku risshi hen*.⁵⁹ This was several years before such issues became a matter of wide intellectual debate during the movement for liberty and people's rights.

Individualism and individuality were two important concepts appearing in *Self-Help* that were not well-articulated in either Confucian or samurai traditions. Thus, when Smiles quoted J. S. Mill to the effect that "even despotism does not produce its worst effects so long as individuality exists under it; whatever crushes individuality is despotism by whatever name it is called," Nakamura wrote, "Whatever form of government destroys the self-reliance [*jiritsu*] of a people must be called a tyrannical government [*kyakusei*]."⁶⁰ While this translation would make it appear that Nakamura limited

57. Travers, "Samuel Smiles," p. 144.
58. *SKRH*, 1:6.
59. Nakamura Keiu, "Jijoron dai-ichi hen jo," in *Meiji keimō shisō shū*, pp. 283–284; "Sho Saikoku risshi hen go," ibid., p. 286; and "Jinmin no seishitsu o kaizō suru setsu," ibid., p. 300.
60. *SKRH*, 1:4, and *SH*, p. 3.

the broad concept of individuality to mere economic self-reliance, that was not the case. The limitation was made by Smiles, who used this quotation as support for his arguments against legislated aid to the working class. Nakamura translated correctly for the context but not for the original concept.

An examination of his paraphrase of Mill's *On Liberty* shows that Nakamura was very much interested in the concept of individuality.[61] Having no equivalent for the term, he used a circumlocution, "that which makes each one distinct" (*dokuji ikko naru mono*), or equated individuality with "character" (*hinkō*), something Mill himself did. Although cutting *On Liberty* far more severely than *Self-Help*, Nakamura struggled to render the full range of meanings Mill attached to individuality, including "eccentricity," which became "character that is out of the ordinary, disobedient, and evil" (*kaiheki hijō no hinkō*).[62] That he sought to introduce these concepts is more significant than are the difficulties he experienced. He was taken by Mill's justifications of individualism in terms of national and social progress. Nakamura emphasized such statements as one that explained European progress (in contrast to Chinese stagnation) in terms of the "remarkable diversity of character and culture" existing in European countries.[63] Perhaps this may be regarded as a distortion of what *On Liberty* was about, giving it a nationalistic interpretation when it was focused on the individual, but it must be noted that Mill specifically avoided asserting individuality or liberty as absolute rights and instead argued in terms of social utility.[64] Although the social focus may only have been an argumentative strategy for Mill, Nakamura was not wrong to emphasize this aspect of his thought any more than he was wrong to add references to the nation when he translated *Self-Help*.

Although the absence of an articulated concept of individualism and individuality might be imagined to have been a significant prob-

61. I have used John Stuart Mill, *On Liberty*, ed. David Spirtz (Norton, 1975). For the translation, see Nakamura Keiu, *Jiyū no ri*, in *Jiyū minken hen*, vol. 2 of *Meiji bunka zenshū* (Nihon hyōron sha, 1969), pp. 1–84.
62. Nakamura, *Jiyū no ri*, p. 52, corresponding to Mill, *On Liberty*, p. 63. In this passage Mill stated, "That so few dare to be eccentric marks the chief danger of the time." By translating this passage faithfully, Nakamura indicated his acceptance of the idea, which might otherwise have been left out.
63. Nakamura, *Jiyū no ri*, pp. 55–57, and Mill, *On Liberty*, pp. 66–68.
64. Mill, *On Liberty*, p. 12.

lem in translating *Self-Help*, that was not in fact the case. Smiles's concept of individualism was narrower than that of Mill. Smiles did not celebrate eccentricity, and he was not at all interested in dealing with people who might engage in behavior that went against social norms simply because it was their prerogative to be deviant. In *Self-Help* behavior deemed odd and eccentric was always justified by the subsequent contribution that the individual made to technological and social progress. When Smiles used the term "individualism," he meant individual initiative or self-reliance, nothing more. Such expressions as "energetic individualism" or "strenuous individual application" had nothing to do with philosophical or romantic individualism and were easily handled with conventional Japanese or Chinese terms. Nakamura had no trouble in rendering literally a statement such as "steady application to work is the healthiest training for every individual [*jinmin no tenten hitori*], so it is the best discipline of the state."[65] However much Confucian thought worked to place the individual in a social context, it nevertheless began with the individual's rectifying his own conduct through individual effort.

Nakamura had no traditional word for self-help and had to coin one: *jijo*;[66] but he had little trouble rendering constituents of it, such as self-culture (*mizukara mi o osamuru*), self-control (*mizukara onore ni katsu*), and self-development (*jiko no chikara ni yorite shitaru*), because an emphasis on individual effort was quite traditional in such a context. It was part of popular Confucianism in Japan and China to advocate a moral scorecard, rather like that associated with Benjamin Franklin, on which the individual recorded his own successes and failures as he strove to cultivate himself.[67]

The samurai ethos had no particularly strong group-orientation

---

65. *SKRH*, 2:2, and *SH*, p. 27. Other examples of his translations of phrases involving "individual" or "individuality" may be found in *SKRH*, 1:9, 1:24, 2:2, and 13:1, corresponding to *SH*, pp. 6, 18, 27, and 383.

66. The lack of an existing vocabulary item does not by itself point to the lack of a concept. "Self-help" could not be literally translated in French, but it would be difficult to argue that French culture lacked individualism. Even in English, "self-help" was not a term of great antiquity. The earliest example given in the *Oxford English Dictionary* is 1831 from Thomas Carlyle. Travers suggests, however that the term came to Smiles from Emerson. Travers, "Samuel Smiles," p. 187.

67. For an exceptionally interesting account of this aspect of popular Confucianism, see Tadao Sakai, "Confucianism and Popular Educational Works," in *Self and Society in Ming Thought*, ed. Wm. Theodore de Bary (Columbia University Press, 1970), pp. 331–366. For examples of this score-keeping in samurai writing, see Udono

when it came to achievement. As R. P. Dore has pointed out, the traditional popular literature of the samurai celebrated the exploits of individual heroes, and pre-Tokugawa samurai had been notorious for their individual glory-seeking and unwillingness to work in disciplined units.[68] Europeans who sought to train Japanese in Western military drill during the last years of the Tokugawa and first years of the Meiji eras found peasants much easier to train than were samurai.[69] Similarly, the late Tokugawa ideal of patriotism as developed by men such as Yoshida Shōin was one of unaffiliated patriots acting according to their own sense of right and wrong.[70] Because they insisted on their own selflessness and proclaimed their acts to be in service to the nation, they cannot be said to have advocated absolute individualism. Nevertheless, they did not think of "organization men" all pulling together for some collective goal.

Smiles, Nakamura, and late Tokugawa activists all regarded the individual as the unit of performance and achievement. Group action versus individual action was not an issue for them. The man who benefited society did so as an individual, not as a member of a working collectivity. The linkage of individual acts to social benefit was essentially amorphous, rather like the "invisible hand" of Adam Smith but with the background assumption that individuals would act morally rather than selfishly. Nakamura was content with what Smiles had to say on this linkage because his Victorian formulations fit Japanese patterns. Smiles wrote, "No individual in the universe stands alone. . . . No man's acts die utterly; and though his body may resolve into dust and air, his good and bad deeds will still be

---

Chōkai, "Kanyō kōfu," in *Bushidō sōsho*, ed. Inoue Tetsujirō (Hakubunkan, 1905), vol. 3, p. 263; Yoshida Shōin, "Bukyō zensho kōroku," in *Yoshida Shōin*, vol. 31 of *Nihon no meicho*, ed. Matsumoto Sannosuke (Chūō kōron sha, 1973), p. 146; and Kaibara Ekiken, "Yamato zokujun," p. 74.

68. Ronald P. Dore, "The Legacy of Tokugawa Education," in *Changing Japanese Attitudes Toward Modernization*, ed. Marius B. Jansen (Princeton University Press, 1965), p. 126; and Ienaga Saburō, *Nihon dōtoku shisō shi* (Iwanami shoten, 1954), p. 80.

69. Marius B. Jansen, *Japan and China from War to Peace* (Rand McNally, 1974), p. 62. See also R. J. Kirby, "Dazai on *Bubi* or Preparation for War," *Transactions of the Asiatic Society of Japan*, series 1, vol. 31 (May 1905), pp. 29–30, for the complaints of Dazai Jun (Shundai) about the inability of samurai to function in organized groups.

70. Harry D. Harootunian, *Toward Restoration: The Growth of Political Consciousness in Tokugawa Japan* (The University of California Press, 1970), pp. 219–245.

bringing forth fruit after their kind, and influencing future generations for all time to come." He emphasized that "every act we do or word we utter" would influence "not only the whole of our future life" but would also make itself felt "upon the whole frame of society."[71] Such statements were similar to the admixture of Buddhist and Confucian precepts found in Tokugawa-era popular ethical writing.[72]

Nakamura was well prepared to translate such passages more or less literally, although he added somewhat to their Confucian sound. Thus, "the whole frame of society" became "posterity [*shison*], friends [*hōyū*], other people, and the customs of the whole [*ittai no fūzoku*]."[73] Nevertheless, the message came through because there was little to differentiate Smiles's ideas from those held within Confucianism. Nakamura cannot be criticized for translating "our forefathers" as "our ancestors" (*senzo*) when Smiles declared that "our forefathers still to a great extent influence us." When Smiles wrote of the "vast importance of domestic training" and asserted that "the nation comes from the nursery," corresponding statements by Nakamura that "the way of managing one household is the way of managing the country" (*ikka no jihō wa sunawachi hōkoku no jihō*) and "public morals [*fūzoku*] are the amalgam of house customs [*kafū*]" were reasonable approximations although certainly not literal renderings of what Smiles had to say.[74]

Thomas A. Metzger has asserted that the pattern of "Western" individualism is one that has emphasized the separateness of the indi-

71. *SH*, pp. 363–364.
72. Throughout the course of research I encountered statements linking Smiles to Puritanism, Protestantism, or Calvinism. See, for example, Hirakawa Sukehiro, "Franklin to Meiji kōgō," *Shokun* (July 1975), p. 229. This article styles both Smiles and Franklin as representing a "Puritan ethos." Those who make this linkage apparently feel that because Smiles stressed hard work and frugality and occasionally mentioned God or heaven, his thought belonged to one of these traditions. In one sense this is true. Smiles came from a Protestant background (his family were Cameronians), and he was born in the same city as John Knox. He was, however, hostile to his childhood tradition. See Smiles, *Autobiography*, p. 27. More important, his concept of heaven was only vaguely Christian and not at all Protestant. His orientation to this-worldly material and cultural progress is the antithesis of any of the three traditions. It was the lack of any specific Protestant color in his thought that made it so easy and generally correct for Nakamura to apply Confucian terminology to the translation of "heaven" as it appeared in *Self-Help*.
73. *SKRH*, 12:6–7.
74. *SKRH*, 12:1, corresponding to *SH*, p. 361.

vidual from the divine and one that has gone so far as to celebrate evil in the case of romantic individualism. In contrast, he has postulated a Confucian individualism that emphasized uniting with the divine and stressed social interaction and benefit.[75] Although such a division may be a useful description of the overall differences between the two traditions at the higher levels of philosophical discourse, this does not appear to be appropriate at the level of popular morality. Certainly, within Western thought there is a tradition of absolute individualism, which celebrates all individual activity— good and evil, social and antisocial—and which has no ready analog within Confucian thought. But, to find such absolute formulations of individualism totally divorced from social utility, one must look beyond popular moralists like Smiles and even beyond major intellectuals like Mill. Especially at the level of popular morality, the cross-cultural comparison yields not the black and white contrast of an individualistic tradition versus a collectivistic tradition but, rather, shows many shades of gray. At least in Japan, the area of shared ground was sufficiently great that the absence of anything directly comparable to the romanticization of the individual in Western thought was in no way a bar to the translation of *Self-Help* nor to the understanding of the concept of self-help.

Beginning in August 1871 (Meiji 4), after the publication of *Saikoku risshi hen*, the government began to take steps that had the effect of realizing the pledges made in the Charter Oath. Samurai and aristocrats not holding government office were permitted to follow any occupation they chose. Whether the popularity of *Saikoku risshi hen* had any direct influence in bringing about this change is impossible to document. Nevertheless, it must be noted that in the months immediately before these reforms were announced, *Saikoku risshi hen* was being read and debated widely among government officials and educators.[76] Even the Emperor Meiji was exposed to *Saikoku risshi hen*. Katō Hiroyuki, advisor to the emperor at this time and subsequently chancellor of the (Tokyo) Imperial Univer-

---

75. See Thomas A. Metzger, *Escape from Predicament* (Columbia University Press, 1977), pp. 42 ff. There are of course many different definitions of individualism that might be used. For some of the many and often contradictory definitions of individualism found in American and European writing, see Stephen Lukes, *Individualism* (Harper and Row, 1973).

76. Maeda Ai, "Meiji risshin shugi no keifu," *Bungaku* 33:4 (April 1965): 11.

sity, gave a series of lectures to Meiji, using *Saikoku risshi hen* as his text.[77] The content of these lectures is unknown, but others in the series dealt with statecraft, and presumably this was the case with Katō's lectures on *Saikoku risshi hen*. Quite likely the theme of these lectures was that which had attracted Nakamura to *Self-Help*: the relation between national and individual independence.

Another high official, Nishimura Shigeki, who was at this time head of the compilation section of the Ministry of Education, considered *Saikoku risshi hen* one of the most important works available for enlightening the people. He quoted extensively from it and other works by Smiles in the ethics texts he wrote.[78] It was also during this period that the Ministry of Education distributed *Saikoku risshi hen* as an ethics text and produced a series of woodcut prints illustrating stories from it for instruction of even the youngest children.[79] Such easily documentable uses of *Saikoku risshi hen* are doubtless only a small fraction of what could be found by combing biographies and government documents of this period. At the very least, this association of *Saikoku risshi hen* with relatively high-placed figures in the Meiji government suggests that its ideas were acceptable to those who were determining the direction that the new Meiji order would take.

Nevertheless, nationalism and official sponsorship cannot begin to account for the popularity of *Saikoku risshi hen* in the early Meiji period, let alone explain its staying power. The base for its popularity must be sought in its audience. Nakamura did not explicitly state for whom *Saikoku risshi hen* was written, but the title is suggestive of a samurai audience. Almost untranslatable into English, it might loosely be rendered as "Lofty Ambitions in Western Countries." The key word in the title is *risshi*, a term used by Mencius to

77. Kimura Ki, "Meiji tennō no shin-teiōgaku—*Saikoku risshi hen* denrai hyaku-nen o kinen shite," pp. 83–100 in Meiji bunka kenkyū-kai, ed., *Meiji bunka kenkyū* (Nihon hyōron sha, 1968), vol. 2, pp. 86–87.

78. His appreciation of *Saikoku risshi hen* is cited in Donald H. Shively, "Nishimura Shigeki: A Confucian View of Modernization," in *Changing Japanese Attitudes Toward Modernization*, ed. Marius B. Jansen (Princeton University Press, 1965), p. 207. For a discussion and reproduction of these texts, see Miyata Fumio, ed., *Dōtoku kyōiku shiryō shūsei* (Dai-ichi hōki shuppan, 1959), vol. 1, pp. 16–17 and 93–115.

79. Karasawa Tomitarō, *Meiji hyaku-nen no jidō shi* (Kōdansha, 1968), vol. 1, p. 192, describes a series of prints featuring Palissy, Arkwright, and Watt, that appear to be derived from *Saikoku risshi hen*. Reproductions are given on pp. 24–25. See also Maeda, "Risshin shusse," p. 13.

mean righteous determination that would inspire others. *Risshi* was used in samurai writing and was closely associated with the *shishi*, or men of high moral purpose, as late Tokugawa activists styled themselves.[80] The format and language also suggest a samurai audience. The prefaces Nakamura wrote were in Chinese (*kanbun*), and the text itself was in a rather stiff Sino-Japanese style (*bungotai*) similar to that used in government documents at the time. There were no glossings for characters except in the case of foreign names, and there were no illustrations. *Saikoku risshi hen* looked very much like a serious, scholarly work, and there is no indication that Nakamura intended it to be anything else.

Reading *Saikoku risshi hen* demanded a level of literacy that was largely but not exclusively a possession of the samurai. Only wealthy peasants (*gōnō*) and wealthy merchants (*gōshō*) among the mass of commoners would generally have had the literacy to read *Saikoku risshi hen*. Although Japanese scholarship tends to associate the work with the notorious robber baron Ōkura Kihachirō, documentary evidence to link *Saikoku risshi hen* to capitalists in general or merchants in particular is nonexistent.[81] The merchant class had an ongoing tradition of writing on advancement and profit-making. It did not need *Saikoku risshi hen* either to guide it or to validate its activities and would find nothing in it to do either. Wealthy peasants

80. Concerning the *shishi*, see Marius B. Jansen, *Sakamoto Ryōma and the Meiji Restoration* (Stanford University Press, 1971), pp. 95–104. For a good example of *risshi* as defined by a *bakumatsu shishi* (one who was executed for his activities), see Hashimoto Keigaku (Sanai), "Keitō roku," in *Bushidō sōsho*, vol. 3, pp. 588–589.

81. Most Japanese scholars have cited the popularity of *Saikoku risshi hen* without considering who could and did read it. Those who go further have usually linked it to Ōkura Kihachirō, a notorious Meiji merchant. The basis for this is a single statement in which Nakamura recorded a gift of appreciation from Ōkura. See Asukai Masamichi, "Keimō shugi minken ron *nashonarizumu*," in *Kindai Nihon shakai shisō shi I* (Yūhikaku, 1968), p. 124; Minamoto Ryōen, *Tokugawa shisō shōshi* (Chūō kōron sha, 1973), pp. 86–87; and Kosaka, *Japanese Thought*, p. 115. Although Ōkura may have been inspired by *Saikoku risshi hen*, it was more likely that he was trying to improve his image through association with Nakamura. This one case is hardly enough evidence to link *Saikoku risshi hen* to Japanese capitalism, although Asukai does just that. If but a single reader is to stand for the whole readership of *Saikoku risshi hen*, one might just as well choose the late Meiji antipollution activist Tanaka Shōzō or cofounder of the Japan Communist Party Yamakawa Hitoshi. Both were readers of *Saikoku risshi hen*. See Kenneth Strong, "Tanaka Shōzō: Meiji Hero and Pioneer Against Pollution," *Bulletin of the Japan Society* 67:10 (June 1972): 7, and Thomas D. Swift, "Yamakawa Hitoshi and the Dawn of Japanese Socialism," (Ph.D. dissertation, University of California, Berkeley, 1970), p. 70, note 33.

had both the literacy to read *Saikoku risshi hen* and a natural affinity for its ideas. Nakamura himself is a prime example of this. It is questionable whether the son of a well-off peasant who had purchased samurai status ought properly to be called a samurai. Moreover, there were many such first- and second-generation samurai at the end of the Tokugawa period.[82] A specifically wealthy-peasant interpretation of *Saikoku risshi hen* was found in the writings of Tokutomi Iichirō (Sohō), discussed in chapter three. Nevertheless, because of the format of *Saikoku risshi hen* and because of recollections that link it to the samurai in the broad, popular sense of that term, it is appropriate to consider what there was in *Self-Help* as rendered by Nakamura Keiu that might have appealed to stipend-receiving gentlemen warriors, not just as patriots but as ambitious men.

Self-Help and *Saikoku risshi hen* received their most explicit linkage to samurai in the form of the Risshisha (Society of Lofty Ambition).[83] This organization was formed in 1874 (Meiji 7) in Tosa by disaffected samurai; later it formed branches throughout the country. The Risshisha took its name and some of its early program from *Saikoku risshi hen*. Its original statement of purpose quoted Smiles's assertion that "the nation is a reflection of its people" (*kuni wa jinmin no hansha hikari nari*) and declared that the country was in jeopardy because the people (the samurai members of the Risshisha) were losing their vigor. To restore the spirit of the nation, they pledged to cultivate themselves, manage themselves, preserve the rights of the people, and become an independent people (*jishu dokuritsu no jinmin*) fully comparable with the free people of Western countries. In part the program to accomplish all this was based on Smilesean principles, and the Risshisha distributed texts based on *Saikoku risshi hen*. The association engaged in various self-help projects for samurai, including a tea plantation, forest management, a school, and a loan fund to keep samurai out of the hands of usurers. Most of these projects came to naught. The samurai did not want to become farmers or woodsmen or businessmen, and they seldom had the knowledge or application required.

82. Beasley, *Meiji Restoration*, p. 32. See also Ray A. Moore, "Adoption and Samurai Mobility in Tokugawa Japan," *Journal of Asian Studies* 29:3 (May 1970): 617–632, and Ray A. Moore, "Samurai Discontent and Social Mobility in the Late Tokugawa Period," *Monumenta Nipponica* 24:1–2 (1969): 79–92.
83. For the background of the Risshisha, see Suzuki Yasuzō, *Jiyū minken kenpō happu* (Hakujō sha, 1939), pp. 13–27.

THE SELF-MADE MAN IN MEIJI JAPANESE THOUGHT

The Risshisha had political interests from its inception, and it became increasingly political over time. It rationalized political activity through ideas taken from Smiles. It argued that the samurai alone among the Japanese people had intelligence (*chishiki*) and a spirit of independence (*jishu no kifū*) because the other three classes had been oppressed during the years of Tokugawa rule. Because of their economic difficulties after the Restoration and because the government denied them a voice in decision-making, the samurai (from Tosa, who had little role in the Meiji government) were losing their independent spirit. If the nation were denied their spirit, the prosperity of Japan would suffer. To preserve their independence, it was necessary that they be allowed to participate in government through a representative assembly and be given economic aid so that they would not become meek and servile like commoners.[84]

The use to which the Risshisha put the formulas it took from *Self-Help* by way of *Saikoku risshi hen* was vastly different from the purpose Smiles had intended those statements to serve. Hereditary privilege and ability were asserted, political activity was justified, and legislated aid was sought. Nevertheless, while the Risshisha usage was extremely selective and went against the grain of the original *Self-Help* and even *Saikoku risshi hen*, it did possess a certain tortured logic. Recognition of this selectivity and the inversion of the formulas from *Self-Help* does not, however, explain how it was that a still partially feudal, hereditarily privileged warrior caste could associate itself with ideas taken from a work intended for industrial laborers and craftsmen in a country that had already passed through the industrial revolution.

This association was not as bizarre as it might first appear. There was substantial congruence between what *Self-Help* said and what significant elements of the mid-nineteenth-century samurai class were doing and thinking. The workmen to whom *Self-Help* had been addressed were what one history of the period aptly styled "the upper crust of the working classes."[85] Smiles himself recorded that those to whom he lectured had been teaching themselves and each

---

84. This section is based on two untitled documents reproduced in Gotō Yasushi, "Risshisha shimatsu kiyō," *Shigaku zasshi* 65:1 (January 1965): 64–69.

85. J. B. Conacher, *Waterloo to the Common Market*, vol. 5 of *The Borzoi History of England* (Knopf, 1975), p. 107.

other "reading and writing, arithmetic and geography; and even mathematics, chemistry, and some of the modern languages."[86] The many samurai who were at this time struggling to acquire the rudiments of Western learning could well find a congenial self-image in the descriptions of self-education and self-cultivation contained in *Saikoku risshi hen*. More important, because of the time lag between "humble origins" and ultimate achievement, the actual models in *Self-Help* were not nineteenth-century factory workers but eighteenth-century artisans, craftsmen, or petty functionaries. By the end of the Tokugawa period, most middle- and low-ranking samurai fell into these categories. Low-ranked samurai had moved into artisan occupations in considerable numbers.[87] Certain occupations were reserved for them as a relief measure to supplement their limited stipends. *Saikoku risshi hen* had an obvious appeal in that it promised advancement out of such circumstances, or at the very least, respect and betterment within rank.

The possibility of samurai identifying with the models and values in *Self-Help* was increased by the vocabulary of *Saikoku risshi hen*. In discussing rank Nakamura relied almost entirely on permutations and combinations of a compound (*fūki hinsen*) meaning "wealthy and honored, impoverished and despised." When Smiles declared that "great men belong to no exclusive class or rank," Nakamura wrote that "great heroes come regardless of being honored or despised, being impoverished or wealthy."[88] This captured the sense of what Smiles had said except for one peculiarity. This compound and the components of it were usually used when writers described the divisions within the samurai class, between those who had high rank and wealth and those who had low rank and were impoverished. Popular Tokugawa texts specifically defined the "honored" portion of this formula as formal rank (*kurai*) and the wealth portion as the emoluments that came with rank. The phrase was explicitly

86. *SH*, p. vii.
87. Concerning this transformation of the samurai, see Fukuchi Shigetaka, *Shizoku to shizoku ishiki* (Shunjū sha, 1956), pp. 70–72. Sasama Yoshihiko, *Ashigaru no seikatsu* (Yūzankaku, 1969), pp. 195–197. Fukuzawa Yukichi, "Kyūhanjō," trans. Carmen Blacker, *Monumenta Nipponica* 9:1–2 (1953): 320–321; and Fukuzawa Yukichi, *The Autobiography of Yukichi Fukuzawa*, trans. Eiichi Kiyooka (Schocken, 1972), pp. 9–11.
88. This example is from the table of contents of *Saikoku risshi hen*.

Confucian and was from the Analects.[89] Using such terminology could not help drawing the models in *Saikoku risshi hen* into samurai concepts of the social order.

There was substantial precedent in Japanese thought for asserting the merits of those from humble circumstances. Early writers had found it expedient to ignore the Confucian emphasis on men of talent and instead to devote their energies to justifying the existing distribution of wealth and honor under the Tokugawa order. Even they had warned of the debilitating effects of hereditary wealth and occasionally asserted the merits of those of low birth without, however, questioning the claims of current holders. In the early eighteenth century, Ogyū Sorai and disciples of his such as Dazai Shundai (Jun) came to emphasize the inherent Confucian notion of promotion by merit. Ogyū argued that the "absence of hardship and tribulation" had caused the "upper classes" to become "increasingly stupid." Sounding distinctly like Smiles, he had claimed that "through the study of history . . . we may see, as clearly as in a mirror, that men of intelligence and talent have all come from below; rarely have they come from hereditarily privileged families." According to Ogyū, it was the overcoming of hardship that tempered those without

---

89. For the Confucian context of this term, see Arthur Waley, *The Analects of Confucius* (George Allen & Unwin, 1938), pp. 102–103. This term appears throughout the writings of Kaibara Ekiken. For a discussion of Kaibara and his intended audience, see Sakurai Shōtarō, *Meiyo to chijoku* (Hōsei daigaku shuppan-kyoku, 1971), pp. 112–130, esp. pp. 113, 120. In later writers, examples of this limited usage may be found in the following: Fujita Tōko, "Hitachi obi," in *Fujita Tōko—Aizawa Seishisai—Fujita Yūkoku*, ed. Hashikawa Bunsō, vol. 29 of *Nihon no meicho* (Chūō kōron sha, 1974), p. 156 (*daimyō* and *hatamoto*), pp. 167–168 (samurai of the *han*), p. 169 (those with large stipends versus those with small stipends); Yoshida Shōin, "Kō Mō yowa," in *Yoshida Shōin*, ed. Matsumoto Sannosuke, vol. 31 of *Nihon no meicho* (Chūō kōron sha, 1973), pp. 90–92 (sovereign versus vassals), and "Bukyō zensho kōroku," in *Yoshida Shōin*, pp. 177–178 (*bushi* families). The main reason for this terminology's being associated with samurai is that when they wrote, they simply did not think about the common people unless the commoners happened to be in rebellion. Concerning this general samurai attitude, see Harry D. Harootunian, "*Jinsei, jinzai,* and *jitsugaku*: Social Values and Leadership in Late Tokugawa Thought," in *Modern Japanese Leadership: Transition and Change,* ed. Bernard S. Silberman and Harry D. Harootunian (University of Arizona Press, 1966), pp. 83–120, esp. note 4. The term does appear to have been linked with commoners in some popular texts, and the reader is cautioned that the point here is to establish the probable associations of the term for a reader of the samurai class, not to establish that the term could mean only divisions within the samurai class.

high hereditary rank and made them more suited for office.[90] As T. C. Smith and R. P. Dore have demonstrated, such ideas were fairly widespread in Tokugawa Japan, receiving especially vociferous treatment near the end of the period.[91] Readers of *Saikoku risshi hen* were well prepared for the emphasis on special merit among those of low birth, especially with the vocabulary chosen by Nakamura.

Even without modification through translation, *Self-Help* matched well with samurai vocational preferences. Although a few late Tokugawa writers had worked to modify the Confucian-reinforced prejudice of the class against commercial activities, recollections, comments, and subsequent performance suggest that the first vocational choice of samurai was government service, followed closely by academia.[92] Neither *Self-Help* nor *Saikoku risshi hen* fundamentally challenged this set of preferences. Smiles was critical of businessmen in general and refused a number of lucrative offers to write panegyrics of contemporary merchants. Although the ninth chapter of *Self-Help* was titled "Men of Business," only one model was specifically a merchant (David Barclay). Those given greatest weight were military: Napoleon and Wellington. The "business" Smiles described was almost exclusively managerial or governmental: military logistics and state fiscal affairs. Nakamura captured the sense of what Smiles was describing by rendering "men of business" as "men who carry out affairs of office" (*shokuji o tsutomuru*) or "men who carry out official duties" (*jimu o tsutomuru*). Only in the case of

---

90. Ogyū's basic argument is given in Tsunoda, de Bary, Keene, *Sources*, vol. 1, pp. 421–424. See also Ogyū Sorai, "Seidan," in *Ogyū Sorai*, ed. Bitō Masahide, vol. 16 of *Nihon no meicho* (Chūō kōron sha, 1974), pp. 466–475. Dazai is discussed in Tetsuo Najita, "Political Economism in the Thought of Dazai Shundai," *Journal of Asian Studies* 31:4 (August 1972): 821–839.

91. Ronald P. Dore, "Talent and the Social Order in Tokugawa Japan," in *Studies in the Institutional History of Early Modern Japan*, ed. John W. Hall and Marius B. Jansen (Princeton University Press, 1968), pp. 349–361, and Thomas C. Smith, "'Merit' as Ideology in Tokugawa Japan," in *Aspects of Social Change in Modern Japan*, ed. R. P. Dore (Princeton University Press, 1967), pp. 71–90.

92. Some rethinking was evident in the thought of Kaiho Seiryō. See Tsunoda, de Bary, Keene, *Sources*, vol. 1, pp. 488–493. For data on samurai preferences and performance in the early Meiji period, see Hiroshi Mannari, *The Japanese Business Leaders* (University of Tokyo Press, 1974), pp. 133–145, and Kozo Yamamura, *A Study of Samurai Income and Entrepreneurship* (Harvard University Press, 1974). For typical expressions of prejudice against commerce, see Ienaga, *Dōtoku*, p. 103, and Fukuzawa, *Autobiography*, p. 3.

Barclay did he use the somewhat pejorative "one who trades" (*shō-bai suru*).[93]

The strength of this prejudice may be seen in contemporary treatments of Benjamin Franklin. Brief biographies of him and translations of some of his moral precepts appeared in ethics texts popular in those years when *Saikoku risshi hen* was most associated with the samurai. Franklin's precepts were divorced from commercial significance in these texts, and his career was described primarily in terms of government service. One popular text simply styled him "a famous government official" (*kōmyō naru kanchō*),[94] a rather limited description that ignored not only his mercantile activities but also his scientific experimentation. Because Smiles was heir to a genteel rather than a commercial tradition, his ideas needed no separation from any commercial context in order to fit the occupational conceits of the samurai-Confucian tradition.

The specific virtues and ideals that Smiles preached generally matched with those common in samurai writing. Frugality is a prime example of this. Frugality in *Self-Help* was described in terms of maintaining consumption within the limits of one's income, consuming appropriate to one's station in life without false and costly display, and avoiding debt through careful budgeting. It was a frugality that was more concerned with limiting consumption and providing a surplus for emergencies or for humanitarian activities than it was a frugality designed to generate capital. In *Self-Help* Smiles did not talk about turning pence into pounds, compound interest, or other such topics as might be included in an ethic of frugality directed at capital accumulation.[95] This was precisely the ethic of frugality found throughout Tokugawa-era writings directed at samurai from Yamaga Sokō in the mid-seventeenth century down to Yoshida Shōin in the mid-nineteenth.[96] Nakamura could there-

93. *SKRH*, 9:1 and 9:32.
94. Mizukuri Rinshō, "Kenzen junmō," in *Nihon kyōkasho taikei kindai hen*, vol. 1, pp. 122–123. The merchant aspect of Franklin may explain why his writings were known but not particularly popular in early Meiji Japan.
95. Concerning Smiles's concept of frugality, see Travers, "Samuel Smiles," p. 129, and *Self-Help*, chap. 10, "Money—Its Use and Abuse." Only much later did Smiles expound on a more capitalistic concept of frugality in his book *Thrift*. See Bendix, *Work*, pp. 110–111.
96. On samurai frugality, see Yoshida Shōin, "Bukyō zensho kōroku," in *Yoshida Shōin*, pp. 163–167. Yoshida remarked that if he could find the time, he would write a

fore render such passages without change simply by using traditional vocabulary.[97] The same thing may be said of the saving of time. Smiles did mention the idea that "time is money," but he put greater stress on time as an opportunity to acquire knowledge or pursue an experiment.[98] This was an emphasis similar to that found in samurai writing where time and its saving were urged in a context of acquiring knowledge or pursuing self-cultivation, not in the production of wealth.[99] The only peculiarity to be noted in this context was that Nakamura had no simple word for punctuality and had to resort to a phrase such as "not mistaking the agreed time" (*teiki o ayamarazaru*).[100] Although the idea of punctuality was found in Tokugawa writing, writers had not developed a single word for it, perhaps because Japan was not yet a machine-paced society.

When Smiles stressed experience over formal education, Nakamura translated such passages well and frequently added emphasis of his own indicating agreement. Even though Nakamura had been educated at the Shōheikō, he had picked up on that widening current within Tokugawa Confucianism that had emphasized practical learning (*jitsugaku*) over the abstract philosophical and metaphysical debates that characterized much of Neo-Confucianism.[101] Smiles looked on formal education, including classical education, as good intellectual training, but he also declared that learning and talent without experience and practice were meaningless.[102] Had Smiles gone as far as some American writers on advancement who declared education, especially classical and liberal arts education, to be worthless or even harmful to the individual, he might have generated some resistance from Nakamura or other contemporary Japanese.[103]

---

book on the subject. See also Fujita Tōko, "Hitachi obi," in *Fujita Tōko*, pp. 154–161 and 172–175.

97. *SKRH*, book 10, esp. 10:7. 98. *SH*, p. 274, and *SKRH*, 9:21.

99. Kaibara, "Yamato zokujun," in *Kaibara Ekiken*, p. 75; Yoshida Shōin, "Bukyō zensho kōroku," in *Yoshida Shōin*, p. 146; "Jitsugokyō genkai," in *Kyōjun* pp. 182 and 185–186.

100. *SH*, p. 270, and *SKRH*, 9:13; *SH*, p. 274, and *SKRH*, 9:22.

101. This is discussed throughout Harootunian, "*Jinsei, jinzai*, and *jitsugaku*." Specific late Tokugawa examples may be found in Yoshida, "Bukyō zensho kōroku," pp. 149–150, and Fujita Tōko, "Kōdōkan kijutsugi," in *Fujita Tōko*, pp. 267–269.

102. *SH*, pp. 27–28, and *SKRH*, chap. 11, "Self-Culture—Facilities and Difficulties," esp. pp. 324 ff., and *SKRH*, book 11, esp. 11:14 ff.

103. Richard Hofstadter, *Anti-intellectualism in American Life* (Knopf, 1963), pp. 255–257. American businessmen were often of the opinion that classical studies

As it was, Smiles provided additional support for what an important segment of Japanese thinkers had been saying to each other.

This matching of values and virtues between the Confucian and Victorian traditions was especially close in the last chapter of *Self-Help*, "Character—the True Gentleman." There Smiles stressed the importance of a good name, temperance, benevolence, loyalty, truthfulness, bravery, and of course, good character. All these virtues were to be found in texts on the ideal samurai gentleman, and it is not surprising that Nakamura rendered the title of this chapter as "Character—the True *Chün-Tzu*," indicating quite specifically that he saw the gentlemanly ideal in *Self-Help* and the Confucian ideal as identical.[104] In only one instance did Nakamura indicate that he believed that the message of *Self-Help* might not be compatible with Confucian or samurai values. In a special preface to chapter four of *Saikoku risshi hen* ("Application and Perseverance" in *Self-Help*), Nakamura emphasized that the true scholar (*shinsei gakushi*) should not be embarrassed by menial tasks (*sengyō*), and he provided several examples of Chinese literati who had engaged in manual labor.[105] Subsequent chapters will show just how justified this fear was, but at this point it is more important to note how much of *Self-Help*, despite its vastly different social milieu, was intelligible without difficulty to an early Meiji samurai audience and, judging by government promotion of *Saikoku risshi hen*, how much was compatible with the thinking of top Meiji officialdom.

Given the case that has been made here for *Self-Help* and *Saikoku risshi hen* as works that were basically compatible with the Confucian samurai tradition, the question arises why Nakamura bothered to translate *Self-Help* or why readers bothered to read *Saikoku risshi hen* when much the same thing could be found in their own tradition. The answer is that the situation is comparable to that noted by R. P. Dore in his comments on the relation between Tokugawa and Meiji educational policy. "To emphasize the ancestry of such ideas in the schools and their subtle subversion of the estab-

---

were worthless. Smiles, however, considered such subjects as Latin and Greek useful for "polishing intellect."

104. *SKRH*, book 13. In Japanese this is *kunshi*. For the Chinese associations, see Waley, *Analects*, pp. 34–38.

105. Nakamura Keiu, "Jijoron dai-yon hen jo," in *Meiji keimō shisō shū*, p. 284.

lished hierarchy, is not to deny the boldness of the final challenge; it merely goes some long way to explaining it."[106] So too for *Saikoku risshi hen* and the ancestry of the ideas found in it. There were precedents for most of the concepts in *Self-Help*, but in many cases these precedents were found, not in the modal instance of Tokugawa writing, but in dissident and critical traditions, almost but not quite "underground" traditions. In *Saikoku risshi hen* the same ideas are very much above ground and are repeated over and over again. The merits of those of "humble origins" is a case in point. So much writing on the subject is found in the works of dissident authors in the last years of the Tokugawa regime because little had been done to institutionalize merit selection since Ogyū Sorai and others first gave explicit expression to the concept. Instead of defensively worded proposals for the advancement of men of low station based on the principles of remote antiquity, *Saikoku risshi hen* justified such advancement through its linkage to the prosperity of Great Britain and the anticipated future prosperity of Japan.

The same could be said for the other points made in *Saikoku risshi hen*. There was no quantum leap over the most progressive of Tokugawa writing but rather an intensification and a generalization of existing themes. There was moreover an immediacy and a concreteness in *Saikoku risshi hen* that was lacking in Tokugawa writers. Tokugawa writers had had to make their assertions as pure abstractions or link them to Sage-Kings and mythic Japanese or Chinese kingdoms. Smiles explained the wealth and power of the far more real British world presence and offered a promise of similar prosperity through the generalization of the values in *Self-Help*. Even more important, there was a special role for those of "humble origins," phrased in terms that made it easy for the lower-ranked samurai to fit their personal ambitions into the overall framework of national prosperity.

106. Dore, "Talent," p. 350.

2 | Study for Wealth and Honor

Readers do as much to make a book popular as does its author, and if readers could misinterpret the original *Self-Help* as a tract on material success, there is no reason to believe that Japanese readers would not so misinterpret *Saikoku risshi hen.* While not an overtly materialistic interpretation, the use made of *Saikoku risshi hen* by the Risshisha (Society of Lofty Ambition) is a clear warning that at least some of its readers did not find in it precisely what Nakamura intended, to say nothing of reading it as Smiles had intended *Self-Help*.

To determine the probable modal interpretation of *Saikoku risshi hen* in the absence of modern reader surveys requires the use of indirect evidence. A number of sources exist that may be used to determine the matrix of aspiration into which *Saikoku risshi hen* fit. The institutional reforms affecting social mobility made after the Meiji Restoration may be considered to be the statements of samurai officialdom on the direction aspirations for advancement should ideally take. Critical comments voiced at this time and other contemporary works on self-advancement aimed at samurai provide clues to their overall values and preferences, particularly with respect to their departures from ideal patterns. Finally, there exists a limited body of direct evidence on contemporary interpretations in the form of schoolboy (and -girl) compositions based explicitly on *Saikoku risshi hen* or on personal aspirations in general. Taken together, these various sources form a reasonably comprehensive picture of

STUDY FOR WEALTH AND HONOR

the early Meiji audience for the Japanese version of *Self-Help* and their probable interpretation of it.

One contemporary work aimed at samurai and dealing with individual aspirations stands out because of its very large circulation. This competing tract was *Gakumon no susume* [An Encouragement of Learning] by Fukuzawa Yukichi, a well-known Meiji educator and pamphleteer.[1] Differing considerably in structure from *Saikoku risshi hen*, *Gakumon no susume* was not one work but rather a series of pamphlets loosely related to the series title. The series came into being in December 1871 (Meiji 4) when Fukuzawa and Obata Tokujirō, a fellow educator, sent a communication to commemorate the opening of a school in Nakatsu, the castle town of their fief. In February 1872 (Meiji 5) this oration was issued in pamphlet form by Keiō Gijuku, an academy operated by Fukuzawa. When this first pamphlet enjoyed good sales, Fukuzawa attempted to capitalize on its popularity by issuing additional pamphlets until by November 1876 (Meiji 9) he had published a total of seventeen under the original title. None of the subsequent pamphlets achieved the sales of the first, but its performance was truly outstanding. By 1880 (Meiji 13) it had sold some 200,000 copies in legitimate reproductions, and Fukuzawa estimated there had been as many as 20,000 reproduced without permission. He calculated that this meant that 1 out of every 160 Japanese had read it. Actually, this claim was all too modest. If due allowance is made for the fact that the original *Gakumon no susume* was no less difficult to read than *Saikoku risshi hen* and that this level of literacy was far from widespread, perhaps as many as 1 out of 10 or even 1 out of 5 who could read it had done so.[2]

1. The structure and circulation of *Gakumon no susume* are analyzed in greater detail in Earl H. Kinmonth, "Fukuzawa Reconsidered: *Gakumon no susume* and Its Audience," *Journal of Asian Studies* 37:4 (August 1978): 677–696.
2. For a rough calculation of potential audience, I assumed, as did Fukuzawa, a total population of 35 million. From this I deducted one-third for infants and nonliterate juveniles, one-half of the remainder for females, and assumed that 20 percent of the remaining population (2.3 million) could read *Gakumon no susume* in its original form. Ronald Dore has placed late Tokugawa literacy at 40–50 percent for males, a figure that has been criticized by Japanese scholars as being somewhat overly optimistic. See Fukaya Masashi, *Gakureki shugi no keifu* (Reimei shobō, 1969), p. 55, n. 127. Considering that in the 1890s conscription tests were turning up total illiteracy rates

THE SELF-MADE MAN IN MEIJI JAPANESE THOUGHT

As did *Self-Help*, *Gakumon no susume* began with a statement about the relation between heaven and man.³ Its subsequently famous first line declared, "It is said that heaven does not create one man above or below another man. This means that when men are born from heaven they are in the same rank." After postulating equality at birth, Fukuzawa went on to observe that men were nevertheless divided into honored and despised, high and low, clever and foolish, rich and poor. Describing these categories as comparable to the difference between clouds and slime, Fukuzawa continued by asking rhetorically what was the source of this disparity among men. The answer he gave was simple. All differences in status among men depended on whether or not they had the "power of learning" (*gakumon no chikara*). Citing a Japanese saying somewhat similar to the first line of *Self-Help*, he declared:

> A proverb says that heaven does not give wealth and honor [*fūki*] to men.⁴ Rather, man adds wealth and honor to himself by his work. If this be so, as I said before, when man is born, he is without distinction of honor or baseness [*kisen*], nor of poverty or wealth. It is merely by employing himself in learning, knowing many things well, that a man becomes respected, that he

---

of 25 percent (see Fukaya, *Gakureki*, pp. 285–286) and that *Gakumon no susume* was fairly difficult in its original form (so much so that some illicit versions were simplified), 20 or even 10 percent seems a more reasonable rate. Concerning these illicit texts, see Tomita Masafumi, "Gakumon no susume," in *Fukuzawa Yukichi Zenshū*, ed. Tomita Masafumi and Tsuchibayashi Shunichi (Iwanami shoten, 1959), vol. 3, pp. 644–646. As for the relative difficulty of Saikoku risshi hen and *Gakumon no susume*, a crude index may be made by sampling and comparing the ratio of characters (*kanji*) to each one-hundred elements of text. This calculation gives an index number of 100 for a *kanbun* text (most difficult) and 0 for a text entirely in *kana*. Using this system, *Saikoku risshi hen* has a rating of 44, the original *Gakumon no susume* a rating of 46, and the fourth pamphlet (aimed at intellectuals) a rating of 48. By way of contrast, the *Jitsugokyō genkai* has a rating of only 30, or 0 if allowance is made for the fact that all the characters that appear in it are glossed.

3. Because of the concentration of circulation in the first pamphlet and the knowledge that only themes from it generally appeared in student compositions (discussed below), I have largely limited the following discussion to the original *Gakumon no susume*. It is reproduced in *Fukuzawa Yukichi zenshū*, vol. 3, pp. 29–35. Two translations into English of this pamphlet are also available: Fukuzawa Yukichi, *An Encouragement of Learning*, trans. David A. Dilworth and Umeyo Hirano (Sophia University, 1969), pp. 1–7, and Fukuzawa Yukichi, "Encouragement of Learning," in *The Autobiography of Yukichi Fukuzawa*, trans. Eiichi Kiyooka (Schocken, 1972), pp. 391–397. The latter translation is more faithful to the tone of the original than is the former.

4. This formula is to be found in some Bakumatsu texts aimed at samurai. See Udono, "Kanyō," *Bushidō sōsho*, vol. 3, pp. 245–246.

becomes a rich man. The man without learning becomes a poor man, an inferior man.

Learning as defined by Fukuzawa was basically academic study. He did not make the distinction that Smiles made between learning and wisdom, but he did emphasize "useful" studies rather than speculative and artistic learning. This meant basic literacy, ordinary arithmetic, and an essentially liberal arts course of geography, physics, history, economics, and ethics. For each of these fields he emphasized the use of translations from Western languages. For brighter students, he suggested the study of Western languages.

That such a program could indeed bring wealth and honor was Fukuzawa's personal experience.[5] He had been born into the family of a relatively low ranked retainer of the Nakatsu fief. Had his elder brother not died, he could not have even looked forward to succeeding to his father's position, that of handling the rice transactions of the fief in Osaka, a job that his father, a frustrated Confucian scholar, very much detested. In his *Autobiography* Fukuzawa recorded that his father considered sending him out to the priesthood in order to give him a chance at a career greater than that permitted within the confines of the hereditary system.[6] His subsequent career was not, however, in the priesthood, but in Dutch Learning (Rangaku), a field he turned to shortly after Perry came to Japan in 1854. Correctly perceiving that Western contact would mean greater opportunities, Fukuzawa soon gained a position with the Tokugawa government, serving on several missions to foreign countries.

What seemed to have been a substantial rise in the making was cut short by two events. First, Fukuzawa was investigated (and later cleared) on charges that he had misused government funds while abroad. Second, the Meiji Restoration saw the overthrow of the Tokugawa and the rise to power of a government that Fukuzawa misread as rabidly antiforeign. Soured on the Tokugawa and fearful of the new government, Fukuzawa bided his time as an educator at

5. Despite an enormous volume of writing on Fukuzawa, there exists no reliable, critical, and comprehensive biography of him. For the years of his career under discussion here, Hirota Masaki, *Fukuzawa Yukichi kenkyū* (Tōkyō daigaku shuppan-kai, 1976), esp. pp. 17–92, is very good and supplants all previous work.

6. Fukuzawa, *Autobiography*, pp. 5–6. The reader is warned that this *Autobiography* tells more about what Fukuzawa liked to think he had done rather than what he had in fact accomplished.

his academy. This academy had been founded with the profits he had made by capitalizing on his knowledge of foreign countries while still a Tokugawa retainer. After realizing that the new government was favorable to things foreign, he returned to his pamphleteering and translation. In the years immediately after the Restoration, these activities made him wealthy and relieved him of any necessity of following the Tokugawa into exile, as Nakamura had done.

In this limited sense, Fukuzawa's career was proof that study could lead to wealth and honor, even under the Tokugawa system. Nevertheless, as a description of what it was that had determined the overall distribution of wealth and honor in society as of 1871 (Meiji 4), the assertions made in *Gakumon no susume* appear as not merely simple but simplistic, his own experience notwithstanding. Fukuzawa was not, however, a simpleton, and the one-sided emphasis in *Gakumon no susume* was part of a sophisticated effort to divert attention away from the actual causes of inequality and to channel potentially destructive energies into striving for wealth and honor through schooling.

Unlike Nakamura, who had been abroad at the time, Fukuzawa had actually experienced the overthrow of the Tokugawa, and the violence of the period seems to have left an indelible impression on him. His *Autobiography*, written many years after the fact and designed to show Fukuzawa at his best, nevertheless reveals a man who was terrified by social and political disorder.[7] Rather than settling discontents that had existed under the Tokugawa, the Meiji Restoration had increased those tensions and, more important, had demonstrated the possibilities for rearranging the distribution of wealth and honor by violent means. Both peasant and samurai discontent continued at a high level after the Restoration, and the latter was of special concern to Fukuzawa. In a later recollection, he declared that one reason he had promoted the school in Nakatsu— the opening of which was occasion for the original *Gakumon no susume*—was that he hoped that through education war between upper and lower samurai could be avoided.[8]

The same fear of discontent based on grievances concerning the

7. Fukuzawa, *Autobiography*, pp. 162–165, 225–260.
8. See Fukuzawa Yukichi, "Kyūhanjō," trans. Carmen Blacker, *Monumenta Nipponica* 9:1–2 (1953): 324.

distribution of wealth and honor in society pervaded that portion of *Gakumon no susume* that dealt with commoners. In addressing them, Fukuzawa decried some of the abuses of the former regime and even encouraged a limited amount of political opposition in the future, provided it was open, quiet, and in accord with "the reason of heaven and the principles of humanity," a style he later defined as martyrdom.[9] He did not think, however, that commoners had any real cause for discontent under the new regime and emphasized the great strides he claimed they had made. According to Fukuzawa, the status of commoners had risen a hundred times over what it had been under the former regime, for commoners could now ride horses, have surnames, and even get government jobs. He did not mention that samurai still had their stipends, their swords, their monopoly on military service, and a practical monopoly of high government positions. Again, his emphasis and selectivity was designed to divert attention away from the actual distribution of wealth and power in contemporary society.

Although admitting the possibility of commoner mobility, Fukuzawa was not comfortable with the idea, nor did he expect very much of it. Essentially, he saw the new, emerging Meiji social order as continuing to be made up of the four formal classes of the Tokugawa period, each with a distinct ethos but with some measure of formal equality. Fukuzawa explained that all men had an equal right to live out their own lives provided they did not infringe upon others, but he explained this in terms of each person's properly knowing his or her "place" (*bungen*). Such a concept did not differ much from that found in Tokugawa-period ethics texts, and the terminology was identical.[10] Fukuzawa linked "place" to rank (*mibun*) and declared that there were "talents and ethics" (*saitoku*) for each and every rank. To know the talents and ethics of one's rank requires knowing the principles of things; to know the principles of things, one must study. If the people do not know that study is the key to wealth and honor, dire consequences will result. In the world there is nothing so pitiful as a people that is illiterate, nothing that is so

---

9. Fukuzawa's political ideas are discussed in Kinmonth, "Fukuzawa Reconsidered," esp. pp. 682–684.

10. There is much in this portion of the original *Gakumon no susume* reminiscent of a Chinese text, *Rikuyu engi tai-i* (introduced in 1722), which was promoted by the Tokugawa government. It is reproduced in *Kyōjun*, vol. 5 of *Nihon kyōkasho taikei* (Kōdansha, 1969), pp. 410 ff.

evil. The extremity of being without wisdom goes so far as to not know shame (*haji*). Because they lack wisdom, when they fall into poverty, when they are pressed by hunger and cold, rather than taking the blame upon themselves, they unreasonably become angry at some nearby rich man or in extreme cases go so far as to form bands (*totō*) and engage in direct petition (*gōso*) and rebellion (*ikki*). If the people failed to operate on the assumption that poverty was entirely their own fault, they could expect a harsh government. If, on the other hand, everyone (and here samurai are probably included) followed his directives and turned their energies to learning, they could expect (and Fukuzawa hoped) that

> this will make it easy for the government to rule and the people will accept its rule [*shihai*] without pain [*kurushimi*], government and people each taking their proper place in preserving the great peace [*taihei*] of the whole nation.

Had *Gakumon no susume* been readable only as a defense of the existing distribution of wealth and honor in society, it is unlikely that it would have achieved the circulation that it did. The main factor in its popularity was doubtless the desire on the part of samurai to rise through academic endeavor. This desire had manifested itself almost as soon as the Tokugawa peace had eliminated opportunities for military aggrandizement in the early seventeenth century.[11] It was further encouraged by the scholastic orientation and the bureaucratic ideal contained in Confucianism. The realities of the Tokugawa system and the gentlemanly ideal of Confucianism worked to keep the pursuit of wealth and honor at the level of a somewhat suspect theme throughout the period, even though there were those who declared that the Confucian de-emphasis of ambition was simply "the customary line of fabrication formulated by those who covet fame."[12]

A few Confucian scholars, such as Ogyū Sorai and Dazai Jun, did see ambition in a positive light and sought to use the promise of rewards as an incentive to encourage study.[13] Their professed goal was

11. See Dore, *Education in Tokugawa Japan*, p. 22, for an example of the early samurai response to Confucianism.
12. This cynical observation was made by Motoori Norinaga, a thinker of merchant-class origin, in his 1794 *Tamakatsuma*. See Minami Hiroshi, *Psychology of the Japanese People*, trans. Albert R. Ikoma (University of Tokyo Press, 1971), pp. 91–92.
13. For Dazai, see R. J. Kirby, "Translation of Dazai Jun's Essay on *Gakusei*," *Transactions of the Asiatic Society of Japan*, First series, 34 (1907): 138; and for Ogyū

to increase the available pool of talented men with a properly moral education; they did not eliminate the moral aspect of learning from their discussion as thoroughly as did Fukuzawa. Popular (as opposed to elite) writers did, however, begin to do this well before the Meiji Restoration. By the late eighteenth century, common school texts were teaching quite explicitly that study was a way to wealth and honor, that learning was a source of profit (*ri*) rather than just the way to know principle (*ri*).[14] Thus, as R. P. Dore has rightly observed, the message of *Gakumon no susume* was a culmination of and not a break with Tokugawa tradition.[15] It was a message designed to appeal to a frustrated ideal within the samurai class and, by so doing, to be more effective in diverting samurai energy from the most traditional route to wealth and honor, violence.

The Tokugawa tradition from which Fukuzawa developed differed at a number of crucial points from that which Nakamura Keiu and his translation of *Self-Help* derived. Fukuzawa was decidedly more elitist. He held no brief for those of humble origin or those who performed manual labor. He defined manual labor as "easy work" and consequently as naturally valued lightly by society. Intellectual work was by contrast appropriately valued highly by society. Although Nakamura Keiu as a Confucian scholar might have been expected to hold to this Mencian formula even more tightly than Fukuzawa, Nakamura had not only translated and emphasized those portions of *Self-Help* celebrating the merits of manual labor, he had also written a special preface in which he used several rather strained examples of Chinese literati who had worked at menial tasks, in order to demonstrate the compatibility of manual work and intellectual accomplishment.[16] Fukuzawa did nothing comparable. He did not tap the indigenous traditions found in the writings of

---

Sorai, "Seidan," in *Ogyū Sorai*, ed. Bitō Masahide, vol. 16 of *Nihon no meicho* (Chūō kōron sha, 1974), esp. pp. 455–459.

14. This connection is made in a 1794 work, "Shingaku ōrai," in *Kyōjun*, pp. 680–683. It is possible that this was an exclusively merchant-class text, although the content does not suggest this. Moreover, studies of Tokugawa elementary education have shown that merchant-class texts were often used in schools aimed primarily at samurai. See Karasawa Tomitarō, *Meiji hyaku-nen no jidō shi* (Kōdansha, 1968), vol. 1, pp. 86–87.

15. Dore, *Education in Tokugawa Japan*, p. 312.

16. Nakamura Keiu, "Saikoku risshi hen dai-yon hen jo," in *Meiji shisōka shū*, vol. 13 of *Nihon gendai bungaku zenshū* (Kōdansha, 1968), p. 90.

Ogyū Sorai and his followers that asserted the special merits of those born in humble circumstances. Fukuzawa's basic thrust was to emphasize final and not initial status and, with the exception of academic study, to ignore the means by which that status had been obtained.

According to Fukuzawa, those people properly respected by society were "doctors, scholars, government officials, merchants who buy and sell on a large scale, and farmers who use [*meshitsukau*] many servants." Although the inclusion of merchants and farmers might suggest that Fukuzawa held to a somewhat equalitarian definition of status, the first three categories were basically samurai monopolies, and both wealthy merchants and farmers often had some samurai privileges and followed samurai customs. In an 1881 (Meiji 14) essay Fukuzawa made it clear that he thought the samurai were the locus of all that was good in Japanese society past and present.

> The great difference in the natural endowments of men are not random. They come from the blood line of mother, father, and ancestors. This is proved by looking at the seeds of trees and grasses, the eggs of fishes and birds, types of horses and cattle, etc. . . . That the *shizoku* [samurai] transcend others in endowed intelligence is clear. This is not the random event of a single day. It is the product of hundreds of years of education handed down within the family. Moreover, this "education" is a matter not solely of reading and writing but of so-called family traditions [*kafū*], something those of other groups cannot expect to know.[17]

Although Fukuzawa did allow that a few wealthy peasants and merchants might share the samurai ethos, the samurai were still the source of everything superior and edifying in Japan. Even when the samurai went into business or agriculture, they did better in these unfamiliar fields, Fukuzawa claimed, than did merchants or peasants, thanks to the natural superiority of samurai. The best thing that Fukuzawa could find to say about commoners in any of the pamphlets of the *Gakumon no susume* series was to suggest that they were "not all foolish, spiritless, and powerless."[18] Nevertheless, for all the superiority that he claimed for the samurai, and for all his reliance in this passage on concepts from Social Darwinism,

17. This quote is from "Jiji kogoto," as reproduced in Fukuchi, *Shizoku*, pp. 236–238.
18. This grudging admission was made in the fourth pamphlet in the series. See Fukuzawa, *Encouragement*, p. 23.

Fukuzawa did not see the samurai as capable of preserving their position in truly free competition with commoners. The passage cited was part of a justification for continued government subsidy of the samurai.

Although much more explicitly elitist than Nakamura Keiu, Fukuzawa did share the former's concern with national strength and independence. The linkage of individual striving to national welfare in *Gakumon no susume* is essentially the same as that found in *Saikoku risshi hen*. That is, the independence of the nation depends on the independence of the people, and the wealth and honor of the nation flows from the wealth and honor of its people.[19] The individual independence he saw as supporting national independence was, of course, purely economic. The issue of individualism in thought or behavior was not raised in the original *Gakumon no susume*, and Fukuzawa later went on record as being specifically opposed to more eccentricity.[20] Fukuzawa, in fact, despite his emphasis on each person's being allowed to live his own life (made in his discussion of "position"), was not willing to permit the individual to spend his wealth freely. He condemned dissipation because such an individual would become a bad model for others and would disturb social customs (*seken no fūzoku*). His arguing against dissipation was, however, the only hint in *Gakumon no susume* that the person of wealth had any responsibility to society at large. Fukuzawa offered nothing comparable to Smiles's discussions of individual philanthropy, social activism, the improvement of life through invention, and the creation of employment opportunities through productive activity. Only in later pamphlets in the series and then only in token fashion did he make up for these omissions.[21]

Failure to discuss social responsibility is striking, not merely with reference to *Self-Help* but also with reference to traditional ethics. Fukuzawa explicitly cited the *Jitsugokyō* [Practical Words for In-

19. This linkage is rather diffuse in the original *Gakumon no susume*, where the emphasis is primarily on not being rebellious. The connection between personal and national independence is first made explicit in the third pamphlet in the series. See Fukuzawa, *Encouragement*, pp. 16–20.
20. See Fukuzawa, *Encouragement*, p. 50.
21. In the tenth pamphlet of the series, Fukuzawa explained that there was more to life than personal profit but that he had not advocated what he called "higher learning," because samurai were incapable of understanding such a concept. See Fukuzawa, *Encouragement*, p. 66.

struction], a popular Tokugawa moral treatise, using it as backing for his claim that the divisions in society were founded on study. He did not, however, offer anything comparable to the exhortations to beneficence and responsibility on the part of those with wealth and rank that were an important part of the *Jitsugokyō*.[22] Missing too from *Gakumon no susume* were any warnings about the transience of wealth and honor, a repeated theme in the *Jitsugokyō*, which had a heavy tinge of Buddhism in its basically Confucian formulations.[23] Whereas the *Jitsugokyō* encouraged learning because it made you a gentleman and a moral man, something that had meaning beyond this life, Fukuzawa looked solely to this world and its material pleasures. In another writing of this period, he advocated study "if you want to live in a stone house and ride in a horse carriage."[24]

Taken together, *Saikoku risshi hen* and *Gakumon no susume* represent the most important and popular writing on advancement directed at the samurai in the first years of the early Meiji. The coincidental popularity of these two rather different works indicates the relative breadth of the samurai tradition at that time. Clearly it was a tradition capable of accepting a wide definition of what constituted advancement (with the notable exception of commercial activity) and which in *Saikoku risshi hen* could be fairly equalitarian in formulation. It was intensely nationalistic but also capable of supporting a strong social and humanitarian consciousness in which personal advancement was subordinated to social good. This was not necessarily the modal case, however, and the popularity of *Gakumon no susume* indicates the existence of a substantial audience eager to read about a narrowly materialistic, extremely elitist concept of advancement based on an underestimation of the difficulties involved, one focused solely on the achievement of government affiliation through academic endeavor. This audience could be expected to read *Saikoku risshi hen* selectively in the light of the values revealed in *Gakumon no susume*.

Just as there was more to the samurai concept of self-advancement than could be found in *Saikoku risshi hen*, there was more to

22. See *Jitsugokyō genkai*, in *Kyōjun*, pp. 200–203.
23. Ibid., pp. 181–183 and 203.
24. Cited in Sakuda Teiichi, "Tekiō no shokeitai," in *Jiga to kankyō*, vol. 6 of *Kindai Nihon shisō shi kōza* (Chikuma shobō, 1972), p. 278.

government reforms than simply giving freedom of occupation to samurai. In terms of future aspirations for self-advancement, the most important reform was to create an institutional framework in which the desire for wealth and honor through academic attainment and bureaucratic affiliation could be realized. The first major step in this direction was taken in late 1872 (Meiji 5) when the government announced a new system of educational control (*gakusei*). It was in the preface to the regulations establishing the new school system that the Meiji government made its most affirmative statement on the pursuit of self-advancement. Here it was proclaimed that henceforth the "goal of life" was to be for a man to "raise himself in the world" (*mi o tateru*), employ his property wisely, and make his endeavors to prosper on the foundation of "striving in the line of his natural aptitudes." Learning (*gakumon*) was declared the capital (*zaihon*) for rising in the world.

Lest anyone miss the point that this new system was to see a break with traditional practice, the proclamation went on to specifically criticize past customs. The purpose and nature of learning had been misunderstood. It had been regarded as a thing only for samurai and above, and they had regarded learning as being for the state, thought it to consist of empty philosophizing and discussion, and moreover expected to be paid to study. From now on learning was to consist of practical subjects: basic literacy, the abacus, vocational skills, law, politics, astronomy, and medicine. Education would be supported by those who received its benefits, and all were ordered to receive those benefits. The proclamation demanded that "every man shall, of his own accord, subordinate all other matter to the education of his children." Aristocrats, warriors, peasants, artisans, merchants, and even women and girls were to receive this education.[25]

Interpretation of this proclamation has been a matter of some controversy among Japanese scholars. Particularly difficult to explain is what has been seen as an almost revolutionary emphasis on individual personal advancement (*risshin shusse*) to the exclusion of national interests, an exclusion that is notable because of its apparent contrast with earlier thinking and that found in later government proclamations. The document is also marked by several statements that seem rather odd by contemporary standards or simple logic. It

---

25. This preface is reproduced in Monbushō, *Gakusei hachijū nen shi* (Monbushō, 1954), pp. 710–711.

stressed freedom of choice but *ordered* all to pursue education. It called for equal education but listed the future recipients in the same order in which they were ranked in traditional documents (samurai, peasants, artisans, merchants), putting females at the bottom of the list. It condemned the impracticality of past learning but defined ordinary education to include law, politics, astronomy, and medicine, subjects of limited use for many segments of society.

Various explanations have been offered for the apparent emphasis on individualistic personal gain. Some have seen the document as a brief triumph of Western individualistic and utilitarian thought which was followed by a conservative reaction to this early infatuation. Others have noted the apparent similarity between the basic message of *Gakumon no susume* and the proclamation and have stressed the persuasive powers of Fukuzawa Yukichi. Yet another explanation is that the government emphasized individual benefit because the system was to be financed largely (90 percent, as it turned out) by those who used it, and to stress personal benefit was to forestall opposition.[26] Each of these explanations has some merit, especially the last, but they all suffer from a misunderstanding of the degree to which the proclamation was indeed a break with previous thought, and from an even more serious misunderstanding of what were the associations of the term *mi o tateru* at this time.

Far from being an expression of any Western contribution, the emphasis on *mi o tateru* (*risshin*) in the proclamation was a reflection of Tokugawa samurai and Confucian thought patterns. The term *mi o tateru* occurs throughout Tokugawa-period writings, especially in works on samurai ethics and in instructions for samurai families. Initially the term appears to have been used to refer to the samurai who had distinguished himself on the battlefield.[27] Later it came to be associated with bureaucratic position during the Tokugawa peace.[28] So acceptable were the connotations of *risshin* that it was often defined as a constituent of filial piety, a formula which

---

26. For the various interpretations of the 1872 proclamation, see Makino Kichigorō, *Meijiki keimō kyōiku no kenkyū* (Ocha no mizu shobō, 1968), pp. 37–47, and Yasukawa Junnosuke, *Nihon kindai kyōiku no shisō kōzō* (Shin-hyōron sha, 1970), pp. 31–38.

27. This is suggested by the usage of the term in "Kuroda Nagamasu yuigon," in *Kinsei buke shisō*, vol. 27 of *Nihon shisō taikei* (Iwanami, 1974), pp. 31–38.

28. The term that thinkers such as Ogyū Sorai used when arguing for the promotion of men of talent was *risshin*.

doubtless reflects the fact that the term is found in the Classic of Filial Piety (*Kōkyō* in Japanese, *Hsiao ching* in Chinese). The person who made a name for himself and rose in the world was properly serving his parents and his ancestors.[29] Only if the individual thought of *risshin* to the exclusion of all other things was there any unfavorable connotation attached to the term.[30] The proper gentleman thought first about knowing the Way, but the same virtues that made one a gentleman were also depicted as instrumental for advancement. The same texts that warn against thinking only of *risshin* also tell the reader what it is that will harm his chances for advancement.[31]

In both Chinese and Japanese writings, *risshin* meant only the acquisition of rank from which proceeded wealth in the form of the emoluments that came with office. It had no connotation of moneymaking, at least among samurai Confucian writers. This was not the case with a closely related term, *risshin shusse*. This word was a peculiar coupling of the Buddhist phrase *shusse*, which meant to go out of the world for the purpose of spiritual enlightenment, and the term *risshin*. According to one theory, this coupling had been made in pre-Tokugawa Zen when separation from the world leading to enlightenment brought a rise (*risshin*) within the hierarchy of the Zen establishment.[32] Since the very temporal *risshin* was coupled to the very spiritual *shusse*, this usage perhaps reflected a bit of medieval

29. See, for example, Honda Tadakazu, "Kyōsei ron," quoted in Dore, *Education in Tokugawa Japan*, p. 63. The terms Dore translates as "ambition" and "to raise one's status" are *risshin* and *mi o tateru*, respectively. The original text is in *Bushidō sōsho*, vol. 2, pp. 249–250.

30. For a general discussion of the formal attitude of Confucian scholars in Japan to self-advancement, see Dore, *Education in Tokugawa Japan*, pp. 62–63.

31. Kaibara Ekiken is an example of a writer who shows such a dualistic attitude. See Kaibara Ekiken, "Yamato zokujun," in *Kaibara Ekiken*, pp. 55–182. Much of the dualism in Tokugawa thought is to be explained by considering the position of the writers. Kaibara, for example, was a hired ideologue writing in behalf of his lord. It was not in the interests of feudal lords to stimulate ambition on the part of their vassals, for the samurai had a long tradition of advancing themselves by any and all means, including treachery. This concern was also evident in samurai house precepts (*kakun*), which often took a negative attitude to *risshin*. For a discussion of this phenomenon, see Sakurai, *Haji*, pp. 88–130. Other writers (Ogyū Sorai, for example) who were more favorable to the principle of promotion were in part seeking to advance their own careers. See J. R. McEwan, *The Political Writings of Ogyū Sorai* (Cambridge University Press, 1962), p. 83.

32. This thesis is advanced in *Nihon kokugo dai-jiten* (Shōgakkan, 1974), vol. 20, p. 342.

cynicism about Zen, which had grown rather affluent under warrior patronage. Cynical or not, the associations of *risshin shusse* were apparently somewhat vulgar throughout the Tokugawa period, and the term almost never appears in moralistic writings.[33] Subsequently, the original Buddhist association was lost. The *shusse* component appears to have been used ambiguously to mean to go out of the world (*yo o deru*) and to go into the world (*yo ni deru*). During the Meiji period, *risshin shusse* was applied to the aspirant to advancement who had to leave his village world (*yo o deru*) and go out into the larger world (*yo ni deru*) that constituted the framework for his advancement. The latter usage still exists. The contemporary term *shusse shita* ("he's made it") refers to the person who has achieved publicly recognized success, including commercial success.[34]

Thus, the 1872 proclamation was not making any quantum leap either in the direction of Western materialism or individualism or even in the direction of indigenous materialism just because it used the term *mi o tateru* (*risshin*). The proclamation said only that learning would lead to an advance in rank, little more. No suggestion was made that learning would be directly profitable. Indeed, the proclamation did not go so far as *Gakumon no susume* and define rank (*mi*) in terms of wealth and honor. At most, the proclamation sought only to generalize an essentially samurai concept of education and advancement, its criticism of past samurai practices to the contrary notwithstanding. This may be seen in its definition of practical education. Only a samurai could think that law, politics, astronomy, and medicine were practical education. Indeed, this is a definition of practical learning (*jitsugaku*) found in late Tokugawa critics. The addition of ordinary arithmetic and the *soroban* to this

33. The only Tokugawa-era use of *risshin shusse* in a moralistic context that I am aware of is found in Yoshida Shōin, "Bukyō zensho kōroku," in *Yoshida Shōin*, p. 146. Yoshida uses it in place of *mi o tateru* as a constituent of filial piety. The term may have been more prevalent in writing of and for the merchant class.

34. Japanese scholars frequently use the term *risshin shusse* with respect to early Meiji aspirations of the type discussed here (academic and bureaucratic rather than capitalistic). In terms of Meiji usage, this would appear to be incorrect. The term *risshin shusse* is common in writing for and by educated youth only *after* the Sino-Japanese War, although it may have been popular in colloquial situations. It does not appear in either *Gakumon no susume* or *Saikoku risshi hen*. It is also of interest to note that the term *risshin* was *not* common in *Saikoku risshi hen*. For one of the few cases where it is used, see *SKRH*, 1:2. Whatever the interpretation of the work, it was not a self-conscious manual explaining how to achieve *risshin* or *risshin shusse*.

list (also found in *Gakumon no susume*) was no less reflective of a samurai perspective. As early as Kaibara Ekiken in the eighteenth century, writers had been telling samurai that they should know practical arithmetic in order to properly manage their finances.[35] Certainly no merchant needed to be told the importance of the abacus.

During the last years of the Tokugawa, a number of thinkers had also proposed various plans for comprehensive education quite similar to that actually implemented by the Meiji government.[36] Just as did the 1872 proclamation, these proposals assumed the continued existence of the Tokugawa status system and phrased their calls for general education in similar language. Finally, it may be noted that the imperious demand that all pursue education was doubtless based on the assumption that it was better for the nation to have all educated by samurai standards than to leave this up to individual decision.

When it was formulated into law, the new school system had no overt limits on the class origins of those who might obtain the capital for rising in the world. As the system developed in fact, it primarily served samurai interests. The grandiose building plans of the 1872 system were only partially realized. Some 53,610 primary schools, 256 middle schools, and 8 universities (*daigaku*) were envisioned.[37] Neither the funds nor the teachers were available for the planned number of elementary schools, and by 1879–1880 (Meiji 12–13) the original goal for new schools had been recognized as impossible. Previously existing schools, such as *terakoya*, and their teachers were incorporated into the system.[38] Only one university was established, and no middle schools. This was *not* a matter of deliberately limiting higher education; there was simply insufficient demand. Both the costs of elementary education and a general disbelief in the promise of advancement as a result of education contributed to this.

35. A samurai tendency to despise arithmetic is condemned in Kaibara Ekiken, "Yamato zoku-dōji-jun," *Kaibara Ekiken*, p. 196. A case for family budgeting is made in Yoshida Shōin, "Bukyō zensho kōroku," in *Yoshida Shōin*, pp. 169–170.
36. See, for example, the proposals of Yoshida Shōin described in Nakaizumi Tetsutoshi, *Nihon kinsei kyōiku shisō no kenkyū* (Yoshikawa kōbunkan, 1966), pp. 108–117.
37. Ogawa Tarō, *Risshin shusse shugi no kyōiku* (Reimei shobō, 1968), p. 100.
38. Dore, "Legacy," p. 104.

Although the elementary-school plan had called for attendance between the ages of six and fourteen, this was not mandatory, and in fact actual attendance was very low.[39] The attrition rate was also extremely high, with more than half of those who entered elementary school leaving after a year and a half or less.[40] Peasants could spare neither the money (50 sen per month for elementary school and 5 yen 50 sen per month for middle school)[41] nor the labor of their children. Moreover, the school system taught little that was of use to the peasant's child as a peasant. To get a return on his investment, the peasant family would have to see its aspirant *shusse* (leave the village) and rise high enough in the world to justify an outlay that might demand virtual starvation for the rest of the family. As Ogawa Tarō has observed, the peasants did not refuse to send their children to school simply out of sheer stupidity or stubbornness; there were good economic reasons not to send them.[42] To most peasants survival was a more immediate concern than advancement, and they demonstrated this, not merely by not sending their children to school, but by rioting against the schools and the tax burden caused by them.[43]

In addition to the high attrition rate that obtained for elementary school, the proportion of those advancing into the upper level of elementary school (*kōtō shōgakkō*) or further into secondary schools was quite small. For example, while there were roughly two million elementary-school students in 1875 (Meiji 8), by 1877–1882 (Meiji 10–15), when most of this two million might be expected to have been in middle school, there were but ten to fifteen thousand such students in all. A very few received a much larger stock of educational capital for their rise in the world than the very many. In this context it is important to note that this low advancement rate was *not* a matter of too many aspirants for too few positions. Competi-

---

39. Japanese National Commission for UNESCO, *The Role of Education in the Social and Economic Development of Japan* (Ministry of Education, 1966), 64–65.
40. Ogawa, *Risshin*, p. 102.
41. Fukuchi, *Shizoku*, p. 229.
42. Ogawa, *Risshin*, pp. 102–104.
43. See Dore, "Legacy," p. 102, and Herbert Passin, *Society and Education in Japan* (Columbia University Press, 1965), pp. 78–80; also Michio Nagai, "Westernization and Japanization: The Early Meiji Transformation of Education," in *Tradition and Modernization in Japanese Culture*, ed. Donald Shively (Princeton University Press, 1971), pp. 54–61.

tion rates to enter even the best schools were not high at this time.[44] Lack of interest, lack of money, and the disruptive effects of the internal political disturbances were far more important than was the ratio of applicants to positions in determining the small number receiving higher education.

By all indications, those for whom education had the most appeal were the sons of samurai and the sons of middle and wealthy peasants (gōnō). Though samurai cannot account for all the roughly one-third of school-age children who were actually in school during these years, being but 6 percent of the population, statistics indicate that at higher levels they were clearly in the majority. In 1878 (Meiji 11), three out of four students at the Imperial University (Teikoku Daigaku at this time, later called Tōkyō Teikoku Daigaku or Tokyo Imperial University after the founding of other imperial universities beginning with one in Kyoto in 1897) were reported to be of shizoku (samurai) origin. This ratio declined steadily until roughly half of the Imperial University students were commoners and half samurai in 1885 (Meiji 18), but this still left samurai over-represented relative to their position in the total population, a situation that persisted for several decades.[45] Not until the turn of the century did commoners come to constitute a majority at some higher- and middle-level schools that fed into the imperial universities.[46] Those of samurai descent were also a large proportion of the teachers at this time—not at all surprising, since this was a logical field for the old order's most literate class. In 1883 (Meiji 16) samurai were more than 70 percent of the middle-school (chūgakkō) and 40 percent of primary-school (shōgakkō) teachers.[47] Samurai were also dominant among those receiving the rank of hakushi (doctor) between 1888 (Meiji 21) and 1902 (Meiji 35), receiving over 70 percent of the degrees bestowed.[48] Statistics for other groups seem to be unavailable, but the well-known interest of the middle and wealthy peasants in education and their possession of the necessary financial means suggests that they

44. These rates are discussed in chapter 5.
45. Asō, Education, p. 6 and Wagakuni no kōtō kyōiku (Monbushō, 1964), p. 35.
46. Karasawa Tomitarō, Gakusei no rekishi (Sōbun sha, 1955), pp. 163–167, discusses the available evidence.
47. Asō, Education, p. 6. This percentage declined rapidly as elementary-school teaching became a route to petty risshin for those attracted by the essentially free normal-school education. See Ogawa, Risshin, p. 113.
48. Fukuchi, Shizoku, pp. 243–244.

made up most of the commoners who were in the upper levels of education at this time.[49] Though not excluded by law from the system, poorer peasants were for the most part barred by financial circumstances. Merchants, according to contemporary observers, had little interest in sending their children for more than a small amount of education, even if they were financially capable of more.[50]

The material to plumb the thoughts of those who were in the school system just described consists of a number of magazines belonging to a popular though unrecognized and unstudied genre which flourished throughout the Meiji era.[51] Essentially, these magazines published compositions by readers, either as a supplement to their regular articles or, in some notable instances, as their sole editorial matter. Individual magazines operated on various principles. Some indicated the topics to be written on while others seem to have left the choice of subject to the writers. Some offered prizes, such as books, magazine subscriptions, or even money.[52] In others the only reward was publication. This was apparently more than enough incentive for most readers and writers. *Eisai shinshi* [Talent Forum], one of the most popular and widely read of this genre, offered this incentive alone, but it survived for almost twenty-five years, an exceptionally long life for a Meiji magazine. Started as a second line of business by a papermaking firm, the first issue appeared in 1877 (Meiji 10), and the last in 1901 or 1902.[53] The circulation was impressive by Meiji standards, reaching almost half a million total for 1878–1879 (Meiji 11–12), twice that of the next most popular magazine, *Marumaru chinbum*.[54] Although *Eisai shinshi* was the most popular and longest lived, it was by no means the only

---

49. See chapter 3 and the works of Irokawa Daikichi cited.
50. Fukuchi, *Shizoku*, p. 229.
51. My attention was called to the existence of this genre by the truly seminal work of Maeda Ai. See Maeda Ai, "Meiji risshin shusse shugi no keifu," *Bungaku* 33:4 (April 1965): 10–21.
52. Kimura Shōshū, *Shōnen bungaku shi Meiji hen* (Dōwa shunjū sha, 1949), vol. 1, p. 17. This work is one of the few sources of information about these magazines.
53. Ibid., p. 20.
54. *Marumaru chinbun* was an immensely popular satirical magazine published from 1877 to 1907 (Meiji 10–40). It reminds one of *Mad*. Kōtoku Denjirō (Shūsui) was one of its writers. The circulation figures on *Eisai shinshi* are from Maeda, "Meiji risshin," p. 15.

Front page of *Eisai shinshi* [*Talent Forum*]. The example is from the 1890s, but the same format was used throughout its existence.

such magazine of this type, even during the early Meiji era. These other magazines, though available only in limited number, provide a check on the themes found in *Eisai shinshi*.⁵⁵ Because many of the compositions appearing in these magazines in this period were explicitly based on topics drawn from *Saikoku risshi hen* or *Gakumon no susume* or give internal evidence of having been so based, they provide a contemporary (rather than recollective) survey of what these works meant to early Meiji Japanese.⁵⁶

Though it is not possible to give a complete demographic breakdown on the *Eisai shinshi* audience, something of a profile may be gotten from a survey of the data given for the composition writers, who were drawn exclusively from the ranks of the readers. (The magazine had no other editorial content at this time.) For the years in question, 1877–1879 (Meiji 10–12), the writers on advancement were largely but not exclusively male (74%). Their ages ranged from seven to eighteen, with the modal age being thirteen. This in turn indicates that most were in the upper form of elementary school, which, given the attrition rates of the day, implies that they came from families of some financial means, had well-off patrons, or were from poor families with a desperate desire to see a son rise through education.⁵⁷ Where class was indicated, roughly half claimed to be

---

55. The Meiji Shinbun Zasshi Bunko has many magazines devoted to student essays but usually only two or three numbers of each. I tried to examine all such magazines as a check on the themes found in *Eisai shinshi*. I found nothing to suggest that its themes were unusual.

56. Several objections may be raised to the use of compositions in such a magazine as source material. The most obvious question is that of editorial intervention, not just by the staff of the magazine, but by relatives, parents, and teachers. There definitely was coaching. Kimura Shōshū, who had experience in editing late Meiji magazines of this genre, has pointed out that the essays use language beyond the likely capability of the ten-to-fifteen-year-olds who nominally contributed the articles. Kimura, *Shōnen bungaku*, vol. 1, p. 29. This intervention does not invalidate these compositions as a source. One "learns" by telling the teacher what he wants to hear. Reward comes for the correct responses, punishment for the incorrect. The compositions indicate the values to which these youth were being socialized. A second objection involves the "representativeness of the sample." This is not really a problem, however, for the concern here is not with all Japanese youth but with those pursuing self-advancement through education.

57. The large number of compositions in *Eisai shinshi* by youth who later became well known indicates the type of audience it attracted. Kimura has claimed that 8 or 9 out of every 10 who later achieved some fame had written for the magazine. Kimura, *Shōnen bungaku*, vol. 1, p. 17. This is perhaps an exaggeration, but it is not difficult to

STUDY FOR WEALTH AND HONOR

samurai, and half, commoners (*heimin*). The largest number were from the Tokyo area, but all regions of the country with the exception of Hokkaido were represented.[58]

Those who contributed essays to *Eisai shinshi* wrote on topics ranging from such simple schoolboy subjects as "My summer vacation" or "My trip to Mt. Fuji" to more weighty issues, such as equal rights for women or the merits of avoiding alcohol and tobacco. Compositions concerning personal advancement were less diverse and tended to repeat certain basic themes:

> Study is the capital from which one receives wealth and fame.
> Study is the base for rising in the world.
> Study is the base for prosperity and good fortune.
> Learning is the base for enriching the household.
> Time is the capital for the creation of wealth and honor.
> Even one second is the foundation of a great activity.
> Learning is the key to receiving the price of wealth and honor.
> Explaining the power of endurance.
> Explaining the relation between diligence-endurance, laziness, and wise men and fools.
> Why we must strive for good character.

As this selection of titles indicates, the most frequently stated goal of the *Eisai shinshi* composition was the acquisition of wealth and honor (*fūki*), the same term noted in the previous discussions of *Gakumon no susume* and *Saikoku risshi hen*. Many of the essays simply repeat the term over and over again in an amuletic fashion. The meaning is not explained, doubtless because all knew what wealth and honor were. Occasionally, however, an essay does define

---

find the names of various middle and late Meiji figures attached to *Eisai shinshi* compositions. The labor leader Sakai Kosen (Toshihiko) and the critic Ōmachi Keigetsu published compositions in it. Ishii Kendō, "Meiji shoki no shōnen zasshi," *Taiyō* 33 : 8 (June 1927): 411. A number of figures later associated with the Genyūsha, the dominant literary society of the 1890s, first broke into print in it. Kimura, *Shōnen bungaku*, vol. 1, p. 30. In general, the magazine appears to have been an outlet for the brighter and more ambitious students of the period. Uchida Roan was one of its avid readers and claimed that it was must reading among his elementary-school contemporaries. Uchida Roan, "Meiji jū nen zengo no shōgakkō" *Taiyō* 33 : 8 (June 1927): 418.

58. Information concerning the demographic characteristics of the *Eisai shinshi* contributors is tabulated in the appendix. In considering the geographical spread of *Eisai shinshi* readers and the large circulation, it must be remembered that this was before the national railroad and postal network was fully developed, making the diffusion of this journal all the more remarkable.

wealth and honor by describing the situation of those with neither. Here are the words of a fourteen-year-old writing in *Eisai shinshi*:

> When I look at the aspects of the types of men in this world, I see that there are two types, an upper and a lower. Who are these people of the upper class of society? They are the ones who receive the greatest fortune and prosperity [*kōfuku-eiga*] or the greatest wealth and highest honor. Who are the people of the lower part of society? These are the people who spend the greater part of their time running from right to left in order to gain the needs of a day. These poor types ought generally to be pitied, for they never have a chance to eat delicious foods or to experience those things which delight the ear.[59]

In this statement more than money is included in the term "wealth," and more than respect in the term "honor." There is a clear division of society into an upper and obviously ruling class and a lower and equally obviously subservient class. Further, the wealth pictured is that which leads to freedom from work or daily struggle. It is not the wealth and honor depicted in *Saikoku risshi hen*, which carried with it the responsibility to be and remain active and productive. It is wealth and honor that results in leisure, a reflection of an aristocratic and not a bourgeois value system.

This statement presents the basic value system of the samurai class with respect to advancement and its reward. Such thinking is to be found in many Tokugawa writings directed at the samurai. For example, Tokugawa Yoshimune (1684–1751) charged the samurai of his day to remember their ancestors, for those ancestors gave the present generation the stipend that freed them from having to work like peasants, artisans, and merchants. As Yoshimune and others stressed, samurai did not work but they never had to face starvation or cold.[60] In theory the freedom from work was supposed to allow the samurai time to cultivate virtue,[61] but that portion of the traditional formula did not appear in essays. There was instead only a

---

59. "Kinben wa kōfuku no moto," *Eisai shinshi*, no. 24 (August 18, 1877), p. 2. This essay did not carry a class designation, but the reader is cautioned that I am not saying that all such essays were by samurai, only that they represented an essentially samurai ideal. Since four of the six essays on wealth and honor having class designations were written by samurai, a case can be made for saying that this was probably written by a child of samurai background.

60. Ienaga, *Nihon dōtoku*, p. 103.

61. Yamaga Sokō was a pioneer in such justifications of samurai parasitism. See Yamaga Sokō, "The Way of the Samurai," in *Sources of Japanese Tradition*, vol. 1, pp. 389–391.

repeated concern with wealth and honor coupled to an almost grim determination to acquire that wealth and honor. In large measure this emphasis on wealth and honor without any traditional responsibility is to be explained by two factors. First, these youth were not moralists (though doubtless many of their teachers were) and were less prone to hide ambition in a moralizing rhetoric. Second, many samurai had come down in the world as a result of the Meiji Restoration. While a few had made it in the new government, as a whole the Restoration had taken away the last shreds of honor which had been hiding the rather threadbare conditions in the lower ranks of the class.

As Ossowski has noted in another context, "A gentleman is not supposed to care about money. But one must have money in order not to care about it."[62] By having their stipends commuted to bonds in 1876 (Meiji 9), the former warriors had most of the pedestal they stood upon pulled out from under them. Eighty-six percent of them had received less than 1,100 yen in bonds, which in turn meant an interest income of 6 yen 33 sen a month or less, hardly enough to give them the economic base to lord it over merchants or others with money.[63] Even more important than loss of stipend for many had been the loss of perquisites and opportunities for petty graft, which, according to Fukuzawa Yukichi, had been a major element of samurai income. This had come about earlier with the elimination of the alternate service (*sankin kōtai*) system and the shift to more centralized administration.[64] When the loss of stipends was added to this earlier reduction in income, the position of many samurai became grim. In the worst instances, they were, according to many contemporary accounts, reduced to such menial tasks as pulling rickshaw in Tokyo. Doubtless, few children of samurai so reduced were included among the *Eisai shinshi* contributors, but even for those whose deprivation was relative rather than absolute, the change in circumstances was an important incentive to seek a renewal of family fortunes through education. Subsequently, this would become a common literary motif.

Another popular essay topic divided men into two different categories, the wise (*ken*) and the foolish (*gu*). A whole series in one maga-

62. Stanislaw Ossowski, *Class Structure in the Social Consciousness* (Routledge & Kegan Paul, 1963), p. 49.
63. Fukuchi, *Shizoku*, p. 75–76.   64. Fukuzawa, "Kyūhanjō," p. 307.

zine dealt with the theme "What determines wisdom and stupidity in man?" All answered in similar terms: "He who studies from childhood becomes clever; he who does not study becomes a fool."[65] This was not a simple question of securing knowledge through study, for as other compositions made clear, the *kengu* (wisdom/stupidity) distinction was closely related to the *fūki-hinsen* (wealthy and honored, humble and despised) distinction with its connotations of rulers and ruled. Consider the words of a twelve-year-old:

Is there anyone who does not desire wealth and fame? Is there anyone who does not hate being poor and despised? Since there are always people sunk into poverty and obscurity and always those who have wealth and fame, how do these differences come about? Is it not that what makes the difference between wealth and fame, poverty and obscurity among men is whether they studied or did not study when they were children? If you study, you become a clever man [*kenjin*]. On the other hand, if you do not study, you become a fool [*gujin*]. If you become a fool, you become poor and wretched.

To this youth the difference between wise men and fools was no mere academic distinction. He continued by saying, "If we carry through the hard work of being a student, bear up under the load, study and work like a lion, it will not be the least difficult to be a great man." And this meant nothing less than becoming prime minister (*dajō-daijin*).[66]

To a certain extent the essays on *kengu*, with their promise of a rise into the ruling elite on the basis of study, seem to have come more often from commoners (*heimin*) than from the sons of samurai. The sample of essays with clear class indications is quite small, but it may be surmised that the compositions on *kengu* represented the hopes and beliefs of commoner sons (probably middle and wealthy peasants) that they too could rise into the ruling strata through the adoption of samurai conceits.[67] If this is true, then it would suggest that the promise of advancement through education went beyond the samurai but only at the price of accepting their definition of the social order. There are very few essays to be found in

65. *Shōgaku sakubun zasshi*, no. 1 (May, 1878). This was also a theme in 19 percent of the *Eisai shinshi* compositions.
66. Maeda, "Meiji risshin," p. 16. The quotation is from *Eisai shinshi* (July 5, 1879).
67. Of essays on *kengu* indicating class, six were from commoners and two from samurai.

this period which deal with commercial or agricultural activities. Learning is rarely described as that which could be used to make a family business prosper or to increase the profit derived from agriculture. The only specific applications for learning involve government affiliation.

The samurai value system is much in evidence in those compositions that deal with the individual virtues said by the writers to lead to wealth and honor. A particularly striking instance of this involves those essays that deal with the saving of time. There are many compositions which at first glance might be thought to be part of a merchant's view of time. They stress that "even a second of time" is important and that the failure to begrudge time leads to poverty. This was not a merchant's view of time, however, for the opposite of poverty is always wealth and honor. A typical composition on this subject used Napoleon as an example of a man who knew the value of time—because he used every spare second to study to get into military school—and presented a Napoleonic ambition as well. The preface to this essay stated: "Generally, if man wants to accomplish a meritorious task and hand down for a thousand generations his fame, there is but one way, and that is by not wasting time."[68]

Equally important to the composition writers was the idea of perseverance (*nintai*), a subject that many explained by using examples drawn from *Saikoku risshi hen*. One typical composition explained perseverance as follows:

> Perseverance is according to the health of the body. Health is born of perseverance. They are mutually related. The three characters [*nintairyoku*] must be the basis for accomplishing one's ambition [*risshi*], carrying out a great work, and thus writing one's name in history.
>
> Stephenson required fifteen years before he first invented the steam engine. Did it not take thirty years before Watt was able to reveal the great achievement of his steam engine? Many were the difficulties and misfortunes on their path to achievement. They endured these great misfortunes. If they had not endured these great misfortunes, could they have been content? Would they have been able to pass a shining accomplishment to posterity?
>
> Men of ancient times did not call victory over the enemy courage; rather, courage was victory over self. It is said a hundred things can be done with perseverance. The necessity of mankind is perseverance.[69]

68. "Kōin kaseki setsu," *Eisai shinshi*, no. 207 (May 14, 1881), pp. 7–8.
69. "Nintairyoku no setsu," *Eisai shinshi*, no. 105 (May 17, 1879), p. 3.

It cannot be denied that Smiles used Watt, Newton, Stephenson, and others as examples of perseverance, but Smiles was more concerned with showing that technical discovery and innovation require time rather than with simply demonstrating the merit of grinding away.

To the young man of Meiji, at least those writing for *Eisai shinshi*, the important issue was neither discovery nor scientific method. Rather, there was always a return to the standard refrain of wealth and honor, wise men and fools. This may be seen in another essay probably based on *Saikoku risshi hen*.

Although it is natural that study [*benkyō*] has been said to be a necessity, now, when these two characters are brought up, it is in view of the fact that wisdom and folly [*kengu*] and wealth and honor [*fūki*] are based on perseverance and study.

For example, while there are people with superior genius, if they do not use this talent and study, their knowledge is invariably not wisdom. Their genius [*sai*] is not genius. This is certainly the truth.

People's good fortune invariably comes from being diligent [*kinben*]. The diligent person is like the ship skillfully sailing with the wind. Is this not natural? Therefore if one employs his faculties [*shinryoku*] and undertakes an endeavor, will attaining that goal, that success, be difficult?

As in olden times when Newton discovered the motions of the heavenly bodies on the basis of extreme perseverance [*nintai*], one ought eventually to be able to enumerate the grains of sand and the stars in heaven.

Saying genius [*sai*] does not mean there is only one kind. Even the activities of the common man should be so called. When this is seen, it is called courage [*eiyū*], but it is the product of perseverance. Ought we not to strive in such a manner?[70]

While this essay is somewhat out of the ordinary in that it gives some recognition to the fact that *"even* the activities of the common man" can have value (Smiles would say "particularly"), it is quite typical in that Newton has been turned into an example of a long, tedious struggle, with the relationship between perseverance and scientific experimentation and discovery largely attenuated. One doubts that Smiles would consider merely counting stars or grains of sand a worthwhile endeavor.

Maeda Ai, one of the few Japanese scholars to examine the *Eisai shinshi* compositions, has suggested that the emphasis on perseverance in these essays represents a bureaucratic ethos, the expectations of those who think in terms of bureaucratic careers. Certainly,

70. "Hito no kengu wa tainin-benkyō to taida ni kansuru setsu," *Eisai shinshi*, no. 6 (April 14, 1877), p. 3.

the essential characteristic of bureaucratic advancement is that it is more or less predictable at the same time that it comes rather slowly.[71] An assumption that the youth who wrote for *Eisai shinshi* thought only in terms of bureaucratic careers not only explains the absence of references to business, but also explains the peculiar interpretation of that virtue which most (61%) of the compositions cite, *benkyō*.

Benkyō is a term soon learned by beginning students of Japanese as an equivalent for the English word *study*. This is indeed the case for contemporary Japanese, but it was not true for Tokugawa usage of the term or even for early Meiji usage. In Tokugawa scholarly writing the term meant "industry" or "hard work."[72] As a consequence, Nakamura Keiu consistently used the term *benkyō* to translate "the spirit of industry" in *Saikoku risshi hen*.[73] Nowhere did he come close to using it as an equivalent for *study*. Neither of the other sources, *Gakumon no susume* and the 1872 school-system proclamation, which furnished inspiration to *Eisai shinshi* writers, used the term *benkyō*. Both used the colloquial term *manabu* to mean study or learn. The same was true of Tokugawa ethics texts, the only other sources that were likely to have been as widely read as *Gakumon no susume*, *Saikoku risshi hen*, or the 1872 proclamation.

Thus, the probable source for the popularity of the term is *Saikoku risshi hen*, where it appears very often, more often than in any other common early Meiji or Tokugawa text.[74] Nevertheless, the interpretation of *benkyō* in the student compositions is rather different from its usage in *Saikoku risshi hen* and that portion of the Tokugawa tradition which Nakamura drew upon. Consider the following essay by a thirteen-year-old:

---

71. Mannheim, *Knowledge*, pp. 249–250, notes this aspect of bureaucratic careers.

72. *Benkyō* is not all that common in Tokugawa texts. One which did use it as described here is Minagawa Kien, "Kien tōyō shōroku," in *Bushidō sōsho*, vol. 2, pp. 229–244. The term was also used by merchants to refer to selling goods at low cost, a usage still to be encountered in Japan.

73. For example, Nakamura translated "spirit of industry" as *shokugyō ni benkyō suru seishin*. *SH*, p. 27, and *SKRH*, 2:1. Numerous similar examples appear throughout *Saikoku risshi hen*. See *SKRH*, 1:6; 2:2; 5:28; 6:1; 12:7; etc.

74. Another contemporary text that might have popularized *benkyō* meaning study is Aoki Hosei, "Minka dōmō kai," in *Nihon kyōkasho taikei kindai hen*, vol. 1, pp. 383–416. See pp. 390 and 401 for *benkyō* used to mean *study*. This work was used as a guide for teachers and may have determined the interpretation of *benkyō* and *Saikoku risshi hen* in some schools.

The earth is filled with we know not how many millions of plants and animals. Man alone has a soul [tamashii]. The difference between poverty and wealth, wisdom and foolishness, is a matter of study or non-study [benkyō] from preschool age. The fundamental nature of man is good like a jewel. Therefore, from childhood, without a moment of laziness, polishing the knowledge of arts and sciences is the way to make clear the principles of heaven and the way of man. Moreover, while it may be said that those who invented such things as the water wheel and the windmill, which gave great profit to later generations, were poor and despised at the time of invention, they eventually received great wealth.

If one is lazy from childhood, uses his days in idleness or play, by adolescence he will not be able to achieve one single endeavor. While he may have been born into a household [ie] of wealth and honor, in the end he will sink to poverty and deprivation so bad that he will not even have a morning and evening fire. Will he not be ashamed, inferior even to beasts, unable to carry out humanity and justice [jingi] and the five virtues [gojō] which ought to be the soul of man? This man will know shame and insult [chijoku]. He will be like a firefly passing its days among the snows. Will such a one as this receive the benefits of study? This is my idea.[75]

Most of the sense of productive industry and invention contained in benkyō has been lost with the term's being absorbed into the traditional rhetoric of ethical cultivation. All of the clichés in this composition—and it is basically a collection of clichés—are, with the exception of the reference to invention, straight out of Tokugawa-period ethics texts.[76]

Once again, this change in the meaning of benkyō would seem to be, as Maeda Ai has suggested, a manifestation of the samurai ethos.[77] Although some samurai, such as Nakamura, could understand the "spirit of industry" contained in Self-Help, for the Eisai shinshi youth and for their teachers and parents, who presumably coached many of these essays, industry and invention were rather remote concepts. Wealth and honor, family fortune, shame, and traditional ethical precepts were much more familiar. The references to wealth and honor in Saikoku risshi hen and its basically ethical orientation linked it to traditional expectations and thought patterns. The readers then absorbed what fit their traditional expectations and thought patterns and left the rest behind. None of the

75. "Fūki benkyō yori shōzuru no setsu," Eisai shinshi, no. 4 (March 1, 1877), p. 3.
76. The Jitsugokyō and the Rikuyu engi tai-i texts are good sources of these phrases.
77. Maeda, "Meiji risshin," pp. 17–18, 18, n.5.

compositions in this period celebrate humble origins, hard work (in a physical sense), frugality (other than time), attention to detail, scientific experimentation, or any of the host of virtues in *Saikoku risshi hen*. What was intellectually acceptable in *Saikoku risshi hen* was not necessarily what was popular.

The modal case in these essays was closer to *Gakumon no susume* than to *Saikoku risshi hen* in the sense that academic study was seen as the primary route to wealth and honor. They also shared Fukuzawa's lack of concern with the responsibilities of wealth and honor. As Maeda Ai has also perceptively noted, the extensive warnings against the misuse of wealth in *Saikoku risshi hen* do not appear in a single *Eisai shinshi* composition.[78] Even traditional references to "humanity and justice" of the type found in the essay above are relatively rare. Most of the essayists were concerned, as was Fukuzawa Yukichi, with the acquisition of wealth and honor, not with what was to be done once these were attained. Doubtless this orientation was behind Nishimura Shigeki's observation made in 1880 (Meiji 13) that it was part of the mood of the times to "despise the honest and upright poor and out of covetousness revere the wealthy and honored."[79] As would be subsequent Japanese fashion, he blamed this on Western influences, conveniently ignoring the tradition of indigenous materialism reflected in *Gakumon no susume*. Nishimura did not, however, reject things Western completely. The text he wrote in order to correct the contemporary emphasis on wealth and honor drew heavily on Nakamura's versions of *Self-Help* and *Character*. The passages he used were those stating the major themes the young essayists ignored, such as hard work and respect for those working at menial tasks.[80]

The *Eisai shinshi* essayists were selective, not merely with respect to *Saikoku risshi hen*, but also with respect to indigenous writing on personal advancement. Most notably, they gave no attention whatsoever to interpersonal relations as a determinant of advancement. This omission is particularly striking, since the very texts that contained the traditional clichés found in the *Eisai shinshi* compositions presented what amounted to a "personality" (as contrasted to character) ethic of advancement. Tokugawa ethics

78. Ibid., p. 18.
79. Quoted in Miyata, *Dōtoku kyōiku*, vol. 1, p. 15.
80. This text is reproduced, ibid., pp. 93–115.

texts stressed the importance of observing precedence, addressing people properly according to their rank, and cultivating proper relations with superiors and inferiors. The observance of proper decorum was a major theme, and numerous manuals on the subject were published. In part this emphasis on decorum and form was inherent in Confucianism and was also a reflection of the ceremonial nature of government, but there was another basis for such an emphasis.

A stress on interpersonal relations and personality can be associated with certain environments for striving: where there is a surplus of aspirants over opportunities; where there are no clear-cut standards for performance and advancement; where the work situation involves relations between people of widely varying status and power. The Tokugawa samurai faced all three conditions, and in some writers the relation between the Confucian-sanctioned values of decorum and propriety were rather specifically linked to personal advancement. Kaibara Ekiken's writings are a good example of this. He warned against getting into arguments (even if one was correct), carrying tales, and bad-mouthing associates, and explained such vital issues as how to praise other people and the importance of avoiding any display of one's own talent and ability, especially where it might show up duller associates. Proper reciprocity to those aiding in one's advancement was counseled.[81] With only a little reading between the lines, Kaibara's advice appears as a more or less complete ethic for the functionary who will rise through his congeniality and contacts rather than his ability.

Closer in time to the *Eisai shinshi* essayists, Fukuzawa Yukichi had also stressed the importance of interpersonal relations. The last pamphlet in *Gakumon no susume* gave three keys to "popularity" (*jinbō*): a smooth public-speaking style, a countenance that would produce empathy, and a careful attention to connections and acquaintances.[82] Nevertheless, despite both traditional and proximate models for emphasizing interpersonal relations, the *Eisai shinshi* essayists, no matter how far they were from *Saikoku risshi hen* and no matter how traditional their rhetoric, never deviated from their basic emphasis on performance. The reasons for this are not entirely

---

81. See "Yamato zokujun," in *Kaibara Ekiken*, pp. 104 ff. Many of the same themes appear in Yoshida Shōin, "Bukyō zensho kōroku," in *Yoshida Shōin*, pp. 135–192.

82. Fukuzawa, *Encouragement*, pp. 107–113, esp. pp. 110–113.

clear. Their schoolboy (and -girl) status was perhaps a major factor. An ethic focused on personality depends on an employment situation, and while they wanted to be government functicnaries, that was some years in the future. Study was a matter of far more immediate import, especially since testing and rates of failure under the early Meiji system were severe, and because study was directly linked to wealth and honor by the system.[83] Prestige awards (honor) and cash (wealth) were common.[84] Nevertheless, schoolboy status is not enough to explain the absence of themes on interpersonal relations. Ethics texts in this period, even by such Confucian writers as Nishimura Shigeki, put more emphasis on performance than on human relations. Some weight must therefore be given to two other factors: the general climate of the period, and the ratio between aspirants and positions. This was a period of intense nationalistic concern, at least on the part of older writers. The toadying attitude implied in the personality ethic must have seemed out of place when the immediate goal was national independence and strength. The relative scarcity of youth with even a token amount of modern education was not conducive to an emphasis on personality. Recollections indicate that a seller's market existed in this period for educated young men,[85] and in such a market the purchasers lacked the leverage to enforce demands for certain types of conformist personalities.

Despite placing full responsibility for success or failure on the individual acting alone, the *Eisai shinshi* writers were not individualistic. Their continual expressions of concern with rank, honor, and fame—socially recognized success rather than objective achievement—indicate that they could not conceive of their quest apart from society. The traditional validation of *risshin* as the highest form of filial piety was social and nonindividualistic. Their social orientation was not, however, to society at large but was limited to the household. *Eisai shinshi* youth did not seek to bring any specific benefits to society at large or to the nation. Only one in five essays made any effort to link the activities of the individual to the national interest, and only three out of more than two hundred com-

83. Fukaya Masashi, *Gakureki shugi no keifu* (Reimei shobō, 1969), p. 75.
84. Uchida, "Meiji jū nen," p. 417, and Nagai, "Westernization," pp. 55–56.
85. Fukaya, *Gakureki*, pp. 110–111.

positions contained any mention of the emperor. Where the nation was mentioned, it was usually somewhat after the fact. An essay in *Shōgaku sakubun shinshi* [Elementary-School Composition Magazine] is typical of this type of composition. Under the title "Learning is the Base for Receiving Valuable Rewards," a young man explained that failure to study led to becoming a fool. A fool could not receive respect. One who studied would, however, become wise and receive respect, passing his name down to future generations. If the country had many such men, it would prosper.[86]

Although it has been suggested that in the early Meiji period the "usual argument" was that "the individual through his success—*risshin shusse*—first improves his family's position and then the nation as a whole,"[87] the majority of 1870s youth represented in the *Eisai shinshi* compositions did not in fact make such an argument. Because they did not speak of national benefit, these youth were not "community-centered" in the sense that this term has been used with respect to the alleged character of Meiji entrepreneurs. Nor were they specifically concerned with benefits to local or provincial society. Few essays promised benefits to their own communities as a result of their quest, and to the degree that the provinces in effect exported capital when youth went off to Tokyo or other urban centers to study, the local communities actually lost. Not until the 1890s did a few commentators begin to express concern that the quest for *risshin shusse* was depriving the provinces of talent and leading to an excessive concentration of educated youth in the cities, especially Tokyo.[88] To the extent that these early Meiji youth had any community orientation, that was limited to the idea of a "return wearing brocade" in which the individual, after a suitable *risshin*, returned to his place of origin, showed off his acquired status, basked in the appreciation of family, relatives, and friends, and then returned to the city.[89]

Only one out of ten *Eisai shinshi* compositions specifically mentioned the family or household (*ie*) as a beneficiary of the individ-

---

86. "Gakumon wa kichō no shō o uru kihon no setsu," *Shōgaku sakubun shinshi*, no. 2 (June 1878), p. 5.

87. Herbert Passin, *Society and Education in Japan* (Columbia University Press, 1965), p. 68.

88. This concern is discussed in chapter 4.

89. Kamishima Jirō, *Kindai Nihon no seishin kōzō* (Iwanami shoten, 1961), pp. 249–252, discusses this type of group orientation.

ual's quest, but given what is known about the role of the household and family in Japan, it is reasonable to regard a number of other theme topics as being implicitly linked to the family.[90] According to anthropologist Nakane Chie, the household in Japan has been conceptualized as a "continuum from past to future, including not only the actual residential members with some projection toward those yet unborn." During these years the idea of "becoming an ancestor" through gaining *risshin* and being able to found a household was used to encourage youth in the pursuit of self-advancement.[91] In youth compositions implicit concern with the household was behind the frequent warnings that those who did not study would not only fail to receive wealth and honor but would also bring shame and embarrassment to the household.[92] All those themes that were concerned with leaving a name to the ages must also be credited to this household consciousness, for it was subsequent veneration by members of the household that gave the most meaning to this concern.

Some feeling for the force of household consciousness and its application to early Meiji youth may be seen in the novel *Omoide no ki* [A Record of Remembrances] by Tokutomi Kenjirō (Roka). It describes the efforts of its hero Shintarō, the son of a rural samurai (*gōshi*), to restore his family name. Along the way to *risshin*, the young hero falls into bad company at school and begins to neglect his duties. To set him back on the road to *risshin*, his mother escorts Shintarō to the ancestral grave. There she offers the young boy a knife so that he might kill himself in atonement for his conduct, all the while scolding him for "dragging the family name still lower" and asking if he cannot "feel the humiliation" that his conduct is causing. Suitably impressed by his mother's determination and the lingering ancestral spirits in the graveyard, Shintarō pledges to

90. Generalization about the role of the family in *risshin* aspirations is made difficult by the fact that despite the existence of a coherent, homogeneous "Japanese family system" in ideology and popular writing, kinship and family practices varied greatly, depending on social class, rank, region, and individual families. It can be assumed, however, that samurai family customs and those who sought to emulate the samurai were less diverse. The comments below are generalizations not about Japanese but about samurai and those who followed similar customs and thought.

91. See the discussion in Chie Nakane, *Kinship and Economic Organization in Rural Japan* (University of London, 1967), pp. 2–11.

92. For example, "Yūda wa hyaku aku no oya," *Eisai shinshi*, no. 17 (June 30, 1877), pp. 2–3.

buckle down to his studies and do his best to restore the family name.[93]

This restoration was, it must be noted, essentially a financial operation. As is made clear in the novel, the family name had not been lost through slander, libel, rumor, or the willful actions of family members. The family had lost its money *and then* from this came the "loss of name." After Shintarō's father had been forced to sell all of the family assets, having been done in by his own kindness, the people of the village began to regard the family house as a "rotten tree that might fall on them at any moment." This and other similar statements in the novel indicate that without money there could be no honor. One could be poor but proud, but society would not recognize this. Name and family fortune were not divisible.

Possibly the financial aspect of this fall was more important to the rural samurai, for the novel declared, "A country-man come down in the world is like a gibbeted head stuck on a pole for all to see—only worse, since he is still alive to feel the pain."[94] But, in other novels that portrayed the quest of samurai sons to "restore the family name"—a theme that became a cliché by the end of the period—the loss of name always proceeds from a financial loss. Novels do not treat with such possible themes as a son trying to repay the debts of a father who has embezzled public funds or who has caused losses to others through his own attempts to profit himself.

Thus, while the phrase *na o kaifuku suru* translates literally as "restore the [family] name," a somewhat better translation might be "restore the [family] balance sheet." The point in stressing the financial implications of this concept of restoration is to forestall any idea that by being "family-centered" the early Meiji aspirant to wealth and honor would be any less mercenary or behave in a manner substantially different from someone pursuing self-advancement purely in his own name. Japanese students of family customs have observed that far from being a moderating force, acting in the name of the family could provide a justification for almost any conduct.[95]

93. Tokutomi Kenjirō (Roka), *Footprints in the Snow* [Omoide no ki], trans. Kenneth Strong (Tuttle, 1971), pp. 61–63.
94. Ibid., pp. 53–54.
95. See Isono Fujiko, "Ie to jiga ishiki," in *Jiga to kankyō*, vol. 6 of *Kindai Nihon shisō shi kōza* [Chikuma shobō, 1972], pp. 83–84.

The strained circumstances families found themselves in did not automatically result in encouragement for the pursuit of *risshin shusse* where that quest involved education gained outside the home town. Going off to study was regarded as a speculative venture, and recollections and studies point to many early Meiji youth struggling for months to convince their parents that they should be allowed to leave home for study. It also appears that not a few simply went off without permission.[96] Later in the period, youth seeking to pursue *risshin* in opposition to family wishes became an issue for magazines that advised young men on how to find success.[97] Even in this context, parental opposition could, however, function as an indirect stimulus to the pursuit of *risshin*, for the young man who did disobey would be under that much more pressure to fulfill his quest and to validate his deviance by coming home "wearing the brocade."

That such opposition does not appear in *Eisai shinshi* compositions at this time doubtless reflects the writing of these essays as school projects or with parental help. Failure of such conflict to appear in *Eisai shinshi* does not mean it did not exist.

Another type of conflict was, however, hinted at in *Eisai shinshi* compositions. This involved the question of what type of advancement should be pursued. The samurai class ethos contained two distinct ideals for raising one's name in the world: one was associated with bureaucratic advancement; the other was associated with military activity. Essentially this duality reflected the fusion of the literary and military arts (*bunbu*) that had taken place during the Tokugawa era. The violent spirit of the samurai had been tamed through institutional restraints and Confucian ideology, but the military ethos lingered in their popular literature celebrating warrior heroes. Recollections indicate that in these years both ideals were very much alive. The poet Kitamura Tōkoku, who was in the same age group as the *Eisai shinshi* composition writers, later recalled such a conflict with his mother. She wanted him to make a great name (*kōmyō*) for himself as a functionary. His own dreams and aspirations came from those Tokugawa classics which celebrated individ-

96. Taoka Reiun records his own experience in "Sukiden," in *Taoka Reiun zenshū*, ed. Nishida Masaru (Hōsei daigaku shuppan-kai, 1969), vol. 5, pp. 45 ff. See also Yoshida Noboru, "Meiji jidai no jōkyō yūgaku," in Ishiyama Nobuhira, ed. *Kyōiku no shiteki tenkai* (Dai-Nihon yūbenkai kōdansha, 1953), pp. 429–442, esp. pp. 434–435.
97. Discussed in chapter 5.

ual warrior heroes. As he was dreaming of being a great general and planning heroic deeds (including a suitably glorious death), his mother was standing over him, forcing him to study past midnight each day.[98]

Eisai shinshi compositions hint at this duality in terms of the essays by young men fretting over lost seconds while citing Napoleon as their model and in the terminology used to describe the name they planned to make for themselves. Many young writers expected to make nothing less than a "thunderous name" (*raimei*) to be passed on to the ages.[99] Such grandiose desires could hardly be realized within ordinary bureaucratic careers, probably not even if one became a minister of state. Grander visions were behind such declarations, and given the stability and bureaucratization of the Tokugawa order, the only source for heroic models was traditional fiction and biography.

98. *Kitamura Tōkoku—Yamaji Aizan*, vol. 6 of *Gendai Nihon bungaku taikei* (Chikuma shobō, 1969), pp. 206–209, for his recollections.

99. "Jigyō no seihi kokorozashi no ikan ni aru setsu," *Eisai shinshi*, no. 193 (January 29, 1881), p. 4, and "Yagaku o moyoosu bun," *Eisai shinshi*, no. 24 (August 18, 1877), p. 4.

Political Youth | 3

After 1880 (Meiji 13), essays on study for wealth and honor largely disappeared from the pages of *Eisai shinshi* [Talent Forum]. In their place came articles and speeches by youth of as little as twelve and thirteen years old calling for liberty, freedom of speech, and a national assembly under a constitution. The appearance of political themes in *Eisai shinshi* was a reflection of the success of the movement begun by the Risshisha (Society of Lofty Ambition) in 1874 (Meiji 7).[1] Spreading beyond its initial provincial base (Tosa) and class base (samurai and *gōshi*), this movement had, by 1880 (Meiji 13), become nationwide with substantial commoner participation. Wealthy peasants (*gōnō*) in particular had been attracted to the movement. Meiji centralization had taken away prerogatives they had enjoyed under the Tokugawa. Meiji economic policies hit them in their role both of landlord and of petty industrialist. The liberal sources used by the samurai in their attacks on the oligarchs contained ideas that answered to wealthy peasant resentments and frustrations.

With the growth of the movement, the age distribution of the participants changed. Articulate youth in general were caught up in the spirit of the times; the young essayists in *Eisai shinshi* were not exceptional. For approximately a decade, politics, and particularly par-

1. I have relied primarily on the narrative of the movement given in Gotō Yasushi, *Jiyū minken* (Chūō kōron sha, 1972). In English, see Nobutaka Ike, *The Beginnings of Political Democracy in Japan* (Johns Hopkins Press, 1950).

liamentary politics, was an abiding concern of youth, so much so that Japanese historians, generalizing from the young men of this period, have referred to the whole of early Meiji youth as political youth (*seiji seinen*). Although this description cannot be applied as broadly as some historians are prone to do, it is nevertheless an apt description of *educated* youth at this time.[2] Because the appearance of these political youth brought about a disappearance of the study-for-wealth-and-honor theme, it can be surmised either that there was an abrupt shift in the values and priorities of youth or that study-for-wealth-and-honor and politics were really one and the same thing. Examining the imagery of advancement associated with the political youth in order to determine which was the case is a necessary chapter in the story of Japanese thought about self-advancement; it also tells much about a movement that is still controversial among contemporary Japanese historians.

Despite the documentable broadening of the movement for liberty and people's rights after 1877 (Meiji 10) to include wealthy peasant participation and demands on economic issues directly tied to their participation, the concerns of that portion of the political youth represented by the *Eisai shinshi* writers were more narrowly focused. They had nothing to say about taxation or local government issues. They concerned themselves solely with the idea of a parliament. Essay after essay called for one to solve internal and external problems in one fell swoop. A fourteen-year-old in an essay entitled "Speaking to My Fellow Geniuses" described Japan as beset by currency and balance-of-payment problems, making no progress in treaty revision, and generally in a bad state. In his view, all that was needed to correct this situation was "parliament and patriotism."[3] A fifteen-

---

2. For example, see Uchida Yoshihiko and Shioda Shōbee, "Chishiki seinen no shoruikei," in *Kindai Nihon shisō shi kōza*, ed. Itō Sei, et al. (Chikuma shobō, 1959), vol. 4, pp. 268–270. Usually, early Meiji youth are described as "political youth" in contrast to late Meiji youth, who are styled "literary youth" (*bungaku seinen*). While these terms have some descriptive utility, it must be kept in mind that they apply only to conspicuous elements of educated youth, not youth in general, that even many educated early Meiji youth were not political, as is demonstrated by *Eisai shinshi* compositions before 1880 (Meiji 13), and that the political fever of youth burned out well before the appearance of the "literary youth." Moreover, as the subsequent analysis demonstrates, "politics" often simply was a version of study for wealth and honor.

3. "Eisai shokun ni tsugu," *Eisai shinshi*, no. 209 (May 28, 1881), p. 2.

year-old noted the same problems and added the foreign threat from Russia and China, but his formula was similar when he said, "There is nothing better for a wealthy nation and a strong army than a parliament," and by his definition, liberty, a strong army, and national expansion were all of one piece.

> In the morning I want to stand in the wind of liberty [*jiyū*]. In the evening I want to be drenched in the rain of liberty. I want to breathe the air of liberty. I want to swim in a sea of liberty. What is it that will make the light of national power to shine brilliantly throughout the world? It is setting up a parliament and uniting the people.

In this youth's formulation, more than the nation's light was to go overseas; parliament was the means to a strong country to extend national power and authority. He declared, "The light from Japanese swords will cause our flag to be known abroad."[4]

Another writer, possibly thinking of earlier compositions which had stressed family fortunes, scored people for being concerned with small, private matters. In calling for youth to join him in a Young People's Neutral Liberal party (Chūritsu seinen jiyūtō), he advised youth to abandon private concerns and join him in the quest for people's rights in order to "extend the authority of the country." His proposed party would "spread the idea of liberty," recruit "capable and active youth," foster a free spirit, and "show the glories of the flag of our Japan to the far corners of the ocean."[5]

In *Eisai shinshi* compositions romantic heroism was the basic means to the achievement of parliament, and despite the suggestions of foreign adventure contained in a few essays, the locus of heroism was Japan, not abroad. A particularly striking example of the personal expectations produced by the quest for a parliament among youth is the essay of one Yamada Kyūsaku, whose compositions in *Eisai shinshi* had the virtue of being a compendium of ideas scattered throughout other essays.[6] At the ripe age of thirteen years and eight months, Yamada proclaimed his dedication to the cause of liberty.

4. "Kōkokkai ronsha bōsho," *Eisai shinshi*, no. 197 (March 5, 1881), p. 2.
5. "Chūritsu seinen Jiyūtō boshū no shisho," *Eisai shinshi*, no. 223 (August 3, 1881), pp. 2–3.
6. Yamada Kyūsaku, "Enzetsu-kai ron," *Eisai shinshi*, no. 207 (May 14, 1881), p. 2. My attention was called to Yamada by the discussion of him in Okawada Tsunetada, "Seinen ron to sedai ron," *Shisō*, no. 514 (April 1964), p. 41.

THE SELF-MADE MAN IN MEIJI JAPANESE THOUGHT

Wrapped in the black smoke from the explosions of bouncing cannonballs, I will stand against the armor-plated battleships and monstrous waves, and I will advance courageously. I will make my way with murderous spirit [*sakki*] shining like a three-foot fall of snow in autumn. And, should some apparition or disaster fall on my head, how will I deal with this? Why I must certainly put out the strength of my own arms and fight against it.

Having gotten through the apparently mandatory display of verbal pyrotechnics—Yamada was no more flowery than any of his contemporaries—he turned to the specifics of what he wanted to accomplish.

Before the masses I want to display patriotism, indignation, and resentment [*aikoku, hifun, kōgai*]. I want to speak out on things that will move the people to action. I want to sweep away completely the fog of confusion that is in the masses [*shūjin*]. If we can put forward the thought that will preserve this, then with the unanimous cooperation [*kyōdō itchi*] of the people, we will vanquish the enemy and we will do it well. We will defeat the enemy and we will do it well.

The enemy Yamada refers to, it is important to note, was not the repressive Meiji government but rather the Western nations who were forcing numerous and sundry indignities on Japan. His goal was to "cleanse away the great shame" (*dai-chijoku o sosogu*) that had resulted from Japan's weakness before foreign powers. His conception of liberty and rights was not only nationalistic, it was Confucian and authoritarian. He continued by observing that the accomplishment of his goal depended on "causing the masses to know the true principle of liberty and autonomy" and on "making clear the true relation between subject and ruler [*taigi-meibun*]." The latter idea was thoroughly Confucian and referred to the situation in which subjects spontaneously performed the ethical duties appropriate to their subordinate positions.

According to Yamada, the means for producing this understanding among the masses was the making of speeches by patriots to arouse the sluggish, superstitious people. But, before the patriotic youth could give speeches, they must, Yamada cautioned, study the techniques of speechmaking because "no good result can come without training." To prove his point, Yamada gave the examples of Demosthenes and Patrick Henry, both of whom he described as men who "vanquished the superstitions of the masses to a nether region with the power of a single tongue." That both men died because of their political activities did not figure in his essay. Yamada was definitely not thinking of becoming a martyr for his principles. He went on to lament the recent government prohibition on student participation in political meetings. He must wait until *after* graduation before he can start dodging cannonballs. Nevertheless, this he pledged to do in order to repay his debt of gratitude to society (*hōon*) and "to pass a name down for ten thousand ages, to write my name in the pages of history."

The combination of Yamada's concluding expectations and his portrayal of his heroes as powerful, almost glib, orators rather than as martyrs makes it difficult to think that he was really concerned with the achievement of political principles rather than the achievement of personal aggrandizement through politics. Recollections by more noted figures who grew up during this period suggest that this pattern was the norm, not the exception. The novelist Futabatei Shimei, for example, recalled how as a young man he had gone to see visiting agitators from the political parties because he was impressed by the dashing figures they cut, although "I knew nothing about the real conditions of the political world. . . . Such things as what kind of party the Liberals were or how they differed from the Progressives." The real excitement, according to Futabatei, was "not for politics, but for political discussion."[7]

Taoka Reiun, a late Meiji political and social critic, said much the same thing. In his autobiography, he recalled he could remember the speechmakers but not the speeches, and he pitied the police who had had to monitor the long, florid, and empty speeches by children like himself, some so young they could not see over their own lectern.[8] Tokutomi Iichirō, a noted journalist of the same age group, later described what he saw as a tendency to grandstand, "to look on politics as a kind of sport, a form of amusement like setting off fireworks."[9]

Given this understanding of politics and fundamental concern with personal advancement, it is not surprising to find compositions

---

7. Futabatei Shimei, *Mediocrity* [Heibon], trans. Glenn W. Shaw (Hokuseidō Press, 1927), pp. 75–76.
8. Taoka Reiun, *Sukiden*, in *Taoka Reiun zenshū*, ed. Nishida Masaru (Hōsei daigaku shuppan-kai, 1969), vol. 5, pp. 507–508, 511–512.
9. Quoted in Dore, "Legacy," p. 117.

and recollections coupling such figures as George Washington and Toyotomi Hideyoshi or equating Gladstone, Bismarck, Macaulay, Lincoln, and Napoleon.[10] That such men were associated with rather different political ideas and systems was of no significance; they had done great things for their nations and made themselves famous in the process. In the scheme of values held by early Meiji youth it was the fame that was important. No historical figure was ever mentioned in compositions of this period without his name being prefaced by some indication of his fame ("the well-known ———" or "——— of high fame"). Although this type of thinking was doubtless to be found among commoners, the historical origins of this conception of heroism and the actual vocabulary used owe more to Tokugawa stories of heroic warriors than to any literature associated with a bourgeoisie, be it defined as the old merchant class or the early Meiji wealthy peasantry. Indeed, some essayists linked themselves to Tokugawa samurai traditions by styling themselves *shishi* ("men of lofty ambition").

Because of this commitment to personal advancement rather than the achievement of specific political ideas or forms, *Eisai shinshi* youth responded very rapidly to the 1881 (Meiji 14) proclamation that promised a constitution and an assembly for 1890. Barely was the ink dry on this announcement when compositions in *Eisai shinshi* turned from heroism in the name of liberty (however defined) to the celebration of the possibilities for youth as members of the future parliament. As one young writer asked rhetorically, "When the parliament is formed, if the members and participants are not today's youth, who will they be?"[11] Other essays dealt with various youth parties that were seen as preparation for future advancement as a parliament member. A composition calling for participation in a Youth Liberal party (Seinen jiyūtō) proclaimed it to be a study society which would "research politics and nourish the talents demanded by the path ahead, so that we might one day have the schol-

---

10. For a composition coupling Washington and Hideyoshi, see "Risshi ron," *Eisai shinshi*, no. 130 (August 30, 1879), p. 2. The second coupling is that of Noma Seiji, founder of the publishing house Kōdansha, as cited in Karasawa, *Gakusei*, p. 34. See also Dore, "Legacy," p. 117, for Tokutomi's criticisms of the heroes of contemporary youth.

11. "Tei *Eisai shinshi* shain shokun," *Eisai shinshi*, no. 253 (April 8, 1882), p. 6.

arly attainments necessary to receive the honor of becoming a member of the parliament."[12] Typically, this essay had nothing to say about being a representative of the people. Composition writers were more concerned with the becoming than with the doing.

This abrupt shifting of gears was all the more remarkable because the government had only committed itself to a constitution and an assembly, structure and content to be determined at its convenience. Such a one-sided issuance was a direct denial of demands made by the movement for the opening of decision-making and the consideration of public opinion. It was not even a victory for the advocates of parliament as a device to unite public opinion and strengthen the nation. The needs of the nation were contemporary and ongoing, but the promised parliament was a decade away. Nevertheless, *Eisai shinshi* contributors generally failed to note these contradictions. If anything, they celebrated the achievement of constitution and parliament without struggle as in the United States or Great Britain and emphasized making good use of the ten-year wait in order to prepare for future triumphs as members of parliament.

This shifting of goals was somewhat more rapid in *Eisai shinshi* composition than among youth at large. Even after the 1881 proclamation, movement activities continued, reaching a peak in 1883 and 1884 (Meiji 16 and 17) in the form of several fairly large-scale incidents of demonstration, rioting, and government repression. Behind these incidents was a combination of specific local grievances on the part of the peasantry and the organizational efforts of various young men known to their contemporaries as *sōshi*. This term originally meant simply a young man in the prime of life, but it had come to be applied to the more active and heroic elements of the movement. Often quixotic in their exploits, they did have a certain amount of success in building on peasant grievances. This sort of real death-defying activity was, however, short-lived. The more extreme elements among the *sōshi* were suppressed or else they shifted to exclusively nationalistic concerns. Many later became involved in antigovernment agitation over what they saw as its weak-willed efforts to secure revision of the unequal treaties. One achieved

12. "Seinen Jiyūtō setsuritsu no shii," *Eisai shinshi*, no. 233 (November 12, 1881), pp. 2–3.

considerable fame in an attempted assassination of Ōkuma Shigenobu in 1889 (Meiji 22).[13]

With the exception of the *sōshi*, the bulk of the political youth were tamed by the promise of a constitution and a parliament. Their expectations with respect to parliament were revealed in a genre of fiction known as political novels (*seiji shōsetsu*).[14] This genre may be said to have started with a loose rendering by Niwa Jun'ichirō in 1879 (Meiji 12) of E. B. Lytton's *Ernest Multravers*. When this novel enjoyed substantial popularity, it was followed by other renderings of works by Lytton, Dumas, and Disraeli. The term *rendering* must be used with respect to the Japanese works because they were not translated even as well as Nakamura had translated *Self-Help*. Commonly, the process of producing a Japanese version was by a system in which the translator made a sight reading of the English text directly into Japanese, which was copied by a stenographer.[15] Since the language used in the Japanese versions employed many Chinese loan words and had whole passages in Chinese, slips were made in taking the dictation.[16] Such errors were, however, not as serious as those which resulted from sheer ignorance of the English language. When Lytton used the Latin term *ergo*, Niwa misread this as *Iago* and added a parenthetical note which explained that Iago was a character in a famous play by Shakespeare![17] In passages pertaining to religion and religious institutions, he used the terminology of Buddhism, translating church as temple (*tera*), for example, leaving the reader with the impression that England and Multravers were Buddhist.

13. The *sōshi* are discussed in Fukuchi, *Shizoku*, pp. 215–228, and Okawada, "Seinen ron," pp. 42–44.
14. The basic work on the political novels is Yanagida Izumi, *Seiji shōsetsu kenkyū*, (Shunjū sha, 1967). A brief summary and typology of the genre is found in Yanagida Izumi, "Seiji shōsetsu no ippan," in *Seiji shōsetsu shū I*, vol. 5 of *Meiji bungaku zenshū* (Chikuma shobō, 1966), pp. 414–434, and *Seiji shōsetsu shū II*, vol. 6 of *Meiji bungaku zenshū* (Chikuma shobō, 1967), pp. 445–476.
15. This style of translation in the specific case of *Endymion* is discussed in Yanagida, *Seiji shōsetsu*, vol. 2, p. 191.
16. The main texts of most political novels were somewhat more difficult than *Saikoku risshi hen*. In addition, many had long passages entirely in Chinese (*kanbun*). They were most definitely aimed at a high literacy, not a mass, audience.
17. Niwa Jun'ichirō, *Karyū shunwa*, in *Meiji honyaku bungaku shū*, vol. 7 of *Meiji bungaku zenshū* (Chikuma shobō, 1972), p. 51. The original passage is in book 5, chapter 3, of *Ernest Multravers*.

Aside from these errors and failures, which do much to enliven these otherwise tedious works for the contemporary reader, the translations are marked by a curious duality. The titles of the novels often incorporated the words *spring* and *willows*. *Ernest Multravers* became "A Spring Tale of Flowers and Willows," and *Coringsby* (by Disraeli) became "Spring Warblings." The literary allusions in these titles were not to nature but to eroticism. Both spring and willows had very specific erotic connotations. "To sell spring" (*baishun*) is a euphemism for prostitution, and "bright flowers under dark willows" (*ryūan kamei*) is a euphemism for licensed quarters. The content, on the other hand, was rendered in a style that recalls the master-disciple dialogues in Confucian texts. Conversations were given in an extraordinarily stilted fashion and were introduced by the term *iwaku*, which might be translated as "thus spake." This didactic tone was intentional. Kimura Ki records that Niwa regarded *Ernest Multravers* much in the way that Nakamura Keiu regarded *Self-Help*, as a text for teaching British virtues to Japanese.[18]

To anyone who has read *Ernest Multravers*, the suggestion that it could have been regarded as a text for national strengthening may sound preposterous.[19] It is a romance, or a novel of manners. At the opening of the novel, the hero, Ernest, is a young man of eighteen freshly returned from being a student in Germany. He chances to meet Alice, the illiterate daughter of a drunken thief and extortionist. Taken by Alice's plight, Ernest proceeds to educate her as a lady, gradually falling in love with her and eventually fathering a daughter by her. When Ernest goes home to see his ill father, Alice is abducted by her father. Returning after his father's death, Ernest is unable to locate Alice, and to recover from his sorrow he goes to Italy. There he falls in love again, this time with a woman of aristocratic status. Rebuffed, he returns to England to begin a career as a popular novelist and politician in a rise to fame marked by a series of complications involving Alice, her daughter, deceitful friends, past and subsequent loves, and a mad Italian.

Nevertheless, despite the apparently thin base for didacticism in the interests of the nation, the translator managed to find such. Ernest's efforts to educate Alice are the opportunity for a discourse on

18. Kimura Ki, "Kaidai," in *Meiji honyaku bungaku shū*, p. 395.
19. *Ernest Multravers* is available in many editions. I read Sir Edward Bulwer Lytton, *Ernest Multravers* (Lippincott, 1889).

the proper education of women and the value of education in general. The journey Ernest makes to Italy provides numerous opportunities for contrasting the character of the English gentleman as represented in Ernest with the Italian character, and of course Ernest's character is linked to British greatness. A typical statement observes, "There are no young men who in response to the moral duty [*seigi*] realize high purpose [*seiun*] and advance themselves [*mi o tatsuru*] more than do Englishmen."[20] Much of this didacticism was actually already in *Ernest Multravers*, but the modern reader is likely to miss these points, since they are intertwined with the romantic story line.

Niwa took care of this problem for the Japanese reader. He cut whole chapters, tossed aside descriptive sections, and compressed narrative passages until *Karyū shunwa* was less than one-fifth the length of the original.[21] He missed few passages that could be turned to didactic use. Often not content to simply translate the original moral, he added parenthetical comments, and in some cases changed the text completely to make it more instructive. Songs of Italian boatmen that were about the beauties of nature in the original became in *Karyū shunwa* songs of a wealthy country and a strong army (*fukoku kyōhei*).[22] The emphasis was not, however, entirely nationalistic. *Karyū shunwa* also became a tract on the attainment of wealth and honor. The term *risshin* (*mi o tateru*) was used often, and many of the didactic passages had to do with advancement. As a consequence, *Ernest Multravers*, a romance with a number of moralistic and didactic passages, was converted into a treatise on English morals and manners as they contributed to national wealth and power and personal wealth and honor. The original plot served as a vehicle to carry the work from one didactic exposition to another.

The nationalism injected into a work such as *Karyū shunwa* was important to contemporary readers, but the primary appeal was neither in nationalism nor in the implied but largely undelivered eroti-

20. Niwa, *Karyū*, pp. 26–27. This section is based on *Ernest Multravers*, book 2, chapter 4.
21. Strictly speaking, *Karyū shunwa* is based on *Ernest Multravers* and a sequel, *Alice*. Together these amount to about 1,000 pages of English text. *Karyū shunwa* in the *Meiji bungaku zenshū* version is only 106 pages. Even allowing for some greater conciseness in highly Sinified Japanese, Niwa's work is little more than a skeleton of the original.
22. Niwa, *Karyū*, p. 29.

cism of the title. What really attracted youth was the image of self-advancement contained in these novels. The novelist Shimazaki Tōson recorded the impact of Disraeli's *Endymion* in his semi-autobiographical novel *Cherry Ripening Time* [Sakura no mi no juku suru toki].

> It seemed as if everything could be done freely, easily, just as one willed. If one thought to ascend to heaven in a single bound, why that too was possible. The life of the impoverished Disraeli, who in a single bound leaped upon the stage of life and politics, achieved high court rank, and became well known to a beautiful widow, stimulated Sutekichi's imagination. He even thought to write another *Endymion* on his own way up.[23]

Sutekichi is Shimazaki himself describing the mood among young men in the early 1890s. Doubtless others shared this reaction to *Endymion*, which was translated in 1886 (Meiji 19) on the eve of the promulgation of the constitution.[24] Offered under the title "Billowing Waves of Passion in the Sea of Politics," the original differed only in detail from *Ernest Multravers* and appears to have received the same sort of translation seen in *Karyū shunwa*.[25]

As Shimazaki's recollection suggests, these works provided an image of self-advancement that could be achieved with little effort. Although Lytton, Disraeli, and Smiles were all Victorians, the value system revealed in the novels was very different from that presented in *Self-Help*. Ernest Multravers and Endymion lived on unearned income, and they were not the least bit troubled by that fact. Not only did they not work for what they had, they gained more without working. At one point Lytton wrote of Multravers that "the world doubled his income."[26] Nothing was said of hard work, frugality, perseverance, or even study—the world just doubled his income. Certainly this had to be a more attractive image for youth than the long-drawn-out grind described in *Self-Help*. Moreover, it could not fail to resonate with traditional samurai expectations, for when describ-

---

23. Shimazaki Tōson, *Sakura no mi no juku suru toki* (Iwanami bunko, 1972), pp. 11–12. Also quoted in Kosaka, *Japanese Thought*, pp. 195–196. The setting of the novel is 1891 (Meiji 24). It first appeared in 1919.

24. According to Yanagida, contemporary newspaper comments emphasized the *risshin* aspect of *Endymion*. See Yanagida, *Seiji shōsetsu*, vol. 2, p. 191.

25. I was not able to compare the original and the translation, and have instead relied on the discussion of *Endymion* in Yanagida, *Seiji shōsetsu*, vol. 2, pp. 174 ff.

26. Niwa, *Karyū*, p. 49, is even more generous. Multravers is given millions (*kyoman*). The original is in book 5, chapter 2.

ing the income of such characters as Multravers, Niwa used the terminology of samurai stipends (*fuchi*). *Karyū shunwa* even went so far as to style Multravers's Norman ancestors as warriors (*bushi*), leaving no doubt about the degree to which the novel fitted into a universe of traditional samurai expectations.[27]

The heroes of these novels not only did not work for their living, they did nothing to bring about their rise in politics. They did not engage in speechmaking, so the reader never knows what their political ideas were, or even if they had any.[28] The novels did not describe political wheeling and dealing, but they did treat in some detail the importance of marital connections. Indeed, it was these connections that were the primary means by which both Multravers and Endymion rose in the world, and the importance of these connections was stressed in both novels. What was perhaps most curious about the characters was that they did not consciously seek to manipulate these connections for their own gain. That was done for them. Both Multravers and Endymion were essentially passive figures pushed along by those who advised them, most often by females. So passive was Endymion that one scholar of Disraeli's novels has styled him "a mere toy" in a "female-dominated world."[29] Apparently this was part of the appeal of these novels. The translator of *Endymion* thought Japanese civilization was not up to modern standards because in planning their rise in the world (*risshin*) Japanese youth did not give sufficient attention to women. If they read *Endymion*, they would understand the importance of women to advancement in politics.[30]

That the dream of a magical advance through female assistance was a key factor in the popularity of these novels is also suggested by the fact that this same theme was picked up in those political novels written by Japanese. In 1887 (Meiji 20) the journalist Tokutomi Iichirō observed the crop of political novels coming out on the eve of the constitution and parliament and from his reading offered a model plot:

27. Ibid., p. 16.
28. Concerning the politics of Disraeli's heroes, see Arthur H. Frietzsche, *The Monstrous Clever Young Man: The Novelist Disraeli and His Heroes* (Utah State University Press, 1959).
29. Ibid., p. 54.
30. Yanagida, *Seiji shōsetsu*, vol. 2, p. 189.

Here we have one student [*shosei*], alone and shivering with poverty. Unexpectedly, at some hot spring, he happens to come to the notice of some daughter of the aristocracy. There is a meeting of hearts which gives birth to a feeling of compassion. There are all kinds of difficulties, but after their triumphing over various and sundry problems, there is a wedding. With his wife's money, the impoverished student becomes a man of substance, and together they plunge into politics. Without turning aside, his reputation grows until he is the head of a nongovernment [*minkan*] party.

In Tokutomi's view the political novels, particularly those written shortly in advance of the first Diet, were merely a vehicle for putting out political speeches, and the novels themselves were the product of what he called a "vulgar, mutual advancement association."[31]

Quite close to this pattern was the novel *Plum Blossoms in the Snow* [Setchūbai] and its sequel *Nightingales among the Flowers* [Kakan'ō] written in 1886 and 1887 (Meiji 19 and 20) by Suehiro Tetchō.[32] Said to have sold some 300,000 copies, the novel described the rise of one Kunio Motoi, a destitute political activist and recent graduate who rose primarily because of his relations with the highborn Tominaga O-haru, who was at once his fiancée and financial backer. After various complicated adventures, including a meeting at a hot spring and a sequence of mistaken identities and chance meetings, Kunio was elected to parliament. The novel did differ a bit from the Disraeli-Lytton pattern: Kunio stated his political ideas in numerous speeches, and he was celebrated for his eloquence in a manner that recalls Yamada Kyūsaku and his concern with speech-making. Otherwise, the novel was basically within the pattern seen in *Ernest Multravers* and *Endymion*, and its heroes and heroines were similar. Kunio is much like Endymion and Ernest Multravers: a naive student prone to bouts of mental instability and dependent on wealthy women for what little coherent direction his life has.[33] Nevertheless, despite their frailties, they were regarded as symbols

---

31. "Kindai ryūkō no seiji shōsetsu o hyō suru," *Kokumin no tomo*, no. 5 (July 15, 1887), p. 12.

32. I have relied on the summary of *Setchūbai* and *Kakan'ō* given in Yanagida, *Seiji shōsetsu*, vol. 2, pp. 414–456.

33. Feldman has aptly observed that "although they are eager idealists the heroes and heroines of these political novels can hardly be called strong characters. They are the muddled intellectual type, vociferous but naive and ineffectual in most cases." See Horace Feldman, "The Growth of the Meiji Novel" (Ph.D. dissertation, Columbia University, 1952), p. 83.

of that character leading to national greatness. Kunio Motoi means "foundation of the nation."

So strong was this pattern of the ineffectual hero dependent on outside aid that it appeared even in a novel that specifically cited *Saikoku risshi hen* and that attempted to portray its hero and heroine as possessed of Smilesean virtues. This novel was *The Diary of Life* [Seiro nikki], written in 1884 (Meiji 17) by Kikutei Kōsui.[34] In the story one Hisamatsu Kikuo is a schoolteacher in his native village. Despite having worked hard to build up the school from a state "where half the people did not even know where it was," he is going nowhere and well aware of that fact. In particular he is stymied in his romance with a wealthy and highborn student because the girl's stepmother thinks Kikuo too low in status to warrant attention. After a great deal of indecision, Kikuo decides to go to Osaka in order to gain the knowledge to get on in the world. In a tearful scene he parts from his beloved Take as they quote Samuel Smiles to each other. "Adversity is the whetstone on which a man's life is honed. Moreover, a man's dreams for the future come only from perseverance. In the past you read and loved *Self-Help*; you must remember the golden words of Western philosophy in it."[35]

Kikuo then goes to Osaka in a spirit of "self-management and independence" to endure two long years of hardships, the principal one of which is "being away from his mother's knee." Just when all seems dark, a friend introduces Kikuo to one Akita Utaka, a rich merchant, who bankrolls the publication of a book Kikuo has been writing while braving hardships. Entitled "Stories of Social Morality" [Shakai dōtoku hen], the subject is, appropriately enough, how a student far from his mother's knee is to conduct himself. The contents are based on Kikuo's experience and sterling character. Most impressed by Kikuo's book, his sponsor takes him in, and after a few more adventures he is able to finish school, go home, and get married (the wicked stepmother turning out to have been not so wicked after all). In the meantime Kikuo acquires a new interest. After a

---

34. My attention was called to this novel by the discussion in Maeda, "Risshin shusse," 19–21. The author (actual name Satō Kuratarō) and the work are also discussed in Yanagida, *Seiji shōsetsu*, vol. 1, pp. 208–226. The novel itself is reproduced in *Meiji kaikaki bungaku shū II*, vol. 2 of *Meiji bungaku zenshū*, pp. 354–398.

35. *Seiro nikki*, p. 366.

brief rest at his mother's knee, he is off to Tokyo to preach "liberty and reform," at which point the story ends.

Because the novel is focused on Kikuo's adventures as a student, the reader never learns what "reform and liberty" mean to the hero. In the absence of specification, advancement (*risshin*) and a chance to get out of the village (*shusse*) must be assumed. Although *Self-Help* is mentioned in the text, the pattern of advancement is similar to that found in the political novels. The real base of Kikuo's advance is finding a wealthy patron. He does not succeed through self-help. In this sense, his pattern of success is rather like that found in the stories of Horatio Alger (1832–1899).[36] Although Horatio Alger is often mistakenly associated with the idea of self-help, the heroes in his stories succeeded less by their own efforts than by their virtue, which caused them to come to the attention of some wealthy patron. Nevertheless, Alger does not appear to have been either read or translated in Meiji Japan, and it is unlikely that the educated youth of this period could have found a self-image in Alger's heroes, who usually ended up as clerks in mercantile establishments. The pattern of success through virtue rewarded and patron found must be traced to indigenous invention or the novels of Lytton and Disraeli, whose political heroes were more compatible with samurai occupational conceits than were Alger's.

More important than the question of whether this pattern was indigenous or not is the question of how such heroes could be seen as effective either for national strengthening or for the achievement of people's rights. Dependent as he was on fortuitous aid and direction from a wealthy woman, Kunio Motoi of *Setchūbai* seems hardly an inspiring model either as a leader of the struggle for people's rights or as "the foundation of the country." Kakuo of *Seiro nikki* seems an even more unlikely leader. The modern reader has difficulty understanding how someone who had great difficulty separating himself from his mother's knee could have been seen as an effective combatant for liberty and people's rights. Such concerns did not trouble contemporary readers, however, for the novel was not only highly praised but was very popular among intellectuals and was reprinted a number of times.[37]

36. The basic Alger plot is discussed in Cawelti, *Apostles*, pp. 115–120.
37. Maeda, "Risshin shusse," p. 21, n. 1.

The weakness of the heroes in the novels about parliament is all the more striking when they are compared with the heroes appearing in those novels more explicitly concerned with national rights (*kokken*). *Beautiful Tales of Managing a Country* [Keikoku bidan], written in 1883 (Meiji 16), is a prime example of the latter variety of political novel.[38] It describes the heroic efforts of one Epaminondas and other youths who save their native Thebes both from an external attack and from the machinations of a radical party. Written as an allegory for contemporary Japan, the novel presented a hero who was far more virile and decisive than those found in the novels on parliamentary themes. That the novel in fact produced such a response among youth was indicated in various recollections. For example, Katayama Sen, later known as a labor leader, recalled:

When I borrowed it, I stayed up at night to read it. Really, it was a book that excited my spirit and made my blood flow. I have never been so stimulated. And it was not just me alone. Other youths were also much impressed by it. For the sake of freedom and independence, the Te-ba [Thebes] youth strove for their country. In making that country independent, it was indeed a rich historical story.[39]

Eisai shinshi compositions show essentially the same interpretation. A youth saw *Keikoku bidan* as a great story of young men "withstanding a hundred difficulties, transcending a thousand adversities" in a struggle to "vanquish the evil party and restore the nation." It was, in his words, a story of brave men of purpose (*eiyū shishi*).[40]

The authors of the political novels were almost without exception of samurai origin. Since the novels were at least as difficult and usually more difficult to read than *Saikoku risshi hen*, it is likely that the readers too were samurai. An assumption of samurai authorship and readership does much to explain the two types of heroes and the popularity of the Kunio Motoi type in novels on parliamentary themes. In the samurai value system, two elements stood dominant: nationalism and the desire to secure status and prestige. Whatever promised the most of each, particularly the latter, captured

38. *Keikoku bidan* is discussed and summarized in Yanagida, *Seiji shōsetsu*, vol. 1, pp. 186–193.
39. Quoted in Karasawa, *Gakusei*, p. 32.
40. "Doku *Keikou bidan*," *Eisai shinshi*, no. 451 (February 3, 1886), p. 5.

their imagination. First, this was study for wealth and honor. Then, when the movement for liberty and people's rights arose, politics moved to the fore, but politics was not a matter of specific ideas rooted in their class situation, such as "no taxation without representation," but rather whatever promised the prestige of government affiliation, be that heroism for the nation or making a name as an exponent of people's rights and a parliament. Since the real motivation behind the quest for people's rights and a parliament was the personal quest for wealth and honor, it is natural that the Lytton-Disraeli model of a magical rise should appeal to them.

Perhaps the sharpest testimonial to the fundamental commitment to personal advancement rather than the advancement of political ideals was that there were no Japanese martyrs in the novels on parliamentary themes. A few went to jail, but no one was sufficiently committed to die for his beliefs. Posthumous fame and the satisfaction of having worked to the realization of idealistic goals was simply not as attractive as temporal wealth and honor. That the heroism depicted for both nation and parliament was more often verbal and romantic rather than real and sacrificial reflected the fundamental commitment to personal advancement in the here and now and the fact that during the Tokugawa peace most samurai had known combat only from what they had read about it in historical romances. That the heroes amounted in the end to somewhat timid student intellectuals was a reflection of the real situation of much of the samurai youth. Few would really brave a hail of cannonballs as long as there were other alternatives to wealth and fame.

In the late 1880s, on the eve of the promised constitution and assembly, a second wave of political youth began to make their presence known in contemporary journals and newspapers. In contrast to the samurai romantic political visions found in *Eisai shinshi* and the political novels, this second wave of political youth held to a self-consciously commoner politics based on commoner virtues. Many writers and several distinct groups were involved in the promotion of this alternative political vision, but by far the most important was Tokutomi Iichirō (Sohō) and the Minyūsha (Friends of the People), a group that he founded. This group and their writings garnered the most attention of those proposing a new politics, and they were the most consistent in advocating a political order based on commoners and their virtues. In so doing they put forward the most Smilesean self-made man to be seen in early Meiji thought.[41]

Tokutomi Iichirō has already been introduced through his criticism of the political novels. Nevertheless, despite his criticism of the political aspirations of others, he himself had such dreams and shared the idea of advancement in parliamentary politics with many of his contemporaries. His ideal was British parliamentary politics as he believed it to exist.

> We want to adapt the so-called English style of politics to Japan. We want to create one political group based on government officials in office. We want to make another political group based on our own ranks. On the basis of the relation between the in and the out groups, we want to emulate the relations of the English parties. Together we will preserve the courtesy, order, and ceremony which is born of this relation. On the basis of this proper and correct relation we will confront one another.[42]

Even at the rhetorical level, Tokutomi was definitely not a member of the *Eisai shinshi* cannonball-dodging school of politics. His ideal was a gentlemanly exchange of power.

The actual occasion for this particular statement was hardly auspicious; the government had just expelled some five hundred assorted opposition types from Tokyo. Despite this latest instance of government repression of dissent, Tokutomi did not call for violence or heroism in response. Instead, he called upon the government to recognize that among contemporary opposition groups there were peaceful (*heiwateki*) and orderly (*chitsujoteki*) groups that ought to be encouraged. He was particularly critical of the *sōshi* ("stalwart

---

41. The other major group holding to approximately the same ideas was the Seikyōsha (Politics, Education Society). It and its writers are excluded from this discussion because of the relatively small circulation of its journal *Nihonjin* [The Japanese], and because few themes traceable to its writers appeared in journals such as *Eisai shinshi*, suggesting a relatively low level of influence. Basic works that deal with the two groups include Uete Michiari, "'Kokumin no tomo' to 'Nihonjin,'" *Shisō* no. 453 (March 1962), pp. 112–122; Kano Masanao, "Kokusui shugi ni okeru shihon shugi taisei no kōsō," *Nihon shi kenkyū* no. 52 (1961), pp. 23–44; Irokawa Daikichi, "Meiji nijū nendai no bunka," in *Iwanami kōza Nihon rekishi* (Iwanami shoten, 1968) vol. 17, pp. 269–315; Kenneth B. Pyle, *The New Generation in Meiji Japan* (Stanford University Press, 1969). Pyle, it must be noted, in contrast to most Japanese treatments, emphasizes the differences between the groups.

42. "Zaiyatō ni taisuru kongo no seisaku," *Kokumin no tomo*, no. 14 (January 28, 1888), pp. 3–4.

youth") who had gone from agitation among the peasants to confrontations with the government over treaty revision. Although he did hint that if the government did not allow peaceful opposition groups some peaceful and orderly opponents might go over to the *sōshi*, this was only a device to emphasize the polite nature of those for whom he claimed to speak. He promised that if the peaceful and orderly opposition were "allowed" participation, they would become "ardent allies" of the government. Moreover, Tokutomi assured the government he and others like him did not have any preconceived notions about current policy. They only wanted to "take on the burden of everyday administration" along with those now in office and to have a say in the "Second Restoration" that Tokutomi saw coming with the promised constitution. Likening those who shared his beliefs to Richard Cobden and John Bright, he asked rhetorically if the government wanted to keep their Japanese equivalents out of office.[43]

In this article, Tokutomi did not explain just why the government should feel obliged to allow the participation of the Japanese equivalents of Cobden and Bright. Nor did he explain how the peaceful exchange of powers between ins and outs was to come about in the face of the explicit opposition of major government leaders even to the idea of political parties, let alone the question of sharing power.[44] Tokutomi had, however, a theory of history with which he had convinced himself that Japan in fact would develop along British lines, not just in terms of political institutions and political behavior, but in terms of economic and social structure, dominant classes, ethics, and morality.

This theory—vision is perhaps a better term—was largely stated in his 1886 (Meiji 19) manifesto *The Future Japan* [Shōrai no Nihon].[45] This work was an extremely optimistic synthesis of various strands of nineteenth-century Anglo-American thought. It had economics based on the so-called Manchester school, politics based on

---

43. Ibid., p. 6.
44. Tokutomi's lack of concern with practical organizing is noted in Irokawa, "Meiji nijū nendai," p. 296.
45. I have relied on the reproduction of this work in *Tokutomi Sohō—Yamaji Aizan*, ed. Sumiya Mikio, vol. 40 of *Nihon no meicho* (Chūō kōron sha, 1971), pp. 59–184. It is also reproduced in *Tokutomi Sohō shū*, vol. 34 of *Meiji bungaku zenshū* (Chikuma shobō, 1974), pp. 50–114. For a discussion of the work in English, see Peter

an idealization of recent British trends, morality and ethics from Samuel Smiles, and most important, a theory of history taken largely from Herbert Spencer's genre of Social Darwinism. In best Spencerian fashion, Tokutomi worked by analogy and found numerous parallels between Japan and Great Britain. Citing similarities in geographical situation and natural-resource endowment, he concluded that Japan was to become the Great Britain of the Orient.[46] Japan was to "blossom out like a bud freeing itself from the snow in the spring" to become the heart of the East, a shop for all the nations of the world.[47] As a consequence of this shift in economic organization, the social and political structure would also change. "In response to the inevitable logic of the development of productive facilities, it [the nation] must become a commoner society," he declared, and with the coming of the commoner society there would also develop the British style of politics he desired.[48]

Even as a good Spencerian in his dependency on analogies, Tokutomi made one important change in Spencer's thought. The latter had postulated two alternative and coexistent patterns of social organization: the military and the civil-commercial. Tokutomi made these into a sequential pattern with the military giving way to the civil-commercial.[49] In so doing, he gave himself a powerful tool for criticizing contemporary Japanese society. Anything that could be associated with the military past of Japan, including the continued political dominance of the samurai, could be branded as out-of-date and subject to change lest Japan be left behind or even destroyed in the international struggle for existence.[50]

Duus, "Whig History Japanese Style: The Minyūsha Historians and the Meiji Restoration," *Journal of Asian Studies* 33:3 (May 1974): 415–436, and John D. Pierson, "The Journalist Tokutomi Sohō: Problems of Westernization and Modernization in Meiji Japan," (Ph.D. dissertation, Princeton University, 1972), pp. 156 ff.

46. Tokutomi, *Shōrai*, pp. 138–148. It must be noted that Tokutomi was not entirely consistent in his description of the economic future of Japan. At some points he emphasized a mercantile future and at other points he talked about manufacturing.

47. Ibid., p. 145.   48. Ibid., p. 146.

49. This shift and its significance is noted in Duus, "Whig History," pp. 421–422 and 429, and in Pierson, "Tokutomi Sohō," pp. 178–179.

50. Overall, Tokutomi did not stress, as did some contemporaries such as Katō Hiroyuki, the more violently competitive rhetoric that was often a part of social Darwinism. He also paid little attention to the more absurd features of Spencer's analogies which traced in great detail the alleged parallels between biological and social evolution.

On this logic various aspects of contemporary Japanese society came in for harsh criticism from Tokutomi, none so much as what he described as the prevailing attitudes toward government and politics. According to Tokutomi, the basic Japanese attitude was one of "honor the official and despise the people" (*kanson minpi*). Officials and bureaucrats were regarded as deities, and the people were passive or cringing before them, a carry-over from the feudal period when there had been only high and low, when those at the top were limitless masters and those below were limitless slaves.[51] Because these attitudes still persisted, Japan was a paradise for officials, while the people existed in hell (*jigoku*). As a consequence, people sought government affiliation, and Tokutomi lamented, "Even if a man of lofty purpose [*yūshisha*] accidentally manages to start some endeavor independently, the majority of such men will somewhere put up various excuses and invite the patronage of the government, all the while trying to appear as if they did not want to receive the favor or intervention of the government for themselves." Thus Japan had no true independent commercial enterprises. Banks, railroads, shipping—all were tied to the government in one way or another, and he declared himself at a loss to see how contemporary "self-styled merchant princes" differed from those merchants who had had semiofficial positions under the Tokugawa.[52] Logically, if these attitudes continued to prevail, it would be difficult if not impossible for the British style of commercial society Tokutomi envisioned to come about.

Politics was equally marked by the continuation of feudal patterns and attitudes. The whole movement for liberty and people's rights had had little or no influence on this. Tokutomi observed that "when Anglo-Saxon ideas of liberty moved to our country, they changed by themselves into something that one would not be off the mark in calling 'liberty, feudal style.'" He scorned the parties that had emerged from the movement, saying they were "nothing but the unions of feudal powers. Other than the clashes of feudal factions, I can see no true political feeling."[53] Tokutomi and other writers of the group were particularly harsh in their denunciations of what they called "Oriental heroism and daring" (*tōyōteki ziyū gō-*

---

51. Tokutomi, *Shōrai*, p. 164.
52. Ibid., pp. 172–173.   53. Ibid., pp. 174–175.

ketsu),⁵⁴ which in effect was the kind of samurai romanticism talked about in *Eisai shinshi* compositions and personified in the *sōshi*. Such a political style was even more out-of-date and more incompatible with a British style of commercial and economic order than was the attitude toward government affiliation.

The remedy for these combined political and economic defects of contemporary Japanese society was for Tokutomi nothing less than the total restructuring of Japanese society. Feudalistic and militaristic elements were to be replaced by commoner and commercial elements. The very spiritual core of the Japanese people was to be reworked along British lines, and like Nakamura Keiu, Tokutomi saw the writings of Samuel Smiles as the actual texts to be used in this spiritual transformation.

> Now I desire that our society become current Western society. However, if the Western moral law which dominates those societies is not imported, what will Japan amount to? What I desire is that the morals of *Self-Help* [Jijoron] and *Character* [Seiyō hinkō ron] take the place of those in [Chu Hsi's] *Elementary Education* [Shōgaku or Hsiao-hsüeh] and [his] *Reflections on Things at Hand* [Kinshi roku or Chin-ssu lu].⁵⁵

Tokutomi used Nakamura's rendering of *Self-Help* and *Character* in his own academy,⁵⁶ and after he arrived on the Tokyo journalistic scene, he preached Smilesean virtues from the pages of his journal, *Kokumin no tomo* [Friend of the People].

Articles in *Kokumin no tomo* touched on all the Smilesean virtues, but none figured as prominently as respect for labor. Tokutomi was fond of quoting Thomas Carlyle to the effect that "work is life" or "true labor is holy."⁵⁷ In one essay, he went so far as to proclaim the need for a "new religion" (*shūkyō*) for Japan, which he termed "the sanctity of work" (*shokugyō no shinsei*).⁵⁸ As one means of spreading a work ethos, Tokutomi called for a program of what he styled "work education" (*rōsaku kyōiku*). In this system students would do most of the janitorial work at their schools and might even

---

54. This aspect of Minyūsha group thought is discussed in detail in Kano Masanao, "'Inaka shinshitachi' no ronri," *Rekishigaku kenkyū*, no. 249 (1961), p. 7.
55. Tokutomi Iichirō, "Shin-Nihon no seinen," in *Tokutomi Sohō shū*, p. 149.
56. Concerning his academy, Ōe Gijuku, see Kano Masanao, "Ichi minken shijuku no kiseki," *Shisō*, no. 536 (February 1969), pp. 54–75.
57. "Rōsaku kyōiku," *Kokumin no tomo*, no. 133 (October 13, 1891), p. 1.
58. "Nihon kokumin no shin-shūkyō," *Kokumin no tomo*, no. 201 (September 13, 1893), pp. 1–6.

construct their own dormitories and make their own soap. Each student, no matter how cerebral his specialty or inclination, was to learn some productive trade.[59] He emphasized that all people, regardless of rank, be they company president or eminent politician, had to work as hard as the lowliest employee or citizen in order to justify their position. Moreover, this work had to continue even after one achieved some sort of rank or recognition.[60]

In so stressing work, Tokutomi demonstrated that he was heir to a very different value system from those youth who wrote in *Eisai shinshi* about study as the route to leisured wealth and honor, and from Fukuzawa Yukichi, who had declared in *Gakumon no susume* that physical labor was not deserving of respect. This attitude of disrespect and the tendency to separate education from productive activity, he described as a carry-over of the warrior (*bushi*) value system, and it was this that his system of work education was designed to correct.[61] Whether it would have in fact done this if implemented is open to question. Features of his system were being used in some schools, but contemporary accounts indicate that such work duty was a cause of student rebellion.[62] Although perhaps naive, his proposals and criticisms are at least further testimony to the grip of samurai values on the concept of self-advancement held by contemporary youth.

So great was the appreciation of labor on the part of Tokutomi and the Minyūsha writers that *Kokumin no tomo* endorsed, albeit rather theoretically, mutual-aid societies and even some features of a Saint Simon style of socialism, as devices to help workers gain the respect and compensation they deserved.[63] Nothing could have been farther from the consciousness of either Fukuzawa or the *Eisai shinshi* essayists. The responsibilities of those with wealth, another major issue in the Smilesean concept of the self-made man, was also taken up by the Minyūsha writers. Here they tended to rely on the writings of Andrew Carnegie, and *Kokumin no tomo* was perhaps the

---

59. "Rōsaku kyōiku," pp. 3–5.   60. Ibid., pp. 6–7.   61. Ibid., p. 1.

62. An account of such a rebellion is found in the news item "Miyagi nōgakkō no funpun," *Nihon no shōnen*, no. 1 (February 23, 1889), p. 35. In the normal schools, which were run according to military discipline, cleaning lamps was a usual punishment. See Karasawa, *Gakusei*, pp. 66–68, for details.

63. See the articles "Rōdōsha no koe," *Kokumin no tomo*, no. 95 (1890, pp. 6–12, and "Heiminteki undō no shin-genshō," *Kokumin no tomo*, no. 69 (January 3, 1890), pp. 5–9.

first journal to introduce the idea of "the stewardship of wealth."[64] Although hardly a radical critique of the wealthy, Carnegie's notion that those with wealth had a responsibility to dispose of it in a socially responsible manner was infinitely more than Fukuzawa or the *Eisai shinshi* youth had had to say on the subject.

As might be expected from Tokutomi's bourgeois view of work, he also placed great emphasis on frugality. His frugality was not, however, the frugality of the *Eisai shinshi* essayists: Napoleon saving time for study. It was saving for unexpected events and it was the saving which provided the capital for national economic growth.[65] When Tokutomi talked about Napoleon, it was to lament the fact that contemporary youth looked up to such men as Bismarck and Napoleon, whom he styled "nation destroyers and murderers." Instead, he urged youth to venerate such men as James Watt and Adam Smith, whom he styled "uncrowned kings." Although he shared Watt as a hero with the *Eisai shinshi* youth, Tokutomi did not celebrate him as a model of perseverance to the distant goal of wealth and honor. Watt attracted Tokutomi because he had been technologically productive and his discoveries had benefited mankind as a whole. Adam Smith was to be revered because he provided an explanation of how it was that individual activities could work to mutual benefit, why it was that one person's gain was not another's loss.[66]

In seeing Smilesean virtues as the basis for a moral regeneration of Japan, Tokutomi shared with Nakamura Keiu the assumption that the nation was a reflection of the individuals composing it, and for Japan to be an independent nation the people must be independent. The linkage between a commoner morality based on Smiles and national independence was his ultimate justification for a commoner society. As Tokutomi explained, "In implementing our commoner society today, the necessity of a commoner morality cannot be doubted. Rich country! Strong army! What are these if they are not the result of the promotion of a commoner morality."[67]

64. "Tomi no fukuin," *Kokumin no tomo*, no. 69 (January 3, 1890), pp. 25–26, and no. 70 (January 13, 1890), pp. 32–33, and "Kinsen o shiyō suru michi ikani," *Kokumin no tomo*, no. 70 (January 13, 1890), pp. 10–13.
65. "Rōsaku, setsuyō, chochiku," *Kokumin no tomo*, no. 94 (September 13, 1890), pp. 10–16.
66. Tokutomi, *Shōrai*, pp. 117–118.
67. "Heimin no dōtoku," *Kokumin no tomo*, no. 170 (October 23, 1892), p. 6.

Tokutomi's appreciation of Smilesean virtue as revealed in *Self-Help* and *Character* was not, however, exclusively nationalistic or theoretical. In large measure, Tokutomi appreciated Smilesean virtues because he came from one of the strata of Japanese society that, unlike the samurai, had a natural affinity for such virtues based on their own economic activities. Tokutomi's family were *gōshi*, or rural samurai.[68] They were described, and not a little bit idealized, in *Omoide no ki* [A Record of Remembrances], by his younger brother Kenjirō (Roka).[69] As depicted in this novel, the Tokutomi family and the *gōshi* in general were well-off peasants who had acquired certain samurai privileges in exchange for services under the Tokugawa regime but had done so without becoming obnoxious, overbearing, or lazy, as was the wont of true samurai. Instead, the *gōshi* was a benevolent father figure to the less well-off in the village. He promoted education and engaged in small-scale mining and manufacturing, always giving considerable weight to employee and community welfare rather than thinking only of personal profit. Above all he was a model of self-help, of the virtues demanded by a commoner society.

Not depicted in the novel, but also a part of the *gōshi* mentality, was a very strong resentment of full samurai. Often the *gōshi* were wealthier and better educated than the lower ranks of the urban samurai but did not receive social recognition in proportion. Tokutomi Iichirō recorded his resentment at being taunted during his childhood by urban samurai who called him "bumpkin warrior" (*zaigōhei*) or "small fry" (*keihai*).[70] In his own writings, he chose to ignore the samurai elements in his background. Instead, he championed those whom he styled "rural gentlemen" (*inaka shinshi*), and "rural men of lofty purpose" (*chihō yūshisha*), a range of active rural types known to contemporary historians as wealthy peasants (*gōnō*).[71] According to Tokutomi, these were the people with "prop-

---

68. Tokutomi's rather complex and ambiguous class background is discussed in Pierson, "Tokutomi Sohō," pp. 1–7.
69. See Tokutomi Kenjirō, *Footprints in the Snow*, trans. Kenneth Strong (Tuttle, 1971), esp. pp. 73 ff.
70. Tokutomi's resentment is noted in Pierson, "Tokutomi Sohō," p. 40 and Irokawa Daikichi, *Shinpen Meiji seishin shi* (Chūō kōron sha, 1973), p. 370.
71. In recent years a great deal of work has been done concerning the *gōnō* by Irokawa Daikichi, Kano Masanao, and others. In many ways their work is a modern version of what Tokutomi was doing: looking for a Japanese equivalent to the Euro-

erty, reputation, character, and intellect" among the Japanese people. They were the one preexisting locus of the values he felt were essential to the commoner society. They were that "middle class" (chūtō kaikyū) which was nothing less than the chief source of national spirit and health.[72] This was precisely what Fukuzawa had claimed for the samurai, but in Tokutomi's view the samurai had been nothing but parasites during the Tokugawa regime, not even capable of living within their unearned incomes and responsible for suppressing such talented men as did appear under the old order.[73]

Thanks to the Meiji Restoration the rural middle class had before it, Tokutomi believed, an especially bright future. He believed this because he had read T. B. Macaulay's *History of England* and saw his rural gentlemen as functionally equivalent to the English gentry.[74] He expected his rural men of purpose to progress in the future as he believed the English gentry had progressed, to be the middle class and to dominate the commoner society, which he himself had declared was the future of Japan. As evidence of their advance, he noted the rural middle class had acquired much from the Meiji Restoration, including control of village government and the right of electing prefectural assemblies, while the samurai had suffered only reduced privileges.[75] The rural middle class had moved forward economically after the Meiji Restoration. Not only were they ever more active in traditional areas such as the production and marketing of tea, silk, and sake, but they were also moving into new areas such as railroad investment and mining.[76] By Tokutomi's reading of history and his analogies with what he believed to be the history of Great

---

pean liberal bourgeoisie. These historians and their concerns are described in Carol Gluck, "The People in History: Recent Trends in Japanese Historiography," *Journal of Asian Studies* 38:1 (November 1978): 25–50.

72. Tokutomi's ideas concerning the rural middle class are developed most specifically in "Chihō yūshisha," *Kokumin no tomo*, no. 33 (November 2, 1888), pp. 1–5, and "Chūtō kaikyū no daraku," *Kokumin no tomo*, no. 172 (November 13, 1892), pp. 697–702.

73. Tokutomi, "Shōrai," pp. 155–156 and 161–162.

74. Concerning Tokutomi and Macaulay, see Pierson, "Tokutomi Sohō," p. 231. Concerning the expectations of other Minyūsha writers, see Duus, "Whig History," pp. 426–427.

75. Tokutomi, "Daraku," p. 697.

76. The economic developments behind Tokutomi's vision are noted in Irokawa, "Meiji nijū nendai," pp. 298–299.

Britain, it seemed that it would be only a matter of time before the rural middle class emerged as dominant in Japan. He gleefully noted the *rural* banking and mining interests behind Gladstone and other British politicians.[77] As the British gentry had progressed, so too would the Japanese country gentlemen, and those who sought to speak for them, the Japanese equivalents of Cobden and Bright, or so Tokutomi hoped.

Giving Tokutomi's vision a broader appeal than it would have had simply as an idealization of the rural middle class was the special role he posited for youth. In a tract entitled "Youth of the New Japan" [Shin-Nihon no seinen] Tokutomi charged youth (*seinen*) with responsibility for bringing about the commoner society. "We must advance to a true, pure commoner society. Who will take the first step? I will decide this. It is the youth of Meiji. Those youth must stand at the head of society's movement." He attacked what he called the "old men of Tenpō" (those born between 1830 and 1844). This covered most of the oligarchs in government, party leaders, and noted intellectuals. Tokutomi declared, "Whatever the age, whatever the country, old men are allies of the social order. Youth are the friends of advancement." The rapid pace of change taking place in Japan would mean that however much the old men had contributed, they would soon be so out-of-date that they would naturally have to be replaced by the new Meiji youth. "Meiji youth are not the ones to be led by the old men of Tenpō. They are the ones to lead the old men," he unequivocally asserted.[78]

Those youth who would lead the old men were not Meiji youth in general but those who embodied commoner virtues. Tokutomi harshly condemned those many contemporary youth whom he described as trying to advance (*risshin*) by the art of kowtowing (*kōtō-gaku*). He called upon youth to realize that "the people of the commoner society are responsible animals" (*sekininteki dōbutsu*). In other words, they recognize and take responsibility for managing

77. Tokutomi, "Chihō yūshisha," p. 1.
78. Tokutomi Iichirō, "Shin-Nihon no Seinen," in *Tokutomi Sohō shū*, p. 118. This tract was a combination of his 1885 (Meiji 18) essay "The Youth of Nineteenth-Century Japan and Their Education" (Dai-jūkyū seiki Nihon no seinen oyobi sono kyōiku) and a prefatory chapter, "Youth of the New Japan," written in 1887 (Meiji 20). All of the citations below are to the prefatory chapter.

their own affairs by themselves. By way of explanation, Tokutomi quoted Longfellow's *Village Blacksmith*.

> His brow is wet with honest sweat,
> He earns whate'er he can,
> And looks the whole world in the face.
> For he owes not any man.[79]

According to Tokutomi, the type of character described in the poem was the model (*tenkei*) for Western commoner society and should be the model for the Meiji youth who would take the great responsibility of realizing the commoner society. Their character and their fate would be that of the new Japan.[80]

For about a five-year period beginning with the publication of *Shōrai no Nihon* in 1886 (Meiji 19), Tokutomi and his formulas enjoyed great popularity among a substantial segment of contemporary educated youth. *Shōrai no Nihon* established his reputation and gave him an opportunity to leave remote Kyushu and found his own journal, *Kokumin no tomo*, in Tokyo. This soon had a circulation of over ten thousand, quite large by contemporary standards, and his group, the Minyūsha, grew into a major publishing enterprise.[81] Not all of this success is to be attributed to the promises for advancement (*risshin*) contained in his writing, but there is evidence to suggest that such were a major factor. Just by itself, the glowing promise of his vision for youth should have accounted for substantial popularity.[82] It appealed to the young men of *Eisai shinshi* who had been studying to be parliamentarians the day the constitution was promised, for Tokutomi referred to parliament and the constitution as a Second Restoration in terms of the opportunities that would be provided to bright young men.[83] It appealed to those who had with-

---

79. Ibid., p. 119.   80. Ibid., p. 122.

81. There was a considerable element of personal *risshin shusse* in this, for the success of *Future Japan* not only helped Tokutomi get out of the provinces (*shusse*) but also rise in the world (*risshin*) and restore his family fortunes. See Pierson, "Tokutomi Sohō," pp. 192–196.

82. Okawada discusses how Tokutomi's special charge built on a youthful self-consciousness that had been growing since the movement for liberty and people's rights. See Okawada, "Seinen ron," pp. 51–52.

83. See Tokutomi, "Zaiyatō," p. 5, for the claim that parliament would be a "Second Restoration," and Okawada, "Seinen ron," p. 52, for the mythologizing of the Restoration which was taking place.

drawn from the movement for liberty and people's rights in the face of government repression, because Tokutomi postulated a new politics of peace and gentlemanly exchange that would come about through the forces of history whether the oligarchs wanted it or not.[84]

Tokutomi's writing also opened up a new channel for expectation: enterprise itself and enterprise as an entry to politics. Commoners could find a special place for themselves and a previously denied sense of superiority, but because Tokutomi talked about spiritual values as much or more than actual class origins, samurai were not excluded from his vision. Samurai could ignore his attacks or see themselves in possession of the values Tokutomi emphasized and find for themselves an appealing self-image in his vision for youth.

Each of the elements suggested here can be documented as having provided a portion of Tokutomi's appeal, but each of them also proved to be based on dreams rather than reality. By 1891–1892 (Meiji 24–25), the whole grand vision was in disarray, and Tokutomi's popularity declined rapidly thereafter. His class vision was largely in a shambles by 1892 (Meiji 25), as he himself indicated in an article entitled significantly "The Decadence of the Middle Class" (Chūtō kaikyū no daraku).

The country gentleman had indeed advanced in industry and politics, but not as Tokutomi had expected. Rather than developing as idealized Smilesean self-made men, they had become corrupt and decadent. The stalwart country gentlemen who used to walk ten miles in straw sandals now rode in a jinrikisha to go to the neighboring village. Homespun and home brew had been supplanted by purchased foreign goods. Those with some petty village government job were soon bureaucratized. Others went to the regional assemblies and were soon citified and soft. After a spell in the provincial capital, they wanted to go to Tokyo, where they spent for whores and drink the money gotten by the sweat of their ancestors. Family heirlooms were going to decorate city whores, and forests were being turned into gold watches, which would soon end in pawnshops to finance another round of debauchery. Others turned to speculation, and if they made money, they sought to set themselves up as a one-

84. Irokawa notes that "The Youth of Nineteenth-Century Japan and Their Education" closed with a charge to youth not to be discouraged, that "inevitable victory" (hisshō) would be theirs. See Irokawa, "*Shinpen seishin shi*," pp. 404–406.

tenth or one-hundredth scale Ōkura Kihachirō or Fujita Denzaburō. In other words, they were seeking to become "political merchants" (*seishō*) of the type that he had condemned earlier. Worse yet, many of his rural elite were turning away from the productive figure described in *Omoide no Ki* and becoming parasitic landlords. In Tokutomi's vivid words, they had turned to "sucking the blood of the small people."[85]

Tokutomi had misread contemporary economic developments. In making his analogies between the English rural gentry and the Japanese, Tokutomi had neglected to consider the very different type and scale of agriculture in Japan and the relative profitability of parasitic landholding. Even as he had been formulating his vision, falling rice prices and the Meiji land-tax system had been decimating the ranks of the rural middle class. Between 1881 and 1890 (Meiji 14–23), their numbers had fallen by a third, and some contemporary observers thought that the middle-rank group would disappear, with only very small holders, tenants, and landlords remaining.[86] Those remaining had the franchise and advanced politically under the Meiji constitution, but their politics were anything but gentlemanly. They confronted the hostile government in raucous contests over the issue of budget and land-tax reduction while paying less attention to their traditional roles in the countryside. For all this, Tokutomi had no answer other than to express the hope that out of the depths of their depravity, the rural gentry would see the light and return to the true morality of the common man.[87] Since he did not even consider the possibility of institutional remedies to the concentration of holdings, he in effect became a defender of the rural landholder.[88]

During this period Japan was beginning that economic growth which in some senses would indeed make it a Great Britain of the Orient, but the reality of economic growth was not as Tokutomi had expected. Writing in 1891 (Meiji 24), he described society as "caught up in a wind of enterprise," with people selling their property to dress up and parade around with a walking stick, trying to look the part of what they imagined an entrepreneur to be. Further, it was in

85. Tokutomi, "Chūtō kaikyū," pp. 700–701.
86. Irokawa Daikichi, *Meiji seishin shi* (Ōga shobō, 1964), p. 286.
87. Tokutomi, "Chūtō kaikyū," p. 701.
88. Irokawa, *Meiji seishin shi*, pp. 288–289.

Tokutomi's eyes an age of get-rich-quick schemes (*ikkaku-senkin*), of trying to imitate the success of such "evil merchants" as Fujita Denzaburō and Ōkura Kihachirō, whom he condemned not only as harming the country but also as not being all that different from common criminals.⁸⁹ Tokutomi observed that many people imagined enterprise to be digging for buried treasure or picking up manna from heaven.⁹⁰ In part this reaction reflected the fact that Tokutomi's idea of a commercial society was largely theoretical. He had never been abroad, and he knew modern capitalism only from what he had read about it in idealized and uncritical treatments in Western writing, including *Self-Help* and *Character*. Otherwise, his knowledge was derived from seeing the small-scale activities his family and those of similar background engaged in.⁹¹

Compositions in *Eisai shinshi* in these years are testimony both to the enterprise fever that Tokutomi cited and to his own influence on youth. A rare subject during the 1870s and early 1880s, enterprise (*jitsugyō*) was such a popular topic that one essayist in *Eisai shinshi* in 1891 (Meiji 24) commented, "Today every time a youth opens his mouth, it is to insist upon enterprise."⁹² Often the rhetoric in these compositions, such phrases as "the old men of Tenpō" or "future Japan," indicates that the writer had been influenced by Tokutomi. Nevertheless, in filtering down to the *Eisai shinshi* essayists, Tokutomi's ideas changed somewhat in nuance. The compositions were more stridently nationalistic than Tokutomi's original writings. The expression "wealthy country and a strong army" came every few sentences, and there was much more use of the Social Darwinistic "survival of the fittest" (*yūshō reppai*) than had characterized Tokutomi's original writings.⁹³ Occasionally, there was a crudity that was completely absent from Tokutomi's own writings. One essay based on themes from Tokutomi proclaimed, "If we say what is

---

89. Tokutomi Iichirō, "Kyogyōka," *Kokumin no tomo*, no. 131 (September 13, 1891), pp. 5–7.

90. Tokutomi Iichirō, "Shakai ni okeru shisō no san-chōryū," *Kokumin no tomo*, no. 188 (April 23, 1893), pp. 2–3.

91. Irokawa, *Shinpen seishin shi*, p. 419.

92. "Seinen jitsugyōka," *Eisai shinshi*, no. 729 (July 18, 1891), pp. 1–2.

93. For example, "Jūkyū seiki no seinen fūshū no dorei to naru nakare," *Eisai shinshi*, no. 549 (January 14, 1888); "Dokuritsu wa shōnin no kanjō," *Eisai shinshi*, no. 572 (June 23, 1888); "Shōnin no shikaku," *Eisai shinshi*, no. 503 (February 19, 1887).

to be the method for advancing the civilization of Japan, the answer is gold.... Anything that puts gold into the hands of Japanese brings gold to Japan."[94]

Moreover, for all the advocacy of enterprise on the part of the well-educated youth who contributed to *Eisai shinshi*, there is little indication that composition writers really saw private enterprise rather than government as a career. The bulk of the compositions simply plugged a new amuletic word into earlier formulations. The same values were celebrated, especially perseverance (*nintai*), and the ambiguous *benkyō*, which could mean either study or hard work. Frugality and capital accumulation did not appear as subjects, nor did composition writers discuss specific careers or enterprises. There was much advocacy of enterprise in the abstract but no declaration of intent to follow such a career on the part of the author. Essays advocated commercial education, but there was no evidence of any interest in such education. Business schools in this period advertised for applicants but were consistently unable to fill more than one-half or two-thirds of the available positions.[95] In short, it appears that Tokutomi's writings gave ambitious youth another composition subject but not a real career goal. In other cases, enterprise was merely a temporary outlet for frustrated ambitions for political *risshin*. Kitamura Tōkoku recalled his own switch of this type and observed, "It was not a matter of having a stimulating plan and trying to reverse complete defeat."[96] By defeat, Kitamura meant the spiritual letdown that came with the failure of the movement for liberty and people's rights.

Tokutomi's promise of an unlimited future for youth fared no better than any of the other portions of his vision when tested against actual developments. By 1891 (Meiji 24) he was complaining that youth were deserting his cause, a development that he explained as being due to a conservative shift on the part of youth.[97] Perhaps this was a factor, but it would seem more likely that youth lost interest when the grand vision of their leading the old men of Tenpō around failed to materialize. Just as he had never quite explained how the

94. "Shōgyō shinki ron," *Eisai shinshi*, no. 510 (April 9, 1887), pp. 5–6.
95. "Yūgaku no kan," *Shōnenen*, no. 20 (August 18, 1889), pp. 18–20, and Karasawa, *Gakusei*, pp. 182–189, for recollections of those who went to such schools and were ridiculed for doing so.
96. Quoted in Maeda, "Meiji risshin," p. 37.
97. Pyle, *New Generation*, pp. 136–137.

British political system was to be achieved in Japan—his theory of history notwithstanding—he had never really explained how youth would come to power. Certainly the working of biology would *eventually* bring some of those who were youth in 1887 (Meiji 20) to positions of power. The old men of Tenpō could not live forever, even though some survived the Meiji era itself. By the same logic these youth would no longer be young, and presumably neither Tokutomi nor those who were inspired by his writings were thinking of simply waiting until the elder generation died; his writings have much more of a sense of imminent leadership. After all, if youth were going to lead the old men around, they had to come to power *before* the old men died.

Since Tokutomi had carefully and repeatedly made it clear that the transfer of political power was not to come about by violence or means outside the system, in the end this leadership boiled down to a declaration of faith backed only by the same breathless optimism that pervaded his overall historical vision. Here again Tokutomi's reading of the future proved wrong. The Progressive party (Kaishintō) Tokutomi favored soon developed a distinct seniority system, and its leader Ōkuma Shigenobu himself lived until 1922 (Taishō 11), dying at the ripe age of eighty-four. The old men of the Tenpō era neither died during the Meiji era nor relinquished power. Those who kept the faith despite the development of a raucous parliament and an oligarchic gerontocracy had it completely shattered when Tokutomi himself joined the oligarchs in 1897 (Meiji 30). This event was widely interpreted as a sellout to personal desires for advancement (*risshin shusse*), Tokutomi's claims to the contrary notwithstanding.[98]

An even more basic reason for the brief popularity of Tokutomi's vision was that the bulk of Meiji youth well enough educated to read his works were fundamentally committed to self-advancement and not to the advancement of political visions other than an amorphous nationalism. Tokutomi himself frequently lamented and condemned the tendency of contemporary educated youth to think only of their own advancement, but his pronouncements of an alternative value system did not alter this situation. Just what Tokutomi's

---

98. See Uete, p. 119, for contemporary reaction, and *Uchimura Kanzō zenshū* (Iwanami, 1933), vol. 16, pp. 257–259, for an extremely bitter satirical attack on Tokutomi, which says in part, "[The] poor fools took me for my words, bought and read my books with avidity, responded to my flatteries, and danced to my pipings."

vision had to compete with is suggested in the career of one Ishizaka Masatsugu.[99] Had Tokutomi's concepts of the self-made man been more descriptive of Japanese reality, Ishizaka Masatsugu should have become famous. He combined the two elements that Tokutomi thought most important in his future leaders. Ishizaka was of rural gentry origin, and he was literally a youth of the new Japan, having been born in 1868 (Meiji 1). In 1884 (Meiji 17) at age seventeen Ishizaka placed in his diary a "Plan for My Life" [Jinsei sekkeizu].[100]

For ten years or so diligently apply myself to learning. Graduate from a university in literature, politics, or political economy. Afterwards tour various countries. Broadly see and hear actual conditions. Meet with various people (and develop connections).
For two years compare the realities of politics to the academic. Examine the condition of society. Enumerate my own great ism [shugi]. Print and distribute this to society. . . .
After three years charge into political society and lead a political party. On the basis of heroism [eiyū shugi] take responsibility for cleaning up the world. . . .
Having ripened in experience, construct a unified government of the nations of the world by clearing away evil and advancing knowledge. Labor to make the peoples free. Pass a name down to the ages after death.
A man who preaches the difficulties of the world! Walk the path of justice by true principle. Will anyone under heaven oppose this? I will turn my eyes to the sun and the moon. I will make my voice a thunderclap. My bones will become those of a prophet. I will be called a true great man. I will be called the best of many. I will be called a god ascended to heaven.
When I carry out the reform of one house, I will set grandmother and parents at ease. I will make pleasant their honorable poverty [seihin].

What is more striking than the naive optimism that pervades Ishizaka's plan is the complete absence of any political ideas. Beyond the vague pronouncement about "a unified government of the nations of the world," he glibly puts off the question of his political thought for the future. He was most specific about those social values that gave meaning to his plans—name, fame, family, nation— and he was already certain of the institutional framework and content with it. Only his ideas were left undefined. He had no core other than his own commitment to his aspirations for self-advancement. This commitment to self-advancement was further illustrat-

---

99. Ishizaka is discussed throughout Irokawa, *Meiji seishin shi* and *Shinpen seishin shi*. He was the brother-in-law of Kitamura Tōkoku.
100. This document is reproduced in Irokawa, *Meiji seishin shi*, pp. 68–69.

ed by his subsequent career. He failed the entrance examination to the preparatory school that would have led him to the Imperial University. Later, after several more failures, he gave up his political quest and went to the United States to seek a fortune he did not find, eventually dying in a concentration camp at Manzanar, California, in 1944.[101]

That Ishizaka would give up his dreams largely because he failed to get into one particular education channel is more significant than his subsequent career. It indicates that he viewed electoral politics as something closely akin to the bureaucracy, for in aiming at the Imperial University he was aiming at an organ specifically intended to produce higher civil servants. This bureaucratic view of politics is further demonstrated by the fact that when he wrote his "Plan for My Life" the area in which he lived was experiencing the unrest that culminated in the Chichibu Incident, a massive peasant-based political rebellion.[102] Nevertheless, despite the presence of peasant politics at his very doorstep, his diary ignored these events. His own political dreams were focused entirely on the central bureaucratic establishment.

That electoral politics and bureaucratic affiliation were generally considered equivalent by educated youth is suggested by the popular contemporary ditty "Song of the Student" [Shosei bushi].

> Don't make fun of the student, the student
> In the future an administration official.
> Don't make fun of the student, the student;
> Great generals and parliamentarians, all students.[103]

The subsequent fate of the many "law schools" that developed out of the movement for liberty and people's rights further confirms the interchangeability of electoral and bureaucratic politics. First formed to teach the latest Western legal and parliamentary ideas to be used in attacks on the government during the movement for liberty and people's rights, these schools shifted—once the constitution was promised and even more so after the bureaucratic system was solid-

---

101. Irokawa, *Shinpen seishin shi*, pp. 42, 124.
102. Ibid., p. 37. In this sense he somewhat resembled Tokutomi, who was writing his "The Youth of Nineteenth-Century Japan and Their Education" during the same period that the Kaba, Iida, and Takada rebellions were going on but who talked only of a "spiritual revolution." See Irokawa, *Meiji seishin shi*, p. 230.
103. This ditty is noted in Mita Munesuke, *Gendai Nihon no shinjō to ronri* (Chikuma shobō, 1971), p. 187.

ified in the 1880s—to teaching those courses that would help aspirants like Ishizaka pass the entrance examinations to the preparatory school of the Imperial University.[104] Rather than continuing as a private alternative to the central establishment, they shifted to feeding in to that establishment.

Overall, the political fever among youth cooled very rapidly after the opening of the parliament as the idealistic became discouraged and the careerist reverted to study-for-wealth-and-honor. Compositions proclaiming political ambitions (parliamentary or electoral) are not to be found in youth-oriented publications after the early 1890s. Editorials in youth-oriented magazines continued to warn against overindulgence in politics as late as 1892–1893 (Meiji 25– 26),[105] but these too soon disappeared. By the Sino-Japanese War of 1894–1895 (Meiji 27–28), a consuming interest in electoral and parliamentary politics was definitely a thing of the past. Those few mentions of politics that appear in youth-oriented publications after the war are singularly devoid of any passion. A 1904 (Meiji 37) article in *Chūgaku sekai* [Middle-School World] is typical. It explained that in Japan there were two kinds of politicians: bureaucratic and popular (*minkan*). The bureaucratic type could get to be prime minister, said the article, but he ought to have graduated from the Imperial University and had to spend years working up through the ranks. The "popular" politician could either work himself up through a party apparatus or go it alone if he had four or five thousand yen in capital, but the "popular" politician, although he could rise to the Diet, could not get to be prime minister as a party member.[106] Thus, one had to pick between the alternatives, depending on capital and education. In either case, ideology and ideals had no role. Politics was just another road to advancement (*risshin*) with no more and no less appeal than any of a number of other careers with which the article dealt.

---

104. These schools are discussed in Masumi Junnosuke, *Nihon seiji shi ron* (Tōkyō daigaku shuppan-kai, 1966), vol. 2, pp. 46–50. For an advertisement indicating the conversion of one of these schools, the Shinbun Gakusha, see *The Student*, no. 131 (November 1885).
105. These editorials are discussed in the next chapter.
106. "Seijika," *Chūgaku sekai* (November 20, 1904), pp. 12–23.

The Stabilized Social Order | 4

Even as dreams of parliamentary *risshin* were dancing before the eyes of youth in the 1880s, the earlier motif of study for wealth and honor through government affiliation was growing in intensity. Politics in general and the movement for liberty and people's rights in particular provided less an alternative than a stimulus to the conception of advancement found in early *Eisai shinshi* [Talent Forum] essays. Compositions on the need for academic preparation in order to become a parliamentarian, the political novels with their student heroes, and the plans of Ishizaka Masatsugu were all testimony to this.

During the early stages of the movement, young men seeking to make their way in the world looked to a number of centers for education and political action. The Risshisha (Society of Lofty Ambition) had started in Kōchi on the island of Shikoku, and Kakuo in *Seiro nikki* [Diary of Life] had looked to Osaka for his education. As the movement progressed, however, attention was focused on Tokyo. After all, if there was to be an assembly, it would be in the capital, and the petitions calling for it and the petitioners themselves naturally "went up to Tokyo" (*jōkyō*).

Compositions on the theme "sending off a friend to study" peaked in 1881 (Meiji 14), just as did the movement itself.[1] In 1886 (Meiji 19) the ultimate incentive for going to Tokyo was provided when the government revised the educational system, making the Imperial

---

1. Maeda Ai, "Meiji risshin shusse shugi no keifu," *Bungaku* 33:4 (April 1965): 15.

University in Tokyo clearly the top of the educational order and the most desirable route into government service by extending preferential treatment to its graduates.² From this point on, the *shusse* portion of *risshin shusse* became synonymous with going to Tokyo.

Those going up to Tokyo were called *shosei*, a term that translates literally as "student," but which carried a special mystique in this period not unlike that attached to the *shishi* ("men of lofty purpose") of the late Tokugawa period. The *shosei* were often seen, by themselves and society in general, as carrying the future hopes of their family lines (*ie*) and the fate of the nation on their shoulders. Tokutomi's charge to youth to create the commoner society was only one of many such directives that placed special responsibility on youth. In addition, the *shosei* had their own desires for personal fame, desires that were marked by the duality of the samurai ethos. Although oriented to bureaucratic service with all that such a life implies in terms of routine, regulations, and paper-shuffling, they were also heirs to the samurai romantic traditions, which added to their natural youthful spirit. *Shosei* in the 1870s and 1880s were often a rough lot: eccentric dressers, riotous, hard-drinking, and frequent patrons of the brothel quarters.³

The excesses of the early *shosei* soon aroused the didactic instincts of the more bourgeois members of the samurai class. In 1885 (Meiji 18) Tsubouchi Yūzō (Shōyō), a samurai from Nagoya, published *The Character of Present-Day Students* [Tōsei shosei katagi], a combination exposé and moral lecture concerning the activities of the *shosei*.⁴ Based on his experiences at the Imperial University several years earlier, the work was intended to tell parents just what was happening to their children in Tokyo, why it was that so few were reaching their goals. Armed with the information in the book, par-

---

2. Concerning the educational system at this time, see Karasawa, *Gakusei*, pp. 64–65, and Kikuchi Dairoku, *Japanese Education* (John Murray, 1909), p. 356. Concerning exemptions and privileges for Imperial University students, see Robert M. Spaulding, Jr., *Imperial Japan's Higher Civil Service Examinations* (Princeton University Press, 1967), pp. 59, 88–99.

3. See Karasawa, *Gakusei*, pp. 29–30.

4. This novel exists in numerous editions. I used Tsubouchi Yūzō, *Tōsei shosei katagi*, in *Meiji-Taishō bungaku zenshū* (Shunyōdō, 1928), vol. 3. Useful biographical and background information is found in Yanagida, *Seiji shōsetsu*, vol. 2, pp. 1–20 and 42–45.

ents could avoid being deceived by their progeny and would know how to set their sons back on the straight and narrow path to advancement.[5]

Cast as a novel—the author had intended it to be a model of a new, nonmoralizing fiction—the work consisted mostly of a series of dialogues interspersed with the author's own didactic comments. These dialogues, rendered in the argot of mispronounced English that constituted the "in" language among *shosei* of the day, usually pitted one student who was something of a wastrel against another who was a model of propriety and bourgeois virtue. In a typical scene, one student lectured another, who had failed to arrive on time. "Yes, that's the way of Japan. Never think of the value of time. Really, Japanese are so *anpankuchuaru* [unpunctual] we ought to be afraid."[6] In another case, a student was busy writing a letter to his parents in which he claimed to have fallen ill with a sickness that could only be cured by a few weeks at a hot-spring resort. Again the friend launched into a lecture about how "Japanese are poor in the spirit of independence [*jiritsu dokkō*]" and thus would scheme to avoid acting by themselves. As an additional admonishment, the friend reminded that such conduct was also unfilial because it would cause worry to one's parents.[7] Other bad habits that were illustrated and preached against included falling into debt,[8] spending too much on fine clothes while one's parents were slaving away,[9] and too numerous excursions to the Yoshiwara brothel area, an activity called *purei* ("play") in the students' jargon.

For all their faults, the students in *Tōsei shosei katagi* were styled by the author as representing the "upper two-thirds" of all *shosei*. The bottom third, those to be found in private schools rather than the Imperial University, were more, the author lamented, than he could stand to treat.[10] This statement was a veiled attack on the Jiyūtō (Liberals), for private academies were more associated with it than with the Kaishintō (Progressives) that Tsubouchi supported.[11] There was also a status split and a rural/urban differential implied, for the private academies were associated with wealthy peasants, as was the Jiyūtō, while the Kaishintō represented a generally urban

5. Tsubouchi, *Tōsei*, p. 453.   6. Ibid., p. 469.   7. Ibid., pp. 470–471.
8. Ibid., pp. 477 and 495.   9. Ibid., p. 492.   10. Ibid., pp. 453 and 497.
11. Concerning Tsubouchi's politics, see Yanagida, *Seiji shōsetsu*, vol. 2, pp. 13–18.

samurai constituency. *Tōsei shosei katagi* was thus addressed to the more urban and affluent elements of the samurai class and was intended to reinforce the bourgeois elements of the samurai ethos.

In the United States didactic fiction played a major role in socializing youth to the demands of urban living and modern society. Aside from being inspiring stories, Horatio Alger's books were literally guides to city life, crammed with useful information on urban living.[12] Despite the model of *Tōsei shosei katagi*, the bulk of the didactic and directive literature concerning the quest for success in Tokyo was not fiction. Prejudices against the writing of fiction by those with an elite education were strong in Japan. Whereas the activities of Alger, a Harvard Divinity School graduate, were not regarded as degrading, the fact that Tsubouchi, an Imperial University graduate, had stooped to writing fiction generated much adverse comment.[13] Further discouraging the growth of a didactic fiction concerning personal advancement in Japan at this time was the nature of the advancement being sought by youth. Oriented as they were to academic preparation and bureaucratic affiliation, Japanese youth needed specific information on a changing institutional environment, a type of information that could not be well supplied by fiction.

As a consequence, the late 1880s (early Meiji 20s) saw the appearance of numerous periodicals that combined didactic lectures with specific and current information about institutional opportunities and requirements, especially with respect to education. In some cases these magazines were directed to promoting the rise in the world of a regional group or, even more narrowly, the rise of one class from some region. The *Aichi gakugei zasshi* [Aichi Arts and Sciences Magazine] is an example of this type, its concerns being a combination of tub-thumping for the Bishū area (Nagoya and vicinity) and guidance to *risshin* for samurai sons. Others were broader in orientation, being concerned with giving youth in general information needed for their rise, if not in the world, in Tokyo at least. In this group fell such now forgotten efforts as *Chishiki* [Knowledge], which carried the slogan "Knowledge is Power" on its cover and

---

12. Cawelti, *Apostles*, pp. 117–118, and Huber, *American Idea*, p. 48.
13. See Marleigh Grayer Ryan, *Japan's First Modern Novel: Ukigumo of Futabatei Shimei* (Columbia University Press, 1967), p. 54.

Cover of Shōnenen [A Garden for Young People], the first successful magazine catering to students facing the examination barrier to higher education.

Cover of Shōnen bunko *[A Library for Young People]*, a spin-off from Shōnenen *[A Garden for Young People]*, specializing in essays submitted by its readers.

THE STABILIZED SOCIAL ORDER

sprinkled misspelled quotes from Samuel Smiles throughout each issue; *Gakusei no shiyū* [Student Friend and Teacher], which revealed clearly in its compositions that the thinking seen in 1877–1879 (Meiji 10–12) issues of *Eisai shinshi* still lived ten years later; and the many *manabi* ("learning") magazines, such as *Manabi no tomo* [Friend of Learning] and the quaintly named *Manabi no teguruma* [Wheelbarrow of Learning]. Most came and went with remarkable speed, being characterized as "three-number magazines" (*sangō zasshi*) because most survived no longer.

The most important youth-oriented publication appearing in this period was *Shōnenen* [A Garden for Young People], published from 1888 (Meiji 21) until at least 1895 (Meiji 28). It commands attention as the prototype of the still-popular youth-oriented journal combining advice for examination preparation with entertainment and student compositions. The magazine was the effort of Yamagata Teisaburō, former Ministry of Education official, later translator of *Self-Help* (1912), and textbook publisher. Aimed at middle-school students and their parents and teachers, the magazine enjoyed a circulation of twelve thousand or so and published contributions by such noted figures as Mori Ōgai, Yamada Bimyō, Tsubouchi Yūzō, Nakamura Keiu, Tokutomi Iichirō, and Shiga Shigetaka.[14] Like *Eisai shinshi*, it also published reader's compositions. This proved so popular that the magazine was swamped and eventually split the composition section off into a separate magazine *Shōnen bunko* [Library for Young People].[15]

The basic editorial line of *Shōnenen*, indeed the raison d'etre of the magazine, was to guide youth to advancement in a society which, to use a favorite phrase of its editorial writers, was "becoming stabilized" or "being made correct" (*chitsujo tadashiku naritsuru*). An early editorial proclaimed:

Around the time of the Restoration or the opening of the ports. by some kind of good fortune, or by the patronage of some famous person, or by en-

14. *Shōnenen* is discussed in Kimura Shōshū, *Shōnen bungaku shi Meiji hen* (Dōwa shunjū sha, 1949), vol. 1, pp. 62–93. The circulation figure is actually the press run for the first issue. Ibid., p. 67. An advertisement for *Shōnenen* appearing in a rival publication, *Nihon no shōnen*, spoke of "the twenty thousand friends" of the magazine. *Nihon no shōnen* 2:4 (February 15, 1890): 82.

15. Kimura indicates that in two months the magazine received 237 articles, 1,727 letters (*shokan-bun*), and 2,043 "impressions" (*kansō-bun*). Kimura, *Shōnen bungaku*, vol. 1, p. 81.

tering the gate of some dignitary, it was possible to go to the United States or Europe without a bit of one's own capital and, before half a year had passed, make a great amount of money. Although there were not a few who did this, things are completely different today. Because the social order is being stabilized, this kind of good fortune is hard to find even in dreams. If you do not tread the proper path when you come to Tokyo, you will not be able to do or know even a single thing.[16]

Although this statement contained hints that the social order was becoming rigid and opportunities were declining, that was not the point the magazine wished to make. It stressed that there was still a vast range of opportunities available to youth. Only irrational and chance routes to advancement had disappeared with the stabilization and correction of the social order. Those already beyond middle school and out in the world could still enjoy the disorganization produced by the Meiji Restoration, but those now in middle school and below would have to count on systematic advancement.[17]

In terms of the mechanics of advancement, the most important feature of the 1886 (Meiji 19) reform of the educational system was the establishment of a system of higher middle schools (*kōtō chūgakkō*). Later to become the famous "number schools," these higher middle schools were the basic route into the Imperial University. Entry to the university was virtually assured if you had graduated from one of these schools, especially the First Higher Middle School (Dai-ichi Kōtō Chūgakkō).[18] Getting into one of these schools was the most important issue facing a youth who would study for wealth and honor. In 1889 (Meiji 22) *Shōnenen* reported that of approximately a thousand applicants to the First Higher Middle School, only about two hundred could expect to pass the test. Most of those who passed would have spent two or three years in private schools preparing to take the exam, and many would not pass on the first try. A few would succeed (or give up) after taking the exam six or seven times.[19]

16. Quoted in Okawada, "Seinen ron," pp. 48–49.
17. "Sōkan no ji," *Shōnenen*, no. 1 (November 3, 1888), p. 2.
18. As of 1892 (Meiji 25), ordinary middle school was for students aged twelve through seventeen and covered years seven through eleven. Higher middle school covered ages seventeen through twenty and years twelve through fourteen. In practice students were often much older than what the system called for, and this should be kept in mind when considering the audience of journals such as *Shōnenen*.
19. "Yūgaku no kan," *Shōnenen*, no. 16 (June 18, 1889), pp. 20–23. An article in *Nihonjin* gave more precise figures for the previous year. It noted that 800 had taken

In some respects this situation represented the first appearance of the so-called examination hell for which Japan is currently famous. There was one important difference: even with these high competition rates, up to 55 percent of the available places in the higher middle schools went unfilled.[20] The Imperial University and the schools that fed into it had high standards, and the examination tested qualifications. It was not yet an elimination contest designed to reduce a surplus of qualified candidates to the number of available seats. The problem for ambitious youth was at this point less their absolute numbers than the poor quality of secondary education jinjō chūgakkō), which as yet was not well developed and not capable of producing graduates of sufficient quality.[21]

The practical information *Shōnenen* gave its readers consisted primarily of data on entrance requirements, including subjects to be studied, dates of examinations, sample questions, and short articles on various subjects, particularly science and mathematics, and evaluations of schools where they could study to prepare for the entrance examinations to the higher middle schools. The reader of *Shōnenen* would find that a mere three out of dozens of preparatory schools accounted for almost 90 percent of the successful students admitted by examination to the First Higher Middle School.[22] This was in spite of the fact that the contemporary newspapers were filled with advertisements from a large number of schools describing in glowing terms each school's ability to place its graduates in higher educational tracks. According to *Shōnenen*, many students came to Tokyo with no more knowledge of the situation than that gotten from some enticing advertisement placed by a Tokyo school in a regional newspaper. It warned in its "Study Away from Home" (Yūgaku no kan) feature column that the prospective student's preparation "ought not to stop at just reading the advertisements in newspapers."[23]

The problem was not simply that some schools had a better place-

---

the exam and 155 (19%) had passed. See "Nyūgaku shiken no kekka," *Nihonjin*, no. 13 (October 3, 1888), p. 24.

20. Fukaya Masashi, *Gakureki shugi no keifu* (Reimei shobō, 1969), p. 204.

21. The disorganized state of mid-Meiji secondary education is discussed in detail in Fukaya, *Gakureki*, pp. 139–144 and 197–203.

22. "Yūgaku no kan," *Shōnenen*, no. 4 (December 18, 1888), p. 23.

23. "Yūgaku no kan," *Shōnenen*, no. 1 (November 3, 1888), p. 21.

ment record than others. Some were out-and-out frauds. Some of the private schools were waiting to take the young scholar for everything they could. Though *Shōnenen* did not go into details on this point, Kimura Shōshū has noted some of the practices of what were called *inchiki gakkō* ("bogus schools"). These included "borrowing" name teachers from other schools to gain accredited status, padding of fees with special charges unmentioned in their regulations, operating dormitories at a profit made by serving the cheapest possible food, requiring students to purchase school-published texts, especially large and impressive editions of foreign authors and foreign-language dictionaries not actually used in class, and various and sundry other frauds. Such schools advertised their having foreign faculty members, but these faculty members appeared but once or twice a month if at all.[24]

Even if they did not resort to outright fraud, it was a competitive world for private schools with only student fees and no government aid to rely on. Even honest institutions had every reason to offer a somewhat rose-colored picture of what they offered their graduates. Intensifying the competition was the propensity of students to jump from school to school if it looked as though they were not progressing to their entrance examination at due speed. As a *Shōnenen* editorial observed, many students came to Tokyo only to feel "dissatisfaction with the school or the teachers and leave one school for another, doing this many times, wasting months and years without accomplishing anything."[25] This situation created problems even for serious schools because, as one contemporary observer noted, "The fear of losing their pupils prevented the directors of such schools from placing their students under strict control and discipline."[26]

Perhaps even more fundamental than the question of where to study was the question of how to pay for study. While no essays or editorials in *Eisai shinshi* had dealt with this question and Fukuzawa had ignored it in his *Gakumon no susume*, it was a major issue in *Shōnenen* editorials and advice columns. According to the magazine, costs had recently risen by a factor of six or seven, and

24. Kimura Shōshū, *Meiji shōnen bunka shiwa* (Dōwa shunjū sha, 1949), pp. 64–67.
25. "Tōkyō ni yūgaku sen to suru chihō no shōnen shoshi ni tsugu," *Shōnen bunko* 1:5 (May 18, 1890): 1–5.
26. "Professor Toyama at Seiritsu Gakusha Reunion," *The Student*, no. 40 (December 25, 1887), p. 39.

the youth who would go off to Tokyo should be certain of his finances before leaving.[27] Just what the magazine was using as its reference point to claim a six- or sevenfold increase is not clear, but there is no question that secondary education was relatively expensive. Ordinary middle school involved an outlay of three to four yen a month, and attendance at the First Higher Middle School required approximately ten yen a month. Just taking the examination to the First Higher Middle School required a fee payment of five yen, about as much as a day laborer could expect to make in a good month during this period. Preparatory schools were less expensive, but still a burden to less than fairly affluent families.[28]

Despite preaching Smilesean virtues and often using items from Smiles's writings as filler items, *Shōnenen* did not suggest the possibility of students working to earn a portion of their fees. Perhaps this was due to realism. Ordinary middle schools and to a somewhat lesser degree the higher middle schools had strict examinations for passing from one grade to the next.[29] There was little chance a student could earn any portion of his expenses and still survive competition within the schools. A more important reason is that *Shōnenen* appealed to a relatively affluent stratum of readers. One year of *Shōnenen* cost three yen, or 60 percent of what a laborer could earn in a month. Families affluent enough to afford *Shōnenen* were not likely to consider having their sons engage in relatively menial tasks in order to acquire some small fraction of their school fees.[30]

Shōnenen advised students to rely not on self-help, but on friends or relatives from one's home district who had already gone to Tokyo. At first reading, this advice seems a bit odd or at least unnecessary. Biographical accounts of those who were students in the 1870s indicate that relying on friends was a well-established practice, and *Shōnenen* would seem to have been repeating the obvious. Never-

27. "Yūgaku no kan," *Shōnenen*, no. 4 (December 18, 1888), p. 23.
28. For cost estimates, see Fukaya, *Gakureki shugi*, pp. 173–176, and "Yūgaku no kan," *Shōnenen*, no. 16 (June 18, 1889), pp. 20–23.
29. Tough entrance and easy promotion and graduation, the situation typical of contemporary Japanese education, developed late in the Meiji period. At this time, the failure rate on periodic exams in middle schools was as high as 35 percent, and Fukaya has estimated that as few as 10 percent went straight through middle school without failure and without dropping out. See Fukaya, *Gakureki shugi*, pp. 180–183.
30. During my stay in Tokyo (1971–1974), whole sets of *Shōnenen* turned up at book fairs and used-book sales. This suggests affluence, stability, and provinciality (because the books were not burned during the war).

theless, this may not have been the case. *Shōnenen* appears to have been directing itself to a slightly different stratum of student than had gone to Tokyo a decade earlier, when the vast majority of students acquiring higher education were of samurai origin.[31] Thanks to the alternate attendance system, even the most isolated fief had had an establishment in Edo, and as a result samurai from the various fiefs had a natural network of links to Tokyo after the Restoration. In addition, many lords had used portions of their post-Restoration bond settlements to establish promotional associations to assist promising young men from their fiefs. The *Aichi gakugei zasshi*, cited earlier, was the journal for one such organization. Some fiefs even had dormitories in Tokyo for their aspiring young men.[32] Because *Shōnenen* did not discuss such facilities and possibilities, it would appear that its audience did not have access to those facilities, suggesting in turn a rural samurai or wealthy peasant audience. Class origin data for students in this period are extremely sketchy, but what there are suggest that commoners—and they had to be relatively wealthy commoners—were advancing into higher education.[33] These were the probable audience for *Shōnenen*.

Also indicative of a provincial audience is a certain anti-Tokyo stance *Shōnenen* shared with Tokutomi's *Kokumin no tomo*. *Shōnenen* warned repeatedly that Tokyo was not all glitter and opportunities for advancement. Evil lurked behind the façade of civilization and enlightenment the city represented to most. In an 1890 (Meiji 23) editorial on the subject of an exhibition in Tokyo that was drawing people from all over the country, editorials in *Shōnen bunko* advised youth not to be impressed by only the façade.[34] At the same time, *Kokumin no tomo* was advising youth to return to their native villages during the summer vacation as a means of spiritual

31. In 1879 (Meiji 12) 77.7 percent of the students at the Imperial University were samurai (*shizoku*). See Karasawa, *Gakusei*, p. 163.
32. Concerning these provincial urban connections which seem to have benefited *shizoku* more than commoners, see Fukaya, *Gakureki shugi*, pp. 136, 168–169, 189–190; Karasawa, *Gakusei*, pp. 29–30; Kimura, *Meiji shōnen bunka*, pp. 53–63, 130–138; Austin W. Medley, "Student Life in Tokyo," *Japan Magazine*, no. 1 (1910), pp. 44–49; and *The Japan Year Book 1906*, p. 447
33. See Fukaya, *Gakureki shugi*, pp. 208–209, for some of the limited data available.
34. "Tōkyō," *Shōnen bunko* 1:4 (May 9, 1890): 67–68, and "Tōkyō yūgaku suru chihō shōnen shoshi ni tsugu," *Shōnen bunko* 1:5 (May 18, 1890): 1–5.

cleansing, to get rid of the "grit" accumulated when one was in Tokyo for long periods.[35] Neither magazine had much to say about whether the concentration of facilities and talent in Tokyo was good or not, and there was a certain measure of hypocrisy in both, considering that their own success and their raison d'etre was the existence of Tokyo and its attractions.[36]

For *Shōnenen* the problem with Tokyo was less urbanization in the abstract than the temptations it offered students and the probability that these temptations would derail them from their course to advancement. *Shōnenen* was especially concerned about the appearance of *geshuku* ("rooming houses") that took care of those students not attached to any sponsor. The *geshuku* were generally viewed with alarm by *Shōnenen* editorial writers, for they were seen as dens of iniquity where innocent rural youth would be exposed to the bad habits of Tokyo. One such editorial proclaimed, "Truly, all of the hundreds of bad things a student can learn are in the *geshuku*." The magazine did not list these hundreds of bad things, presumably for fear of giving encouragement to those who might be willing to stray from the well-ordered path to advancement. There were some explicitly described evils, however, such as smoking and drinking, and some vague hints of sex.[37] These fears were doubtless another reason for the magazine's urging reliance on friends and relatives.

Even more worrisome to the magazine than the possibility that its young readers would discover sex in Tokyo was the possibility that they would become involved in politics as *sōshi* ("stalwart youth," "bullies"). The magazine attacked the *sōshi* repeatedly, and told youth that politics was not for them, a theme soon picked up by its

35. "Seinen gakusha wa nanzo kokyō ni kaerazaru nanzo inaka ni asobazaru," *Kokumin no tomo*, no. 56 (July 12, 1889), pp. 15–17. Tokutomi's nostalgia for the countryside appears in his review of the novel *Kisei* [Homecoming] by Miyazaki Koshoshi, which is a sentimental description of a young man's homecoming. The novel has many sketches of those who grabbed at *risshin* but missed. See Maeda, "Meiji risshin," p. 21, and "*Kisei* o yomu," *Kokumin no tomo*, no. 88 (July 13, 1890), pp. 9–13.
36. The Seikyōsha and its journal were more concerned about this problem. See "Sotsugyōsei yūzū no issaku—zenkoku chishiki no kin'itsu," *Nihonjin*, no. 14 (May 3, 1894), pp. 8–11.
37. "Yūgaku no kan," *Shōnenen*, no. 3 (November 18, 1888), pp. 23–24. See also Miyazaki Michimasa, "Nihon shosei no zento," *Nihonjin*, no. 4 (May 18, 1888), pp. 8–11.

young readers eager to see their names in print.[38] A typical composition on the subject of avoiding politics took the form of a letter of admonition to a friend who had quit school to join a political party and who had added insult to injury by not communicating this fact home until third parties had already done so. In the usual phrase of the day, the letter writer found his friend's conduct "hard to bear," and he scolded, "Politics is necessary to society, but for inexperienced youth like ourselves, it is just not the thing to be debating." Repeating the editorial line of *Shōnenen*, he warned that one had to study and that "one must first of all acquire the skills" before one goes out into the "political battlefield." To go out unprepared was "to invite destruction in the struggle for dominance [*yūshō reppai*]." Finally, apparently feeling that his friend might not be brought back to the straight and narrow path to advancement by the logic of Social Darwinism, he went on to assert that such conduct was also a transgression of filial piety.[39] Similarly a *Shōnenen* editorial on "the single greatest danger to youth" advised that while party politics was necessary to a constitutional order, there could be nothing more dangerous to youth, for politics was the fastest way to ruin for country and family.[40]

The concern with youth's being caught in the vortex of politics lasted only a few years. Editorials on the subject seldom appeared after 1892 (Meiji 25). More common in all magazines aimed at youth were editorials warning that the nation needed more than would-be functionaries and that better opportunities were to be found in other areas. In lieu of politics, *Shōnenen* provided lists of what it styled "enterprises [*jigyō*] Japanese youth should undertake." Although the term was sometimes used to mean commerce, in the case of *Shōnenen* the word meant much the same as "business" had meant to Smiles in *Self-Help*: governmental, military, and academic activities. Virtually all of the enterprises cited by the magazine had academic prerequisites: medical research, agricultural research, civil engineering, and so forth. Even its recommendations in the military

38. A long, multi-part series on the *sōshi* was featured in 1889 (Meiji 22). See Suekane Imokichi, "Sōshi, seinen, shōnen," *Shōnenen*, no. 12 (April 18, 1889), pp. 3–7, and subsequent issues.

39. Kitamura Saburō, "Yūgaku-chū seito ni kamei seshi yūjin o isameru sho," *Shōnen bunko* 1:1 (March 9, 1890): 100–103.

40. "Shōnen no ichidai kiki," *Shōnenen*, no. 78 (January 18, 1892), pp. 1–4.

area were technological: navigation, meteorology, cartography, and so forth.⁴¹ Although basically Smilesean in content, the recommendations in *Shōnenen* contained no suggestion of independent research or discovery. Youth would study in a formal academic environment and apply preexisting Western knowledge to Japan.

Beyond such recommendations, *Shōnenen* gave very little in the way of hard information concerning employment opportunities. Perhaps employment was too remote a subject to interest its readers. After all, they were from nine to twelve years away from graduation, depending on the number of years of post-middle-school preparation it would take before they entered the track to the Imperial University and eventual graduation. Nevertheless, in reading *Shōnenen* one feels that the main reason for a lack of specific employment information is that both the magazine and its readers looked to the civil service for employment, and conditions and compensation were well known. The market for graduates of the Imperial University in the late 1880s and early 1890s was very good, and starting salaries were pegged to grades according to a formula that was well known and published. Since even those who barely managed to graduate and even some failures were assured of jobs, there was no pressing need for more precise vocational information.⁴²

Overall, graduates of the Imperial University could expect forty to sixty yen a month to start, with rapid increases in both rank and pay after employment. According to one set of calculations, the Imperial University graduate made back the cost of his additional education beyond the middle-school level in just two years after graduation. Middle- and normal-school graduates received much less. Elementary-school teachers ranged from five to thirty yen per month, while low-rank civil servants could expect twelve to twenty yen. Nevertheless, when it is considered that day laborers could make only three to five yen a month, even ordinary secondary education was well compensated. In four years the ordinary middle-school grad-

41. See "Kōmyō fūki no genya," *Shōnenen*, no. 7 (February 3, 1889), pp. 1–4, and Shiga Shigetaka, "Nihon shōnen no nasubeki jigyō," *Shōnenen*, no. 7 (February 3, 1889), pp. 4–6, and no. 8 (February 18, 1889), pp. 4–5.

42. The scale was as follows (monthly figure in parentheses): 85 and up, 600 yen (50 yen); 79–84, 550 yen (46 yen); 65–78, 500 yen (42 yen); below 65 (failing), 450 yen (38 yen). See "Daigaku sotsugyōsei no saiyōhō," *Nihonjin*, no. 31 (August 8, 1889), p. 26, and Spaulding, *Higher Civil Service*, pp. 90–91.

uate made back the cost of his education beyond the elementary level.[43]

The picture was less uniformly favorable for students who proceeded to nonelite higher education. Only one out of six or seven students with higher education graduated from the Imperial University. The vast majority studied at a somewhat amorphous category of institution known in English as professional school or college (senmon gakkō). In theory these schools took middle-school graduates and gave them a quality, higher-level education in such preprofessional fields as medicine, pharmacy, law, business, and engineering. Unlike the Imperial University, they were to teach and use textbooks in Japanese, and thus had no need for the higher-school stage of language preparation, but they were nonetheless to offer a comparable education.

In practice there was great disparity between national (kanritsu) colleges and those in the public (kōritsu) and private sectors. Only national institutions, which were concentrated in medicine, commerce, engineering, and foreign languages, came close to the ideal of offering a quality vernacular higher education. Private schools were poorly funded and concentrated on the fields of law and political economy, which were inexpensive to teach. The formal requirement that students have a middle-school education or its equivalent was not generally enforced, and ability to pay school fees was often more important than academic preparation or ability. Rather than providing preprofessional higher education, these schools served as temporary resting places for students who were studying for higher-school entrance examinations and needed remedial help or simply proof of enrollment for continued draft deferment. Those who graduated were at a disadvantage because of legal discrimination in favor of Imperial University applicants to the civil service as well as because they had received an inferior education.[44]

43. Fukaya, *Gakureki shugi*, pp. 212–213 (graduate compensation), p. 176 (teacher and civil servant compensation), and pp. 214–215 (pay-back calculations).

44. The exemptions and privileges granted to Imperial University graduates are described in great and often confusing detail throughout Spaulding, *Higher Education*. After 1893 (Meiji 26), the discrimination against private-college graduates was strongest in the case of the judical and bar examinations and relatively unimportant in the case of the more popular administrative examinations. The schools in general are discussed in Amano Ikuo, "Continuity and Change in the Structure of Higher Education," in William K. Cummings, Amano Ikuo, and Kitamura Kazuyuki, eds., *Changes in the Japanese University: A Comparative Perspective* (Praeger, 1979), pp. 10–38. As

THE STABILIZED SOCIAL ORDER

The private colleges gained large numbers of students in 1886–1887 (Meiji 19–20) in anticipation of the constitution and all the opportunities it was supposed to bring. At that time *Nihon no shōnen* [Young People of Japan] editorialized that far too many students were studying law at private schools and the market for such youth was bound to decline.[45] In 1890–1891 (Meiji 23–24), the bulk of these students graduated. Over 3,400 private law-college graduates were added to the pool of advancement seekers, and the accuracy of the *Nihon no shōnen* prediction was soon demonstrated.[46]

In 1891 (Meiji 24) both *Shōnenen* and *Nihon no shōnen* reported on the declining market for youth with nonelite higher education. *Shōnenen* recalled that twenty years before, graduation from a private school, knowing a Western language, and reading a few Western books would get you to secretary (*shokikan*) rank in the government in one jump. In the newspaper field it would make you an editor, and in business, a manager. Now graduation from a private college would get you a ten-yen-a-month job as a reporter or maybe into the bottom ranks of the bureaucracy.[47] *Nihon no shōnen* went so far as to claim that half the private-college graduates in politics and economics were unemployed, and both magazines editorialized against the prevailing popularity of law and politics as a field of study.[48] Subsequently, the number of private-college graduates dropped precipitously, especially in law, but not apparently enough to cure the market glut in the short run. *Nihonjin* [The Japanese] claimed in 1893 (Meiji 26) that for fifty sen or one yen students would happily give "three bows and nine prostrations" without embarrassment, because of their desperate situation.[49]

---

for the relative importance of the institutions in terms of graduates, it may be noted that in 1892 (Meiji 25), out of 2,508 *reported* college and university graduates, only 15% were Imperial University graduates, while 60% were from private colleges. Private law-college graduates were 32% of the total, whereas Imperial University law grads were only 3% of the total. *Monbushō nenpō*, no. 20 (1892), pp. 12, 41, and 45–47. These figures are of unknown accuracy, although it may be assumed that the national-sector figures are quite good while those for the private sector may be low.

45. "Kyō no shōnen," *Nihon no shōnen*, no. 2 (March 5, 1889), pp. 6–8.
46. Graduate numbers by field and type of institution were reported in the *Monbushō nenpō* for the fiscal years indicated. See also *Nihon teikoku tōkei nenkan*, no. 12 (1893), pp. 93–94.
47. "Gakumon no chochiku," *Shōnenen*, no. 56 (February 18, 1891), pp. 1–2.
48. "Sotsugyōsei no matsuro," *Nihon no shōnen* 3:3 (February 1, 1891): 2–4.
49. "Gendai no shōsōnen seniki," *Nihonjin*, no. 5 (December 18, 1893), p. 7. Pri-

THE SELF-MADE MAN IN MEIJI JAPANESE THOUGHT

With this change in the market for at least a portion of youth having secondary and higher education, Social Darwinistic rhetoric began to be more prominent both in editorials and in student compositions. As early as 1889 (Meiji 22) a *Nihon no shōnen* editorialist was observing that "along with the progress of society, the ways of dealing with the world [*shosei*] become more difficult." The "struggle for existence," as he phrased it, was getting harsher, and he specifically noted the increased competition to enter select schools.[50] By 1891 (Meiji 24) it is possible to find the English word "victims" being used to describe those who were defeated in the competition for advancement.[51] By 1895 (Meiji 28) even *Kokumin no tomo* was, in an article specifically on *risshin*, speaking of youth as "born naked into the world and the struggle for existence," and, as the editorialist observed, "The person who does not win is defeated."[52] There were no shades of gray. Either you were on top or you were not, and woe be to him who was defeated.

Student compositions gradually came to use more Social Darwinistic rhetoric and apply it to individual competition rather than competition between nation states, the common early Meiji usage of these concepts. More concern was shown with the matter of avoiding failure than with the more positive theme of securing advancement. Such writing reached an extreme in a topic that enjoyed considerable popularity in 1894 (Meiji 27) among contributors to *Gakusei hissenjō* [Battlefield of Student Writing Brushes], a publication dedicated solely to reader-supplied essays. Youth after youth declaimed on the subject "Climbing a Mountain in a Snowstorm."[53] The idea was that rising in the world was as difficult as climbing a mountain in a blizzard, with enormous difficulties to be overcome and numerous chances to slip and fall into the abyss of poverty and low rank. Though essentially a variation on the theme endurance (*nintai*) for wealth and honor found in *Eisai shinshi* in the 1870s, the emphasis was now on what had to be done to avoid falling rather than on what assuredly led to advancement.

---

vate law graduates totaled 1,828 in 1891, 807 in 1892, 1,061 in 1893, 634 in 1894, and 492 in 1895.
50. "Kyō no shōnen," *Nihon no shōnen*, no. 2 (March 5, 1889), pp. 6–8.
51. "Kyōsō jidai," *Nihon no shōnen* 3:9 (May 1, 1891): 8–9.
52. "Risshin," *Kokumin no tomo*, no. 257 (July 23, 1894), pp. 1–3.
53. See, for example, "Setchū tozan ki," *Gakusei hissenjō*, (February 5, 1894), p. 54.

THE STABILIZED SOCIAL ORDER

Goals remained largely unchanged from the earlier period—wealth, honor, and fame—but much more attention was paid to the idea that these were "for the country." It is difficult to say if this change really reflected a growing concern with the affairs of the nation. The bodies of most compositions were unchanged from the 1870s, with only a quick preface added in most cases. An example from *Nihon no shōnen* illustrates one common way in which priorities were stated.

> Why do we study? Why do we labor in real enterprise [*jitsugyō*]? The small reason is that we seek fame, wealth, and honor for ourselves. The large reason is that we seek to cause our Japan to shine among the heavens and the many nations.[54]

Such themes were a bit more common in Hakubunkan publications. The firm was trying to become a textbook publisher and seems to have gone out of its way to emphasize nationalistic themes.[55] It let hardly an issue of any of its journals get out without some reference to Imperial Rescript on Education, and filial piety figured in a notable number of the student compositions as would-be essayists parroted back the editorial line of the firm.

Compared with *Shōnenen*, compositions in Hakubunkan publications gave more attention to both "commerce" (*shōbai*) and the more ambiguous "enterprise" (*jitsugyō*). Two factors may be noted to explain the relatively greater importance of these themes in Hakubunkan publications. Hakubunkan was an old-style merchant firm, while *Shōnenen* was founded by an educator and ex-bureaucrat. The former was in part tooting its own horn in emphasizing commerce, especially commerce for the nation, while the latter reflected intellectual or bureaucratic preferences. Hakubunkan publications also seemed to have been aimed at a slightly different stratum of readers, provincial types no less affluent than the families who subscribed to *Shōnenen* but more directly involved in commercial activities. Nevertheless, the difference is not major. Few compositions in Haku-

54. *Nihon no shōnen*, no. 9 (June 15, 1889), p. 32.
55. For general background on the firm, see Kano Masanao, "Taiyō," *Shisō*, no. 450 (December, 1961), pp. 135–147, and Tsuboya Zenshirō, *Hakubunkan goju̅ nen shi* (Hakubunkan, 1937). Concerning its editorial policies for its youth-oriented (*Nihon no shōnen*) and juvenile-oriented (*Yōnen zasshi*) publications of this period, see Kimura, *Shōnen bungaku*, vol. 1, pp. 158–164, 201–209.

135

bunkan publications (or in *Eisai shinshi*) rise above broad abstraction, and commercial heroes are conspicuous by their absence.[56]

Study for wealth and honor was the dominant motif in all magazines, and as essays in all magazines stressed, study had to be systematic, since the social order was now stabilized. A theme from *Eisai shinshi* in 1894 (Meiji 27) eloquently shows what had happened to the visions produced by the Meiji Restoration and the changes that followed:

> Truly, a time like the recent Meiji Restoration was a time for doing deeds and making a name among the rival camps. Among the men with great ambition who happened to be there, were there any who lacked the will to fight the stag on the contest field? There are not always such chances. . . . The world turns and there are peaceful days even on the four seas. When society has an order [*chitsujo*] it is not possible to leap to the sky in a single bound. In the impetuous days of youth it is easy to be dominated by such greatly mistaken dreams. There are many hero-worshipers who want to imitate the accomplishments of those who have gone before. The danger is that they do not nourish minute [*seikei chimitsu*] thoughts. They go as far as unrestrained and rough behavior. Are there not a great number who fail to gauge the broad trend of the times? If Toyotomi Hideyoshi were born today, he would be just one small animal [*ippiki*]. If Saigō [Takamori] were born today, he would be just one poor student. Really, the chance for one poor student to seize political power in one bound comes just once in a thousand years. Is not the only way to respond to society to expand one's abilities to the fullest? Can the accomplishments of heroes be applied to today's ordered society? What is the profit in trying to imitate the heroes of the past in today's ordered society? Get rid of those dreams![57]

Reading these essays, one often finds it difficult not to feel a certain sympathy for mid-Meiji youth. The 1872 (Meiji 5) proclamation that all would have the educational base for rising in the world, the dreams of becoming a second Saigō or a Disraeli, Tokutomi's grandiose vision for youth—they were all so splendid and inviting, but in a matter of a generation or less, society was back to a stability which, if not the same as that of the Tokugawa era, certainly contrasted with the hopes and dreams that had developed during and after the Restoration. Opportunities remained, to be sure, but the principal

56. One of the few exceptions to this generalization is "Risshi," *Yōnen zasshi* 2:2 (January 17, 1892): 27. Here Toyotomi Hideyoshi and Iwasaki Yatarō (founder of Mitsubishi) were offered as models of "lofty ambition." For an editorial celebration of a businessman, see "Shōgyō gakkō yori daijin idenu," *Shōnenen*, no. 95 (October 3, 1892), pp. 1–3.

57. "Koku eiyū sūhai ronsha," *Eisai shinshi*, no. 875 (May 26, 1894), p. 2.

method of assigning opportunities, the examination system, was inherently destructive of youthful spirits. Futabatei Shimei recalled:

> Truly, in those days I had nothing in my eye but examinations. Studying for examinations, my joy and sorrow depending on my success in examinations, looking upon all things with indifference unless they were related to examinations, I devoted practically my whole life to examinations, so that if they had been taken out of it at that time, it [my life] would have become like insignificant smoke.[58]

After an examination, all he could think of was release from the agony. "I wanted to stick my finger down my throat and vomit . . . and be refreshed if I could."[59] Such was the orientation to examination preparation among aspirants to *risshin* that some magazines felt obliged to remind their readers that eating and sleeping also had a place in their lives.[60]

Such sympathy is largely out of place. Most of those who entered the contest for wealth and honor already had more of both than the vast bulk of their contemporaries. Those who were successful in the most elite track would be very well rewarded for their efforts. Even those who acquired a middle-school education but were unsuccessful in going further were part of a small elite and would acquire more income and status than their less well educated counterparts. Moreover, even if the system was spiritually destructive, most did not feel that at the time. Futabatei's comments were written long after the fact. Many greeted the changes with enthusiasm and were completely satisfied with the system. Here, a composition by one such youth is offered in its somewhat tedious entirety to give a feeling for what it was to be an ambitious youth seeking to advance in the stabilized social order of Meiji Japan in the late 1880s and early 1890s.

Systematic Study

Why should a youth read? Why should he write? Why should he work and study diligently? Some will be quick to say that the answer is because the child's father has said to him that if he gets a good grade on his next examination, come next summer, he will be taken on a trip. For this reason the child studies. This is the answer of one child. There is nothing strange

---

58. Futabatei Shimei, *Mediocrity* [Heibon], trans. Glenn W. Shaw (Hokuseido Press, 1927), p. 65.
59. Ibid., p. 64.
60. "Professor Toyama at Seiritsu Gakusha Reunion," *The Student*, no. 40 (December 25, 1887), p. 39. Original in English.

about this. It is easy to understand. But is this the answer of one who will really amount to something? Is this the answer of one of deep purpose? Is it too much to say that such a child will go into the battle for survival naked?

Take a look at the path lying before us. It is so vast that we can not see its extremity. Is not the 10,000-mile [*ri*] battlefield spread before us? Are not the great schools recruiting us? However, this all comes down to one question, one determination, one examination—the so-called winning post. This means the winning of a woman and the acquisition of wealth [*fujinzainō*].... Whether one's name is carved on monuments and passed down through countless generations is all determined this way. If this be so, will we youth who are proceeding down the road of life expressing hopes and pressing forward with our dreams find our pleasure in the word victory?

Observe. A cute child receives an award, and he shows this to people. He cannot keep the joy from showing on his face. His eyes meet those of others, and he thinks to himself, "I got this prize!" A blush comes to his cheeks. His insides dance with unlimited spirit. He opens and closes his mouth, but he is speechless. He can only quiver. Is this not cute? This is but one student. If you ask what he has learned, you will find that it is not in readers but in ethics texts. It is not in calculation but in the law of elimination. What is his prize? Two or three marks on a paper or just a dozen pencils. The value? A fraction of the trip promised by his father. He is shown to people and praised. It is like listening to the voice of a demon [*oni*]. What is it that is inside of him and gives him so much pleasure? It is said that if one is victorious, one will occupy a throne in fame. The prize he received in the exam is but a trifle, something of the least cost. Yet, what is the way of seeking this? Is it not study? One studies and it leads to happiness. One does what one must. What if one does not study? What if one is neglectful of systematic study? No, never! One must never neglect systematic study!

Systematic study is superior to unsystematic study. To advance the ladder of the system, one must advance by systematic study! Can we advance without systematic study? Can we progress by disorganized study? The first years of Meiji were such a period when there was no systematic ladder. Getting a well-placed wife and wealth was not in the proper road of the great competitive field. It was in the byways. Receiving the prize of admission to some great school was not expected. It was random. Now the great differences in the advancement of the four classes is gone. The time demands systematic study.

Hidden among the inaccessible crags and fog, meandering about the summit, is not the way spread out before us? Are not the masses falling from the cliff, sinking in the swift waters before our very eyes? If we want to ascend to the pinnacle in a single bound, if we want to advance to the summit, is it not dangerous? Look at the people who waste time until an examination draws near before they stop being lazy and start to study. While they sometimes get the prize, they will not be able to pass the real test. They get on by looking at their neighbor's answers and using them as their own. After they have received the prize, they must feel shame in their conscience. They hide their lack of knowledge. Will they have the same pleasure as one who receives the prize with his own efforts? Will they reach the final winning post in the race?

Like the person who seeks to buy momentary pleasure by momentary study, can they really raise up any kind of result in this way? The difference between true pleasure and that of such youth is like that between heaven and mud. The person who will climb the ladder of the system studies systematically. Does he try the dangerous trick of ascending in a single bound? One hour of study gives an hour of profit. However, it is difficult to keep this going for long. One can make disorganized study work briefly but it does not lead to the final victory. Today's youth! Don't study in a disorganized fashion! Do study with a system.[61]

The author of this composition later became an executive in a government corporation. He apparently followed his own advice in the rectified social order.

More of a commentary on youth in the decade before the Sino-Japanese War is the fact that not only did they write many such essays, they also *paid* to read them. Student compositions had been something of an afterthought with *Shōnenen* and its spin-off, *Shōnen bunko*, but Hakubunkan used student compositions as a selling point from the very beginning. It drew upon the desire of contemporary youth for recognition to the fullest possible extent. Large sections of various Hakubunkan publications—*Nihon no shōnen* [Young People of Japan], *Yōnen zasshi* [Magazine for Children], and *Gakusei hissenjō* [Battlefield of Student Writing Brushes]—were devoted to student compositions, which were often collected into special issues and even book form. Given the verbosity of these compositions, the endless repetition of set themes, and the frequent plagiarism in evidence, it is difficult for the present-day observer to understand the appeal of these collections. Nevertheless, they apparently sold, even such efforts as one with a title in "English" of "Literal Exhibision of Janseyouth" that was advertised as a selection of the "best" of some 3,400 compositions received.[62] Young people, or their parents, were willing to pay for works containing "English" compositions like the following:

61. An essay that appeared in *Shōnenen* 1:9, as quoted in Kimura, *Shōnen bungaku*, vol. 1, pp. 85–88.
62. Advertisement for "Shōnen gakujutsu kyōshinkai," *Nihon no shōnen*, no. 18 (November 1, 1889), p. 40.

Our young brethren! your obligation is something that is energy, perseverance about for yourself and mankind, in this juncture and wildeawake world. Keep Smills Maxim, "Heaven helps those who help themselves." Pull your hands from your pockets; spring has neary finished, and summer is comming; none can be brought forwards for young time again. Put away "the nonsense that the world is against you." It is not so! your testing is in your own strong arm.[63]

Only an age of youth absolutely mad with its own rhetoric or desperate to see itself in print could have appreciated such works.

One reason why youth of this period might have felt such a desire to gain publication stemmed from a belief that such publication was a step on the road to *risshin*, a belief that was encouraged in promises made by the magazines. For example, the inaugural issue of *Shōnen sekai* [World of Young People] proclaimed, "The youth who will take charge of the nation and who ought to be the base of an eminent people will be able to discover and nourish morality and intellect by this [magazine] and will further contribute to the glory of future civilization. Your fame [*meiyo*] ought not to stop with this one humble house [publisher]."[64] Another advertisement claimed that participation in the competition for publication sponsored by the magazine (*Yōnen zasshi*) was comparable to participation in the Battle of Hastings or the Battle of Sekigahara.[65] Apparently the youth who was victorious in this "student's Hastings" or "student's Sekigahara" was to consider himself on the way to *risshin*, though given the quantity and quality of the compositions published, it is hard to believe that much selectivity was used to choose winners.

The personality evident in the general run of compositions in youth-oriented publications and in "Systematic Study" was not simply a reflection of the age of the composition writers. Their slightly older brothers, the new intelligentsia that had emerged in the late 1880s, depicted itself both in critical essays and in fiction as basically conformist and concerned with *risshin* to the exclusion of almost all human emotion. A number of writers raised the question whether there was more to life than the pursuit of *risshin* in conformity to social demands; with one exception, they all answered that *risshin*

63. K. Suzuki, "For the Youth of Japan," *Nihon no shōnen* 2:11 (June 1, 1890): 58.
64. Kimura, *Shōnen bungaku*, vol. 1, pp. 354–355.
65. Advertisement for "Nihon zenkoku shōgakkō seito hissenjō," *Yōnen zasshi*, no. 5 (March 3, 1891).

was life itself. Nothing meant more than personal advancement in conformity to social demands.

The question whether life had more meaning than *risshin* was first raised in the novel *Tōsei shosei katagai* [The Character of Present-Day Students] by Tsubouchi Yūzō. The hero, Komachida Sanji, is the son of a samurai fallen on hard times. His father had vowed that his son would never experience the indignity of being hounded by bill collectors, and Sanji is out to "pursue learning to the end" in order to avoid the fate his father met. Along the way to advancement, Sanji falls in love with a "singer" named Ta-no-ji. When he spends too much time too openly with her, he is suspended from school.[66] After a brief interval under suspension, he is offered the chance to redeem himself for "causing unforgettable shame" to his family and to his school.[67] The price for being allowed to return to school is abandonment of Ta-no-ji. With little hesitation, Sanji returns to his pursuit of *risshin*, refusing to have anything to do with the grieving Ta-no-ji. She pledges nevertheless to wait ten or even twenty years until Sanji has achieved his goals. Then he can take up with her again without harming his chances for *risshin*.[68]

In a tedious detour in the novel, fellow students discuss the *risshin* implications of Sanji's behavior. They decide that "disgrace is an impediment to rising in the world. Taking a singing girl [*geigi*] for a wife is a disgrace. Therefore taking a singing girl is an impediment to rising in the world."[69] This logical exercise is more or less irrelevant to the story because Sanji has already decided he would rather have *risshin* than love. It does serve the purpose of letting the reader know where the author stands, however, and during the interval when it seems that Sanji might choose love, a harshness creeps into the narration. When Sanji elects *risshin* in conformity to social and family demands, the narration becomes more sympathetic. Tsubouchi was editorializing on which was more important.[70] His preference for *risshin* and conformity is clear. Nevertheless, he did allow Sanji to have both. Ta-no-ji is discovered to be the long-lost sister of one of Sanji's friends. She is of samurai descent and, once rescued

66. Tsubouchi, *Tōsei*, p. 484.
67. Ibid., pp. 538–539. 68. Ibid., p. 553. 69. Ibid., p. 579.
70. Marleigh G. Ryan arrives at just the opposite view of Tsubouchi's preferences. Marleigh Grayer Ryan, *The Development of Realism in the Fiction of Tsubouchi Shōyō* (University of Washington Press, 1975), p. 44. Nevertheless, I believe the overall thrust of the novel is to encourage *risshin* in conformity with social norms.

from her fate as a singing girl, is certified as compatible with Sanji's *risshin* quest.[71]

Sanji's cavalier treatment of Ta-no-ji when it appeared she would harm his chances for *risshin* is exceeded by the brutal treatment of another woman for the same reason in the partly autobiographical story *Maihime* [Dancing Girl] by Mori Ōgai.[72] The story is cast in the format of a recollection by a young Japanese student who is returning from study in Germany. The student, Ōta Toyotarō, is the product of a regular *risshin* ladder: domainal school, Imperial University, government service. Always a top student, Ōta soon receives an order to go to Germany for study. This he expects will further his hopes for an uneventful life, a steady rise, and eventual retirement, all of which are part of his desire to "make a name for myself and cause my household [*ie*] to flourish," a formulation remarkably like those found in *Eisai shinshi*. The atmosphere in Germany gradually causes him to become aware of the fact that he has been a "passive machine," first the object of his mother's desires for his advancement, and then as the appreciated *deshi* ("follower") of his bureau chief. This realization leads to secret inner thoughts, a failure to associate with his fellow Japanese, and a platonic relationship with a poor German girl. Nevertheless, fellow students report that Ōta is involved with a "dancing girl," frequenting plays and other entertainments, and generally acting in a way unbecoming to a young bureaucrat on the way up. The bureau chief reports Ōta's alleged deviation, and in quick succession he receives two letters from home. One is from his mother, saying she will pay his way home because she cannot ask the government to pay for a son who has behaved so shamefully. A second letter arrives to tell him of his mother's death.

Fired from his bureaucratic job, he moves in with the family of the girl, Erisu, all the time worrying about returning to Japan with a sullied (*omei*) name. A friend who took notice of Ōta's firing gets him a job as the Berlin correspondent for a Japanese newspaper. Ōta gradually forgets his studies and settles into a routine but warm existence

71. Tsubouchi, *Tōsei*, p. 604.
72. This novel first appeared in *Kokumin no tomo* (January 3, 1890). I have used the version appearing in *Maihime* (Ōbunsha bunko, 1969), pp. 7–35. The personal events behind *Maihime* are discussed in Hasegawa Izumi, "Kaisetsu," in *Maihime*, pp. 173–183. A complete translation of *Maihime* is now available in English. See Mori Ōgai, "Maihime [The Dancing Girl]," trans. Richard Bowring, *Monumenta Nipponica* 30:2 (Summer 1975): 151–176.

with Erisu and her family. Soon the friend, Aizawa, arrives from Tokyo and offers to get Ōta reinstated. Ōta declares he has no further interest in wealth and honor (*fūki*), although he will accept some translation work to help make ends meet. Ōta does such a good job that he comes to the attention of the Japanese ambassador. Soon Aizawa comes with another offer. If Ōta announces that he is finished with Erisu, he will be reinstated, maybe even promoted. This choice throws Ōta into a quandary, and the difficulty of his decision is increased by the discovery that Erisu is pregnant. Vacillating several times, he eventually comes to a decision. When asked by a visiting minister to return with him to Japan, Ōta thinks of "losing my country, cutting off the chance to restore my name" and fears "being put to rest among the great sea of people in this Western capital." Having reasoned thusly, he can but answer, "I will do as you bid."

While this might seem like the ending, with Ōta having proved himself a cad, this is not in fact the conclusion of the story, for having wrestled mightily with the question of *risshin* or love, he proceeds to swoon and fall ill *without* having informed Erisu of his decision. During his sickness, he is nursed by Erisu, who is still unaware of his decision. Only *after* recovering does Ōta get around to telling Erisu, who is by then much weakened from a combination of pregnancy and her efforts on Ōta's behalf. She faints at the news, and when she comes to, she is stark raving mad. A doctor says Erisu is suffering from paranoia and has no prospect for recovery. Ōta's friend gives Erisu's mother money to put her in a lunatic asylum, and Ōta goes back to Tokyo and his *risshin*.

In the novel *Ukigumo* [Floating Clouds] by Futabatei Shimei, *risshin* versus love is given a somewhat different treatment in which the hero discovers that, in mid-Meiji society, without pursuing *risshin* he may not be able to find love either.[73] The nominal hero of the novel is Utsumi Bunzō, the personification of a young samurai who has been educated at great cost in personal suffering on the part of his parents. His father is described as a samurai unable to make the transition to either government service or commerce under the new regime. After Bunzō's father dies, it is only by the heroic efforts

---

73. I have relied on the translation of this novel by Marleigh Grayer Ryan contained in *Japan's First Modern Novel: Ukigumo of Futabatei Shimei* (Columbia University Press, 1967), pp. 197–356.

of his mother that they manage to survive. At age fifteen (in 1878, Meiji 11), Bunzō goes to Tokyo and joins an uncle, who is also a samurai who fell on hard times with the Restoration but who was saved by his shrewd mistress.[74] Thanks to his diligence and application to study, Bunzō is admitted to a new preparatory school and gets on the ladder of the stabilized social order. Unlike most of the students who come from better-off families, Bunzō lacks an allowance and is thus a model of self-help. Moreover, he is talented, never getting less than a second on examinations.

On graduating, he discovers that study for wealth and honor was not quite the whole story; he lacks "connections," and thus it takes six months for him to find a job. When he does get a position, he comes face to face with the realization that all his work and study really count for little. Not only is his learning not needed for his job, but any demonstration of knowledge is dangerous. With little effort, Bunzō manages to get weeded out in the first shakeup that occurs, and the reason is not hard to find. Bunzō has spent too much time on his studies and not enough time on his knees. Only after having been fired does he come to realize the importance of what Tokutomi Iichirō called the "science of kowtow" when he scolded Meiji youth. He muses to himself, "I must have been fired because I wouldn't play up to the boss. The boss is a bastard. And my fellow workers—they're so damned obsequious. It's downright obsequious to be so submissive and grovel for the sake of a little pay."[75]

If it takes getting fired to teach this lesson to Bunzō, this is not true of his "friend," the aptly named Honda Noboru (*noboru* means "to ascend"). Honda Noboru is, in American slang, a "brownnose." His formula for advancement has little to say about study for wealth and honor. Instead, he plays up to the boss at every available opportunity. This means not being merely a passive "yes man," but going so far as to copy the boss's speech and gestures and even the way he clears his throat. Noboru scores by pointing out the mistakes of others and by paying Sunday visits to the boss at his home, being sure to bring presents.[76] Bunzō meanwhile learns that the demand for obsequiousness is not limited to his boss or the bureaucracy. When he

74. Ibid., pp. 206–207.
75. Ibid., p. 226. Retrenchments were common. See Spaulding, *Higher Civil Service*, pp. 94–96.
76. Ryan, *Ukigumo*, pp. 247–248.

loses his job, his friends and his fiancée, rather than supporting him, consider him stupid for not taking Honda Noboru's route. His fiancée loses interest in him, and her mother sums up Bunzō's status by observing, "Bunzō is in an altogether different position now."[77] He is no longer a young man on the long road to wealth and fame, and he can no longer be considered as a prospective son-in-law.

As described so far, *Ukigumo* might seem to be a story describing the struggle of one individual to follow his conscience in a society that does not reward such behavior, but in fact Bunzō is not depicted as someone out to challenge the system. He does not get fired for standing up to the boss; he gets fired for not bothering to bow down often enough. In terms of getting fired, these may be equivalent, but in terms of conscience, they are not. Bunzō's failure to bow down to his boss is not a matter of strongly held principle, and the novel ends with his wondering whether he should crawl to get his job back.[78] His main concern seems to be whether crawling would work at this late date. As depicted in the novel, Bunzō gives little assurance that he will not make the attempt. Given the weakness of Bunzō's character, it seems unlikely the novel was intended, as has been claimed, to sanction a new "independent outlook" among Japanese.[79] The only character in the novel with a true sense of independence is Honda Noboru. Though obsequious and self-effacing before his boss, he is not a passive tool of society. He is cynical and knows how to use social forms for his own purposes.

Tokutomi Iichirō harshly condemned the obsequious personality type and chided youth for seeking to advance by flattery rather than actual ability. He was not critical, however, of the youth who was willing to sacrifice all, including love, for the sake of advancement, and he was not at all successful in providing ethical guidance to those who were placed in a situation where they might have to sacrifice their advancement for the sake of moral or ethical principles. This failing may be seen in a series of articles in 1890 (Meiji 23) in which Tokutomi discussed the responsibilities and ethics of government officials. In his view, the chief danger faced by officials was that of becoming drunk with thoughts of money. This threat was to

---

77. Ibid., p. 243.   78. Ibid., p. 309.
79. This interpretation is found in Pyle, *New Generation*, pp. 14–15.

be met by not thinking of name and fame; these had to come as "by-products" (*fuku-sanbutsu*) of the basic task of promoting the public welfare. As further developed by Tokutomi, the ideal bureaucrat should "have before him only the thing which he ought to be exerting himself in." The good functionary respects others, and most important, "he follows regulations correctly."[80]

While these may seem a reasonable, albeit conservative, set of instructions, what of the issues not raised by Tokutomi? What does the functionary do when he gets an "immoral order," or what does one do if one discovers immoral or illegal conduct on the part of others—a superior, for example? Which is one loyal to, the chain of command and the rule book or one's conscience? Tokutomi is silent, and this omission is particularly glaring because in the third of these short articles he raises the issue of an individual and internalized morality. But when he explains what this morality is, he speaks of it as "defining the system and making an order."[81] The most important aspect of this morality is believability (*shin*), but Tokutomi explains this only in terms of honoring contracts and not telling lies.[82] One might ask, does the morality of not telling lies mean the morality of telling the truth when not asked? Again Tokutomi is silent, and the answer is not to be found elsewhere. Such a sticky question as where and when does one put one's career on the line and accept the fact that to be loyal to some internal moral code will mean the possible or probable end of one's chances for advancement is not dealt with by Tokutomi. To bow or not bow before officials or to seek to advance by performance rather than obsequiousness were questions the individual might face, but not the only ones, and not necessarily the most important. In 1891 (Meiji 24) the Christian Uchimura Kanzō was forced from his position at the First Higher Middle School when momentary questions of conscience caused him to hesitate to offer what might be construed as religious veneration to a portrait of the emperor. Tokutomi was strangely silent.[83]

80. "Gojin no senzo," *Kokumin no tomo*, no. 83 (May 23, 1890), pp. 6–7, and "Shinsei no jimuka," *Kokumin no tomo*, no. 83 (May 23, 1890), pp. 8–9.
81. "Shin no ichiji," *Kokumin no tomo*, no. 83 (May 23, 1890), pp. 10–12.
82. Ibid., pp. 11–12.
83. See Ozawa Saburō, *Uchimura Kanzō fukei jiken* (Shinkyō shuppansha, 1961), for a complete discussion of the incident. Tokutomi also took a weak stance on the Imperial Rescript on Education which was part of a conservative effort to reassert elements of Confucian morality.

THE STABILIZED SOCIAL ORDER

The degree to which even such critical thinkers and writers as Tokutomi were committed to an absolute conformity to social rather than individual goals is seen even more clearly in an exchange with Kitamura Tōkoku on the subject of romantic love (*renai*).[84] As a critic and essayist, Kitamura was instrumental in the 1890s in introducing certain concepts of romantic love that sharply challenged the existing principles of family relations held among samurai and those who shared their family ethos. Put rather crudely, the traditional practices of the propertied strata were governed by a rule which said "keep love and sex out of the family and in the brothel where they belong."[85] Marriage and the family were for the purpose of carrying on the ancestral line and for possessing and distributing property. As long as love did not enter the economic sphere, there was no problem. Kitamura challenged this view of love when he announced, "Love is the key to life. Where there is love there is life. If love is cast off, what is left of life?"[86]

While Kitamura's concept of love was platonic to the point of harming his own marriage, in Tokutomi's eyes *renai* was "dogs in heat chasing one another." He painted a lurid picture of young men reading *renai* novels late at night under the dim light of a lamp in a sordid *geshuku*. Although the reader might expect a denunciation of some "vile habit," what actually agitated Tokutomi was that youth reading such novels would in their dreams become the hero of the novel and "imagine that one can become rich without hard work, that one can make a name without study, that one can raise up a household [*ie*] without a plan for *risshin*!" In fact, despite the implications of his "dogs in heat" image, it was not the sexual implications of *renai* which bothered Tokutomi as much as the *risshin* implications. He thundered that "man cannot serve two masters," and he declared *risshin* and *renai* as an either-or proposition. "If you want to realize the emotion of love, you must suppress any desire

---

84. This exchange is discussed in Makibayashi Kōji, "Kitamura Tōkoku to Tokutomi Sohō," in *Kitamura Tōkoku*, ed. Nihon bungaku kenkyū shiryō kankō-kai (Yūseidō, 1972), pp. 140–151.
85. Rural samurai (*gōshi*), wealthy peasants (*gōnō*), and wealthy merchants (*gōshō*) can generally be considered to have followed similar practices. In Tokutomi's case, it is of interest to note that not only was his marriage arranged but the ceremony was carried out by proxy. See Pierson, "Tokutomi Sohō," p. 119.
86. These are the opening lines of his essay "Ensei shika to josei," in *Kitamura Tōkoku—Yamaji Aizan*, p. 63.

to accomplish great deeds. If you desire to accomplish something great, then you must suppress the emotion of love." Human strength is limited, and for the person who has a calling (*tenshoku*) or a great ambition, love is, according to Tokutomi, just so much baggage that ought to be cast aside.[87] In short, Tokutomi advocated the course taken by the hero of *Maihime*: advancement at any cost.

In response Kitamura observed that Tokutomi had not really understood the meaning of the internalized morality he had talked about. Tokutomi had written, "Do not learn just the enterprise [*jigyō*], learn its spiritual technique. Do not look at the material phenomenon, look at the spiritual phenomenon."[88] But, according to Kitamura, this was nothing but "narrow positivism" that reduced morality to a set of "techniques" when it should be "founded on experience, namely, standing upon the inner life."[89] This was in fact an accurate assessment of Tokutomi because, as was noted earlier, his whole assertion of a commoner morality was part of a program of nationalistic reform. His ethics and values were merely instruments for this purpose and had no justification beyond their social utility. Kitamura's notion of morality founded on individual experience and an inner life was a radical challenge to Japanese thinking in general and even more so to thinking about *risshin*. Kitamura was able to move beyond the usual definition of life as *risshin* in conformity to social demands, but only to a limited degree.

In his most famous essay, "On the Inner Life" [Naibu seimei ron], Kitamura asserted that it is natural for man with his reasoning ability to wonder whether there is really a life (*seimei*) or not.[90] By life Kitamura meant "afterlife," or reason for existence beyond that which looked to the surrounding society and its demands. In raising this question Kitamura was touching on a very weak point of all those who asserted the priority of *risshin*. Was there no other reason for existence? Did one exist merely for family or state or for *risshin* itself? The *Eisai shinshi* youth knew why they existed: to pursue wealth and honor through study in order to raise the family name or to leave their own to the ages. The youth who wrote "Systematic

87. "Hirenai," *Kokumin no tomo*, no. 125 (July 23, 1891), pp. 6–7.
88. Makibayashi, "Kitamura Tōkoku," p. 146.
89. Kitamura Tōkoku, "Naibu seimei ron," in *Kitamura Tōkoku—Yamaji Aizan*, p. 147.
90. Ibid., p. 145.

Study" existed for the sake of winning the applause of society and the material benefits it offered. Tokutomi and others of his generation and group tended to stress the state. Kitamura, thanks in part to Christianity, could wonder whether these were really all there was to life, and as he noted, if there was nothing more to life than the short fifty years of man's existence, there was really not much point in working or planning.

The answer to this meaning of existence and the source of the inspiration and standards by which the individual might decide what he should do was to be found in *individual experience* and in a special momentary separation from the world, which would give the individual an opportunity to think things through and free him from social demands so that he might indeed be able to find a solution for himself.[91] This was in effect a call for a *shusse* in its original meaning: a going out of the world. Unlike all those who wrote on *risshin shusse* and who sought individual fulfillment and the meaning of life through a *shusse* that took them out into the world where their conformity to social expectations validated their quest, Kitamura was saying that the only self-fulfillment lay in the original meaning of *shusse*: to get away from society and think it all through for one's self. Achieving this sort of separation in mid-Meiji society was far from easy, however, and in one essay, "My Jail" [Waga rōgoku], Kitamura lamented that his life had been continually limited by the demands of contemporary society that he pursue fame, power, wealth, and honor. These had been his jail.[92]

Indeed, Kitamura's life up to 1893 (Meiji 26) had been a microcosm of the various styles of thinking on personal advancement observed so far. Kitamura was of samurai origin and combined in almost stereotypical fashion the dual burdens of his class. On the one hand, as a child he was an avid reader of the great classics that celebrated individual heroism, and he dreamed of imitating the heroes and heroism depicted in those stories. On the other hand, he lived in a present dominated by a mother he referred to as "commanding general" in his recollections. Her goal was that Kitamura should through study achieve wealth and honor and raise the family name and fortunes by getting a good government job. Straying from the study-for-wealth-and-honor track after going to Tokyo in 1881 (Meiji

91. Ibid., p. 148.
92. "Waga rōgoku," in *Kitamura Tōkoku—Yamaji Aizan*, pp. 41–43.

14), Kitamura became something of an activist in the people's rights movement and even came to be known as a *sōshi*. Later he dreamt of saving the Orient through philosophy and compared his expected role to that of Christ. Still later he turned to literature with a brief sidetrack into commerce (*shōbai*) as he tried his hand at commodity speculation in Yokohama in what he later described as an attempt to recover from a personal spiritual depression that had come with the end of the people's rights movement.[93]

How strong his "jail" was is illustrated by the fact that when Kitamura expanded on his notion of the inner life, he could not free his thinking from the terminology and concepts that permeated so much of the writing on personal advancement. In his exposition of the inner life he could not refrain from elitism, and he proclaimed, "Poets and philosophers are nothing less than those who *solve* the inner life of mankind."[94] Despite his emphasis on *individual* discovery, there still had to be those who would do the discovering for the masses. More significantly, in an article, "Patterns in Present-Day Literature," he promised literary youth that which the *risshin* youth sought. Admonishing literary youth not to be taken by temporary fame, he proclaimed, "Your world is not the present. It is in the future sometime. Fame and authority [*kenri*] exist in the limitless tomorrow." This was an assured development, for, according to Kitamura, "Carlyle has said you ought certainly to rank among the heroes of tomorrow."[95] Thus Kitamura remained committed to the criteria used for measuring *risshin* in the society at large.

Possibly it was in part a combination of his own ability to escape from his wealth-honor-and-fame jail within the context of contemporary Japanese society and even within his own thought that led Kitamura to hang himself on the morning of May 16, 1894 (Meiji 27).[96] Whatever his actual motive, he did leave behind an example that will be encountered again, that of a turning inward to literature,

---

93. The basic source of information on Kitamura's childhood is his letters to Ishizaka Mina (sister of Ishizaka Masatsugu). These are found in *Kitamura Tōkoku—Yamaji Aizan*, pp. 206–209. See also Tōyama Shigeki, "Nihon kindaika to Tōkoku no kokumin bungaku ron," in *Kitamura Tōkoku*, pp. 40–47; Irokawa Daikichi, "Shin-Tōkoku-zō no shutsugen," *Shisō*, no. 522 (November 1967), pp. 30–44.

94. "Naibu seimei ron," in *Kitamura Tōkoku—Yamaji Aizan*, p. 147.

95. "Tōsei bungaku no ushio moyō," in ibid., pp. 58–59.

96. This is the impression given in Shimazaki Tōson, *Haru* (Iwanami bunko, 1969). This novel was based on Shimazaki's experiences with Kitamura. Aoki in the novel is Kitamura. It first appeared in 1908 (Meiji 41).

philosophy, religion, and suicide to provide a frontier, a not yet stabilized social order, where the individual could seek self-fulfillment without being restricted by social demands for conventional *risshin*. Nevertheless, at the time, although deeply influential on a few close friends, Kitamura's ultimate rejection of the Meiji social order and its values generated no widespread reaction, even among intellectuals.

How far Kitamura was out of step with the general norms of educated youth is best illustrated by what most were doing with Carlyle in the same years he was formulating his inner life. Heroes and hero worship had been a steady feature of youth compositions from the earliest years of *Eisai shinshi*, but the introduction of Carlyle's *On Heroes, Hero Worship, and the Heroic in History* gave such worship extra respectability by linking it with a noted Western intellectual.[97] In 1894 (Meiji 27), the year that Kitamura committed suicide, *Eisai shinshi* had numerous essays on hero worship inspired by Carlyle. Although a few writers were against hero worship, the majority were proponents.[98] Typically, they argued as did one youth who observed, "If hero worship is abandoned, the difference between the honored and despised must be ignored. Fools and wise men must be blended together. Outstanding heroes and mediocrities must be made into one." To avoid this undesirable situation, "inferiority and superiority must be judged. From inferiority and superiority is naturally born the concept of submission. Where there is submission, there is worship."[99] Another proclaimed, "What way is there to lead the masses if not with eminent men [*ijin*]?" and went on to offer as examples "the patriot Jefferson" and the "revolutionary Napoleon" along with Victor Hugo, Confucius, and Toyotomi Hideyoshi![100] An-

97. The whole question of Japanese concepts of the hero is fascinating and largely unexplored territory. Virtually every Meiji thinker at some point penned an essay on the subject of heroes and heroism (*eiyū*). A boom in publishing on the subject seems to have begun around 1890 (Meiji 23) when Hakubunkan began publishing "Collected Stories of World Heroes." See Noguchi Takejirō, ed., *Sekai Hiyaku Ketsuden* (Hakubunkan, 1890). (The romanization is that used by the publisher.) One volume of this multi-volume work offered Toyotomi Hideyoshi, Confucius, Socrates, Plato, Mahomet, Pythagoras, and the Rothschilds.

98. Anti-essayists argued variously that heroism was inappropriate to the rectified order, that venerating men rather than their accomplishments was wrong, or that one should not venerate foreign heroes. See "Eiyū sūhai ron," *Eisai shinshi*, no. 870 (April 21, 1894), p. 2; "Sūhai netsu," *Eisai shinshi*, no. 863 (March 3, 1894), p. 2; 'Futatabi sūhai netsu ni tsuite," *Eisai shinshi*, no. 869 (April 14, 1894), pp. 1–2.

99. "Eiyū sūhai hatashite hiriki," *Eisai shinshi*, no. 867 (March 21, 1894), p. 1.

100. "Eiyū sūhai ron," *Eisai shinshi*, no. 873 (May 12, 1894), pp. 1–2.

other writer put the whole issue very precisely: "Essentially, hero worship is nothing but the attitude the lower class [rank] holds toward the upper."[101] No youth of this period but Kitamura seems to have held to Carlyle's assertion "Fool! The ideal is in thyself, the impediment too, is in thyself." The modal case of educated youth during this period was the hollow personality seeking such wealth, honor, and fame as could be gained in the stabilized social order.

101. "Futatabi eiyū sūhai ni tsuite," *Eisai shinshi*, no. 873 (May 5, 1894), pp. 1–2.

Success! | 5

Even before the Sino-Japanese War had come to an end and its outcome had been made clear, it was being celebrated as a boon to the aspirations of youth. *Shōnen sekai* [World of Young People] went so far as to proclaim that the war would amount to a "second Meiji Restoration" and that it would give contemporary youth the opportunity to follow in the footsteps of such Restoration figures as Iwakura Tomomi, Kido Kōichi, Ōkubo Toshimichi, Saigō Takamori, Iwasaki Yatarō, Shibusawa Eiichi, Fukuzawa Yukichi, and Katō Hiroyuki. Although the Restoration metaphor suggested that contemporary youth ought to overthrow the stabilized social order, as had some of those the magazine enumerated, *Shōnen sekai* had no such idea in mind. The opportunities that the magazine saw coming with the war would come not through domestic political activity but rather through imperialistic expansion. According to the magazine, victory over China was showing Japan to be stronger than such nations as Italy, Spain, and Holland. Having thus demonstrated its fitness for dominance, Japan would now reverse the post-Restoration situation in which the nation had hastily imported knowledge to meet the foreign threat. From now on the nation would be expanding.[1]

The magazine featured a cover in which two young Japanese lads in military uniforms were looking over a map of Asia, Africa, and

1. "Dai-ni no ishin," *Shōnen sekai*, 1:3 (January 15, 1895): 1–3. Similar ideas were expressed in *Eisai shinshi*. See "Shosei risshin dan," *Eisai shinshi*, no. 924 (May 11, 1895), p. 2, and "Gakusei risshin annai," *Eisai shinshi*, no. 909 (January 26, 1895), pp. 2–3.

Australia. In their hands were rising-sun flags. No caption was needed to explain that they were considering where to plant those flags. Later, when the Triple Intervention demonstrated that flag planting was not so easy as had been imagined, the magazine returned to a variation of its earlier globe and scientific-instrument design, which symbolized the Charter Oath and the acquisition of knowledge from throughout the world.[2]

As might be expected, the Sino-Japanese War also produced an emphasis on military heroes. One Shirakami Genjirō was widely depicted in word and picture for his deed of dying with his bugle to his lips.[3] *Eisai shinshi* [Talent Forum] had several articles celebrating local heroes in each issue during the war. After the war, "military" careers figured prominently in *Shōnen sekai* compositions on future goals, although the composition writers seldom saw themselves as following in Shirakami's steps. Usually the young essayists depicted themselves as becoming nothing less than generals or admirals. Apparently, even the relatively young audience of *Shōnen sekai* had already realized that mere heroism and fame without any rank or wealth to go with it was not really *risshin*.[4] Neither imperialism nor militarism proved to be lasting motifs in writing on advancement either from the composition side or from the editorial side. The former did not survive the Triple Intervention, and the latter was limited to the juvenile readers of *Shōnen sekai*. *Chūgaku sekai* [Middle-School World], also from Hakubunkan but appealing to older youth, ignored militarism altogether.

Far more important than the stimulus given to militaristic or expansionistic visions of advancement was the contribution the war made to the growth of the economy and the subsequent definition of advancement in monetary terms. In the short run the war gave rise to a speculative boom of considerable intensity. *Kokumin no tomo* [Friend of the People] lamented that the energy generated by the

    2. A similarly expansive motif was found in the cover of *Taiyō* [The Sun], Hakubunkan's major adult-oriented publication: a bright sun (Japan) emerging from behind dark storm clouds.
    3. See Donald Keene, "The Sino-Japanese War of 1894–95 and Its Cultural Effects in Japan," in *Tradition and Modernization in Japanese Culture*, ed. Donald Shively (Princeton University Press, 1971), pp. 145–154.
    4. See "Shōnen endan," *Shōnen sekai* 5:20 (September 15, 1897): 98–100, and subsequent issues.

Cover of the inaugural issue of Shōnen sekai [World of Young People], a Hakubunkan publication aimed at students seeking to advance to secondary education. The cover design was said to symbolize the Charter Oath of 1868 (Meiji 1) with its commitment to seeking knowledge throughout the world.

Cover of Shōnen sekai *[World of Young People]*, *reflecting the expansionistic mood prevailing during the Sino-Japanese War. Later the magazine returned to its Charter Oath motif.*

war, rather than being turned to science, religion, or academia, had ended up in speculation and get-rich-quick schemes. Peoples' heads were full of stock prices. Even the loss of Liaotung (in the Triple Intervention) was not a matter of national honor sullied but a chance for wealth that had been lost. Whereas the past had seen a surplus of youth dreaming of politics, the postwar era saw them shouting "Gold! Gold!" and "Make Money! Make Money!" or so the editorialist claimed.[5] Uchimura Kanzō made a similar observation about the postwar atmosphere in 1897 (Meiji 30):

Get money; get it by all means, for it alone is power in this generation. Wish you to be patriotic? Then get money, for you cannot better serve your country than by getting money for you and it. Be loyal? Then get money, and add wealth to your Master's land. Be filial to your father and mother? You cannot be so without getting money. The strength of your nation, the fear of your name—all come from money. Morality ever for the sake of money. Honesty is the best *policy* for—getting money.[6]

Whether these were accurate portrayals of all youth just after the war is open to question, but there is hard evidence that the economic growth stimulated by the war had in turn stimulated a new interest in business among even relatively well-educated youth, those who would previously have only considered government affiliation worthy of their efforts.

Prior to the Sino-Japanese War, business schools had had considerable difficulty in filling all their seats. Recourse to newspaper advertisements in an effort to recruit bodies was not unusual even for government schools.[7] After the Sino-Japanese War, not only were the schools in general able to fill their places without recourse to advertising, but some of the better schools came to be in a position of exercising considerable selectivity. By 1897 (Meiji 30) the Tokyo Higher Business School (Tokyo Kōtō Shōgyō Gakkō), later Hitotsubashi University, had 2.8 applicants for each seat, and by 1904 (Meiji 37) it had 4.7 applicants for each seat.[8] Inasmuch as these ratios were even higher than those for entry into the First Higher School, which

5. "Seinen gakumon no keikō," *Kokumin no tomo*, no. 304 (August 21, 1896), pp. 1–2.
6. Uchimura Kanzō, "The Voice of Kishiu," in *Uchimura Kanzō zenshū*, vol. 16, pp. 154–155. Original in English from *Yorozu*, May 21, 1897.
7. Fukaya, *Gakureki shugi*, pp. 114–117, and Karasawa, *Gakusei*, pp. 184–186.
8. See the foldout table "Tōkyō kōtō shōgyō gakkō nyūgaku kyōsō-ritsu," in Karasawa, *Gakusei*, following p. 202.

led into the Imperial University and the bureaucracy,[9] at least among a certain stratum of youth business had risen to a status comparable to that of the traditional bureaucratic course.

The writing on personal advancement which was aimed at youth was relatively slow to reflect this increased status of business. *Chūgaku sekai* took little note of the increased popularity of business, and the first venture aimed at guiding less well educated youth into new business opportunities was not a success. This was the journal *Jitsugyō no Nihon* [Business Japan], which first appeared in 1897 (Meiji 30). At that time it was the organ for something called the Great Japan Business Academy, which sought to sell "higher-school-level lecture courses" in business and agricultural subjects to students who had no chances for further formal education. Although the magazine declared that business was flourishing, and many youth were seeking to rise in the world (*mi o tateru*) through business, they apparently were not seeking to do it through mail-order courses in business; two or three thousand copies sold was considered a good month.[10] Perhaps the students who were really interested in business realized that mail-order courses were not in fact a good substitute for actual education at a school such as the Tokyo Higher Business School, which was internationally known.[11]

This relative indifference to business in general and the specific version that *Jitsugyō no Nihon* had to offer persisted until 1902 (Meiji 35) when the magazine discovered a new audience, who wanted "the secrets of success," not lectures on business techniques and economic theory. The founder of the firm, Masuda Giichi, later recalled how the magazine stumbled into a new and highly profitable venture:

At that time (1902), Koike Seiichi translated the American Carnegie's *Empire of Business* [*Jitsugyō no teikoku*], and it was published by our firm. We advertised it as explaining the secrets of success and the essential ways for meeting the world, and it sold extraordinarily well. In fact I realized that the

---

9. Competition rates for the First Higher School were in the range of 1.9 to 3.0 for the period 1895–1900 (Meiji 28–33). See *Dai-ichi kōtō gakkō rokujū nen shi* (1939), p. 596.

10. Concerning the founding of *Jitsugyō no Nihon*, see Masuda Yoshihiko, *Jitsugyō no Nihon nanajū nen shi* (Jitsugyō no Nihon sha, 1967), pp. 3–13, and Yamazaki Yasuo, *Dai-ni Chosha to shuppansha* (Gakufū shoin, 1955), pp. 134–139.

11. See Jean-Pierre Lehmann, *The Image of Japan* (Allen and Unwin, 1978), pp. 132–133.

"secrets of success" were what people wanted, and I decided to write and publish articles on success. From that point, the numbers [of *Jitsugyō no Nihon*] published and sold increased very rapidly.[12]

Other publishers made the same discovery. Both major general magazines of the period, *Taiyō* [The Sun] and *Chūō kōron* [Central Review], added columns on success, as did a number of other magazines.[13] According to Sakai Kosen, so popular did writing on success become during 1902 (Meiji 35) that there was "not a single place where the word success is not to be seen." There was, he noted in amazement, "even a magazine called *Success* [Seikō]."[14] The next year at least twelve books with "success" in their titles appeared as authors scrambled to cash in on the boom.[15]

As Masuda's recollections suggest, much of the new writing on success had to do with the "secrets" of acquiring wealth comparable to that of Andrew Carnegie. Compared with writing on *risshin* before the Sino-Japanese War, the most striking feature of the writing on success when it first appeared at the beginning of the twentieth century was its concern with money and wealth. Success in any activity, great or petty, was measured by monetary criteria in the new literature, and the greater the wealth, the greater the success. If any word was to be seen as often as "success" itself, it was "multimillionaire" (*fugō* or *dai-fugō*). Articles appeared with titles such as "A Man of 150,000,000 Yen" (about Vanderbilt) or "The Youth of a Man Worth 600,000,000 Yen" (about Carnegie).[16] Advertising copy fairly screamed the theme. Asserted one typical advertisement in *Seikō*:

If you once read this volume, you will find out how to create millions of yen in wealth, how the rich made the foundation of their rise in the world, how

12. Quoted in Masuda, *Jitsugyō no Nihon*, p. 19.
13. For example, "Seikō no hiketsu," *Chūō kōron*, 17:11 (November 1, 1902): 26 ff. *Chūō kōron* did not then have the reputation it has now of being the leading journal of Japan's liberal intelligentsia, but it was nevertheless a serious and adult-oriented magazine. See also "Seitetsuō to 'Jitsugyō no teikoku,'" *Taiyō* 8:11 (September 5, 1902), pp. 107–110. This article is about Andrew Carnegie.
14. Sakai Kosen, "Seikō no niji," *Yorozu* (December 29, 1902) in *Sakai zenshū*, vol. 1, pp. 241–242. For further comment on the fad of success, see "Seikō ni tsuki," *Nihonjin* (August 5, 1903), pp. 9–10.
15. Takeuchi Yō, *Nihonjin no shusse-kan* (Gakubun sha, 1978), p. 109.
16. "Ichioku-gosen-man en no fugō," *Seikō*, 1:1 (October 10, 1902): 9–12, and Abike Teijirō, "Rokuoku en fugō no seinen jidai," *Seikō*, 1:2 (November 10, 1902): 7–11.

they accumulated unlimited capital, how they strenuously overcame obstacles, how on the basis of attentiveness [*chūi*] they expanded their enterprises. You will also be able to learn their house constitutions and their secrets for such an enormous accumulation of capital.[17]

Though the "super millionaires" presented in the advertised volume were all foreign, the only reason for the exclusion of Japanese seems to have been their relatively small standing beside the likes of Carnegie, Krupp, Gould, and Vanderbilt. Other works dealt with wealthy Japanese in only slightly less strident tones.

Because of the seeming infatuation of the literature of success with American multimillionaires, there were those who stood ready to blame this new literature on the United States and American values.[18] Various observers complained that the moral base of Japan was being eroded by the worship of gold brought in from the United States. The possibility of using a modified *bushidō* ("way of the warrior") to stem the tide of materialism became a popular subject.[19] This view of the new literature ignored a number of important points. First, Japanese were not forced to read or translate works that emphasized wealth and materialism. That they did so with such gusto indicates there was more than an adequate base for materialism in Japan. Indeed, Japan's own tradition of literature celebrating the acquisition and ostentatious consumption of great wealth went back to the seventeenth century and predated the existence of the United States. Second, whatever *bushidō* might have had to say about materialism, the *bushi* ("warriors") themselves had never really been against having great wealth and spending it ostentatiously—the gold teahouse of Toyotomi Hideyoshi and the garishly

---

17. Advertising copy for a collection of *Seikō* articles republished under the title *Sekai dai-fugō risshin den* [The Rise of the World's Super Millionaires] found in *Seikō*, 7:1 (July 1, 1905).

18. Numerous writers played on this theme, none so consistently as Uchimura Kanzō. See "American Christianity," *Uchimura Kanzō zenshū*, vol. 3, p. 50; "Bushidō and Christianity," *Zenshū*, vol. 3, p. 56; "Enemies of Christianity," *Zenshū*, vol. 3, p. 72.

19. In addition to Uchimura, numerous other writers discussed this possibility. On the general phenomenon, see Gotō Chūgai, "Bushidō no kenkyū ni tsuite," *Shin-shōsetsu* 10:5 (May 1, 1905): 193–196; Gotō Chūgai, "Shisō wakuran no jidai," *Shin-shōsetsu* 6:6 (June 1, 1901): 169–175; "Bushidō," *Chūō kōron* 19:6 (July 1, 1904): 54. For specific examples, see Nemoto Michiaki, "Nihon to shōrai no bushidō," *Seikō* 4:5 (May 15, 1904): 8–10; Satō Tadashi, "Bushidō to shōgyō dōtoku," *Seikō* 6:1 (January 1, 1905): 20–21; Nitobe Inazō, "Shinshidō," *Seikō* 11:2 (March 1, 1907): 11–12. Interestingly, none of these authors thought *bushidō* appropriate to the new age.

gilded Tokugawa mausoleum at Nikkō were hardly monuments to warrior frugality; rather, they had developed an ideological dislike for gold from commercial sources, not gold in general.

The young samurai sons who wrote compositions on study for wealth and honor in the 1870s were writing of noncapitalistic wealth, but it was wealth that they expected from rank, and this was long before the influx of American literature. American values had not corrupted Japanese traditions so much as capitalistic development had shown that there could be more than one way to the combination of wealth and honor. When businessman Shibusawa Eiichi was inducted into the peerage in 1897 (Meiji 30), recognition was given to the possibility of honor and rank that came from wealth, not just wealth that came from rank.[20]

At the same time that there were those who decried the emphasis on wealth and its alleged undermining of tradition, there were those who argued that this tendency had not gone far enough. For example, Tanabashi Ichirō, a founding member of the Seikyōsha, a group that held to a commonerism (*heimin shugi*) similar to that of Tokutomi Iichirō and his Minyūsha, declared in *Seikō* that wealthy Japanese were setting a bad example for youth when they used their wealth to lobby into the ersatz aristocracy in Shibusawa's wake. Noting rumors that Iwasaki (of Mitsubishi) was to become a baron, Tanabashi scolded, "He ought to be satisfied in being clearly Japan's top millionaire. By thinking that he would want to be among the very lowest ranking of the aristocracy, he deliberately lowers himself from the rank he occupies as Japan's richest man."[21] Such concern, however, seems misplaced. Most other evidence points to a general acceptance of wealth as a standard for measuring *risshin* to at least the degree that governmental or aristocratic rank had occupied.

This shift in values was documented by its critics and the popularity during these years of *Konjiki yasha* [The Miser] by Ozaki Kōyō.[22] In this immensely popular novel Kan'ichi, the hero, loses his fiancée,

20. See Sumiya Mikio, *Dai-Nihon teikoku no shiren*, vol. 22 of *Nihon no rekishi* (Chūō kōron sha, 1966), p. 166.
21. Tanabashi Ichirō, "Seinen to jishinryoku," *Seikō*, 1:1 (October 10, 1902): 23–25.
22. There are many editions of this novel, including several where other authors sought to finish the story left incomplete when Ozaki died. I read Ozaki Tokutarō, *Konjiki yasha* (Shunyōdō, 1915). For comments on the novel's popularity and its relation to social change, see Sumiya, *Nihon teikoku*, pp. 61–63.

Miya, to one Tomiyama, a wealthy young entrepreneur, a character said to be patterned on the founder of Hakubunkan. Although Kan'ichi is still a student, he has an assured but slow rise ahead of him as a functionary, for he has already been admitted to the Imperial University. Moreover, he has an inheritance of 7,000 yen coming to him. This is not enough to satisfy Miya, who leaves Kan'ichi for Tomiyama's flashy wealth. In *Ukigumo* [Floating Clouds], Bunzō, the struggling young functionary who had lost his job, was kicked aside by his calculating fiancée in favor of a fellow functionary, Noboru, who was on his way up. By the turn of the century it was plausible for the assured success of a functionary to be passed over in favor of wealth without rank, a choice that would have been most unusual by early Meiji standards.

To note the emphasis on wealth and moneymaking in the literature of success and to relate this to economic growth is by no means equivalent to saying that the period when this writing first appeared was in fact a time of great economic prosperity. In fact it was not. The interval from 1900 to 1903 (Meiji 33–36) saw a severe depression with substantial unemployment.[23] Businessmen who had only just recently risen to the pinnacle of publicly bestowed honor had to appear in journals that had previously paid them little attention to explain why business was so bad.[24] The more extreme promises in the first wave of literature on success were in part vicarious or even compensatory, a cycle that was repeated in subsequent depressions following booms.[25] There is of course an obvious logic to this: if opportunities really exist in extraordinary number, there is little need for guidance.

The appearance of the literature on success at this time was deceptive in another respect. The word "success" (*seikō*) was being used with two distinctly different meanings. In the instances described so far, the term was being used according to the distinction made by Karl Mannheim between "success" and "achievement."[26]

23. Matsunari Yoshie, et al., *Nihon no sarariiman* (Aoki shoten, 1957), p. 39.
24. See, for example, "Ōkura Kihachirō no dan," *Taiyō* 7:2 (February 5, 1901): 71–73.
25. This is an impression formed from the tenor of newspaper advertising for books after the Russo-Japanese War, World War I, and during the Shōwa depression. See also "Kane kane kane kashoku jidai," *Asahi shinbun* (January 7, 1931), p. 3.
26. Mannheim, *Sociology*, pp. 236–237.

The former depends on social recognition accruing to an individual in the form of fame, rank, or wealth, while the latter involves objective accomplishment, not necessarily with any attached social recognition. According to this distinction, *Self-Help* was about accomplishment, and *Gakumon no susume* [An Encouragement of Learning] and the *Eisai shinshi* compositions were about success. Wealth and honor in early Meiji writing was inherently a matter of social recognition and had little to do with objective accomplishment. Since *risshin* already meant essentially the same thing as *seikō* (taken to mean recognized success), the combination of the two terms (usually *risshin seikō*, rarely *risshin shusse seikō*), a peculiarity of writing in this period, would seem to create a redundancy. Nevertheless, this was not the case, because *seikō* was being used as an antonym for *shippai* (failure). Thus, the phrase *risshin seikō* as it appeared in book and magazine titles and in advertising copy did not usually mean "rise in the world and be a [recognized] success" but rather "to succeed in rising in the world [in a traditional sense]."

Japanese scholars have frequently missed this vital linguistic distinction and have seen the appearance of the success literature as only the coupling of a new idea of monetary success to the older formula of *risshin* or *risshin shusse*.[27] Late Meiji observers saw things differently. For example, Sakai Kosen explained why the idea of success and literature about it had suddenly become so popular in the interwar period. "The way I see it, this [fad of writing on success] appears to be the result of the average man's coming to realize the severity of competition in today's society."[28] This increasing competition was only in small part economic. The competition for higher education which existed in the interwar period was quantitatively and qualitatively far more severe than that which had existed even in the 1890s. It was this increase in competition with a parallel rise in rates of failure which gave meaning to the word "success" in much of the literature aimed at youth. When youth-oriented writing

---

27. Failure to recognize the dual usage of *seikō* mars an otherwise fine article by Oka Yoshitake, "Nichiro sensō go ni okeru atarashii sedai no seichō," *Shisō*, no. 512 (February 1967), p. 137. The same misapprehension appears in Maruyama Masao, "Patterns of Individuation and the Case of Japan: A Conceptual Scheme," in *Changing Japanese Attitudes Toward Modernization*, ed. Marius B. Jansen (Princeton University Press, 1965), pp. 509–510.

28. Sakai Kosen, "Seikō no niji," *Sakai zenshū*, vol. 1, pp. 241–242. For others with the same view, see "Shoseinan," *Bunko* (April 15, 1903), pp. 4–7.

is broken down by the educational attainment and expectations of the audience for the various magazines, the single-minded emphasis on success as the acquisition of wealth through business disappears. In its place comes a situation in which the lower the educational level and expectations of the readers, the greater was the definition of advancement in terms of wealth. The higher the educational level and expectations of the readers, the greater was the usage of "success" as an antonym for "failure" in an academic context.

In these years *Chūgaku sekai* [Middle-School World] had very little to say about success as the acquisition of wealth, and what it did have to say was largely in the form of critical editorials.[29] The only direct reflection of the rise of business to prominence was a somewhat greater concern with starting pay.[30] The magazine was, however, very concerned with success defined as passing entrance examinations, and it devoted whole issues to this subject. This lack of interest in success as wealth reflected the continuation in *Chūgaku sekai* of a magazine aimed primarily at readers who thought only of the study-for-government-affiliation pattern of advancement. For all practical purposes, *Chūgaku sekai* took over from *Shōnenen* [Garden for Young People] in terms of both intended audience and editorial conceits.[31]

Jitsugyō no Nihon [Business Japan] stood at the opposite extreme in terms of both its target audience and its definition of advancement. In *Jitsugyō no Nihon*, wealth was the supreme definition of success. Biographies of rich businessmen, both Japanese and foreign, filled its pages. In the case of Japanese businessmen, there was something of a tendency to present them as models of samurai virtue and merchant talent, and it may be argued, as Byron Marshall has, that the profit motive as such was played down in these portrayals.[32] This lack of stress on the profit motive meant nothing, however, for the

29. Ōmachi Keigetsu, "Ima no seikōsha," *Chūgaku sekai* 5:14 (November 10, 1902): 1–2.
30. "Shoseihō ni tsuite," *Chūgaku sekai* (November 20, 1904), pp. 2–8.
31. Published from 1898 (Meiji 31) until the late 1920s, the magazine was remarkably similar to *Shōnenen* in style and content. In this period it was under the editorship of Ōmachi Keigetsu, an Imperial University graduate.
32. Byron K. Marshall, *Capitalism and Nationalism in Prewar Japan* (Stanford University Press, 1967), chap. 3, "The Meiji Business Elite and the Way of the Warrior." Marshall describes *Jitsugyō no Nihon* as a "business journal" and appears to have been unaware of its intended audience.

specific monetary values applied to any and all endeavors described left no doubt about what constituted the basic criterion for measuring success. Bankrupts, no matter how virtuous, were not dealt with. That the profit motive might be played down is less important than the fact that the magazine used specific monetary standards to measure advancement rather than the vague "wealth and honor" formula, position, or abstract accomplishment.

Jitsugyō no Nihon was not a business magazine but rather a fan magazine with businessmen in place of film stars. It had a gossip column about businessmen and features on subjects such as the smiles of businessmen, the households of the very rich, even the mothers of businessmen.[33] Actual business and economic news was minimal. Although the magazine was definitely a product of the rise of modern capitalism, only the periodical format and inclusion of foreign models was new. Otherwise, the magazine harked back to Tokugawa merchant-class traditions. Most of its readers seem to have been drawn from shop clerks and the like, the Meiji extension of the Tokugawa merchant class. This was explicitly the case with *Jitsugyō shōnen* [Business Youth] from Hakubunkan. Published for five years after the Russo-Japanese War, this journal was similar to *Jitsugyō no Nihon*. A typical feature in the magazine solicited "business secrets" from shop clerks. An award winner in this category explained how he used relatives unknown in his neighborhood to make his store look busy and attract customers.[34]

The third major youth-oriented publication of this period, *Seikō* [Success], offered a mixed definition of that which it celebrated in its name. Capitalistic wealth figured prominently in what it styled success, but at the same time it dealt with the older study-for-wealth-and-honor theme. It served an audience that stood between *Jitsugyō no Nihon* readers and *Chūgaku sekai* readers in attained education and expectations for future education. Because the stratum served

33. The gossip column was entitled "Fūbun hyakuwa" and appeared at various times. For an example of the "fanzine" style of *Jitsugyō no Nihon*, see "Jitsugyōka to aikyō," *Jitsugyō no Nihon* 9:1 (January 1, 1906), p. 82. This article deals with "the smiles of entrepreneurs." Articles on the households and families of entrepreneurs appeared sporadically and were collected in books such as Masuda Giichi, ed., *Nihon fugō no kafū* (Jitsugyō no Nihon sha, 1905).

34. "Nihon zenkoku himitsu hakurankai," *Jitsugyō shōnen* 4:12 (October 15, 1910): 14.

by *Seikō* rapidly expanded in this period, it is more important in terms of social change than either *Jitsugyō no Nihon* or *Chūgaku sekai*; because the magazine drew upon a diverse body of writers, it is more useful as a sample of late Meiji thought on self-advancement than are the other magazines.

Seikō was well known to contemporaries (it even figured in a novel by Natsume Sōseki) and was extensively advertised, yet little is known about the origins of the journal itself.[35] A single recollection by Ishii Kendō (Tamaji), one-time *Seikō* managing editor, provides the only available information about one of the most popular and noted Meiji magazines. According to Ishii, the magazine was entirely the effort of one Murakami Shunzō, who usually wrote under the pseudonym Dakurō. In 1900 (Meiji 33) Murakami came to Tokyo to edit a magazine affiliated with the Christian academy Aoyama Gakuin. When this magazine folded, Murakami founded *Seikō* with his own funds, using his own house for editorial offices.[36] From these humble and obscure beginnings, *Seikō* developed rapidly and claimed a circulation of fifteen thousand by 1905 (Meiji 38).[37] In addition to the magazine, Murakami turned to book publishing,

35. *Seikō* is mentioned in Natsume Sōseki, *Mon* [1910, Meiji 43], trans. Francis Mathy (Tuttle, 1972), p. 58. *Seikō* has been discussed in English in Ronald P. Dore, "Mobility, Equality, and Individuation in Modern Japan," in *Aspects of Social Change in Modern Japan*, ed. Ronald P. Dore (Princeton University Press, 1967), pp. 113–150. Japanese scholars have largely ignored it until recently, but this attitude seems to be changing. After my own study of *Seikō* was completed, two articles concerning it appeared. See Takeuchi Yō, "Risshin shusse shugi no keifu to ronri," *Kansai daigaku shakai gakubu kiyō* 7:1 (November, 1975): 33–49, and Takeuchi Yō, "Risshin shusse shugi no ronri to kinō," *Kyōiku shakaigaku kenkyū* 31 (1976): 119–129. Professor Takeuchi's work generally confirms the analysis given here.

36. Meiji bunka kenkyūkai, *Meiji jibutsu kigen* (Nihon hyōron sha, 1969), pp. 1282–1283. According to Ishii, Murakami used the money he made from *Seikō* to finance Japan's first Antarctic expedition. Ishii himself was an interesting character. He worked for *Seikō*, *Jitsugyō shōnen*, and other juvenile- and youth-oriented magazines. Later he was one of the compilers of the *Meiji bunka zenshū* under Yoshino Sakuzō. Efforts to discover more biographical details concerning Murakami proved abortive. Even the pronunciation of his name is uncertain, being given elsewhere as Goshizō. See "Seikō shugi bōkoku ron," *Hikari* (September 25, 1906), p. 1. This article has some interest, since it appeared after early socialists had broken with *Seikō*. It refers to Masuda and Murakami as "maggots."

37. See Takeuchi, "Keifu to ronri," pp. 43–44, n. 8. This claim was made in *Seikō* 6:4 (April 1905).

Covers of Chūgaku sekai [Middle-School World], a magazine for students seeking entry to national (kanritsu) institutions of higher education. Published from the late 1890s to the late 1920s, it took over the style and au-

dience of Shōnenen *[A Garden for Young People]* and dominated the field until the parent firm, Hakubunkan, experienced financial difficulties in the Shōwa depression.

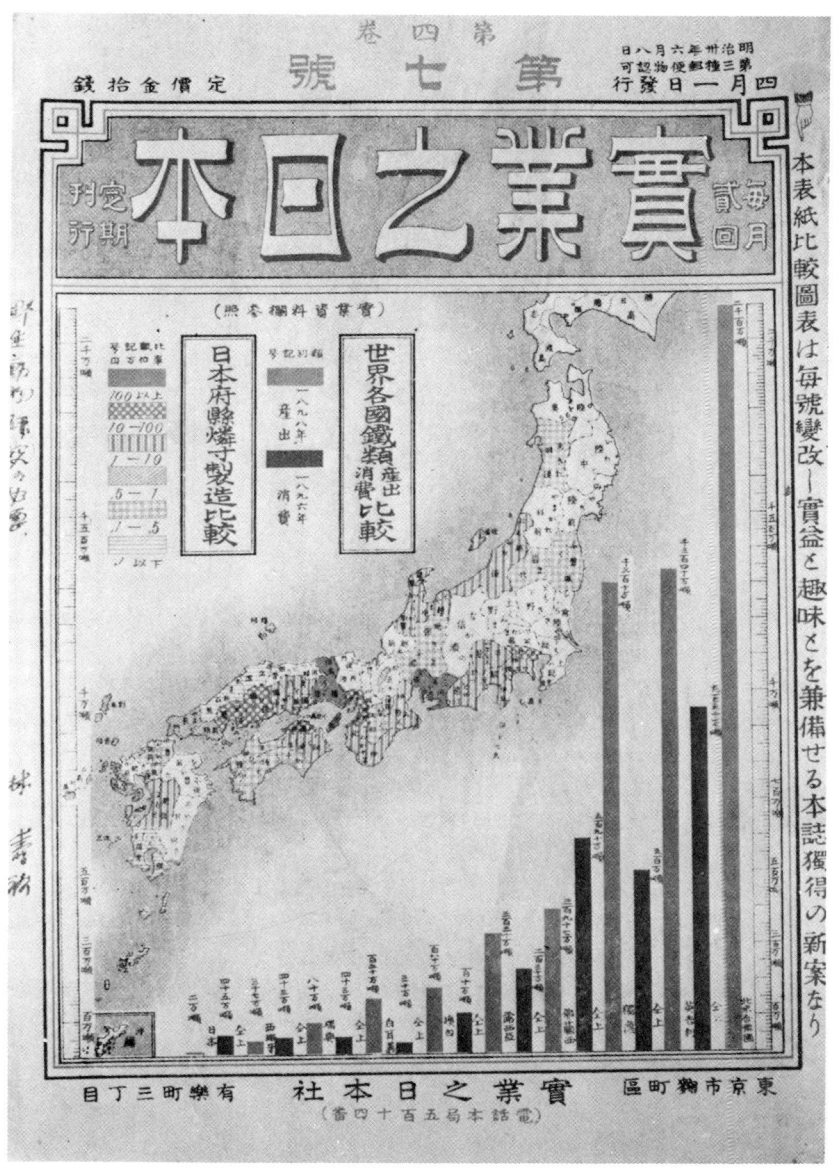

Covers of Jitsugyō no Nihon [Business Japan], a magazine catering primarily to shop clerks and low-level company employees. Covers of regular issues featured graphs and charts, giving the magazine the appearance of being a serious business and economic journal, but the bulk of its editorial

matter was inspirational and success-oriented. Special issues such as the 1905 (Meiji 38) "Survey of Vocations" [Shokugyō taikan] pictured here were entirely devoted to tips on self-advancement. Jitsugyō no Nihon *is still being published.*

and Seikō Zasshi Sha (Seikō Magazine Company) issued large numbers of inspirational works as well as some semischolarly items, including a biography of Nakamura Keiu by Ishii. The inspirational works were advertised extensively and often reviewed in other, more noted journals.[38]

Although Murakami's precise reasons for starting *Seikō* are unknown, the statement of purpose given in early issues of the magazine indicates that he was heavily influenced by Tokutomi Iichirō. Just as had Tokutomi in his *Shin-Nihon no seinen* [Youth of the New Japan], Murakami called for young people to follow a pure character ethic of self-improvement and advancement. He charged, "Just help yourself and raise yourself up. Manage yourself. Work hard by yourself. And, by the power of your own arms, create your own fate. This is the kind of person that is needed."[39] "Needed" here meant both what the youth who read the magazine had to have in order to rise in the world and the sort of youth that Japan ought to have many of for its own sake. In much the same vein as Tokutomi (and Nakamura Keiu before him), Murakami and *Seikō* proclaimed that the nation's fate hung in the balance according to whether it had few or many youth taken by the spirit of self-help. Murakami virtually quoted Tokutomi when he declared youth to have a special role in the reform of society, saying "In any country the old men are conservative and shake their heads when they hear progress and improvement."[40] Again, in parallel to Tokutomi and his *Kokumin no tomo* [Friend of the People], Murakami and *Seikō* were sympathetic to the working class and the labor movement. Many early *Seikō* contributors also wrote for *Rōdō sekai* [Labor World], the organ of

---

38. For example, see "Seikō," *Rikugō zasshi*, no. 263 (November 15, 1902), p. 78, and Kōda Rohan, "Saikaku no seikō ni kansuru kansatsu," *Chūō kōron* 17:12 (December 1, 1902): 55–57. The latter item is a reprint from *Seikō*. Although usually treated in terms of romanticism, Kōda Rohan was a major producer of inspirational fiction on *risshin* themes. This was apparently a matter of belief and not economic necessity. For a discussion of his writings in this genre, see Maeda Ai, "Rohan ni okeru risshin shusse shugi," *Kokugo to kokubungaku*, no. 530 (April, 1968), pp. 36–45.
39. Murakami Dakurō, "Hakkan no ji," *Seikō* 1:1 (October 10, 1902).
40. Murakami Dakurō, "Shisō-ryoku o yōsei seyo," *Seikō* 2:1 (April 10, 1903): 25–28, and "Seikō wa nani o oshien tote yo ni ideshi ya," *Seikō* 1:5 (February 10, 1903): 24–27.

the turn-of-the-century labor movement, and there was cross-advertising between the two journals.[41]

Seikō specifically denied that it was preaching material success,[42] and its connection to the budding labor movement shows that it was not the single-minded purveyor of materialism that *Jitsugyō no Nihon* [Business Japan] was. At the same time, that connection points to the extreme immaturity of the socialist and labor movements, for self-help is an inherently conservative idea, one which places all responsibility on the individual. Nevertheless, those who were at this time identified as socialists or would be so identified in the future were still thinking in terms that allowed them to support *Seikō* or similar ventures. Sakai Kosen, later to found the Japan Communist party, was at this time advising "middle-class youth," "You ought to want to be a Diet member. You ought to want to be a minister of state. You ought to want to be a millionaire."[43]

Nishikawa Kōjirō, another important figure in the early labor and socialist movements, was writing in *Seikō*, "No matter how ardent the youth is to make money, if he fails in the accumulation of pennies, with the exception of one or two rare cases, he can never expect to reach his goal of wealth."[44] Katayama Sen, the prime mover behind *Rōdō sekai* and an "Asian Revolutionary" who would be honored by burial in the Kremlin Wall, was principally engaged at this time in telling young men how to emigrate to the United States in order to acquire education and wealth.[45] Even Kōtoku Denjirō (Shūsui), who would become perhaps the most sophisticated politi-

41. Murakami Dakuro, "Seinen to shakai kairyō mondai," *Seikō* 2:6 (September 10, 1903): 29–31.
42. The first issue of *Seikō* carried an advertisement for *Rōdō sekai* and shared many writers with it, including Horiuchi Shinsen, a writer of inspiration fiction with titles such as "The Value of Sweat." For other works by Horiuchi, see the advertisement in *Seikō* 26:3 (November 1914). Judging by the number of reprints listed for his works, Horiuchi was a very popular novelist, although standard literary histories either ignore his existence or list him as a "poet."
43. Sakai Kosen, "Chūtō shakai no seinen," *Yorozu* (April 29, 1902) in *Sakai zenshū*, vol. 1, pp. 174–175. Also cited in Sugai Yoshinobu, "Shakai shugi," in *Meiji kyōiku seron no kenkyū*, ed. Motoyama Yukihiko (Fukumura shuppan, 1972), vol. 2, p. 234.
44. Nishikawa Kōjirō, "Seikō no hito to shippai no hito," *Seikō*, 1:1 (October 10, 1909): 43–44.
45. Katayama's promotional activities are discussed below.

Cover of Jitsugyō shōnen [Business Youth], a short-lived Hakubunkan publication that apparently sought to compete for the audience served by Jitsugyō no Nihon [Business Japan] in the years after the Russo-Japanese War.

cal thinker of this early group (and be executed for his troubles), was only at the level of editorializing on the plight of those aiming at higher-school education, a tiny minority of Japanese youth and those with the greatest drive to become part of the central government establishment.[46]

There was nothing in their background or thinking to turn them away from fairly conventional concepts of advancement, and if anything, those who came from a Christian background (Kōtoku was the only prominent non-Christian) had an even greater dose of *risshin* orientation than did most of their contemporaries, thanks to missionaries. As Rudyard Kipling observed of American missionaries in Japan, "They . . . instil into the Japanese mind wicked ideas of 'Progress,' and teach that it is well to get ahead of your neighbour, to improve your situation, and generally thrash yourself to pieces in the battle of existence."[47] Contact with missionaries and Christianity also predisposed social activists to see problems in terms of moral reform, which coincided with the Smilesean revival intent of *Seikō*.[48] Thus one finds in *Seikō* a declaration such as the following by Kozuka Kuya, assistant editor of *Rōdō sekai*:

> Character is the base of all human conduct. Character is the fountain of success. Thus more than anything, saying success and thinking of *risshin* involves first of all building one's self. Rich country and strong army, the reform of society—all are founded on first improving the individual.[49]

This formula was equally acceptable to the great majority of contemporary academics and journalists, especially those who had come of age during the first decades of the era (1870s and 1880s). *Seikō* listed such "special" supporters as the romantic novelist Kōda Rohan, the Christian journalist and leader in women's education Iwamoto Zenji, the Shinshū priest Murakami Senjō, as well as To-

---

46. Kōtoku Shūsui (Denjirō), "Kōtō kyōiku no kyōnetsu," *Yorozu* (September 6, 1901) in *Kōtoku zenshū*, vol. 3, pp. 307–310. Also cited in Sugai, "Shakai shugi," p. 228.

47. Quoted in Lehman, *Image of Japan*, p. 34.

48. Concerning this general tendency, see Sugai, "Shakai shugi," p. 221. For an especially severe example of this, see the writings of Abe Isoo, including "Ikanishite shippai o sakubeki ya," *Seikō* 2:3 (June 10, 1903): 25–27, and "Kōfuku naru shōgai," *Seikō* 3:5 (February 10, 1904): 28–30.

49. Kozuka Kuya, "Nakamura Keiu sensei no heizei," *Seikō* 1:1 (October 10, 1902): 20.

kutomi Iichirō, Inoue Enryō, and Shiga Shigetaka of the Minyūsha and Seikyōsha groups. In its list of merely "eminent supporters" were such men as Katō Hiroyuki, past president of the Imperial University and holder of numerous high government posts, Ebina Danjō, Christian leader and later president of Dōshisha University, Inoue Tetsujirō, conservative ideologue and an Imperial University professor, and Matsumura Kaiseki, Christian journalist.[50] Just what role each of these played in the magazine varied according to the individual. In some cases the articles attributed to them were "recordings of conversations" or speeches, but in other cases it was expressly indicated that they had written the article that appeared under their name.[51]

That such a diverse group of intellectuals would write on success was in no way inconsistent with their other roles. To the degree *Seikō* phrased its goal in terms of uplifting youth morally, it was natural that it should attract such a community of supporters. This cannot be seen as a peculiarity of the Meiji intellectual community. In the United States the idea of the self-made man had found such spokesmen as Thomas Jefferson, Ralph Waldo Emerson, and Walt Whitman.[52] The self-made man was an essential element of their conceptions of the ideal society. This was true in the Japanese case as well. Politically conservative figures such as Katō Hiroyuki, who had lectured the Emperor Meiji from *Saikoku risshi hen*, could support the call in *Seikō* for a Smilesean revival because he believed that national character was a function of individual character. Socialists, who were usually Christian at the same time, could support moral reform and also see in it the potential for social reform. This wide range of contributors is in striking contrast to both *Chūgaku sekai* [Middle-School World] and *Jitsugyō no Nihon* [Business Japan]. The former drew almost exclusively on the Hakubunkan literary establishment, and the latter relied mostly on its founder and on reporters who worked for the magazine.

50. These lists were given in each issue of the magazine, usually on the first or last page. For reasons discussed below, early lists included more labor and social activists.
51. "Conversations" (*danwa*) were a standard feature of late Meiji journals. Doubtless some fabrication was involved, but it is also likely that most of those approached by *Seikō* welcomed the chance to pontificate.
52. Emerson is perhaps the leading example of an American intellectual who also celebrated success. For a discussion of his activities and writings in this area, see Cawelti, *Apostles*, pp. 80–95.

From this potpourri of authors as filtered through the editorial intervention of Murakami and later Ishii, the *Seikō* reader received a continual reassertion of the various virtues associated with self-help, just as its statement of purpose promised. As was true of earlier writing, this was not strictly the same as *Self-Help*. Even with its labor movement contributors, the self-help that appeared in *Seikō* was scholasticized and aimed at schoolboys, not workers. It was also somewhat Americanized and partially monetized. *Seikō* championed what doubters have referred to in the American case as "the log cabin myth," the idea that being born in a log cabin and humble circumstances were an advantage and not an impediment to personal advancement.

The first issue of *Seikō* featured a bust of Abraham Lincoln on its cover and a picture inside of the log cabin in which Lincoln was born.[53] The magazine's emphasis on Lincoln's self-education was within the range of American usage, although with its statement of purpose influenced by commonerism (*heimin shugi*), it might have given some attention to his political accomplishments. When it dealt with Benjamin Franklin and made him into a model student, not a crafty merchant, clever inventor, or senior statesman, it was showing even more selectivity.[54] In a biography of Jay Gould written by Murakami, the magazine further demonstrated its scholastic conception of self-help when it described Gould as a young man who "did not waste time playing with tops or sailing paper airplanes like other children but instead put all his energies into study."[55] At the same time that the magazine scholasticized models who had

---

53. *Seikō* covers indicate a rather catholic concept of success that changed somewhat over time. A few examples include Lincoln (October 10, 1902); Grant (November 10, 1902); John Hay (July 10, 1903); Theodore Roosevelt (August 10, 1903; June 1, 1905; December 1, 1911); Cecil Rhodes (March 10, 1903); Thomas Edison (October 10, 1903); Andrew Carnegie (July 1, 1904); Hegel (September 1, 1904); Ibsen (December 1, 1904); Marco Polo (May 1, 1904); Cromwell (February 2, 1906); Toyotomi Hideyoshi (October 10, 1910); Christ and Buddha (May 1, 1911)! Covers of issues during the period of the Russo-Japanese War were largely of military figures, and these continued sporadically after the war; but in general, postwar covers featured Restoration-era politicians, especially Ōkuma and Itō.

54. Murakami Dakurō, "Furankurin seinen jidai," *Seikō* 1:4 (January 1, 1903), pp. 4–8.

55. Murakami Dakurō, "Dai-fugō Gōrudo no risshin den," *Seikō* 1:6 (March 10, 1903): 4–8.

Cover of the inaugural issue of Seikō *[Success], which appeared in October 1902 (Meiji 35). Just as had its American namesake, Orison Swett Marden's* Success, *it featured Lincoln on its cover and a version of "the log cabin myth" in its editorial matter.*

nothing much to do with study, it also went in the other direction, monetizing models not primarily associated with wealth. The first issue of *Seikō* featured a biography of Nakamura Fusetsu, the artist who illustrated Yokoyama Gennosuke's pioneering works on the lower classes of Japan. It presented him as a model of frugality and diligence for having saved three thousand yen in order to study art abroad.[56] Articles and themes on frugality were by no means new, but putting a cash value on such accomplishment was a reflection of the changing of attitudes with respect to wealth.

In making its biographical models into students, *Seikō* tended to make them into what were called "struggling students" (*kugakusei*) who worked to support themselves in school. In this emphasis the magazine was not alone. *Seikō* and other journals carried advertisements for a variety of handbooks on the subject, and there was even a tabloid newspaper, *Kugakukai* [Struggling Student World], dedicated specifically to the needs of such students. Like other themes to be found in the new writing on success, "study by struggle" (*kugaku*) was not a totally new idea. Ten years earlier *Eisai shinshi* [Talent Forum] had had a brief spate of compositions on the subject, but like "enterprise" (*jitsugyō*), "study by struggle" had been basically an abstract topic for composition purposes and not something essayists saw themselves doing. In this period, the situation was rather different. Young men were explicitly declaring their intent to seek an education through "study by struggle," and they addressed to the consultation columns of *Seikō* concrete questions about the possibility of studying at this or that school by working as a paper boy or milk deliveryman in Tokyo.[57]

This new interest in study by struggle was not, however, indicative of a generalization of Smilesean virtues among the same stratum that had toyed with the idea in the 1890s. *Chūgaku sekai* served that stratum and it largely ignored the theme.[58] The idea gained currency because by 1901–1902 (Meiji 34–35) the dream of *risshin* through education had spread beyond those who had family wealth, connections, or a *han* support network to aid them. By 1906 (Meiji

56. "Risshi gaka Nakamura Fusetsu," *Seikō* 1:1 (October 10, 1902): 1–5.
57. "Kisha to dokusha," *Seikō* 2:4 (July 10, 1903): 49–51.
58. *Jitsugyō no Nihon* had a few articles on the subject, but since it assumed that its readers were full-time employees who would rise in their shops or companies, study by struggle was not a major topic for it.

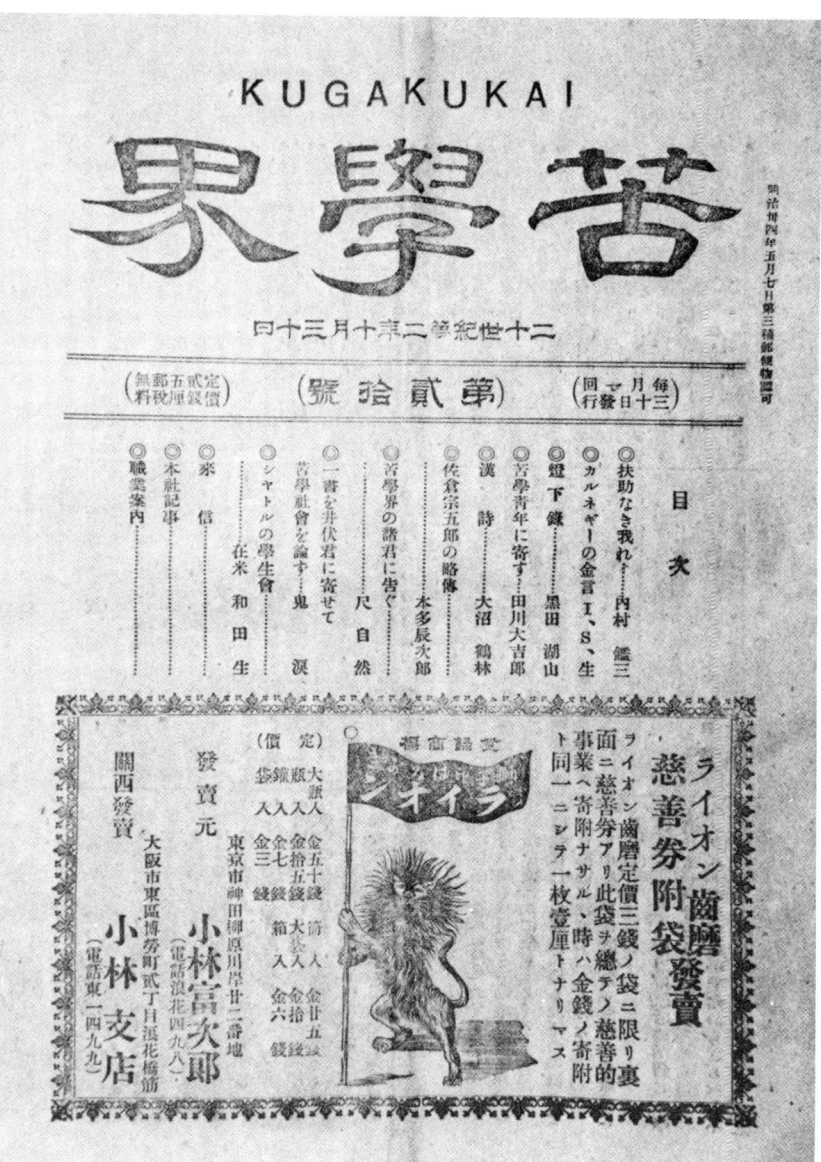

Cover of **Kugakukai** *[Struggling-Student World], a magazine for students trying to work their way through school. This issue for "the thirtieth day of the tenth month of the second year of the twentieth century" features an inspirational article by the noted Christian critic Uchimura Kanzō. The lower third of the page is an advertisement for Lion Toothpaste, a firm that patronized various "good causes."*

39) observers were noting that the fever for success had spread to the point where rural people were, according to one commentator, muttering "Success! Success!" in their sleep.[59]

In the years 1887–1891 (Meiji 20–24) there had been an average of only eleven thousand middle-school students enrolled in any one year. A decade later, in 1902–1906 (Meiji 35–39), the average was one hundred thousand.[60] While not all of these students came from impoverished or even less than affluent backgrounds, this expansion could not take place without a shift downward in the social and economic background of the students. This was not necessarily a shift in "class" origins but rather a shift within existing groups to include less-affluent members. Middle-school education was still expensive. Guides for the latter part of the period suggest monthly costs of ten yen for boarding students and four-to-five yen for commuting students. These costs effectively excluded blue-collar workers and poor peasants, even those with any income that might come from struggle, and were high enough relative to income to be a major burden for lower-paid white-collar workers such as teachers and petty civil servants.[61] If there was any class shifting involved, it was more likely to have been in terms of those who thought about study by struggle but who did not try it or in the many who tried and quit: approximately half of those who attempted middle school dropped out without graduating.[62]

The image of the poor boy working his way through school had considerable appeal to those of a Christian, humanitarian, or socialist persuasion. The contributors to *Kugakukai* were almost identical with the group known as the idealist band (*risōdan*) at the *Yorozu chōhō*, the leading contemporary newspaper of social concern: Kinoshita Naoe, Sakai Kosen, Uchimura Kanzō, Kuroiwa Ruikō,

---

59. Yokoi Tokiyoshi (Jikei), *Tokai to inaka*, in Sumiya, *Nihon teikoku*, p. 352.
60. Calculated from table 4, "Chūgakkō (kyūsei)," in *Gakusei hachijū nen shi* (Monbushō, 1954), p. 1047.
61. Cost estimates are from Fukaya, *Gakureki shugi*, pp. 345–349. See also *The Japan Year Book 1906*, p. 446, which estimated middle-school costs at 136 yen per year. This cost amounted to 70% of average *yatoi*, 39% of average *hannin*, and 11% of average *sōnin* class civil servant pay in the period 1906–1910 (Meiji 39–43). Civil servant pay calculated from *Meiji Taishō kokusei sōran* (Tōyō keizai shinpō sha, 1927), table 737, p. 664.
62. Fukaya, *Gakureki shugi*, pp. 360–361.

and others.⁶³ *Kugakukai* was the "organ" of a society of the same name which had as its official purpose the "raising up of a spirit for study by struggle among impoverished students and the looking out for the spiritual and material needs of those who have elected this course."⁶⁴ The paper proclaimed that it would advertise work suitable to the needs of the struggling student, organize lecture series for him, and teach him how to get along on the least money. It also solicited contributions to be used for this program and listed a number of worthy figures who had contributed to the cause.⁶⁵ Spiritual sustenance proved easier to produce than did material help. The columns of *Kugakukai* that promised to list jobs suitable for the student seeking to work his way through school—the essential prerequisite for the whole scheme—were more often than not editorials bewailing the fact that currently there were no such jobs. Readers had to be content with inspiration rather than useful information. A reprinted article by Uchimura Kanzō included the refrain "Advance, advance to the end! Without fearing the path ahead, advance without falling, without retreating."⁶⁶ Kuroiwa Ruikō, editor of the *Yorozu*, advised struggling students to value highly the difficulty of their road, for "nothing worthwhile is accomplished without pain."⁶⁷

Other social activists who wrote on the subject of study by struggle were less convinced of the merits of this approach to an education. Kōtoku Denjirō (Shūsui) argued against study by struggle in his contribution to a book entitled *Kugaku no hanryo* [Comrade of the Struggling Student]. According to Kōtoku, many of those claiming to be struggling students were not in fact students at all but were merely pretending to be such in order to win sympathy and money. Because struggling students in the past had not been given special treatment, there was no special reason to provide such for contemporary students. Moreover, many of these young people were, Kōtoku claimed, leading a life of dissipation. Better in his view to become a so-called eating guest (*shokkaku*) who did odd jobs in exchange for

63. The "idealist band" is discussed in Kosaka, *Japanese Thought*, pp. 339 ff.
64. *Kugakukai*, no. 14 (May 10, 1902), p. 1.
65. These included Inoue Tetsujirō, Ōi Kentarō, Katō Hiroyuki, Yokoyama Gennosuke, Katayama Sen, and Ebina Danjō.
66. Uchimura Kanzō, "Susume," *Kugakukai*, no. 15 (May 20, 1902), p. 2.
67. Kuroiwa Ruikō, "Kugaku no hito ni shimesu," *Kugakukai*, no. 15 (May 20, 1902), p. 1.

room and board. The "eating guests" were less likely to fall into evil company.[68]

This was not a very realistic answer to the needs of would-be struggling students. The numbers involved were far too great relative to the number of families sufficiently affluent to support such "eating guests."[69] Moreover, one must wonder about Kōtoku's own political sophistication at this time. The "eating guest" relationship was essentially a patron-client relationship and hardly one geared to generating either a spirit of self-help or social consciousness. Fellow *Yorozu chōhō* [Complete Morning News] columnist Sakai Kosen took a similar stance but argued that while borrowing money or becoming an "eating guest" were preferable to study by struggle with its potential for falling into evil ways, these were at best stopgap measures until cooperative ventures for struggling students could be created.[70] Sakai's suggestions show a bit more sophistication in that he recognized the limits inherent in the "eating guest" system, both practical and in terms of social consciousness.

For *Seikō* there was a somewhat different conflict between the principle of study by struggle and the realities of contemporary Japan. While the idea was at once a logical part of the magazine's encouragement of Smilesean virtues, it was potentially disruptive of family discipline. Many of the early inquiries about study by struggle in *Seikō* indicate that the idea often appealed to youth whose plans for going off to Tokyo were opposed by their families. Where the need for self-support came because of family opposition, *Seikō* sided with the family.[71] Where no such opposition existed and the *risshin* aspirants expressed sufficient commitment, *Seikō* did encourage study by struggle. Whether this was really to the benefit of such youth is, however, open to question. For example, a 1913 (Taishō 2) editorial presented what it called a "not at all unreasonable

68. "Kugaku to jikatsu," *Kōtoku zenshū*, vol. 5, pp. 334–337, and "Iwayuru 'kugakusei,'" *Kōtoku zenshū*, vol. 4, pp. 260–262. For a similar view, see Taguchi Ukichi, "Seinen to jikatsu shūgaku," *Seikō* 1:4 (January 1, 1903): 19.

69. On the decline of this system, see "Kugakusei no zento," *To-Bei* (November 12, 1907), pp. 6–8.

70. See "Shosei o yashinau no fū," *Sakai zenshū*, vol. 1, pp. 83–84; "Chūtō shakai no seinen," *Sakai zenshū*, vol. 1, pp. 174–175; "Gakusei chinpi seidō oyobi kugakusei no mondai," *Sakai zenshū*, vol. 1, pp. 235–237.

71. "Kisha to dokusha," *Seikō* 2:4 (July 10, 1903): 49–51, and 2:5 (August 10, 1903): 50.

plan" for study by struggle: holding two part-time jobs, subsisting on bean-paste soup, and living with at least four others in a single six-mat room (10 square meters). Even by Japanese standards of that period, it would seem that the aspirant to *risshin* would be literally risking his life for an education, and a very marginal education at best. With this degree of effort a young man could expect to finance himself through the Iwakura Railroad School (Iwakura Tetsudō Gakkō), the Southern Odawara Short Course School (Minami Odawara Kōshū Gakkō), or the Waseda Short Course School (Waseda Kōshū Gakkō).[72] These schools were not frauds, but they were so far down on the *risshin* pecking order of the day that offering them in the context of *risshin* essentially devalued the word.

This was the case with correspondence courses that began to appear around the time of the Russo-Japanese War. They promised a middle-school education and *risshin shusse* by mail. A typical advertisement for one of the more notable sources of such materials proclaimed:

Becoming an eminent man like General Nogi is a matter of the power of education. Becoming first among the rich men of Japan is also based on the power of education. From here on in today's world, if you do not graduate from middle school, it's hopeless [*dame*]. "Middle school" is *the one key to risshin shusse*. Look for yourself—are not all young men trying to grasp this key? And, the least expensive and least time-consuming route is to enter the Great Japan Youth Middle School Association (Dai-Nippon Seinen Chūgakkai) and study the association's latest lecture notes.[73]

That such "schools" could pay what must have been a substantial bill for advertising—full pages month after month in several magazines at fifteen-to-thirty yen per page plus newspaper advertisements as well[74]—indicates even more directly than do middle-school enrollment figures that the message of study for wealth and honor had spread among a vast new body of believers.

The *risshin* that these new believers could get from such courses was limited at best. Some of the better "schools" had periodic exams and issued certificates upon successful completion of the course.

72. "Tsuki zuki jū en no gakuhi de nani o manabu ka," *Seikō* 29:6 (September 1, 1915): 46–47.
73. Advertisement for Dai-Nihon seinen chūgakkai in *Shōnen*, no. 110 (November 1912).
74. These are the published rates for *Seikō* in 1907 (Meiji 40).

These were supposed to be the "equivalents" of a middle-school diploma, but as *Seikō* candidly admitted in its consultation column, this was not the case.[75] The advertisements were not, however, entirely fraudulent. There were several ways to capitalize on the courses, but doing so was considerably more difficult than was implied by the advertising copy.

The study-by-mail courses of Waseda University (Tokyo College or Tōkyō Senmon Gakkō at this time) were potentially the most useful. Waseda was an institution of some quality, only incidentally in the study-by-mail business, and it could offer partial credit for its correspondence courses when they were followed by actual attendance.[76] Those aspirants to *risshin* who purchased the courses of other vendors could make use of them in several ways. Those who were able to acquire an education equivalent to completion of one year of middle school might be able to gain admission to a military preparatory school (*rikugun yōnen gakkō*) and eventually work their way up through the military education system. Others who completed the equivalent of two years of middle school could take a test and become low-level employees of the Ministry of Communications (Teishinshō) or the Ministry of Railroads (Tetsudōshō). With extreme effort, the aspirant might even succeed in passing the college certification examination required of all applicants without a middle-school diploma. So certified, the young man dreaming of *risshin* could potentially become a clerk (*hanninkan*) in the national civil service, a privilege open without examination to those possessing a middle-school diploma.[77]

Whether any of these alternatives really should have been considered a path to *risshin* is, however, highly questionable. Only 2.5 percent of public-sector middle-school graduates in the years 1907–1911 (Meiji 40–44) entered government service, probably because of the

75. "Kisha to dokusha," *Seikō* 1:2 (November 10, 1902): 51.
76. On Waseda, see *Gakusei hachijū nen shi* (Monbushō, 1954), pp. 635–636.
77. Concerning the utilization of these mail-order courses and for many examples of their advertising, see Yamamoto Akira, "Kyōyō to ikigai," pp. 183–210 in *Nihonjin no seikatsu*, vol. 4 of *Kōza—hikaku bunka* (Kōdansha, 1976), p. 188 (access to military schools), p. 200 (postal and railroad employment). Concerning the college certification examination and its function as an equivalent for a middle-school diploma, see Spaulding, *Higher Civil Service*, pp. 190–195. Entry without examination to *hannin* status is noted in ibid., fig. 10, p. 104, and *The Japan Year Book 1911*, p. 218.

Advertisement for a mail-order middle-school course. The copy explains that the two paths to risshin shusse are formal education and employment. Those who are employed must study on their own; lectures offered by the firm are the best and least expensive equivalent of a middle-school education; new purchasers (called associates) will receive a special dictionary; the address is "before the gate of the university" (daigaku seimon mae), a location probably chosen for its association with Tokyo Imperial University.

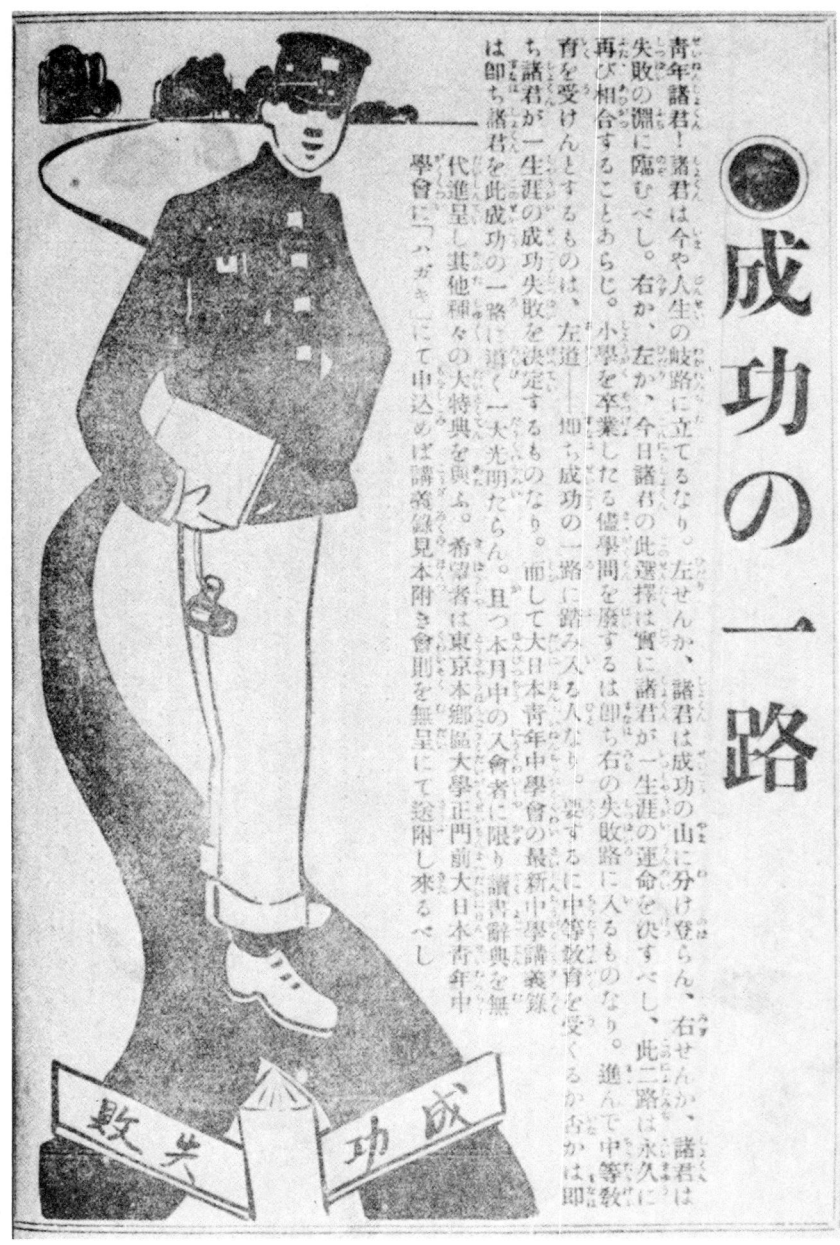

Advertisement for a mail-order middle-school course. The youth in the picture is standing at the fork in the road of life, facing a choice between the path to success and the path to failure. A youth who purchases the firm's lecture notes will be on his way to climbing the mountain of success. Mail-order middle-school advertisements were common in youth-oriented publications and newspapers after the Russo-Japanese War and continued throughout the Taishō and early Shōwa periods.

low pay and prestige associated with *hannin* status.⁷⁸ Nevertheless, from the standpoint of those who would purchase a mail order lecture course, a clerkship, a job in a post office, or a position with the national railroads may indeed have been thought of as *risshin*, but overall this was not true. Middle-school teachers and writers on success generally urged young men to "aim for the top," and this generally meant the higher schools followed by the imperial universities.

In contrast to the explosive growth of middle-school education, there was no comparable expansion in the higher-school system, and there was even a short-term contraction in 1908 (Meiji 41) when one school was closed. As a consequence, admission rates, which had actually risen in the years just before the Sino-Japanese War as middle schools improved in quality, once again started moving downward. In 1895 (Meiji 28), 67 percent of higher-school applicants were admitted, but in 1901 (Meiji 34), one year before the beginning of the success literature fad, only 34 percent of the applicants were admitted. In 1908 (Meiji 41), the worst year of the late Meiji period, the rate was down to 20 percent.⁷⁹ For those seeking admission to the First Higher School (Dai-ichi Kōtō Gakkō), the change was even more dramatic. The rates for the same three years were 52, 23, and 14 percent respectively.⁸⁰

For those who passed the higher-school examinations, there were few problems ahead. Although the relative advantage of higher education was declining, such students still had a fairly assured *risshin* ahead of them. Even if capitalistic wealth was rivaling bureaucratic honor, students of the higher schools were still greatly respected in society at large. They had little trouble becoming "eating guests" or finding patrons if they needed money, and to judge from some recollections, they might have to virtually fight off adoption offers from wealthy families who saw in higher-school students the perfect candidate for an adoptive son-in-law (*muko-yōshi*). Temporary teaching, tutoring, and other jobs dependent on education were

78. In contrast to the small numbers going into the lower ranks of the civil service, 9.4% became teachers, 4.9% joined the military, and 14.1% were employed in business. For data, see Sakurai, *Chūgaku kyōiku*, p. 431.
79. Data from the *Monbushō nenpō* for the years indicated. The 1895 rates are actually for admission to higher middle school (*kōtō chūgakkō*).
80. *Dai-ichi kōtō gakkō rokujū nen shi*, p. 595.

available to them.[81] Problems came from those who failed the examinations or who could not hope to even attempt them because they lacked funds for the requisite period of cramming. For these young men there were basically three alternatives. They could give up and seek employment, which is what *Jitsugyō no Nihon* urged.[82] They could keep studying and try again next year or the year after next or the year after that, an increasingly common pattern for those with enough money. Or they could seek alternatives to higher education. *Seikō* dealt primarily with the last possibility.

The most extreme choice available to those seeking higher education was to quit Japan entirely and go off to the United States. That such an alternative was much in vogue in Japan at this time is further testimony to the generalization of the desire for personal advancement through education; at the same time, it speaks to the narrowing of opportunities within Japan. A number of authors wrote in this area, but none approached Katayama Sen in sheer output. Katayama first appeared on the *risshin* scene in 1901 (Meiji 34) as the author of *Gakusei to-Bei annai* [Student Guide for Going to America]. This small pamphlet was immensely popular, selling as many as two thousand copies in a single week.[83] From this Katayama progressed through a series of guides, which he claimed attracted over a hundred thousand readers.[84] Advertisements for his various guide books were a certain item in the journals devoted exclusively to success and in more general-interest newspapers and magazines as well. His articles appeared in *Seikō*, and for a time he had his own magazine, *To-Bei* [Going to America], devoted to the encouragement of emigration.[85]

America, as depicted by Katayama Sen, was a country where self-help really worked the way it should, the way the biographies all said it did. America was the country where the idea that "labor is

81. See the recollections of Kikuchi Kan in his "Han-jijoden," in *Kikuchi Kan— Kume Masao*, vol. 57 of *Nihon gendai bungaku zenshū* (Kōdansha, 1967), pp. 162–168, and Abe Yoshishige, *Waga oitachi* (Iwanami shoten, 1966), pp. 273–274, 282.

82. "Okite yo dokuritsu jiei no jidai wa koreri," *Jitsugyō no Nihon* 9:1 (January 1, 1906): 12–14.

83. Sumiya Mikio, *Katayama Sen* (Tōkyō daigaku shuppan-kai, 1960), pp. 136–137.

84. Katayama Sen, *To-Bei no hiketsu* (To-Bei kyōkai, 1906), p. 1.

85. Sumiya, *Katayama Sen*, pp. 142–143, contains a list of Katayama's guides. Professor Sumiya kindly lent me copies of the guides cited here.

Cover of To-Bei zasshi *[Going to America Magazine]* for April 1905 (Meiji 38). An English-language section, "The Socialist (Japan)," is included. Mr. Tneo Okasaki [sic] used Katayama Sen, the magazine's labor-organizer publisher, to recruit people and funds for a rice-growing scheme in Texas that later proved to be a fraud.

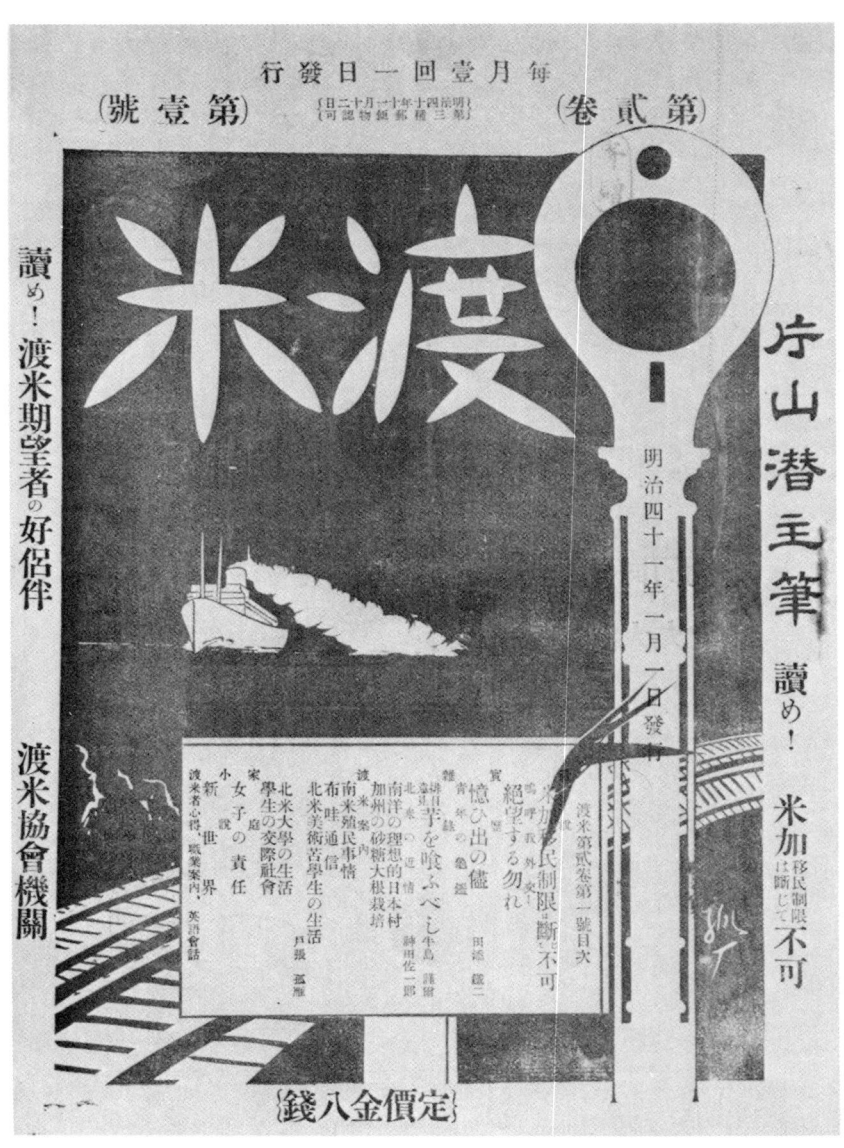

Cover of **To-Bei** *[Going to America]*, successor to **To-Bei zasshi** *[Going to America Magazine]*. This issue of January 1908 (Meiji 41) advises readers not to be discouraged by limitations on emigration to the United States.

holy" was most widely and strongly held.[86] America was where you really could work your way through school, where being a struggling student, though difficult, was not, as in Japan, "next to impossible."[87] America was also where you did not have to face entrance examinations which "denied two-thirds of all applicants aiming at higher education."[88] America was, as Katayama happily noted, the country where you really could work yourself up from shop clerk to multimillionaire, as had John D. Rockefeller.[89]

Because America was a nation where self-help really worked, those who should go to America were, consequently, those youth who most embodied the virtues of self-help. In terms of those who would go to be self-supporting students, the best qualified, according to Katayama, were those who had delivered milk or newspapers or those who had been toughened by other hard work, especially the sons of poor peasants.[90] It was these who had the necessary perseverance to stand up under the hardships that came with study in America. These included racial discrimination and the simple tedium of working as a "houseboy," the employment Katayama described as most suitable for the struggling student in America.[91] Here he drew extensively on his own experiences for illustrations of the power of his favorite virtue, and while there was more than a little element of blowing his own horn in these anecdotes, they did give his writings something that all the other literature lacked: realism. Katayama was no "success" in monetary terms, but he had gotten an education in America. He had done what he sought to advise on, whereas most other writers had not. Moreover, Katayama kept abreast of current developments through correspondence with Japanese in the United States. This currency was in fact one of the points made in advertising for his guides. They were "the most up-to-date."[92]

As one committed to social reform, Katayama should have been presented with something of a dilemma in his advocacy of emigration. At best, emigration was an avoidance of social problems. At worst, it worked to remove potentially politically active elements

86. Katayama Sen, *Gakusei to-Bei annai* (Rōdō shinbun sha, 1901), p. 9.
87. Katayama, *Hiketsu*, pp. 42–43.　　88. Ibid., p. 39.　　89. Ibid., p. 45.
90. Katayama, *Gakusei*, pp. 40–41, 6–7.
91. Katayama, *Gakusei*, pp. 25–28.
92. *Seikō* sent its readers to Katayama because he had "the latest information."

from Japan and encouraged a concern with wealth acquired through individual efforts, both tendencies being inherently counterproductive as far as reform in Japan went. No such reservations seem to have troubled him, although later some contemporary thinkers such as Kōtoku Denjirō were considerably more critical of emigration as an answer to social problems in Japan.[93] Overall, about the only element in Katayama's guides that distinguished him from other writers who did not go on to be styled Asian revolutionaries was that in writing about Japanese who had gone to the United States and had become wealthy, Katayama made much of the paternalism these wealthy emigrants extended to their employees.[94]

Emigration should have presented a similar dilemma to *Seikō*. Since the magazine declared that the more self-helping individuals a nation had, the stronger it would be, encouragement of emigration should have been seen as the exporting of a strategic resource. The magazine in fact had reservations about emigration, but from a completely different perspective. Emigration to the United States was even more of a *shusse* ("going out of the village") and resulted in a greater cutting of the ties between youthful aspirants and their families than did merely going to Tokyo for study. It was this aspect of emigration which bothered *Seikō*. Whenever there was any indication of parental opposition, *Seikō* urged "deep reflection" or counseled against emigration. Only when the aspirants' letters showed no sign of parental opposition did the magazine respond favorably to readers' inquiries and refer them to Katayama Sen for further information.[95]

Thanks to racist opposition to Japanese immigration in the state of California, crossing to America rapidly ceased to be a path to edu-

---

93. Katayama's lack of concern with these issues is noted in Sumiya, *Katayama Sen*, pp. 139–142. Critical comments on emigration are found in Kōtoku Denjirō, "Nihon no imin to Beikoku," *Kōtoku zenshū*, vol. 6, pp. 52–57.

94. See the articles "Hokubei nishi-kaigan dai-seikōsha Furuya-kun hatten etsureki," *Seikō*, 9:6 (September 1, 1906): 30–34, and "Hokubei Tekisasu no seikōsha Okazaki Tsuneo," *To-Bei* (April 3, 1905), pp. 9–12. Okazaki turned out to be more of an entrepreneur than Katayama imagined. Taken in by his proposal to buy land in Texas for rice cultivation, Katayama acted as a recruiter of families and money, but the scheme was fraudulent. See Sumiya, *Katayama Sen*, pp. 152–154.

95. "Kisha to dokusha," *Seikō* 2:1 (April 10, 1903): 46–48, and 3:3 (December 10, 1903): 53–55.

cation and personal advancement.⁹⁶ When Katayama wrote his first guide in 1901 (Meiji 34), besides perseverance, the America-bound youth did not need much more than such simple advice as "When it's hot on the boat, don't take off your clothes and wander about naked as if you were at home."⁹⁷ In subsequent editions there were detailed explanations of forms to be filled out, regulations to be met, and minimum capital requirements.⁹⁸ After Japanese victory in the Russo-Japanese War allowed racists to raise the spector of a "Yellow Peril," there was effective exclusion in the form of the so-called Gentlemen's Agreement (Nichibei shinshi kyōyaku) of 1907 (Meiji 40). When this agreement went into effect, *To-Bei* advised "Don't Be Discouraged" in its headlines, but the alternatives, such as Australia, Taiwan, Korea, China, were more appropriate for entrepreneurs than for struggling students.

Even before the possibility of emigration to the United States was largely eliminated, the careful reader of Katayama's guide for students would have noted a very good reason for not going to the United States in search of an education. Although higher education could be obtained through self-support in the United States, that education would not sell in Japan and did not confer any special *risshin* advantages on its holder. Here again Katayama was his own best example. As Sumiya Mikio has noted, Katayama's turn to social work in Japan stemmed in part from the fact that his American education (Andover and Yale) did not qualify him for any other work.⁹⁹ The systematization of the Japanese social and educational order which had taken place in the 1880s and 1890s had largely eliminated any place for the person with a Western education. A special *risshin* premium came only to those whose study in a foreign country came in addition to an elite Japanese education, not when it came in lieu of it. Thus, the late Meiji aspirant who looked to education for his advancement in Japan had to take that education in Japan. If he could not get into the higher-school-to-university course, he had to search for a Japanese alternative.

96. The background to the anti-Japanese agitation in California is discussed in Roger Daniels, *The Politics of Prejudice* (Atheneum, 1968).
97. Katayama, *Gakusei*, p. 15.
98. Katayama Sen, *Shin-to-Bei* (Shuppan kyōkai, 1904), pp. 76 ff.
99. Sumiya, *Katayama Sen*, pp. 32–33.

Just such a shift into alternative forms of secondary and higher education was evident before the Russo-Japanese War, although it was not necessarily correctly interpreted at the time. For example, in 1903 (Meiji 36) an observer in *Kyōiku jiron* [Education Review] proclaimed:

> Previously the majority of those who completed middle school held hopes of entering higher school. Industrial, business, foreign-language and other similar practical training schools were the object of relatively few students' attention. In contrast to the situation when such schools could not recruit desired numbers, it looks now as though things have changed. The relative rank of these schools appears to have risen. Students have recognized the evil [*hei*] of blindly aiming at higher school, have understood the true demand of the times [*jisei*], have abandoned false fame and are now nourishing actual power. This must be applauded as a most noteworthy development.[100]

Had this been literally true, it would have meant that at long last, youth with the desire and the means to acquire secondary and higher education had abandoned the basically samurai notion of study for government affiliation and were now following the course which various writers from the 1880s on had been urging.

Statistics on education for the interwar period show that the changes at this time were not as simple or as unidirectional as the journal proclaimed.[101] Such higher educational institutions as higher industrial schools (*kōtō kōgyō gakkō*) and higher business schools (*kōtō shōgyō gakkō*) not only no longer had to advertise for students but had four or five applicants for each entry position offered. The ratio of higher-school applicants to middle-school graduates had indeed fallen from the 70 percent level in 1898 (Meiji 31) to the 35

---

100. "Seinen shibō no itten," *Kyōiku jiron* (September 25, 1903), p. 45.

101. The changes discussed are covered in Fukaya, *Gakureki shugi*, chap. 5, pp. 315–368. I have not, however, followed Fukaya literally, because of reservations about the basic data and his treatment of it. The careful reader will note that Fukaya gives slightly different figures for middle-school graduates in 1901–1903 in tables 72 (p. 239) and 115 (p. 323). The author does not comment or explain this discrepancy, but it apparently comes from using different editions of the *Monbushō nenpō* to create the two tables. Although the discrepancies are not large, the variations (probably due to late reports) indicate that the data cannot be regarded as accurate to the units, the tens, or even possibly to the hundreds level. Therefore percentages and ratios cannot legitimately be calculated to two decimal places, as in the *Monbushō nenpō*, or even to one place, as Fukaya does. I have therefore deliberately used expressions such as "70 percent level" rather than giving the calculated amount, in order to avoid imputing more precision to the data than is warranted.

A more important problem in the discussion at hand is the faulty or ambiguous

percent level in 1903 (Meiji 36). This change was not, however, due simply to middle-school students' switching from higher schools to higher industrial or business schools. The ratio fell primarily because of a rapid increase in the number of middle-school graduates relative to higher-school places. In 1898 (Meiji 31) there were three middle-school graduates for each higher-school entry position; in 1903 (Meiji 36) there were eight.[102]

As a consequence, competition rates for higher-school admission climbed, and as they did, a number of middle-school graduates dropped out of the struggle. Those who dropped out did not, however, flow to the higher industrial and business schools, because competition to enter those schools was at least as severe as that for the higher schools. Instead, they flowed into the private colleges (*shiritsu senmon gakkō*), which still followed a policy of giving admission to virtually all warm bodies who could pay school fees.[103] There those who fled the higher-school competition did not study industrial or business subjects but instead studied law or political economy. The number of students studying these traditional sub-

---

labeling of tables 72 (p. 239), 115 (p. 323), and 139 (p. 350) in Fukaya. The item identified as "middle-school graduates" (*chūgaku sotsugyōsei*) in each of these tables is in fact only the figure for public (*kōritsu*) middle-school graduates. This means that Fukaya's figures understate total middle-school graduate numbers by 30 to 50 percent with a corresponding effect on the ratios he calculates. Failure to include private-middle-school graduates does not invalidate his discussion but does mean that the magnitude and timing of certain changes are misstated. Because of this problem I have used wherever possible calculations based on total middle-school main-course (*honka*) graduates as given in the *Monbushō nenpō*. For a convenient tabulation of the Monbushō data on the postgraduation status of *public*-middle-school graduates, see Sakurai Mamoru, *Chūgaku kyōiku shikō* (Rinsen shoten, 1975), pp. 397, 431, and 517–518.

102. The proportion of middle-school graduates seeking higher-school entry in their year of graduation is not given and cannot be calculated from Monbushō data. The ratio of higher-school applicants to total middle-school graduates is a rough substitute for the desired ratio, but because of the inclusion of *rōnin* it is larger by a factor that varies from year to year. Only students applying to the university preparatory course (*daigaku yoka*) of the higher schools have been considered in calculating the ratios given in the text.

103. In 1900 (Meiji 33) the government imposed some control on the lax admission policies of private colleges by requiring entrance examinations for applicants *without* middle-school diplomas. Spaulding, *Higher Civil Service*, p. 133. Otherwise, there was no significant barrier to entry, as is indicated by admission rates averaging 80 percent. In contrast, national (*kanritsu*) colleges had stiff competition rates, especially in medicine, with an average of six applicants for each place in the last years of the Meiji era. For other competition rates see Fukaya, *Gakureki shugi*, pp. 258–259, and Karasawa, *Gakusei*, foldout table following p. 202 (see note 8).

jects in private schools climbed from the seven thousand level in 1898 (Meiji 31) to over thirteen thousand in 1903 (Meiji 36).

Five years after *Kyōiku jiron* editorialized, the ratio of higher-school applicants to middle-school graduates was up to almost 70 percent, near the level just after the Sino-Japanese War. Only one out of five applicants was successful, however, and since 50 to 60 percent of the applicants in a given year were *rōnin* (students who had failed an earlier exam), the proportion of graduates successful in their year of graduation was one in twenty or less.[104] Faced with such low probabilities of success, middle-school graduates continued to shift to the private colleges. In 1898 (Meiji 31) only 1 in 9 middle-school graduates had gone to any type of college (*senmon gakkō*), but by the end of the Meiji era 1 in 4 did so, and in some years the proportion was as high as 1 in 3. Most of this college enrollment was in the private sector, since there was little expansion in national or provincial college facilities, and 3 out of 4 private-college students studied law or political economy. Thus, while there was diversification in student aspirations to include applied higher education, most clung to an early Meiji conception of what constituted the proper study for wealth and honor.

Greater interest in applied education is to be seen at the secondary level. Class A vocational-school (*kōshu jitsugyō gakkō*) enrollments grew twice as fast as did those of middle schools, and vocational education in general grew four times as fast.[105] To a limited degree, growth in this type of education was related to the difficulty of getting into middle school. Competition rates for middle schools in general were in the 2 to 1 range, but schools noted for their higher-school preparation capabilities had rates of up to 6 to 1.[106]

104. The 1906 (Meiji 39) *Monbushō nenpō* gave data on the number of successful applicants coming from that and previous years' middle-school graduates. Of the 1,475 successful higher-school applicants in 1906, 55 percent had graduated that year. These 801 successful applicants stood in the ratio of 1:19 with respect to the approximately 15,600 middle-school graduates in that year. Since the proportion of applicants successful on their first try was declining, a ratio of 1 in 20 or worse may be assumed for subsequent years. *Monbushō nenpō*, no. 34 (1906–1907), p. 145.

105. Using 1897–1898 (Meiji 30–31) as a base, calculations of compound growth rates show ordinary middle-school enrollments increasing at 7 percent a year to 1907 (Meiji 40) while class A vocational schools gained at 13 percent, and all vocational schools at 28 percent. Calculated from enrollment figures in Monbushō, *Gakusei hachijū nen shi*, pp. 1046–1047, 1052–1053, and 1056.

106. For some discussion of this, see Fukaya, *Gakureki shugi*, pp. 280 and 345. Gross rates are discussed throughout Sakurai, *Chūgaku kyōiku*.

SUCCESS!

With the possibility of going on to higher school decreasing and the return on a private-college education questionable, the proportion of middle-school graduates going to either form of higher education fell from 1 in 2 in 1898 (Meiji 31) to 1 in 3 in 1908 (Meiji 41). Some parents and students must have felt that if middle school would not lead to elite higher education, it would be better to go into vocational secondary education. At least such education prepared you for a job, unlike the middle schools, which gave an essentially liberal arts education geared to higher-school requirements. Vocational schools were also somewhat less expensive, if not in terms of fees, in terms of proximity.[107] The students in these schools, either by lack of choice or by family background, were more predisposed to "understand the true demand of the times" than were those sufficiently affluent to carry on to ordinary middle schools only to find themselves unable to capitalize on their expensive middle-school education through admission to elite higher education.

After the Russo-Japanese War, *Seikō* [Success] rapidly became a guidebook for those pursuing alternative secondary and higher education and the *risshin* opportunities associated with such education. This is to be seen most dramatically in the consultation columns of the magazine. In columns before the war, the questions were often of cosmic scope, such as What are the personal characteristics of an inventor? Is genius necessary to become an eminent man? How does one become rich like Andrew Carnegie? Soon after the war, the questions became increasingly technical and concerned with what might be called petty *risshin*:

> What level of education is required for the electrical technician certification exam?
> How much is an electrical technician paid?
> Is it possible to get into army officer's school without middle-school graduation?
> What are the good night schools in Tokyo?
> What should I study for the ordinary civil servants exam for Korea?
> Is there a veterinary school that will take a twenty-six-year-old?
> Can an upper-elementary-school graduate enter dentistry school?
> When and where is the exam for tourist guides given?
> What are the pay and employment prospects for graduates of private craft schools?

107. Fukaya emphasizes changing student backgrounds in this context. Fukaya, *Gakureki shugi*, p. 363. *Seikō* advice columns give the impression that both costs and competition ratios were also factors.

197

Which private middle schools carry draft exemption?
Where do I get a study guide for the middle-school teacher certification exam?
Does a court reporter get a pension and what is his starting pay?
Is there an age limit on entry to normal school?

In almost every issue sixty to a hundred such inquiries would be listed.[108] So great was the crush that the magazine had to specify it would not answer questions that could be answered through the published catalogs of schools or questions that had been answered within the last few months. It put severe limitations on the format for asking questions to the point of providing a model postcard that had to be followed exactly lest the magazine throw out the aspirant's letter for such infractions as using pencil rather than ink or for asking more than two questions per card.

The replies the magazine gave to these requests for information were often snappish. A young man who dared to ask a competition rate might be told that someone with a true will to succeed should not be asking such questions.[109] As a matter of principle the magazine gave very little information on competition rates, in striking contrast to *Chūgaku sekai* [Middle-School World] and its multipage statistical tables. Articles on examination study in *Seikō* tended to be largely inspirational, not geared to specific schools as was *Chūgaku sekai*. This difference reflected the concentration of *Chūgaku sekai* on national (*kanritsu*) higher educational institutions and of *Seikō* on private (*shiritsu*) secondary and higher education. Most schools *Seikō* readers aspired to had competition rates near unity and entrance examinations that certified minimal knowledge and ability rather than rejecting excess qualified applicants. Ability to pay was as important for many schools as ability to do the required work.[110]

Tokyo College (Tōkyō Senmon Gakkō), now Waseda University, was the only institution of any quality that regularly appeared in questions from readers and in the recommendations of *Seikō*. Indeed, at times the magazine seemed almost to be an advertisement

---

108. The consultation column "Kisha to dokusha" appeared in all but a few issues of the magazine. The examples given here are loose renderings of questions in *Seikō* 26:2 (November 1, 1913): 89–94, but the pattern appeared much earlier.

109. "Kisha to dokusha," *Seikō* 4:3 (April 15, 1904), pp. 43 ff.

110. For a sense of the schools associated with *Seikō* and its readers, see "Honnen shigatsu nyūgaku subeki Tōkyō kaku gakkō annai," *Seikō* 15:5 (March 1, 1909): 85 ff.

for the school. Many *Seikō* contributors and supporters were affiliated with the school, and given a choice the magazine usually recommended it over other institutions. This relation was, however, a natural one, for the Tokyo College was really the only moderate-cost alternative to higher education. Other private colleges were narrowly focused on law, but Tokyo College was a conglomerate offering everything from middle-school correspondence courses to a "university department" (*daigakubu*) of considerable quality. Keiō Gijuku, Fukuzawa Yukichi's academy, offered a reasonably high quality education, but it was known as a school for the progeny of the corporate rich and seldom figured in *Seikō* exchanges.

In contrast to the often harsh responses to technical questions, *Seikō* gave lengthy and loving responses to the earlier variety of cosmic questions, segregating them from the rest at the head of the consultation column. This curious situation in which *Seikō* was almost openly hostile to its readers is to be explained in terms of two factors: First, the apparently largely rural readers of *Seikō* had no other convenient source of information. Neither *Jitsugyō no Nihon* [Business Japan] nor *Chūgaku sekai* dealt with the schools and subjects covered by *Seikō*. Second, despite being part of the late Meiji journalistic scene, the magazine intellectually belonged to the 1880s portion of the era when all were supposed to be striving to the utmost for their country. Although the magazine specifically charged its readers to look at "second-rank" ("third" would have been more honest) routes to advancement, it also expected them to hold great dreams and to continue striving.[111] Rather than wanting to be just electrical technicians, a *Seikō* reader was expected to want to become an Edison. They were to be like those youth depicted in *Self-Help*, the young craftsmen and mechanics who became the great industrialists who had made England into Great Britain.

As was seen earlier, the Smilesean vision in the early *Seikō* originally included both a nationalistic dimension and a social-reform dimension. The Russo-Japanese War was, however, a turning point, and subsequently *Seikō* editorials and articles talked less about the common role of self-help in reforming society and building an independent Japan and concentrated instead on the importance of these

111. "Kisha to dokusha," *Seikō* 5:2 (August 1, 1904): 49–52.

same virtues to an expanding Japan. At the beginning of the war, the magazine and the socialist movement were still linked in terms of contributors, and the *Heimin shinbun* [Commoner Newspaper], generally seen as Japan's first socialist newspaper, carried advertising for *Seikō*.[112] That portion of the movement represented by the *Heimin shinbun* was, however, antiwar, while *Seikō* was enthusiastically prowar, and in a matter of months, *Seikō* had become critical of the movement for its antiwar stance.[113]

More important than differences over the Russo-Japanese War were differences over the applicability of self-help to social reform. Although originally committed to self-help, most late Meiji social and labor activists gradually became more sophisticated and began to develop a critique of society based on a concern for social structure, not just morality. With this critique came a hostility to self-help. Sakai Kosen, for example, went from telling youth they ought to want to be millionaires to satirizing the success genre. In *Heimin shinbun* in 1904 (Meiji 37), he published an alleged interview between a businessman and a reporter from "Seikō no Nihon," an obvious spoof on both *Seikō* and *Jitsugyō no Nihon*.[114] In the article, the businessman explained his secrets of success. These included marrying the daughter of the company owner, forming a trust, using child labor, and bribing Diet members.[115] Other articles went so far as to suggest that there might be some need for redistributing wealth in Japanese society, that self-help was not sufficient.[116]

It was this last suggestion that really split *Seikō* from the more sophisticated portion of the socialist and labor movements. The satire on ways to success was tolerable. The magazine condemned such dishonorable routes to success as speculation while glossing over or ignoring the other techniques cited in Sakai's satire. To suggest that there ought to be some redistribution of wealth was, however, more

112. See the advertisement for *Funtō shugi* (*Strenuous Life*, by Theodore Roosevelt) published by Seikō zasshi sha in *Heimin shinbun* (February 21, 1904), p. 8.
113. Murakami Dakurō, "Senji to jijoteki seishin," *Seikō* 4:1 (March 1, 1904), pp. 47–49, and "Jihyō," *Seikō* 4:5 (May 15, 1904): 41–42. All *Seikō* covers in this period featured military leaders.
114. Takeuchi notes that this article was attributed to Murakami Giichi, a takeoff on Murakami Dakurō and Masuda Giichi. Takeuchi, *Risshin shusse-kan*, p. 111.
115. Sakai Kosen, "Ōganemōke no hiketsu," *Heimin shinbun* (October 16, 1904), pp. 6–7.
116. "Fusha to shakai shugi," *Heimin shinbun* (May 1, 1904), p. 1.

than could be accommodated within the range of social concern held by *Seikō*. An anonymous "comment on the times," probably by Murakami, declared that while the magazine really wanted to be the friend of labor, it could not continue to be such if labor was not diligent, did not rely on itself, and did not seek to develop its own fate. The magazine could not support labor so long as it looked to such solutions as "sharing the wealth."[117] A subsequent editorial, this time signed by Murakami, explained that such schemes could only work in a society in which the majority of people were morally perfect and would respond to noneconomic incentives.[118]

This sudden emphasis on men as being solely motivated by material rewards should have struck the *Seikō* reader as curious. The steady reader of *Seikō* would have read a great deal about wealth, even from nonbusiness models, but he would seldom if ever have encountered anyone, even a businessman, who was depicted as economically motivated. Even after the magazine's antisocialist declarations, he would still not find such depictions. Apparently, successful men became profit-motivated only when challenged by socialists and not while they were acquiring their wealth. In trying to have its cake and eat it too, the magazine was in good company. Samuel Smiles had also depicted his models as motivated by almost anything but the desire to make personal profits, yet he discovered the value of the profit incentive when faced with socialist challenges. Smiles, too, had become an object of derision and satire on the part of socialists.[119]

At the same time that it was Smilesean both in its beginnings in social reform and in its reaction to socialism, *Seikō* was perhaps the more conservative of the two. In dealing with workers and craftsmen and urging them to better themselves through self-help, Smiles was operating in a context where the relations between the potential for individual advancement and the social structures which oppressed the individual were relatively diffuse. In dealing with aspirants to secondary and higher education, *Seikō* was operating in a context where the relations between the potential for individual ad-

117. "Jihyō," *Seikō* 4:5 (May 15, 1904): 41–42.
118. Murakami Dakurō, "Gendai chōryū shōkan," *Seikō* 5:4 (October 1, 1904): 24–26.
119. Travers, "Samuel Smiles," pp. 269–272.

vancement and the social structures which oppressed the individual were grossly obvious. *Seikō* readers had to seek inferior forms of secondary and higher education because government policy explicitly chose not to expand educational facilities at these levels. *Seikō* seems never to have editorialized on the subject of school expansion, however, and as a consequence, the basic thrust of the magazine—that even a poor boy could raise himself in the world through education—was essentially conservative from the very beginning of the journal. Had there been any body of influential thought in Meiji Japan, as there had been in Smiles's England, which argued that one ought to be content with the status one was born to, the rags-to-riches-through-study-by-struggle theme would have been progressive. Since there was *no* such thought, the failure of *Seikō* to look beyond the individual meant that it had really been supporting the system that denied those it seemed to want to help. The magazine never followed the course of its American namesake, O. S. Marden's *Success*, into muckraking.[120]

If *Seikō* can be said to have followed Samuel Smiles in its separation from the labor and socialist movements, it can also be said to have followed its other source of inspiration, Tokutomi Iichirō, into imperialism. *Seikō* was not merely prowar—it soon became jubilantly expansive. The magazine proclaimed that while Japan had previously been learning from the West, the Russo-Japanese War demonstrated that Japan was ready to embark on expansion. In particular, the war showed that Japan had a special talent for blending Eastern and Western elements. Moreover, Japanese, as Asians, were naturally qualified to expand in Asia and were qualified to do so in a way that no Westerners, especially Americans, could be.[121] In the case of *Seikō*, this change of emphasis continued to the point where in 1915 (Taishō 4) the magazine publicly repudiated its earlier commonerism to advocate instead "strong-man-ism" (*kyōsha shugi*) in which the concept of a Carlyle style of hero was grafted onto a rhetorical base derived from Social Darwinism. The precise motivation for this change is unclear, but *Seikō* covers of the time depicted a

120. *Seikō* and *Success* are compared in chapter 7. On muckraking, see Huber, *American Idea*, pp. 153–154.
121. Murakami Dakurō, "Nihon kokumin to shin-bunmeikoku kensetsu," *Seikō* 11:3 (April 1, 1907): 23–25.

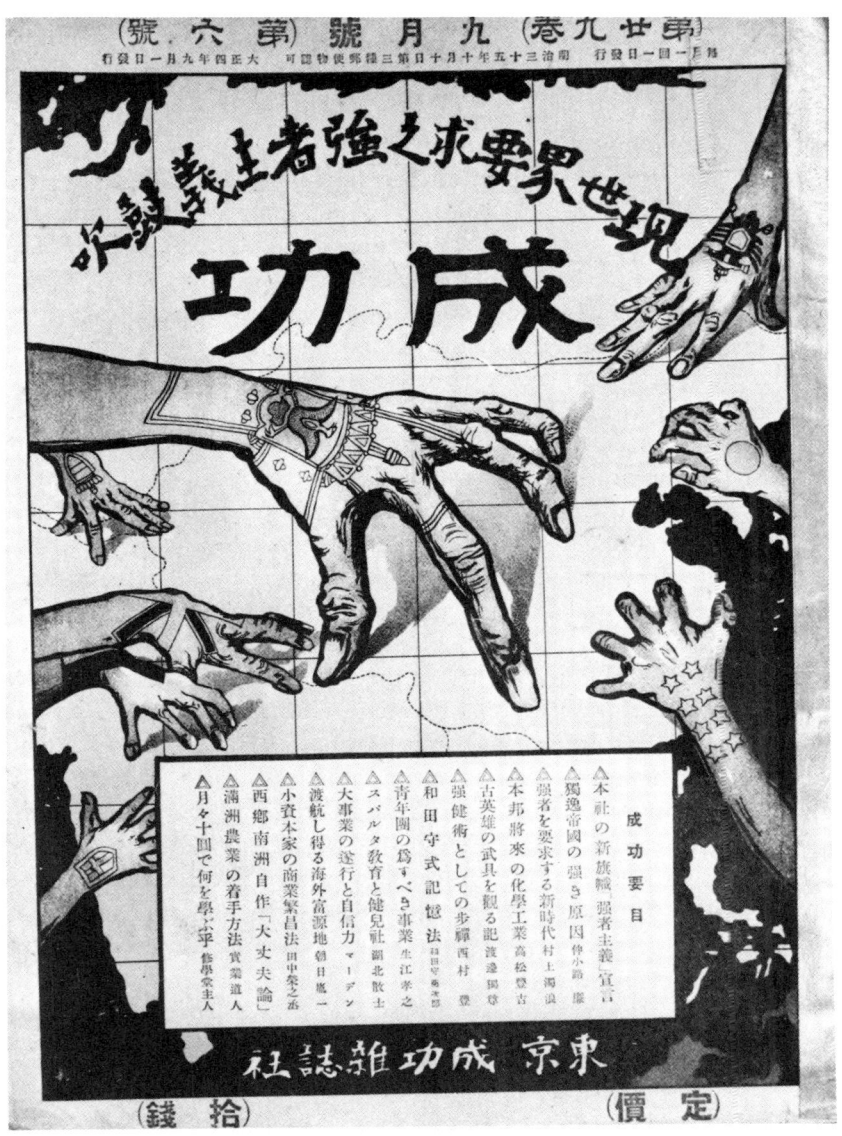

Cover of Seikō [Success] for September 1915 (Taishō 4), announcing its shift from the promotion of success to the promotion of "strongman-ism" (kyōsha shugi). The magazine ceased publication soon after this change.

number of hands labeled with national symbols of European imperial powers and Japan grasping at China. Editorials on the change cite the breakdown of international order with World War I and proclaim that victory will go to the "strong man" (*kyōsha*).[122] Overall, one is left with the feeling that as the editor of *Seikō* aged, he reverted to ideas that had been commonly expressed in the 1890s and after the Sino-Japanese War.[123] This shift in emphasis from the equalitarian and social-reform aspects of commonerism to the nationalistic and imperialistic elements was strikingly similar to that made by Tokutomi at the time of the Sino-Japanese War.[124]

Whatever the precise motivations of Murakami in switching from a commonerism that emphasized equalitarianism to one that emphasized imperialism, the new message of *Seikō* was not seemingly matched by any great response from readers.[125] The initial change to expansionism after the Russo-Japanese War only occasionally generated any expressions of interest in the consultation columns, and these were seldom if ever connected to any great national vision. Readers who expressed interest in going abroad usually noted the financial incentives or lack of competition, not the contribution they would make to an expanding Japan. At best, overseas opportunities appear much the way private colleges stood relative to the higher schools: a second choice for those unable to make it into the first-choice track. Perhaps the most eloquent commentary on reader enthusiasm for the shift in *Seikō* editorial policy is that the magazine went out of business shortly after proclaiming its "strong-man-ism." Contemporary youth wanted hard information on those seemingly insignificant but nonetheless vital issues that ruled their lives: application procedures, deadlines, fees, draft exemptions, and the like. They perhaps perceived better than did Murakami and other *Seikō* writers that because of the vast increase in the number of edu-

---

122. Murakami Dakurō, "Kyōsha o yōkyū suru shin-jidai kitareri," *Seikō* 29:6 (September 1, 1915): 7–9, and "Sengen," *Seikō* 29:6 (September 1, 1915): 1–4.

123. Imperialistic thought in general is discussed in Kano Masanao, "Kokka shugi no taitō," in *Kindai Nihon seiji shisō shi* (Yūhikaku, 1971), vol. 1, pp. 287–305.

124. On Tokutomi, see Pyle, *New Generation*, chap. 8.

125. R. P. Dore suggests that "fervent nationalism" in *Seikō* provided "vicarious alternative satisfactions to those who had been disappointed in the struggle for success." Dore, "Mobility," p. 138. Lack of response from readers indicates that any such satisfaction was limited to Murakami.

cated youth, most of them were destined to become cogs in, not drivers of, Japanese capitalism. As such, they were quite appropriately concerned only with their own specific problems because they, unlike the handful of youth with a Western education in the first decades of the era, could expect to have no significant influence on the course of Meiji Japan.

6 | Anguished Youth

Not all late Meiji youth responded to the conditions that had given rise to the literature of success with further dedication to the pursuit of personal advancement. Among a portion of youth large enough to be a cause of widespread concern among educators, government officials, and editorial writers, there was a rejection of the struggle for *risshin*. Occurring particularly but not exclusively among well-educated youth, this rejection was marked by a search for outlets for self-expression in a society which was less and less geared to providing these opportunities within the framework of traditional *risshin shusse*. Such youth were known to late Meiji observers by a variety of names, including "anguished youth" (*hanmon seinen*) and "decadent youth" (*tandeki seinen*).[1] Responding to these youth became a major problem for writers on the subject of self-advancement. Their appearance signaled a marked change in Japanese thinking about advancement and saw the development of motifs that would figure in writing on the subject throughout the prewar period.

The anguished youth came to the notice of contemporary observers just a few months after the appearance of the "success youth" (*seikō seinen*), those who constituted the audience for the success

---

1. This terminology and characterization of youth is best known today through the comments of Tokutomi Iichirō. See Tokutomi Iichirō, *Taishō seinen to teikoku no zento* (Minyūsha, 1916), pp. 1–22. These terms were in use much earlier, however, and Tokutomi was merely reporting, not making an original analysis.

206

literature. The event that first called the anguished youth to widespread public notice was the suicide of one Fujimura Misao, an eighteen-year-old student at the First Higher School in Tokyo.² In May of 1903 (Meiji 36), he took his own life at Kegon Falls in Nikkō, leaving behind a suicide note entitled "Thoughts upon the Precipice" (Gantō no kan). In this note he declared his inability to understand life and his hope of finding peace on the rocks below.

> The philosophy of Horatio
> What means it in the end?
> All truth is but one word—
>   Unfathomable.
> Anguished, I think of this.
> In the end, I decide on death.
> Quiet. Quiet.
> Heaven and earth, past and present,
> Far, far distant.
> How to measure their greatness
> With my humble self.³

Ordinarily, a suicide by an otherwise unknown youth could have been expected to generate little more than grief among immediate family and friends and possibly a brief note on the "third page" of newspapers where gossipy items and scandals were placed. Fujimura's suicide was not, however, so treated. It was front-page news, and according to one contemporary observer, it was second only to

---

2. The mood and phenomena associated with the anguished youth existed prior to Fujimura's suicide but were not a major journalistic concern. For some of the earlier indications of anguish among youth, see: "Seinen shippai no ichidai-riyū," *Rikugō zasshi* (January 15, 1900), pp. 9–12; "Rakutan suru nakare," *Chūgaku sekai* (July 25, 1899), pp. 80–81; "Handō no seishin," *Chūgaku sekai* (June 10, 1899), pp. 66–68; "Shōnen shakai no aku ryūkō-byō," *Chūgaku sekai* (December 10, 1899), pp. 1–3. The latter is typical. It harshly condemns what it described as the "lamentation fever" (*kōgai netsu*) among youth and urges them to put their noses back to the grindstone. The content is less surprising than the author, Takayama Rinjirō (Chogyū), who appeared a few months later as one of the most visible of the anguished youth.

3. Numerous reproductions of this note exist. I used the one appearing in Sumiya Mikio, *Dai-Nihon teikoku no shiren*, vol. 22 of *Nihon no rekishi* (Chūō kōron sha, 1966), p. 193. Itō Sei suggests that "Gantō no kan" was a plagiarization from *Hamlet*, which Fujimura had been reading shortly before his death. Itō Sei, *Nihon bundan shi* (Kōdansha, 1964), vol. 7, p. 143.

Russian movements in Manchuria in terms of coverage.[4] In short order, the incident generated poetry, songs, and a novel.[5]

Contributing to this coverage were a number of factors that lifted Fujimura's suicide out of the ordinary. As a First Higher School student, he was one of that tiny minority of Japanese youth successful in advancing to the most sought after educational facility in Japan, one that was both officially and popularly seen as producing future leaders. Acts by First Higher School students were automatically a subject for press coverage. Moreover, by virtue of being a first Higher School student, Fujimura seemed to have every reason to live. To these students after their assured passage through the imperial universities (usually Tokyo), the stabilized social order gave its greatest rewards of wealth and honor. This made his suicide particularly difficult to understand.[6] Adding to the interest was the relatively high status of his family: his father had been a well-placed bureaucrat in the finance ministry, and his uncle was a well-known lecturer and historian at the Imperial University.[7] Finally, there was the matter of the peculiar medium Fujimura had chosen for his suicide note: he had carved it into the trunk of a living tree.

Had these been the only features of Fujimura's suicide, the incident would still warrant little more than a footnote in the history of late Meiji journalism as an example of what it was that could capture public attention even on the eve of a major war. What made Fujimura's suicide historically significant was that he almost instan-

---

4. Press coverage is described in Gotō Chūgai, "Kaigiteki jisatsusha," *Shinshōsetsu* 8:9 (September 1, 1903): 209–214; Fujiwara Kiyozō, *Kyōiku shisō gakusetsu jinbutsu shi* (Tōa seikyō sha, 1943), vol. 2, pp. 133–136; and Itō, *Nihon bundan shi*, vol. 7, p. 144. Reproductions of press accounts are found in Ono Hideo, *Meiji wadai jiten* (Tōkyōdō shuppan, 1968), p. 290–292, and Araki Masayasu, *Shinbun ga kataru Meiji shi* (Hara shobo, 1976), pp. 246–247.

5. The novel is Oguri Fūyō, *Seishun* (Shunyōdō, 1906). Unfortunately, it is hostile to the anguished youth and nearly worthless for social history. A character based on Fujimura Misao also appears in the novel *Pillar of Fire* by Kinoshita Naoe. Kinoshita Naoe, *Pillar of Fire* [Hi no hashira], trans. Kenneth Strong (Allen & Unwin, 1972), pp. 104–105.

6. The various explanations offered by the contemporary press for his suicide are discussed in Gotō, "Kaigiteki jisatsusha."

7. Concerning Fujimura's family, see Haga Noboru, *Meiji kokka to minshū* (Yūzankaku, 1974), p. 268, and Matsuoka Hideo, "Fujimura Misao," in *Meiji no shūen*, vol. 8 of *Nihonjin no hyaku-nen* (Sekai bunka sha, 1972), p. 94.

taneously became a model for other youth.⁸ His suicide note was reproduced in a pamphlet with pictures of Fujimura (and the tree) on the cover and quickly became a best seller. Youth were said to have walked around singing "Gantō no kan."⁹ Even more striking, other youth were moved to complete emulation. Reports of youthful suicides in the name of "anguish" or "world weariness" (*enseikan*) continued in the newspapers for years afterwards.¹⁰

Just how many youth actually committed suicide in emulation of Fujimura is impossible to know, but one scholar has claimed that there were forty successful and sixty-seven unsuccessful attempts at Kegon alone in the period 1903–1908 (Meiji 36–41).¹¹ One of the first statistical studies of suicide in Japan was stimulated by the Fujimura incident. According to the author, a comparison of suicide rates for 1890–1897 (Meiji 23–30) and 1898–1904 (Meiji 31–37) led to the conclusion, "In recent years there has been an increase in suicide among all age groups, but the increase has been greatest among sixteen- to twenty-one-year-old males." This increase was, the author observed, related to the appearance of anguish among youth.¹² Although the statistics of suicide in this period are open to serious doubt, there is no question that contemporary officialdom saw a relation between the Fujimura incident and what they perceived to be an increase in youthful suicide. The police prohibited "Gantō no kan" in the hope that this would end suicides in emulation of Fujimura.¹³ This prohibition did not work as it was intended to, and as soon as the Russo-Japanese War had ended and attention was once

8. The response of contemporary youth to Fujimura's suicide is described in Karasawa, *Gakusei*, pp. 74–75, and Itō, *Nihon bundan shi*, vol. 7, pp. 144–146.

9. See Fujiwara, *Kyōiku shisō*, vol. 2, p. 135. This pamphlet is reproduced in *Nihon no gakusei no rekishi* (Kōdansha, 1970), p. 157.

10. Youthful suicides as late as the World War I period would recall Fujimura's act. For an example from the same year, see "Another Suicide at Fatal Fall," *Yorozu Weekly* (September 14, 1903), p. 3.

11. Matsuoka, "Fujimura Misao."

12. For various commentaries that linked an apparent increase in youthful suicide to Fujimura's example, see "Jisatsu ron," *Tōkei shūshi*, no. 315, pp. 259–263; Ōtsuka Soe, "Jisatsu to seinen," *Taiyō* 9:8 (July 1, 1903): 207–213; and Fujikawa Yutaka, "Jisatsu mondai," *Chūō kōron* 21:11 (November 1906): 41–48. These articles did not consider the possibility that the apparent increase might have been due simply to increased reporting or better statistical coverage.

13. For police comment, see "Kegon taki dai-ninki ryūkō," *Tōkyō Nichi nichi* (July 4, 1903), in Araki, *Shinbun*, p. 253.

again focused on domestic issues, the subject of the anguished youth was taken up by the government and the press. Magazines had forums and panels on the subject of how to treat the anguish of youth.[14] The Ministry of Education issued orders, and government officials gave scoldings.[15] None of these measures really worked, and articles on the subject, usually sparked by another suicide, appeared sporadically until World War I. As late as 1916 (Taishō 5), Tokutomi Iichirō was describing the anguished youth as a significant portion of contemporary youth, and some of their writings were popular until World War II.[16]

Suicide was only the most dramatic manifestation of this anguish. There were others, particularly a concern with religion and philosophy. The works of Tsunajima Ryōsen describing his three "experiences of seeing God" were immensely popular among the stratum of youth capable of reading his difficult prose and willing to discount the probability that his experiences were nothing but hallucinations stemming from his soon to be terminal case of tuberculosis.[17] There was a spurt in church membership after 1901 (Meiji 34), largely among members of the new intelligentsia.[18] Certain Buddhist groups that appealed to the same stratum enjoyed considerable success, although one man's report of seeing Buddha did not generate as much excitement as Tsunajima's alleged meetings.[19] Philosophy came to enjoy great popularity, such that the Christian journal *Rikugō zasshi* [The Universe] cited a bookseller who asserted, "If the title doesn't have the words philosophy [*tetsugaku*] or humanity [*ningen*] in it, a book won't sell."[20] This was not quite true. "Success" in a book title also guaranteed sales during this period, but with that qualification, the generalization was valid. It was in these years that the works of

14. See "Ensei to hanmon no kyūji," *Shinkōron*, July 1906, August 1906.
15. See *Gakusei hachijū nen shi* (Monbushō, 1954), pp. 932–933.
16. This was the basic theme of his *Taishō seinen. Santarō nikki* [The Diary of Santarō] by Abe Jirō is an example of such a work. It is discussed in chapter 8.
17. Tsunajima's essays are reproduced in *Meiji shisōka shū*, vol. 13 of *Nihon gendai bungaku zenshū* (Kōdansha, 1968), pp. 390–399. For contemporary comment on Tsunajima and his experiences, see Fujiwara, *Kyōiku shisō*, vol. 2, pp. 172–185.
18. Sumiya Mikio, *Nihon no shakai shisō* (Tōkyō daigaku shuppan-kai, 1968), pp. 37–38.
19. Fujiwara, *Kyōiku shisō*, vol. 2, p. 186.
20. "Tetsugakusho rui no ryūkō," *Rikugō zasshi*, no. 274 (October 15, 1903), pp. 68–69.

Kitamura Tōkoku first began to receive some general appreciation.[21] A number of European romantics became must reading for educated youth, including Carlyle, Byron, Shelley, Goethe, and Nietzsche, to name some of those that appear most prominently in recollections.

Although seemingly far removed from any treatment of Japanese thought concerning advancement, these anguished youth command attention because in one way or another they all rejected that passion which had been consuming educated youth since the beginning of the Meiji period, the pursuit of *risshin shusse*. This was made most explicit in the recollections of Iwanami Shigeo, founder of the publishing firm of that name and a close associate of Fujimura Misao.

It was an age of introspection and despair that focused on such questions as "what is human nature?" and "where did I come from?" and "where am I going?" As men we felt embarrassed about uttering such words as "rise in the world [*risshin shusse*]" and "wealth, honor, and fame [*kōmyō fūki*]." It was an age in which even death was not frowned upon as a way to contact the base of existence [*jinsei*], to grasp at eternal life. In those days I was coming and going with such friends as Abe Jirō, Abe Yoshishige, Fujiwara Tadashi, among others. Since we were always agonizing over the matter of "existence," it was thought by friends that we might commit suicide. In fact Fujimura was a pioneer, and after his death, Kegon Falls was the object of our ambitions. I don't know how many times I wept after Thoughts upon the Precipice.[22]

To have a complete description of Meiji Japanese thought concerning the self-made man, it is necessary to see what it was that could cause a highly conspicuous portion of Meiji youth to reject the pursuit of personal advancement and turn to the pursuits associated with the anguished youth. It is necessary to determine why life no longer meant *risshin* for these youth.

The most educated of the anguished youth were prolific writers. Page after page of their compositions may be found in the First Higher School dormitory magazine and in various literary and philosophical journals of the period. Subsequently, many of the anguished youth who survived their initial brush with melancholy wrote extensively

21. Kitamura's collected works were first published in 1902 (Meiji 35). Concerning their popularity, see Kurita Kakuya, *Shuppanjin no ibun* (Kurita shoten, 1968), p. 25.
22. Quoted in Sumiya, *Nihon teikoku*, pp. 195–196.

in their later roles of novelist, philosopher, or academic, carrying on themes and interests manifested in this period. Autobiographical accounts in which the experience of anguish looms large are to be found for a number of the most prominent of these youth. Nevertheless, little if any of their writing addressed the historicity of their anguish, and none even began to approach the possible sociological background of the phenomenon. To the degree that the anguished youth explained their melancholy, either at the time or subsequently, they did so in terms of the influence of certain personalities, such as Fujimura Misao, or of certain writers, such as Nietzsche.[23]

Japanese scholarly writing on these youth has largely accepted at face value their statements concerning the causes of their anguish. Where some attempt has been made to explain further the appearance of the anguished youth, historians have cited such factors as the breakdown of traditional morality, especially that involving the family, a loss of purpose following the Russo-Japanese War, and a natural reaction to the costs of modernization.[24] Such explanations confuse cause with symptom, however, and the major factor in the appearance of the anguished youth can be demonstrated to have been a shift in the terms of trade for educated youth. This led to a redefinition of *risshin shusse* in terms of a romantic pursuit of self-fulfillment.

Major reasons exist for not assigning a causal role to the items being read by the anguished youth. First, with the possible exception of Nietzsche, most of the writers and writings favored by the anguished youth had been known in Japan since at least the 1880s and in some cases as early as the 1870s but had not been associated with anything resembling anguish except in the isolated instance of Kitamura Tōkoku.[25] Second, expressions of anguish were not by any means limited to the select group at the First Higher School or even

---

23. In addition to Iwanami's comments cited above, see those of Hiratsuka Raichō in *Wakon yōsai*, vol. 10 of *Nihon bungaku no rekishi* (Kadokawa shoten, 1970), p. 25.

24. This view appears to a certain degree in the following: Kamishima Jirō, "Meiji no shūen," in *Kindai Nihon seiji shisō shi I*, vol. 3 of *Kindai Nihon shisō shi taikei* (Yūhikaku, 1971), pp. 381–424; Kano Masanao, *Shihon shugi keiseiki no chitsujo ishiki* (Chikuma shobō, 1969); Sumiya Mikio, "Kokuminteki buijyon no tōgō to bunkai," in *Shidōsha to taishū*, vol. 5 of *Kindai Nihon shisō shi kōza* (Chikuma shobō, 1960), pp. 9–42.

25. For example, Kosaka notes that many of the romantic authors were introduced by Uemura Masahisa beginning in 1887 (Meiji 20). Kosaka, *Thought*, p. 183.

ANGUISHED YOUTH

to those who had been reading European romantics. Anguished young people were to be found expressing their doubts to the editors of *Seikō* [Success], which at best had a would-be elite audience.[26] The editors of *Jitsugyō no Nihon* were particularly worried about anguish among their audience, but that audience had at most little more than an elementary education and had probably not even heard of most of the European romantics let alone actually read any of them.[27] In *Seikō* there were numerous letters similar to the following:

> I have a spirit of wanting to advance. I lead the strenuous life. And, as advocated by *Seikō* magazine, to cultivate my own fate, I intently, morning and night, venerate my elder hero, Fujita Tōko. Still, somehow there is a loneliness in my heart. There is in my heart a fear and a feeling of danger about my own fate that I almost cannot bear. Since I have not yet decided what field [I will rise in], I would like your opinion on how to advance to some quietness of spirit [*ritsumeikan*]. At the same time that I avidly read the Bible, I trust in the writings of Tokutomi Roka [Kenjirō] who reflects the spirit of the Bible. I exhaust myself in crying, crying, crying. I would like to hear your view.[28]

Another *Seikō* reader remarked that "in the quietness of the night" he thought about the path before him. As a result, "I have come to feel apprehensive about this world and wonder what the pleasures of the next might be like."[29]

Letters on the theme of anguish also appeared in magazines that published student compositions. For example, *Chūgaku bundan* [Middle-School Literary Circle] had letters of the following variety:

> I am a future Napoleon!!! A future Commander Hirose!!! A future Washington!!! A future Gorky!!! Actually, I'm just a downtrodden, shivering student. Although I'm five feet [*shaku*] tall, my knowledge is inferior to a three-foot child. I put out my hand to the left and to the right, but this is only the movement of a machine. Both feet are strong, but I have yet to tread the Himalayas. I am gasping for breath with the wide mouth of an alligator caught in a whirlpool. My eyes are flashing, my face is bright, but all

---

26. The prevalence of letters from "anguished students" (*hanmonsei*) in *Seikō* is noted in Takeuchi, "Keifu to ronri," p. 46, n. 8.
27. In 1905 (Meiji 38) *Jitsugyō no Nihon* had a regular feature, "Solace in Life" (*Jinsei no ian*), aimed at anguished youth. See also Nitobe Inazō, "Yo wa naze Jitsugyō no Nihon sha no henshū komon to naritaru ka," *Jitsugyō no Nihon* 12:1 (January 1, 1909): 7–9.
28. Quoted in Mita Munesuke, *Gendai Nihon no shinjō to ronri* (Chikuma shobō, 1971), pp. 211–212. The orignal appeared in *Seikō* (April 1904).
29. "Kisha to dokusha," *Seikō* 8:5 (March 1, 1906), pp. 62–63.

213

under heaven is dark. I am nothing but a puppet on a string!!! What is my future!!![30]

Though the level of sophistication varied enormously between the First Higher School students and those who wrote to *Seikō, Chūgaku bundan,* and other similar magazines, the overall thrust was the same—uncertainty and confusion. The amusing rhetoric in the writings of youth beyond the most elite should not be cause for writing the appearance of such letters off as a simple curiosity of late Meiji culture. Something had happened to make such themes meaningful to youth of the time. Something had happened that prevented them from answering that the meaning of life was *risshin* for family or country. Something had happened to put an enormous gulf between these young people and earlier youth who had entertained no self-doubts as to whether there was more to life than *risshin*. These doubts were to be found spread throughout the spectrum of late Meiji educated youth and were by no means limited to those who had been exposed to Nietzsche or any other element of European romanticism.[31] Causal factors must be sought elsewhere.

Among those close to the anguished youth or sympathetic to them, only Anesaki Masaharu (Chōfū) made any attempt to explain the appearance of anguish in terms other than the influence of specific personalities or European romanticism. In an essay written shortly after he had returned from a study period in Europe, Anesaki analyzed the anguished youth in terms of a number of factors, including the Meiji educational system. He suggested that a major cause of anguish among youth was that late Meiji society was "too well defined," especially in terms of education.

Present-day education has as its goal the turning out of moneymaking machines the way bread is produced. It gives no place for the functioning of

---

30. "Boku no mirai," *Chūgaku bundan*, no. 184 (January 15, 1906). Punctuation as in the original.
31. The reference to Tokutomi Roka (Kenjirō) in the first *Seikō* letter cited above suggests that one model for less well educated anguished youth may have been the character Yabuki in the novel *Omoide no ki*. Although this novel is generally an optimistic and idealized treatment of *risshin*, Yabuki is an anguished youth. In one scene he says, "Why are men born to start with? We don't even know the answer to that one. All right, suppose we graduate from here to go on to the university, become bureaucrats or professors or something, keep our parents alive until they choose to die. Is that what it's for? If so, isn't it meaningless? I only have to start thinking, and it's such darkness." Later he commits suicide. Tokutomi Kenjirō, *Footprints in the Snow* [Omoide no ki], trans. Kenneth Strong (Tuttle, 1971), pp. 189–190.

human beings. Today's youth are thrown into this endeavor, oppressed by examinations and classes, and if they safely pass the obstacle course of examinations, they are graduated as deformities [katawa], not knowing who they are or why they exist.

Worst in this respect, Anesaki observed, were the (professional) colleges (senmon gakkō) and vocational education (jitsugyō kyōiku), though even the imperial universities were not much better.[32]

Anesaki's criticisms of education came closer to dealing with environmental factors, but he did a remarkable job of skirting the actual relation between education and anguish. First, it is to be noted that higher-school students were not especially oppressed by examinations or courses. For the ten-year period 1903–1912 (Meiji 36–45), the average dropout rate from higher schools for academic reasons was approximately 1.4 percent per year, or slightly more than 4 percent for the whole three-year course.[33] Recollections certainly indicate dissatisfaction with courses and teachers, but those same recollections indicate that course and exam requirements could be met by night-before cramming with borrowed notes and imposed no special burden on students. Indeed, to flunk out of higher school, one had to work at it aggressively. Abe Yoshishige, one of the anguished youth at First Higher School, mentions in his autobiography that he flunked out only after failing to attend any classes for a full year![34] The higher schools were already operating on the so-called "pass 'em out" (tokoroten) system found in contemporary Japanese higher education in which entrance assures graduation. If anything, it was the *freedom from* rigorous and continual testing that gave the higher-school students the opportunity to indulge themselves in philosophical and romantic literature. Other students actually in school and

32. Anesaki Masaharu, "Genji seinen no kumon ni tsuite," Taiyō 9:9 (August 1, 1903): 83–84.
33. From the Monbushō nenpō for the fiscal years indicated.
34. Abe Yoshishige, Waga oitachi (Iwanami shoten, 1966), p. 214. At the university level, the situation varied according to school and faculty. Kikuchi Kan, a student at the new Kyoto Imperial University, recalled later that he could pass courses on borrowed lecture notes without once ever attending certain classes or seeing the professor. Kikuchi Kan, "Han-jijoden," pp. 182–183. A Chūgaku sekai report on Tokyo Imperial University in 1907 (Meiji 40) noted few failures except in law, where a combination of tough school examinations plus the task of preparing for the higher civil service examinations saw many students ruining their health and few making it through in the anticipated four years. "Akamonha no gakkō to sono shiken seidō," Chūgaku sekai 10:8 (July 10, 1907): 42–59.

of the same age group were equally unoppressed by examinations. Even the better private schools were in no position to ride roughshod over paying customers, and the propensity to ignore academic performance increased as the quality of the school decreased.

From the turn of the century on, there were only two areas where examinations could be considered oppressive: the periodic exams in middle schools and the entrance examinations to the higher schools. Nevertheless, here again the issue was considerably more complex than Anesaki indicated. Neither type of examination was new, nor was the rote memory work associated with them. Futabatei Shimei's recollections concerning the Meiji teens make the latter point most vividly. The *Shōnenen* [A Garden for Young People] warnings cited in chapter four indicate that high rates of failure were nothing new. If anything, competition was worse before the Sino-Japanese War than immediately after, but there was no comparable anguish in the earlier period. The problem was not the examinations or the failure rates as such but what the examinations had come to mean. Future prospects for advancement rode on the examinations to a greater degree during the latter part of the period than they had in the former. The earlier exams selected from a small number of aspirants those qualified for higher education. Even those who failed were part of a small elite, not without prospect and status even in the stabilized social order proclaimed by *Shōnenen* in the 1890s.

After the turn of the century, the entrance examinations to the higher schools were three-day elimination contests cutting down the surplus of qualified applicants to the artificially limited number of places in higher education. Those who failed fell into the rapidly increasing pool of those with at least a middle-school education. Between 1897 (Meiji 30) and 1901 (Meiji 34), four times as many graduates were produced as in the period 1892–1896 (Meiji 25–29). In the next five-year period, 1902–1906 (Meiji 35–39), ten times as many graduated. By 1902 (Meiji 35) only 1 in 10 would get into higher school in his year of graduation, and as was noted in chapter five, this ratio soon fell to 1 in 20. The examinations themselves were not oppressive. Failure and the resultant condemnation to a second-class education and lowered *risshin* prospects were oppressive.

Much of the anguish among youth at large was to be found centered on the examination barrier to the higher schools. The youth who failed these examinations had before him several alternatives, each of which was conducive to psychological stress. He could simply give up his quest and return home; if he had come from a small, provincial community, the potential psychological stress involved in so doing was enormous. Such youth were few in number, were commonly sent off with some pomp, and were known to all. To come back in failure was not a pleasant prospect. As a popular Meiji poem noted, "The young man sets his goal [*kokorozashi o tateru*] and departs the gate of his home. If he does not accomplish his studies, he cannot return home even after death."[35] Unless he was an heir, he would have little to return to, and if he was an heir, he had probably gone to Tokyo over parental opposition, a combination of circumstances even less conducive to a pleasant return home.

Instead of returning home in disgrace, the seeker after *risshin* could turn away from study-for-wealth-and-honor and go into business. *Jitsugyō no Nihon* urged this course on frustrated middle-school graduates,[36] and it was becoming increasingly common. In 1898 (Meiji 31) one out of thirteen public-sector middle-school graduates was reported in Ministry of Education reports as being placed within one year of graduation in some type of business. In 1908 (Meiji 41) 1 out of 6 was reported to be so placed. This shift was not, however, made without considerable reluctance. Editorials in *Jitsugyō no Nihon* and letters to *Seikō* explicitly indicate that for many youth with a middle-school education, employment without further study was a last and unhappy resort. Giving up on the higher-school-to-imperial-university track and seeking alternative higher education was only slightly less stressful than going to work, although it too became a more common pattern. In 1898 (Meiji 31) 1 out of 9 public middle-school graduates went on to a college (*senmon gakkō*), whereas in 1905 (Meiji 38), a peak year for such schools, 1 in 3 did so.[37] Students who went into the colleges knew that both their long- and short-run prospects were inferior to the prospects of those who succeeded in entering the higher schools unless they had been among the few successful in passing the stiff examination barrier to a national (*kanritsu*) college.

35. This poem is quoted in Irokawa Daikichi, *Meiji no bunka* (Iwanami shoten, 1970), p. 32. There were others to the same effect.
36. "Okite yo dokuritsu jiei no jidai wa koreri," *Jitsugyō no Nihon* 9:1 (January 1, 1906): 12–14.
37. Calculated from Monbushō data reproduced in Sakurai, *Chūgaku kyōiku*, pp. 397 and 431.

Of the alternatives open to youth confronted with the higher-school and national-college entrance examinations, the one most conducive to anguish was the continuation of study as a *rōnin* ("masterless samurai"). This pattern became increasingly prominent just before the appearance of the anguished youth. In 1900 (Meiji 33) 1 out of 5 students successful in passing the higher-school examinations had been *rōnin*. By 1902 (Meiji 35) nearly 1 in 3 had had this experience, and in 1906 (Meiji 39) almost half of the successful applicants had been *rōnin* for a year or more.[38] For all those who were successful, there were many more who were unsuccessful.[39] Those who failed but kept studying were in a situation especially conducive to anguish. They had to spend a full year waiting for another chance, and next year the competition rate was almost sure to be higher and the pool of qualified aspirants larger.

Many of the pressures weighing on the *rōnin* were described in a short story, "Diary of an Examination Taker" (Jukensei no shuki), by Kume Masao.[40] Although written in 1918 (Taishō 7), the system and the experiences that made the story believable and popular existed from the turn of the century.[41] In this story, an aspirant to the First Higher School turns to cramming after failing his first attempt at the examination barrier. Chagrined beyond endurance when his younger brother passes and he fails, the author of the diary commits suicide. As depicted in the story, the *rōnin* was in a situation where friendships were difficult to form, since those students of comparable class and regional backgrounds were likely to become competitors. The distinct prospects that one would fail and another would pass cast a pall over possible friendships. This worked to further iso-

38. Fukaya, *Gakureki shugi*, table 71, p. 238, and *Monbushō nenpō*, no. 34 (1906), p. 145.

39. Available data do not allow ready calculation of the total number spending time as *rōnin*, but it may be noted that the proportion of middle-school graduates (public sector) listed as "unknown" increased from roughly 1 in 6 in 1898 (Meiji 31) to 1 in 3 in 1903 (Meiji 36) and to nearly 1 in 2 in 1914 (Taishō 3). A portion of these were undoubtedly *rōnin*, as were a number of those listed as "advancing to a college." Data from Sakurai, *Chūgaku kyōiku*, pp. 397, 431, and 517–518.

40. Kume Masao, "Jukensei no shuki," in *Kikuchi Kan—Kume Masao*, vol. 57 of *Nihon gendai bungaku zenshū* (Kōdansha, 1967), pp. 227–257. This story is summarized in English in *Introduction to Contemporary Japanese Literature* (Kokusai bunka shinkōkai, 1939), pp. 108–111.

41. I have also relied heavily on Ishikawa Tengai, *Tōkyō gaku*, in *Meiji bunka shiryō sōsho* (Kazama shobō, 1970), vol. 12, pp. 341–514, esp. pp. 481 ff. This was published in 1909 (Meiji 42).

late the individual who was already often far from home and possibly under considerable family pressure to do well, especially if his studies were being financed with difficulty or had involved parental opposition in the first place. Those friendships that could be formed under these circumstances tended to be with happy-go-lucky types who did not appear to be competitors. While such friendships eased isolation, they did not necessarily lead to success in the examinations. Such friends could easily lead more serious students astray, a development all the more probable since Tokyo and boardinghouse (*geshuku*) life in particular provided many temptations.

It is not coincidental that these same years saw a resurgence of warnings about the evils of life in the *geshuku*, a favorite topic of *Shōnenen* [A Garden for Young People] in the early 1890s. There was a spate of newspaper articles on what commentators described as the depravity of students. The allegedly high rate of failure of First Higher School students due to venereal disease sparked considerable press attention about this time, as did a reported gang rape of a hotel maid by middle-school students.[42] Guides to study in Tokyo published at this time repeat all the concerns of *Shōnenen* but with a much greater sense of alarm and add such new warnings as to be wary of those offering help in exchange for sodomy![43]

Whether the quality of students had in fact declined, as some contemporary observers claimed, is debatable given the reputation of earlier *shosei* ("students"), but there was definitely a very large number of students without formal school affiliation and supervision. One survey of the period claimed eighteen thousand such students in Tokyo and argued that only 20 percent of all the fifty thousand middle-school students in the city were virtuous and law abiding.[44] Even allowing for a good measure of hyperbole, there is reason for giving credence to such reports. In addition to the increasing pressure of examination competition, there was a change in the

---

42. Concerning the gang rape and other alleged student depravities, see "Gakusei no daraku," *Rikugō zasshi*, no. 259 (July 15, 1902), pp. 66–67. Concerning V.D. among First Higher School Students, see Inoue Tetsujirō, "Gakusei no fūki mondai ni tsuite," *Taiyō* 12:13 (October 1, 1906): 63–74. This article is in part a refutation of the claims made about student V.D. in the *Yorozu*. According to Inoue, only thirteen had V.D., far fewer than the *Yorozu* claimed. Nevertheless, he was concerned about the apparent deterioration in the quality of students.

43. Yanagiuchi Yoshinosuke, *Tōto to gakusei* (Shinsei sha, 1901), p. 41.

44. Ibid., pp. 21–23. Yanagiuchi's source is a *Yorozu* survey.

demographic characteristics of students. In the 1880s middle-school entrants had ranged upward to as high as age twenty and had included a number of married students. Thanks to the stabilization of the social order in the late 1880s and early 1890s and improvements in lower-level education, the age of middle-school students and hence those cramming in Tokyo declined.[45] This meant a clustering of students in the middle and late teens, years of physiological and psychological turmoil, even without the stresses that came from the ever increasing difficulty of securing what the 1872 (Meiji 5) proclamation had styled the capital for rising in the world.

Other contemporary observers, who had less of a tendency to intellectualize the anguish phenomenon than did Anesaki and modern Japanese historians, early noted the apparent connection between it and the *risshin* crisis of the interwar period. Sakai Kosen, Kōtoku Denjirō, Ishikawa Takuboku, and Tokutomi Iichirō, among others, specifically related the anguished youth to the difficulty of getting into higher education or to the declining market value of educated youth.[46] Nevertheless, at first glance the failure of the Meiji promise of *risshin* for all through education would seem inapplicable as an explanation for the anguish of First Higher School students and those who had recently graduated with an elite education. Such students or graduates were, to use a contemporary Japanese phrase, on an escalator that would take them to the highest positions of wealth and power in Japanese society. How then could they be affected by the failure of *risshin*? The answer is rather simple. Such youth did not look at their less fortunate peers or their own distant future but, as many contemporary observers lamented, compared themselves with youth of the 1880s and 1870s, or even with those of the immediate Restoration period when rises were breathtakingly rapid not frustratingly slow.

45. For data, see Fukaya, *Gakureki shugi*, pp. 183, 239. Yanagiuchi, *Tōto to gakusei*, p. 45, complained that parents were allowing or pushing children into study in Tokyo when they were not mature enough to be away from home.

46. For some of the *many* contemporary observations that link *hanmon* to the changing position of educated youth, see Tokutomi Iichirō, *Taishō seinen*, pp. 17 ff; "Seinen to seizon kyōsō," *Rikugō zasshi*, no. 285 (September 15, 1904), p. 74; Sakai Kosen "Renai bungaku to shakai shugi," *Chūō kōron* 21:3 (1906): 100 ff; "Gyakkyō no seinen," *Shinsei* (June 30, 1901), pp. 8–11; "Seinen shippai no ichidai-riyū," *Rikugō zasshi*, no. 229 (January 15, 1900), pp. 9–12. Kōtoku Denjiro, "Seinen no dai-fuhei," *Shinbun* 1:3 (July 1, 1901), in *Kōtoku zenshū*, vol. 3, pp. 396–400.

ANGUISHED YOUTH

Editorials in a variety of youth- and adult-oriented publications graphically demonstrate that the position of educated youth, even those with the most elite education, was rapidly falling as the Meiji period wore on. On the eve of the Sino-Japanese War *Nihon no shōnen* [Young People of Japan] had observed that the first decade of the era (1868–1877) had been "a very good time" for rising in the world. The second decade (1878–1887) had seen "not a few" rise in the world. Now, however, only one out of ten, or fewer, could expect to achieve their ambitions.[47] In 1893 (Meiji 26) *Kokumin no tomo* predicted on the basis of 1891 (Meiji 24) data that in the near future those achieving their dreams would fall to but one in a thousand, and there soon would be thousands, even tens of thousands of university-educated *rōnin* who would spend years before they eventually found employment in such trivial positions as ten-yen-a-month elementary-school teachers. Already, the magazine claimed, a hundred or so of the some four hundred university graduates were spending some period masterless before they found jobs, and in the future this would grow, especially if plans to increase the number of universities were realized.[48]

There was more than a little hyperbole and speculation in this account. It did not allow for the boom that came with the Sino-Japanese War or for a sharp drop in the number of private-college graduates. As a consequence, the situation did not deteriorate quite as rapidly as was predicted, but when the Sino-Japanese War boom ended, the situation for educated youth began to approximate that forecast in the journal. A *Nihonjin* [The Japanese] editorial in 1899 (Meiji 32) sounded one of the first postwar alarms when it noted that a graduate in medicine "a few years before" could have expected 100

This failure of Japanese scholarship to deal with the material origins of anguish presumably reflects a desire to give the frustrations and criticisms of Meiji society expressed in this period a meaning beyond simple self-interest. However laudable this goal, it makes for poor history. An interesting example of this in operation is the use made of Ishikawa Takuboku's essay "Jidai heisoku no genjō." It is frequently cited in the context of criticizing the oppressiveness of the Meiji state. This it in fact does, but a reading of the *whole* essay reveals Takuboku to have been equally or *more* concerned about the difficulty of getting into higher school and the low pay for educated youth! This essay is found in all collections of his work. I used Ishikawa Takuboku, "Jidai heisoku no genjō," in *Kunikida Doppo—Ishikawa Takuboku,* vol. 12 of *Nihon bungaku zenshū* (Shūei sha, 1967), pp. 390–400.

47. "Shōnen no zento," *Nihon no shōnen* (February 2, 1894), pp. 2–5.
48. "Gakusei no zento," *Kokumin no tomo,* no. 196 (July 13, 1893), pp. 7–11.

to 150 yen a month to start, but this had fallen until the graduate who found a job at over 100 yen a month was "most rare and an object of envy" to his less fortunate peers.[49] A 1903 (Meiji 36) editorialist in *Fukoku seinen* [Youth of a Rich Country] claimed he found it "difficult to recall" the era when a student could expect a 100-yen-per-month job on graduation. "Now," he observed, "they fight for a 25-yen-per-month job in the bureaucracy." Those going into banking, he claimed, could expect but 10 to 15 yen a month.[50] Nakamura Fusetsu wrote in 1911 (Meiji 44) that the difference between the time of the Daigaku Nankō (first-decade predecessor of the Imperial University) and the present was the difference between many offers leading to at least 100 yen per month and a few offers leading to a 20- or 25-yen job *if* one's grades were especially good.[51] When allowance is made for price-level changes, the declining position of educated youth is even more striking. Between 1879 (Meiji 12) and 1911 (Meiji 44), prices nearly doubled, meaning that there was not a 4 or 5 to 1 ratio between early Meiji and late Meiji salaries but rather an 8 or 10 to 1 ratio.[52]

This relationship may be seen more clearly by considering civil service salaries, since by contemporary observations government employment was the usual first choice of those with higher education. In 1887 (Meiji 20) the average monthly pay of the lowest of the three major divisions of the civil service, the *hannin*, was 17.1 yen. In 1897 (Meiji 30) it was 18.4 yen, a decline in real terms of approximately 19 percent in ten years. For the *sōnin* ranks to which college and university graduates aspired, the average monthly pay in 1887 (Meiji 20) was 73.4 yen. In 1897 (Meiji 30) the corresponding amount was 83.4 yen, and in 1902 (Meiji 35), 91.0 yen. In real terms these absolute increases represented declines of 13 and 18 percent, respectively. In 1907 (Meiji 40) the discrepancy was even greater: 29 percent in real terms. If anything, the lower ranks received better compensation for inflation, with the result that the ratio of average

49. "Kanritsu daigaku sotsugyōsei no bunpu," *Nihonjin* (August 5, 1899), pp. 1–3.
50. "Shōkai zappei no gakumon," *Fukoku seinen*, no. 3 (February 5, 1903), pp. 1–4. See also "Hisan naru gakkō no sotsugyōsei," *Hikari* (November 20, 1905), p. 4.
51. Nakamura Fusetsu, "Shoshitsu yori mitaru gendai shakai," *Taiyō*, 17:3 (March 1911): 17–21. See also Dore, "Mobility," p. 132.
52. Price-level data from *Prices*, vol. 8 of *Estimates of Long-Term Economic Statistics of Japan Since 1868*, ed. Kazushi Ohkawa, Miyohei Shinohara, and Mataji Umemura (Tōyō keizai shinpō sha, 1967), table 2, col. 3, pp. 135–136.

sōnin to average *hannin* compensation dropped from 4.3 in 1887 (Meiji 20) to 3.7 in 1902 (Meiji 35).[53]

The ratio of university-graduate earnings to those of minimally educated manual workers also narrowed substantially during and after the Sino-Japanese war. In 1889 (Meiji 22) a barely passing Imperial University graduate could expect a government job paying at least 37.5 yen per month. This was 7.5 times the average monthly earnings of male workers in the manufacturing sector. In 1903 (Meiji 36), the year of Fujimura's suicide and the appearance of the anguished youth, those Imperial University graduates who found only the 25-yen-per-month job that observers claimed was usual, were starting at only 2.3 times the average wage for males in manufacturing and just 1.6 times the average monthly earnings of skilled construction workers. In 1911 (Meiji 44), when Nakamura Fusetsu made his observations, the 25-yen-per-month wage for university graduates was only 1.2 times that prevailing in the construction trades. Although university graduates enjoyed better working conditions and would in the long run have much greater income and incomparably greater career prospects, this situation was quite a comedown for those who had devoted their lives to study under the expectation that it would lead them *directly* to wealth and honor. Moreover, the low initial wage for university graduates was more acutely felt in these years because many graduates were in their late twenties or even early thirties as a consequence of the years they had had to spend as *rōnin* cramming to get into the higher schools.[54]

Along with a decrease in pay, there was a decrease in the power and prestige that accrued to the educated youth upon graduation.

---

53. These *unweighted* averages were calculated from *Meiji Taishō kokusei sōran* (Tōyō keizai shinpō sha, 1975 [1927]), table 737, p. 664.

54. For starting compensation of Imperial University graduates in 1889 (Meiji 22), see Spaulding, *Higher Civil Service*, p. 91. For the wages of blue-collar workers, see *Prices*, vol. 8 of *Estimates of Long-Term Economic Statistics*, table 25, pp. 243–245. To compare the monthly wages of white-collar workers with the daily wages of blue-collar workers, a twenty-five-day month was assumed for the latter. This assumption probably understates their earnings. Although the specific ratios cited here cannot be regarded as precise indications of the magnitude of the changes taking place, they do point to what was most certainly a decline in the earnings premium attached to higher education. Concerning the impact of cramming on graduation age, see *The Japan Year Book 1911*, p. 211; "Waga-kuni no shiken-byō," *Chūō kōron* 17:2 (February 1, 1902): 5–8; and Ōmachi Keigetsu, "Educational Reforms," *The Sun* 7:7 (June 10, 1902): 1–2.

What this meant in a specific field, education, can be seen by comparing observations concerning career possibilities in early and late Meiji Japan. Yamaji Aizan, one of the original Minyūsha group, described the early Meiji era as a period when a youth in his teens with a Western education could become headmaster over men many years his senior simply by virtue of that education. An editorial in *Nihonjin* in 1905 (Meiji 38) observed that at the time even graduates of the Higher Normal School were having trouble finding positions.[55] When Abe Yoshishige graduated in 1909 (Meiji 42) with his even more prestigious Tokyo Imperial University education, the best job he could find was teaching at a middle school for twenty-five yen per month. Although Abe eventually became Minister of Education, he did not achieve that status until 1946 when he was sixty-three years old.[56] Mori Arinori, the first Minister of Education, had gained office in 1885 (Meiji 18) at age thirty-eight, and he had done so on the basis of a fragmentary, foreign education that would not have been recognized in the latter part of the period. There was still advancement to be had, but it would come at a much slower pace than it had early in the period and only after a long time spent in menial positions with little opportunity for self-expression.

Low starting rank and pay were not the only signs of decreased status. Although most histories present unemployment among those with a university education as a phenomenon that first appeared in Japan after World War I,[57] there is much evidence of such unemployment as early as 1900 (Meiji 33). Kinoshita Naoe wrote in *Shakai shugi* [Socialism] in 1903 (Meiji 36) that unemployment during the 1900–1903 (Meiji 33–36) depression was a problem "even for those with a university education."[58] Similarly, Kuroiwa Ruikō, editor and

---

55. Yamaji Aizan is cited in Pyle, *New Generation*, pp. 12–13. For the fate of Higher Normal School graduates, see "Kanshi daigaku no sotsugyōsei," *Nihonjin*, no. 416 (August 5, 1905), p. 1. The Higher Normal School is not to be confused with the First Higher School where Fujimura was a student.

56. Abe, *Waga oitachi*, p. 425.

57. See Henry Dewitt Smith, II, *Japan's First Student Radicals* (Harvard University Press, 1972), p. 17, and Karasawa, *Gakusei*, p. 211–212.

58. Quoted from *Shakai shugi* (August 18, 1903) in Matsunari Yoshie, Izutani Hajime, Tanuma Hajime, and Noda Masaho, *Nihon no sarariiman* (Aoki shoten, 1957), p. 29. See also "Hisan naru gakkō sotsugyōsei," *Hikari* (November 20, 1905), p. 4. This article claims that imperial university graduates were becoming provincial-school teachers in lieu of better jobs.

Cartoon from Chūō kōron [Central Review] depicting hordes of 1902 (Meiji 35) graduates in higher education seeking to board the overcrowded streetcar to success.

publisher of the *Yorozu chōhō* [Complete Morning News], addressed a group of young men in 1903 (Meiji 36), declaring:

> There is an army of young men who are quite willing to work and who know how to earn their daily bread, but employment is not very easy to find. It is not so rare that even men with the proud title of "so and so *gakushi* [university graduate]" fail to secure employment.[59]

A cartoon in *Chūō kōron* in 1903 (Meiji 36) depicted a mass of new graduates waiting to climb on board an already overcrowded streetcar that would take them to success.[60]

Chūgaku sekai [Middle-School World], the journal that catered to those seeking entry into government schools, succinctly described the situation facing educated youth during the years when the anguished youth first appeared. The magazine observed that in the past it had been possible to gain a "very likable rank" on the basis of very little education, but with the increase in those similarly equipped, it was no longer a "seller's market" but rather a "buyer's market." In a decided understatement, the magazine declared that the increase in graduates at all levels "certainly dealt a great blow to today's students and graduates."[61] After the Russo-Japanese War, things were no better, possibly even worse. Nakamura Fusetsu, a socially concerned artist, wrote in *Taiyō* [The Sun] of unemployment even among imperial university graduates, and the question of "educated idlers" (*kyōiku aru yūmin*) or "high-class idlers" (*kōtō yūmin*) became an issue for journalistic and political debate.[62]

No precise index of the market for youth with college and university education is available, but several simple comparisons tend to

---

59. "Mr. Kuroiwa's Advice to Students," *Yorozu Weekly* (November 16, 1903), p. 1. Only students who graduated from the regular degree course of a legally recognized university (only the imperial universities until 1918) earned the title *gakushi*. Prewar sources give "M.A." as the translation for *gakushi* and "B.A." as the translation for *tokugakushi*, the degree awarded by the higher schools. *The Japan Year Book 1920–1921*, pp. 243–244, and *The Japan Year Book 1930*, p. 168. Journalistic accounts do not always observe the legalistic distinction and refer to *senmon gakkō* as *daigaku* and to their graduates as *gakushi*. Adding to the confusion is the presence in the imperial universities of students who entered directly from middle school. Mostly in agriculture and medicine, they were called *seito* to distinguish them from regular degree candidates (*gakusei*).

60. This cartoon is reproduced in the text.

61. "Shoseihō ni tsuite," *Chūgaku sekai* (November 10, 1904), pp. 4–5.

62. Nakamura Fusetsu, "Shoshitsu yori mitaru," p. 17; "Question of the Educated Unemployed," *The Japan Year Book 1911*, p. 411; "Kyōiku aru yūmin no shochi mondai," *Chūō kōron* 27:7 (July 1912): 75–90.

confirm the journalistic descriptions. The ratio of all (Tokyo) Imperial University graduates to the yearly increment in the *sōnin* class of the civil service was near unity in the period 1893–1897 (Meiji 26–30), but climbed steadily after the Sino-Japanese War until it averaged 2 to 1 in the years 1903–1912 (Meiji 36–45). Subsequently this ratio climbed to 7 to 1 for the interval 1913–1917 (Taishō 2–6). If graduates of the new imperial universities (Kyoto, Tohoku, Kyushu, and Hokkaido), which were just entering the market in the early twentieth century, were added to the calculation, the change would be even more dramatic. It is this ratio that helps to explain the increase in (Tokyo) Imperial University graduates listed in Ministry of Education data as "unknown or employment not yet determined" to nearly 40 percent in 1914 (Taishō 3) and to almost 60 percent for law faculty graduates. These rates were two to three times the levels that were usual before the Russo-Japanese War and up to six times those prevailing in the late 1890s. Comparable placement data was not collected for private-college graduates. The ratio of private law-college graduates to the yearly increments in the *sōnin* class of civil servants, always more than unity, climbed to nearly 6 to 1 in the years 1903–1907 (Meiji 36–40) but declined thereafter as the number of such graduates stabilized and then declined from a peak in 1910 (Meiji 43).[63] Students and their parents apparently had second thoughts about the value of nonelite higher education.

Because the anguished youth did not begin to search for meaning in life beyond conventional *risshin* until it was no longer the immediate and automatic product of a certain level of education, a strong suspicion arises that their religious, literary, and philosophical interests were part of a quest for alternatives to conventional *risshin* or compensation for its loss. Examination of themes appearing in youth magazines, autobiographical writings, and critiques from the

63. Readily available statistical compendia do not give the number of civil servants hired or promoted in each year. As a *crude* substitute for this figure, I have used the year to year increase in employment (ignoring years of reported decrease). This figure is doubtless much lower than actual hiring and promotion, but even if openings amounting to five or ten percent of each year's employment are added to the calculations (to allow for hiring and promotion to replace attrition), the pattern described in the text still holds: the ratio of higher education graduates to higher civil service opportunities increased sharply in the latter part of the Meiji period. The data used are from *Meiji Taishō kokusei sōran*, table 737, p. 664, and *Monbushō nenpō* for the *fiscal* years indicated.

years just before the Fujimura incident does much to confirm this apparent relationship between the market for youth with secondary and higher education and their anguished mental state. At the same time, this material discredits the explanations of anguish given in Japanese scholarly writing. Most easily dismissed is the idea that victory in the Russo-Japanese War had fulfilled those early Meiji goals of national security and wealth and as a consequence later Meiji youth were left without direction or were freed to think of themselves rather than the state.[64]

The small number of *Eisai shinshi* [Talent Forum] compositions in the 1870s mentioning the nation suggests that most educated youth had not been pressed to link their aspirations to state goals long before the Russo-Japanese War. It was only in the 1880s and again in the 1890s that declarations of personal ambition in a context of service to the state or the emperor became the norm. This pattern of composition was, however, short-lived, disappearing not after the Russo-Japanese War but during the Sino-Japanese War. *Eisai shinshi* had an essay or two on heroes in each issue during the first war and a few articles on opportunities for *risshin* through imperialistic expansion, but even at the height of the war, the bulk of its material was literary, especially articles on the composition of "new form poetry" (*shintai-shi*). After the war this trend continued. The immediate postwar years saw the founding of a large number of "little magazines" dedicated to the new literary form and something that was called "elegant prose" (*bibun*). Compositions on *risshin* in general and such common prewar topics as enterprise (*jitsugyō*) for the nation in particular became extraordinarily rare. Even with the traditionally nationalistic editorial line of Hakubunkan, both *Chūgaku sekai* and *Shōnen sekai* came to resemble the "little magazines" with their "elegant prose" and poetry.[65]

Taoka Reiun, a critic affiliated with several of the "little maga-

---

64. For examples of this thesis, see Sumiya, "Kokuminteki *buijon*," pp. 14–15; Oka, "Nichiro sensō go," pp. 140–141; Kamishima, "Meiji shūen," p. 385; and Maruyama Masao, "Patterns of Individuation and the Case of Japan: A Conceptual Scheme," in *Changing Japanese Attitudes Toward Modernization*, ed. Marius B. Jansen (Princeton University Press, 1965), p. 510.

65. Some sense of this change may be gained from the theme counts given in Yasuda Saburō, *Shakai idō no kenkyū* (Tōkyō daigaku shuppan-kai, 1971), pp. 434–435.

zines" of this period,[66] specifically linked these developments to the declining position of youth. Taoka observed that youth, and by this he meant rather well educated youth, were turning to literature, seeking what he described as a "quick fame" made possible by the new literary forms that did not require effort and practice.[67] Instead of seeking this cheap fame in literature, youth should have been, Taoka asserted, holding dreams like those expressed in the ditty "Shosei bushi" [Student Song], which was in effect a classic statement of early Meiji *risshin* aspirations. It proclaimed that government officials, cabinet ministers, even Napoleon, were once students (*shosei*). Taoka did not directly explain why this traditional concept of *risshin* was no longer common, but his idea of a "second Meiji Restoration" points at declining opportunities.

Tokutomi Iichirō had promised a "second Restoration" of opportunity with the convening of parliament. *Shōnen sekai* had located this in imperialistic expansion. Taoka instead demanded a "second Restoration" to restore the avenues to opportunity that the first had promised but which had since been closed off. According to Taoka, Japan in the late 1890s was a dead end for youth just as the late Tokugawa had been.

Thirty years after the Restoration revolution [*ishin kakumei*], I see another dead end for talent. Although the Restoration revolution smashed the cliques of the honored and despised [*sonpi*], I see a new grouping distinct from the old. Those who rose before [*kyūshin*] have filled up the places ahead and the latecomers [*shinshin*] cannot advance. The latecomers, who are increasing in number, are falling into the pit of despair while those who rose before remain without moving.

According to Taoka, the only opportunities that existed in contemporary Meiji society accrued to those with "clever tongues," those who would advance "by means of small clevernesses."[68] Precisely what he meant by this is not clear, but the reader should recall the personality types presented in *Ukigumo* [Floating Clouds] and "Systematic Study" in chapter four.

Taoka's own response to this situation was twofold. He chided

66. See Ienaga Saburō, *Suki naru shisōka no shōgai* (Iwanami shinsho, 1955), for a biography of Taoka.
67. Taoka Reiun, "Shinshun no dai-ikkatsu," in *Reiun yōei*, in *Meiji shisōka shū*, vol. 13 of *Gendai Nihon bungaku zenshū* (Kōdansha, 1968), pp. 240–241.
68. "Jinzai no yōsoku," in *Reiun yōei*, p. 235.

youth for celebrating their own melancholies and for creating poetry on hackneyed themes, such as flowers, birds, wind, the moon, and love. He urged them to turn instead to "giving voices to the tragedies and resentments of the poor."[69] Carrying his analogy between the late 1890s and late Tokugawa Japan to its logical conclusion, Taoka argued that because youth at the end of the Tokugawa period had responded to their era's "dead end for talent" by destroying the system, it was the *duty* of present-day youth to act in the same way. He went so far as to call upon youth to "take up the knife" and join him in "destroying the cliques and renovating society." Such action, he declared, would bring an end to the "melancholy" among youth.[70]

Sakai Kosen and Kōtoku Denjirō said much the same thing about the relation between melancholy and the falling position of youth. They too urged a greater social concern,[71] but except for a brief flurry of interest over the Ashio copper-mine-pollution incident, the general tendency until World War I remained that of introspection. Educated youth had not traditionally been popular social activists. The number who looked to the peasantry during the movement for liberty and people's rights had been but a tiny fraction of all youth nominally interested in politics. More typical was the case of Ishizaka Masatsugu. Just because *risshin* was beginning to fail did not mean an automatic shift to social activism. There were no ongoing movements for youth to cleave to, and in the short run, literature and the discovery of self were more attractive than any social activism, which would have required a long-run commitment and a great deal of effort to start something that did not exist.

The diary of the poet and short-story writer Kunikida Doppo provides an example of how the failure of *risshin* and the promise of literary fame could come together to produce an anguish that tended to be at best introspective and at worst suicidal, not social in orientation. Kunikida was, by his own frequent and public admission, an anguished youth. Indeed, his diary, which was a "semipublic" project,

69. "Hyūmanichi," in *Reiun yōei*, pp. 248–249.
70. "Seinen shokei ni gekisu," *Reiun yōei*, pp. 237–238.
71. See Sakai Kosen, "Shōnen shōjo no kyoeishin ni tōzuru shōryaku," *Yorozu* (April 21, 1903), in *Sakai zenshū*, vol. 1, pp. 262–263, and Kōtoku Denjirō, "Seinen no dai-fuhei," *Shinbun* 1:3 (July 1, 1901), in *Kōtoku zenshū*, vol. 3, pp. 396–400. For another contemporary view suggesting that literature was becoming popular as an alternative to conventional *risshin*, see Gotō Chūgai, "Kadoki no gisei," *Shinshōsetsu* 7:7 (July 1, 1902): pp. 151–153.

is one of the earliest examples to be found of the general and repeated use of the term and may well have served to popularize it.[72] This anguish, as it appeared over and over again in his diary, stemmed from a matter of not knowing what course to pursue.

> What am I to see?
> What am I to believe?
> What ought I to do?
> If I ought not to be seeking fame and
>   fortune, then what ought I to be doing?

This confusion came in turn from being torn between two definitions of *risshin*: the conventional one of *risshin* as fame and fortune, derived from the general expectations of Meiji society and his peers; and a more idealistic vision derived in part from Christianity, in part from sources similar to those of Kitamura Tōkoku, and in part from alternative readings of standard materials on *risshin*. He told himself that he ought to go into missionary work, but he still had dreams of fame and fortune through literature, politics, law, commerce, agriculture—something, anything. None was sufficiently enticing to hold his attention. Dreams of conventional *risshin* prevented him from pursuing an idealistic *risshin*, and visions of a higher calling prevented him from following conventional *risshin*. He oscillated between the two, lamenting that his youth was passing without accomplishment. He turned to various sources and asked friends for advice. Tokutomi gave him Franklinesque homilies. Yamaji gave him O. S. Marden's *Pushing to the Front*, which Kunikida read, noting in his diary that he was "impressed." He also read Byron and Burns and recorded in his diary that he cried as he read.

The conflicting advice and values he found in his readings served only to confuse him, and near the end of 1895 (Meiji 28) he wrote:

Ought I to look at the universe (*tenchi*) and life (*jinsei*) in the manner of the Old Testament? Should I look at them in the manner of the New Testament? In the manner of Carlyle? In the manner of Wordsworth? In the manner of Franklin? In the manner of *Saikoku risshi hen*?

---

72. This is his "Azamukazaru no ki," of which at least part was published before his death and before the Fujimura incident. Various reprints exist. I have used the abbreviated version found in *Kunikida Doppo shū*, vol. 18 of *Nihon gendai bungaku zenshū* (Kōdansha, 1962), pp. 336–419.

Marital problems added to his confusion, but throughout the diary his main concern was the difficulty of choice between conventional *risshin* and some idealistic endeavor. He looked to breaking sod in Hokkaido and considered going to America for a new start. He continually considered suicide, though he confessed that he lacked the courage. And, throughout all, he wrote and published his thoughts, egotistically believing as did the later naturalist (*shizen shugi*) novelists that the trivia and frustrations of daily existence constituted the essence of literature. Thus, Kunikida was a complete microcosm of the anguished youth and success youth all in one monumentally confused individual.

Kunikida at age twenty-five in 1895 (Meiji 28) was a transitional figure. He stood between two traditions. He was old enough to have been caught up in early Meiji concepts of *risshin* as political adventure, and he labored under Tokutomi Iichirō, one of the most vocal and articulate spokesmen for *risshin* in conformity to state demands. He was young enough to still have dreams which outran his likely capability for achievement, since he was outside of any defined route to *risshin*.[73] He was too early a figure to be embarrassed about confessing his interest in *risshin* (unlike Iwanami), but like the later anguished youth, his own problems were far more important to him than were those of the nation.[74] He was partially freed from conventional constraints and supports for *risshin*, but as he himself lamented over and over again, he was not entirely so freed. He was not, despite the model of Kitamura Tōkoku and access to the same sources Kitamura used, in possession of a philosophy to give his doubts and frustrations transcendent meaning, to make the repudiation of any and all social norms, especially those pertaining to *risshin*, into a virtue.

Such a philosophy did not come until 1901 (Meiji 34), when it appeared primarily in certain writings from Takayama Chogyū (Rinjirō), a thirty-one-year-old literary critic and editor of *Taiyō*, the main adult-oriented journal from Hakubunkan. Second only to Fu-

---

73. See Maeda Shigeru, "Meiji no seiji seinen," *Tenbō* (December 1948), p. 14.

74. Jay Rubin points out that while Kunikida had been a correspondent during the Sino-Japanese War, he made absolutely no mention of the war after his return to Japan even though it was still going on. See Jay Rubin, "Kunikida Doppo" (Ph.D. dissertation, University of Chicago, 1970), pp. 44–45, 60.

jimura Misao in the recollections of the anguished youth (and as a target of those who were hostile to them), Takayama's most famous essay, "On the Aesthetic Life" (Biteki seikatsu o ronzu). became almost a manifesto for the anguished youth.[75] In this essay, Takayama began by rejecting any notion that behavior was or should be governed by "moral norms." Taking the example of Kusunoki Masashige, the hoariest example of the feudal ethic of sacrifice for one's lord to be found, Takayama declared that Kusunoki would not have acted as he did in response to such abstract moral principles as "loyalty" (chūgi) and filial piety (kōtei). Kusunoki acted as he did because this made him feel something in his own heart, and he could feel this only because he had a real lord, not some moral abstraction to sacrifice for. The relation between motivation and act was not ethical; it was a matter of instinct, as in the case of a baby when it reaches for the breast. Therefore, *if* there was a meaning in life, it had to be found outside of concepts of good and bad, outside of that which society sought to define as valuable. This meant that the individual himself and his instincts were the only source of validation for any activity.

We do not know for what purpose we were born into this world. Nevertheless, it goes without saying that once born into this world, our object is happiness [kōfuku]. What is happiness? It is nothing, I believe, but the satisfaction of instinct. What is instinct? It is the fundamental need of human nature. What fulfills the fundamental need of human nature is what I call the aesthetic life [biteki seikatsu].

All was to be subject to the individual's aesthetic judgment and morality, and even intelligence itself had no role other than to help the individual realize his instinct, which, Takayama noted, was ultimately directed to the satisfaction of sexual desire.

It was not sexual gratification that Takayama emphasized, although this statement in particular was singled out for attack by some contemporary critics. In defining the aesthetic life, Takayama stressed such examples as the scholar who pursues knowledge with-

75. For comments on the impact of Takayama, see: Fujiwara, *Kyōiku shisō*, vol. 2, pp. 130–134; Karasawa, *Gakusei*, pp. 73–74; Kosaka, *Japanese Thought*, p. 360; Abe, *Waga oitachi*, pp. 268, 341. Takayama's writings are reproduced in numerous literary collections. I have used *Takayama Chogyū—Anesaki Chōfū—Sasakawa Rinpū*, vol. 14 of *Gendai Nihon bungaku zenshū* (Kaizō sha, 1928). See "Biteki seikatsu o ronzu," in *Takayama Chogyū*, pp. 206–211.

out regard to the value of that knowledge, the miser who hoards not for a goal but because he enjoys it, and the Trappist monks, about whom he remarked, "How fortunate they are to have found a paradise in life outside of wealth and fame." Still more highly did he praise the poet and the artist who pursued their works in poverty, cut off from home and facing official wrath, although Takayama never took even the smallest step in the latter direction himself. In these diverse examples, the unifying theme was the pursuit of some goal without reference to socially determined criteria such as wealth and fame. "The kingdom is always in your breast. The realization of that kingdom is the aesthetic life," he concluded.

In Takayama's essay, Meiji youth acquired a more complete exposition of the self-made man than that offered by any earlier writer save Kitamura Tōkoku. Takayama's self-made man was more complete in the sense that he could and indeed had to choose of his own free will what it was that he would do in society. All early Meiji writers except Kitamura had demanded that youth seek to alter their position in society, but in so doing, they gave no more recognition to true individual aspiration than did Tokugawa writers. Early Tokugawa ideologues had demanded stasis for the good of society. Early Meiji ideologues began by demanding mobility for the good of the society. Both gave the individual no choice.

Takayama extended absolute recognition to individual aspiration up to and including the rejection of society and social convention so that the individual could become self-made not only in terms of altering his position in society but in defining his relation with society. Takayama gave Meiji youth a vision of complete individualism up to and including eccentricity and hedonism. His individualism was not just that of Tokutomi Iichirō and earlier writers who were interested solely in individual performance for state or social purposes and who did not recognize the supremacy of the individual as such. Takayama clearly belonged to a different generation, one with a sense of self unimaginable by early Meiji standards, when he declared, "If one does not live for one's own sake, then to what purpose ought he to live? While I'm not necessarily one to make light of society and the state, I don't think they compare with my own importance."[76]

76. "Mudai roku," in *Takayama Chogyū*, p. 290.

Nevertheless, for all his apparent repudiation of contemporary social values, especially the general emphasis on the pursuit of *risshin*, Takayama was a product of late Meiji society; his thought was shaped by his own personal *risshin* frustrations, and it gained currency because it provided an answer to the *risshin* discontents of educated youth. Takayama first appeared on the Meiji literary scene in 1894 (Meiji 27) as a lyric poet, author of *Takiguchi Nyūdō* [The Lay Priest Takiguchi], and as a translator of Goethe's *Sorrows of Young Werther*.[77] His lyricism soon gave way to stridency, and in 1897 (Meiji 30) he emerged as the proponent of an expansionistic and imperialistic philosophy that he called Japanism (*Nihon shugi*).[78]

The years after the Sino-Japanese War had seen many different expansionistic and imperialistic philosophies being put forward. Because Takayama switched from lyricism to imperialism after others had popularized expansionistic thought, his own change smacks greatly of opportunism, an impression that is heightened when one notes that he assigned a preeminent position to national culture in the future struggle between nations that he postulated. He seems to have been trying to link his own personal star to the rising sun of Japanese imperialism. He emphasized the role of critics in leading and shaping national culture, and his essays make clear that he saw himself as the director of Japanese cultural development.[79] Nevertheless, while he had *Taiyō* [The Sun], the most important opinion journal of the day, as his monthly platform, his essays continually lament that critics (Takayama himself) were not being heeded. The public, he observed, was too stupid to realize the worth of critics and kept asking why critics (Takayama) did not write examples of the sort of works they believed necessary.[80] Unable to answer this other than by saying that present-day society was "too complex" to per-

---

77. See Kosaka, *Thought*, p. 303, and Harry D. Harootunian, "Between Politics and Culture: Authority and the Ambiguities of Intellectual Choice in Imperial Japan," in Bernard S. Silberman and H. D. Harootunian, eds., *Japan in Crisis: Essays on Taishō Democracy* (Princeton: Princeton University Press, 1974), p. 139.
78. His basic statement of this concept is found in the essay "Nihon shugi," in *Takayama Chogyū*, pp. 202–205.
79. See "Waga-kuni genkon no bungeikai ni okeru hihyōka no honmu," in *Takayama Chogyū*, pp. 243–248.
80. This frustration is expressed in the essay cited above and even more strongly in "Tsuchii Bansui ni ataete tōkon no bundan o ronzuru sho," in *Takayama Chogyū*, pp. 254–259.

mit the dual role of author and critic, Takayama found a way out of his personal dilemma in the writings of Nietzsche.[81]

According to Takayama, Nietzsche was a critic of culture and civilization (*kulturkritiker*) who was at war with statistics, customs, myth, inheritance (genetics), environment, truth, history—all of the "so-called scientific thought" of the nineteenth century, which would place limits on the individual, which would deny subjectivity, instinct, and emotion. In Nietzsche, Japanese youth had found an ally who recognized the value of the soul, of subjectivity, of the individual in the face of nineteenth-century thought, which would seek to destroy these. It was Nietzsche who countered the idea that humanism was to lead to mass equality and prosperity. The true purpose of humanism was in the production of a few model individuals, the *Übermensch* (*chōjin*) for whom the masses existed. What this meant in personal terms is that Takayama found in Nietzsche an ally for his own views and an aura that he could draw down upon himself. He gleefully celebrated the popularity and fame of Nietzsche in Germany and Europe at large, almost echoing early Meiji composition writers celebrating the fame of Toyotomi Hideyoshi or George Washington. Since Takayama had been staking out a position as the critic of Japanese culture, he did not need to explicitly equate himself with Nietzsche. Because his celebration of Nietzsche focused on his criticism rather than his creative works, Takayama had an answer for the problem of his own criticism without creativity. Finally, because the true critic of civilization as postulated by Takayama did not "cultivate the applause of inferior readers" Takayama could make a virtue out of rejecting that which was not offered!

All of this was rather similar to what Kitamura Tōkoku had done

---

81. I have followed conventional wisdom in attributing Takayama's subsequent ideas to Nietzsche, although I suspect that his concept of the superman and the critic of culture owes more to Thomas Carlyle's conception of the "hero" than it does to Nietzsche. Takayama was an avid reader of Carlyle's works, and there are numerous testimonials to Carlyle in his *zenshū*. More important, Takayama's *chōjin* had a social role, precisely as did Carlyle's hero but unlike Nietzsche's Übermensch. On the difference between Carlyle's hero and Nietzsche's *Übermensch*, see Walter Kaufman, *Nietzsche: Philosopher, Psychologist, Antichrist* (Princeton: Princeton University Press, 1968), p. 313. For the social dimension of Takayama's *Übermensch*, see his essay "Waga-kuni," his view of Nichiren in "Kangai issoku," in *Takayama Chogyū*, pp. 72–80, and his description of the role of the critic in "Bunmei hihyōka toshite no bungakusha," in *Takayama Chogyū*, pp. 260–266.

with Emerson and Carlyle a decade earlier, although Takayama was more strident and blatantly opportunistic. What makes Takayama more important in terms of social history is that his ideas and frustrations were now shared by a large number of educated youth, whereas Kitamura's were not. In a context of mass culture represented by the expansion of secondary education and in the face of a sharply reduced premium attached to higher education, the idea of rejecting contemporary national, social, intellectual, and moral norms to become a critic of culture and an absolute individual gained attention because this offered an alternative route to the elite status now so hard to acquire by conventional means.

Individual distinction could still exist in a world of mass education and statistics because the discovery of the self was the one area of accomplishment, the one area of self-expression, the one area of *risshin* ("rising above others") that could not be mass-merchandised or glutted by too many seekers, because the discovery of the self was by definition based on unique personal experience and individual instinct. It was their anguish, as some youth of the day explicitly stated, that made them members of a spiritual aristocracy.[82] Since any analysis of their anguish would have taken away its uniqueness and their ability to believe that in the absence of conventional measurements of transcendent status they were nonetheless unique, it is not surprising that the anguished youth so carefully avoided reflections on their own historicity.[83] Had they done so, they would have run the risk of noticing that German romanticism was a product of the declining status of educated youth,[84] and this would have reduced them to another sociological phenomenon, a product of the statistics Takayama abhorred.

In theory any concept of the self based on the thought of Nietzsche might have been expected to lead to an arrogant personality. This was not generally the case in Japan, however, and as the phi-

82. See Tokutomi Iichirō, "Reply to the Letter from a Youth Who Lives in the Country," *Chūgaku sekai* 9:3 (March 10, 1906): 1–5. Original in English.
83. An interesting example of evading this relationship in an essay nominally on the history of European romanticism and its introduction to Japan is found in Tanaka Ōdo, "Bunmei shi ni okeru rōmanchishizumu no iga," *Tetsugaku zasshi* (July 1910), in *Meiji bungaku zenshū*, vol. 50, pp. 130–140.
84. This relationship is postulated in Henri Brunschwig, *Enlightenment and Romanticism in Eighteenth Century Prussia*, trans. Frank Jellinek (University of Chicago Press, 1974).

losopher Miyake Setsurei observed, it was not the arrogant (*sondai*) aspect of Nietzsche's thought that prevailed but the despairing (*jibō jiki*) chord in his ideas that resonated with the mood of late Meiji youth and colored their formulations of individualism.[85] Miyake did not explain why this should be so, but the observations of the poet Ishikawa Takuboku are suggestive. Meiji youth had, in his words, been "educated to become useful," which was another way of saying that they had been educated for *risshin* for family or state.[86] But when *risshin* was repudiated the individual did not automatically find anything to replace it. Their inherent elitism precluded social involvement of the type championed by Taoka Reiun, and there were no significant political or social movements to which they could attach their energies in this period. As a result, those who repudiated conventional *risshin* were thrown back on their own devices, what they could find within themselves. Often that was precious little, and Takayama was a good example of this. After formulating his concept of the aesthetic life and absolute individualism, he went on to celebrate Nichiren as an example of a Japanese superman, but when he became terminally ill, he retreated into the conventional Nichiren Buddhism of his childhood.

Another pattern of adjustment to the spiritual vacuum created by the repudiation of conventional *risshin* was portrayed in the short novel *Doko e* [Whither], by Masamune Hakuchō, a twenty-nine-year-old writer intimately acquainted with the anguished youth.[87] In the 1880s or even the 1890s Suganuma Kenji, the hero of *Doko e*, would have been a model for the young man on his way to *risshin*. His father is a poor samurai, and Kenji, in best success-story fashion, works hard, never settling for anything less than first place on examinations. He is fired by a passion for raising the family name. Advancing through middle and higher schools, he finds a patron who pays his college expenses. At this point, for reasons not well explained in the story, Kenji comes to regard everything as "stupid" (*kudaranai*). He wants to strip off his school uniform and be free.

---

85. Miyake Setsurei, "Meiji shisō shōshi," in *Kuga Katsunan-Miyake Setsurei*, ed. Kano Masanao, vol. 37 of *Nihon no meicho* (Chūō kōron sha, 1971), pp. 424–426.

86. Quoted in Kosaka, *Thought*, p. 360.

87. *Doko e* exists in numerous editions. I used that in *Masamune Hakuchō shū*, vol. 11 of *Nihon bungaku zenshū* (Shūei sha, 1969), pp. 26–80. The novel first appeared in 1908 (Meiji 41). The hero appears to be patterned on Takayama Rinjirō (Chogyū).

Only the pleas of his patron persuade him to remain in school. Raising the family name and fortunes ceases to have meaning for him, and his view of samurai traditions becomes cynical. Noting his father's longing for the old order, Kenji suggests that the last family heirlooms be sold to buy a horse, that his father put on armor and sword and ride away shouting "Banzai!" Better to do this than lead a life of continual questing after petty satisfactions in a competitive world.

Pressured over the issue of marriage, Kenji escapes to a boardinghouse. His aversion to marriage stems from the pettiness into which he can see his acquaintances slip as they are oppressed by family responsibilities and the difficulty of making a living. Kenji himself finds no satisfaction in work. After graduation he spends three months teaching at a middle school, only to quit because he feels like a "phonograph record or a parrot." Turning to magazine writing, he finds no more opportunity for self-expression because he must write that which sells, not that which he believes. Bored and frustrated, his greatest concern is finding some way to pass each day. "Play" becomes his occupation (*honshoku*), and he seeks suggestions for diversions. Opium seems as though it might offer possibilities for providing the "taste" that is otherwise lacking in his life, but the closest he comes to finding any interest in living is in watching a spirited young Salvation Army preacher harangue a crowd. To a friend he remarks:

Isn't that interesting. That guy has the certainty to tell the world with his own mouth what truth is. Look at his face. There is an ardor for telling the masses about God with his own power. If mankind doesn't have that kind of ardor, it's worthless. . . . I want to join the Salvation Army. Rather than writing what I don't have my heart in, working for a magazine and trying to catch the mood of readers, the Salvation Army looks interesting. That fellow is passing each day without yawning—he's living.

Despite this inspiration, Kenji is never sufficiently moved to any action to end the yawning of his own existence.

Suganuma Kenji was a literary depiction of what some contemporary critics called "decadent youth" (*tandeki seinen*), those anguished youth who had gone beyond doubt to nihilism or hedonism.[88] Although Masamune did not describe Kenji's initial anguish

---

88. For a description of the decadent youth as seen by a contemporary observer, see Tokutomi, *Taishō no seinen*, pp. 20–24.

in terms of frustrated *risshin*, his subsequent discontent was quite specifically portrayed as a product of the limited opportunities for self-expression to be found in the positions available to highly educated youth. Had Kenji been able to graduate into the early Meiji world where men of his age group became policy makers while yet in their twenties, it is most unlikely that he would have been bored and considering opium. Indeed, a novel such as *Doko e* or the many others of the period that depicted bored, indifferent, defeated, or frustrated "heroes" could not have been written in the first decades of the era.[89] Kenji with his total lack of concern for national issues and his repudiation of family desires would have been incomprehensible to that generation which produced and read the political novels and the early *Eisai shinshi* compositions.

But, more important, that generation would have found it even more difficult to understand how someone with a university education could expect at best to be a middle-school teacher. Ishizaka Masatsugu had, after all, expected a similar education to carry him to the leadership of a world political order, and other early Meiji fictional expectations had been only slightly less grandiose. Such dreams did, however, have some potential for realization in the early Meiji period, or at the very least there had been such rises within recent memory in the Meiji Restoration. By the end of the period, the reality and possibilities were very different, and *Doko e* and the anguished youth were a product of those changed circumstances described by the dry statistics of competition ratios and bureaucratic compensation cited earlier.

89. Hiraoka Toshio has described the rather negative features ascribed to heroes in a number of late Meiji works dealing with youth. See Hiraoka Toshio, "Meiji yonjū nendai bungaku ni okeru seinen-zō," *Bungaku* 37:6 (June 1969): 18–36. Most of the works discussed by Hiraoka, including those by Mori Ōgai, Tayama Katai, Tokutomi Kenjirō, and Natsume Sōseki, are excluded from discussion here because these authors were notably older than the youth about whom they wrote. Rather than doing yet another article or monograph on these overstudied authors, the scholar wishing to investigate the image of late Meiji youth should turn to the late Meiji equivalents of *Eisai shinshi* or to the novels and biographies of lofty ambition (*risshi shōsetsu* and *risshi retsuden*) that were ground out by now forgotten authors such as Horiuchi Shinsen.

New Ethics for a New Generation | 7

By the turn of the century, both the definition of self-advancement and the literature concerned with it were more diverse than in the first decades of the Meiji era. Definitions of *risshin* ranged from the early Meiji study for wealth, honor, and bureaucratic affiliation to dreams of vast capitalistic wealth. For some the hedonistic repudiation of conventional *risshin* was the only true form of self-realization. Writers who sought to guide youth no longer had an audience ever ready to parrot their words, and they no longer faced a society for which an emphasis on unlimited pursuit of *risshin* seemed the most appropriate policy.

Would-be leaders of youth were faced with three conflicting tasks. For those youth who were anguished and had rejected *risshin*, they had to reassert the value of striving for traditional goals. For those youth who were still in the competition, they had to provide psychic preparation for the increasingly certain discouragements and slow progress these youth would encounter. For future generations, especially rural youth, they had to provide alternatives to *risshin shusse* as it had been defined and to scale down expectations to the possibilities of late Meiji society.

These partially conflicting goals dominated youth-oriented literature from just after the Russo-Japanese War. They remained important throughout the pre–World War II period, gradually giving way to a still more important task, that of socializing youth to become good employees, to become—as a contemporary phrase put it—those who could be "used by society."

THE SELF-MADE MAN IN MEIJI JAPANESE THOUGHT

When late Meiji observers were first made aware of the anguished youth (*hanmon seinen*), their general reaction was one of disbelief coupled with speculation as to what Fujimura Misao's real motive had been. After the Russo-Japanese War when attention returned to domestic matters, observers discovered that anguish was to be found among what seemed to many to be a large and threatening segment of youth. Consequently, attention was turned to explaining and treating this anguish. Most of the explanations and treatments proposed tell little about the anguished youth, but they do say much about the differences between early and late Meiji youth.

A broad survey of contemporary opinion on the anguished youth, most of it by commentators who had come to intellectual maturity before the Sino-Japanese War, appeared in the journal *Shinkōron* [New Review] in 1906 (Meiji 39). Some of those responding to the anguished youth declared that anguish was only a brief squall that would soon blow over. Others emphasized the corrupting effects of philosophy and speculative thought and argued for the prohibition of the study of philosophy by immature students. Many proposed draconian measures to deal with anguish. Sending anguished youth to the countryside, exporting them to Japan's colonies, or giving them a whipping and sending them out to earn their own pay by their own labor and sweat were among the proposals of this type. In the most extreme case, one author suggested that those prone to suicide should be *encouraged* to act, since this would reduce the number of deviants in society.[1]

Chūgaku sekai [Middle-School World], the chief journal aimed at those seeking entry into the higher schools, offered commentaries on the anguished youth by Tokutomi Iichirō, Inoue Tetsujirō, and Ōmachi Keigetsu, among others. In his long contribution, which the magazine offered in both English and Japanese (presumably to be used as preparation material for entrance examinations), Tokutomi demonstrated that he had no more tolerance for individualism in the 1900s than he had had in the 1890s.

> I hate such a matter as the investigation of the questions of life. Specifically I hate that young people rack their brains on behalf of such foolish attempts. ... If such hard questions had been solved with a man's short life, man must have been more powerful than God! ... Moreover, you seem proud of

---

1. These are the comments of Suzuki, Saji, Yamagata, and Nemoto as they appear in "Ensei to hanmon no kyūji," *Shinkōron*, July 1906 and August 1906.

your mental disturbance which according to you, cannot be understood by vulgar people. What a nonsense! I cannot but laugh at one who advertises his sorrows and regards himself ranked in the spiritual aristocracy.... The people who have such sorrows are the men poisoned by their idleness. If a man toils during the whole day as hard as he sweats in a cold weather, he will have no desire to weep over his causeless sorrows.[2]

There is no evidence that this or similar articles by Ōmachi (editor of *Chūgaku sekai*) and Inoue (an Imperial University professor of philosophy best known for his attacks on Christianity) had any substantial influence on the anguished youth. The style of preaching indulged in by Tokutomi was an object of satire in *Doko e* [Whither], and those First Higher School students who knew Inoue regarded him as a mediocrity and a fool.[3]

When the anguished youth did not disappear or respond to the ridicule and threats of older writers, more attention was given to the phenomenon, its social origin, and its political significance. Writers came to associate anguish with the decline of *risshin* opportunities in the 1900s and to fear that youth might turn to socialism as an answer to their frustrations. Even without making such a social analysis, individualism, decadence, and socialism appeared as all of one piece in the official mind.[4] A paraphrase of the views of Makino Nobuaki, minister of education after the Russo-Japanese War, noted:

The Minister finds among the students actually pursuing their studies some who are known to be content with small successes or given to luxurious living, entirely forgetting their place in life. In some cases they are known to go to such an extreme as to give themselves up entirely to vice and dissoluteness, without shame.

What it was feared that the anguished youth might become is indicated by the article's further comment that "Mr. Makino hears that

2. Tokutomi Iichirō, "Reply to the Letter from a Youth Who Lives in the Country," *Chūgaku sekai* 9:3 (March 10, 1906): 1–5. This article was a transcript of a "Sunday Lecture" by Tokutomi and originally appeared in his newspaper *Kokumin*. The translation is that of *Chūgaku sekai*.

3. Ōmachi Keigetsu wrote extensively on the subject of *hanmon* in *Chūgaku sekai* and other youth-oriented journals. These writings, which include two book-length works, *Seinen jidai* (1911) and *Seinen to hanmon* (1913), may be found in [Ōmachi] *Keigetsu zenshū* (Kyōbun sha, 1923), vols. 9, 10, and 11. For Inoue's view of anguish, see Inoue Tetsujirō, "Seishinteki kiken ni taisuru seinen no keikai," *Chūgaku sekai* 6:9 (July 10, 1903): 9–17. For a retrospective account of how the anguished youth regarded Inoue, see Abe, *Waga oitachi*, p. 342, and Itō, *Bundan shi* vol. 7, p. 143.

4. Oka, "Nichiro sensō go," p. 140.

THE SELF-MADE MAN IN MEIJI JAPANESE THOUGHT

men professing extreme Socialism visit different places of late and attempt by various means to seduce teachers and boys."[5]

There were indeed men who were offering socialism to youth as a way out of their frustrations and anguish. These offers first appeared in the *Heimin shinbun* [Commoner Newspaper], which was published during the Russo-Japanese War. Although its primary message was pacifism and its socialism was based more on Social Darwinism than on a materialist critique of history, the *Heimin shinbun* also revealed a growing sophistication on the part of *some* socialists, who had come to doubt the efficacy of self-help and who had become more critical of *risshin*. Several articles addressed themselves to the student audience that *Seikō* [Success] and the *Heimin shinbun* partially shared. It was pointed out that both the just-graduated young man looking for work and the even more pitiful student taking an entrance examination to get into higher education were being exploited by the capitalistic system.[6] The answer to this was of course socialism, and Nishikawa Kōjirō, one of the founders of the paper and a *Seikō* contributor, urged youth to become socialists so that they could bring about social change and create a society where their "talents could shine."[7] After the Russo-Japanese War and the suppression of the *Heimin shinbun*, Sakai Kosen continued this message in somewhat moderated form. Writing in *Chūō kōron* [Central Review] in 1906 (Meiji 39), he told those youth who were engrossed in their own problems of love (*renai*) and anguish (*hanmon*) that they ought to realize that the only way out of their dilemma lay in socialism.[8]

Despite the logic of the appeals made by socialists, there is relatively little evidence for any response among the intelligentsia in general or among anguished youth in particular. In 1907–1908 (Meiji

---

5. "The Education of Youth," *Sun Trade Journal* (July 1, 1906), p. 24. *The Sun Trade Journal* was the English-language section of *Taiyō*. See also *The Japan Year Book 1906*, p. 448, and *The Japan Year Book 1911*, pp. 411–412.

6. "Shin-sotsugyōsei ni tsugu," *Heimin shinbun* (July 10, 1904), p. 2, and "Jukensei ni tsugu," *Heimin shinbun* (July 10, 1904), p. 2. See also Sugai, "Shakai shugi," pp. 239–240.

7. Nishikawa Kōjirō, "Nan no gaku to chii ni nan no hokori ari ya," *Heimin shinbun* (October 2, 1904), p. 1.

8. Sakai Toshihiko, "Renai bungaku to shakai shugi," *Chūō kōron* 21:3 (March 1906): 100.

41–42), there were several recorded strikes among low-rank government officials,[9] but overall, educated youth were not prone to political activism either for themselves or for others. The basic pattern of response was that found by Taoka Reiun when he had earlier called upon educated youth to "take up the knife" and bring about a second Meiji Restoration. Literary and philosophical pursuits promised more self-fulfillment than did politics, and only a few isolated individuals such as Ishikawa Takuboku and Ōsugi Sakae combined a literary orientation with political criticism and activism.[10] Nevertheless, even if it is possible to demonstrate a consistent pattern of inward direction rather than social activism as a response to the declining position of youth during the Meiji era, this does not alter the fact that government officials and those who wrote to youth operated on the assumption that anguished youth might well turn to socialism and that this had to be fought against.

After the Russo-Japanese War, instruction (*kyōkun*) for youth became a major enterprise; a contemporary observer noted that "Shintō priests, Buddhist priests, Christian ministers, *rōnin*, literary men, and storytellers" were all in the business of trying to guide youth. Others satirically lamented the spirits of the thousands of trees being felled to provide the paper for all this writing.[11] In many instances these writers explicitly stated that they were concerned with the possibility that frustrations in the quest for *risshin* would lead to anguish and hence to socialism. Much of the writing in *Jitsugyō no Nihon* [Business Japan] and *Seikō* came to be less concerned with advancement as such than with the treatment of anguish. *Seikō* offered a column entitled "Success Philosophy" (Seikō tetsugaku), which stressed perseverance and endurance but which drew its quotations and examples from such literary figures as Zola and Carlyle, apparently seeking to appeal to what were perceived as the reading habits of anguished youth.[12]

Both gave much attention to religious answers to anguish. *Seikō*,

9. Matsunari, *Sarariiman*, pp. 34–36. Presumably, there were more strikes that went unrecorded.
10. For their criticism of contemporary youth, see Ishikawa, "Jidai heisoku," p. 397, and Ōsugi Sakae, "Saikin shisōkai no keikō," cited in Arima Tatsuo, *The Failure of Freedom* (Harvard University Press, 1969), p. 61.
11. Oka, "Nichiro sensō go," pp. 366–367.
12. See, for example, "Seikō tetsugaku," *Seikō* 7:1 (July 1, 1905): 30–32.

for example, had at least one special issue on "Religion and Success" plus frequent sporadic articles under similar titles. Although this special issue began by proclaiming that "for the purpose of achieving success, the two best religions are Buddhism and Christianity," the content was geared more to the question of how to find spiritual tranquility (*anshin ritsumeikan*) rather than success.[13] *Jitsugyō no Nihon* featured the "quiet sitting" (*seiza*) of Okada Takeshi for the same purpose.[14] Articles in which noted persons explained their outlook on life (*jinseikan*) were a related genre conspicuous after the Russo-Japanese War. The general tenor of these articles was for some individual to relate that he too had faced hardship, discouragement, and anguish, but when he thought of his mother slaving away to send him to school and of his duty to the nation, he was rescued from his anguish and proceeded on to *risshin*.[15]

All three magazines shared an interest in the works of Theodore Roosevelt, seeing in them a wholesome philosophy useful in countering whatever else youth might be reading. *Seikō* in particular made much of the idea of the "strenuous life," coupling it to more or less traditional concepts of self-cultivation, such as the reading of inspirational biographies and the taking of early-morning cold-water baths. This latter suggestion was eventually moderated when some readers overdid it and harmed their health, adding physical suffering to their mental anguish. The young man in chapter six who found himself "crying, crying, crying" was apparently an instance of this, and the response of *Seikō* to him is typical of the exchanges between it and those among its readers who declared themselves anguished.

It is due to just your own weak spirit that you are suffering. It is due to your very own weakness and not due to the strenuous life. You ought to be reading nothing but the stories of great men and heroes. From now on you ought to consider even looking at novels prohibited.[16]

Relatively similar injunctions can be found in the other two journals, those in *Chūgaku sekai* having some extra interest, since such

13. "Kinkoku," *Seikō* 20:5 (May 1, 1911): 204.
14. Most issues in 1911–1912 (Meiji 44–45) have an article on this subject. This reflected in part a government push to use religion to fill the spiritual vacuum it saw developing after the Russo-Japanese War. See Oka, "Nichiro sensō go," pp. 368–369.
15. Numerous examples may be found in the special issue "Gendai shosei tomoshibi" [Lighthouse for Contemporary Students], *Seikō* 10:6 (January 10, 1907).
16. Quoted in Mita, *Nihon no shinjō*, pp. 211–212.

ideas and the writings of Theodore Roosevelt were championed by Abe Isoo, one of the early socialists who had not become disillusioned with self-help.[17]

Overall, most of these pseudo-philosophical and spiritual answers to anguish were not very sophisticated and could hardly have appealed to any readers who had ventured into the heady realm of Nietzsche or Takayama. There were, however, some writers who reaffirmed traditional values but in a sufficiently sophisticated form and with a sufficiently complex vocabulary that they were indeed read by some of the best educated of the anguished youth. A notable example of this is the writing of Kuroiwa Ruikō, editor of *Yorozu chōhō* [Complete Morning News]. In 1903 (Meiji 36) Kuroiwa had taken time from his editing and writing to read widely in philosophy, partly to answer some doubts in his own mind, but also to keep up with contemporary trends and the issues being debated by some of his more intellectual associates. Out of the "more than one-hundred" philosophical works that he read he distilled his own philosophical synthesis and published it in 1903 (Meiji 36) under the title *Tenjin ron* [On Heaven and Man].[18]

According to Kuroiwa there were two great principles that dominated the universe and gave meaning to existence: anabolism (*kōjō shugi*) and energism (*seiryoku shugi*).[19] He described the universe as ever moving onward and upward in evolutionary terms (anabolism), with each individual playing a role in this great advance. Because of this, the individual was really immortal, his life living on in his children. Of course, to insure immortality, the individual had to have children, and Kuroiwa championed monogamous marriage, an obvious rejection of the instinctualism (*honnō shugi*) associated with Takayama. Similarly, he argued that ethics and morality had to be founded on those principles that governed the universe. Any that were not would lead to a "suicidal future" (*jisatsuteki kyūun*). Al-

---

17. Abe Isoo, "Seikō no shin-igi," *Chūgaku sekai* 6:8 (June 10, 1903): 10–19. Abe was a regular contributor to *Seikō* and *Chūgaku sekai*. *Jitsugyō no Nihon* published and advertised what it claimed were the complete works of Roosevelt. For the strenuous life in the original, see Theodore Roosevelt, *The Strenuous Life* (Century, 1899).

18. Kuroiwa's motivation for writing *Tenjin ron* is described in Itō Hideo, *Kuroiwa Ruikō den* (Kokubun sha, 1975), pp. 156–159. For the text itself, see Kuroiwa Ruikō, *Tenjin ron*, in *Kuroiwa Ruikō shū*, vol. 47 of *Meiji bungaku zenshū* (Chikuma shobō, 1971), pp. 301–348.

19. The translations are those Kuroiwa himself indicated.

though these ethics were supposedly derived from his observations of the cosmos, they sound rather familiar: study and hard work, perseverance, and strenuous effort (rikkō). Pleasure would come from fulfilling one's duty in the cause of universal advancement, in looking back on the obstacles overcome in contributing to this advancement, and in being in conformity with the "great harmony" (daichōwa) of heaven.

Although *Tenjin ron* was not originally written in response to the anguished youth, Kuroiwa later stated that he believed that had Fujimura read the work, it might have saved him from suicide. It subsequently was advertised as an answer for anguished youth.[20] Whether it would have in fact saved Fujimura or any other anguished youth bent on suicide is highly debatable. To a modern reader it seems a rather facile blending of Confucian terminology and concepts with late-nineteenth-century American efforts to square evolution and Christianity.[21] Nevertheless, Kuroiwa was not cynical but sympathetic to the anguished youth, and contemporary views must not be read back to the early twentieth century.[22] *Tenjin ron* was sufficiently interesting and created such a strong impression that Abe Yoshishige, one of the original First Higher School anguished youth, remembered and commented favorably on it more than sixty years later.[23] Since *Tenjin ron* went through ten printings, a rather large number of other relatively highly educated Meiji readers must also have found it interesting.[24]

Although government officials were concerned about the anguished youth, there was little that could be done directly about them, especially when they were not students and when they did not engage in any political activity. Pronouncements were issued and a certain amount of encouragement was given to spiritual reform

20. See Kimura Ki, "Kaidai," in *Kuroiwa Ruikō shū*, p. 387.
21. Among the works used by Kuroiwa were those of Henry Drummond, probably his *Ascent of Man* (1894). Another probable source of some importance is John Fiske's *Outline of Cosmic Philosophy* (1874).
22. Kuroiwa was one of the few of his generation to be sympathetic to the anguished youth. For his view of Fujimura's suicide, see "Fujimura Misao no shi ni tsuite," in *Kuroiwa Ruikō shū*, pp. 370–374.
23. Abe, *Waga oitachi*, p. 339.
24. Fujiwara, *Kyōiku shisō*, vol. 2, p. 156. Kuroiwa wrote a number of similar works after the success of *Tenjin ron*. Advertisements suggest that others wrote in a similar vein, but the whole field of popular (as contrasted with academic) philosophy is unexplored ground.

efforts, but the basic thrust of officialdom was at those who were currently students. Directives were issued concerning the scrutiny of reading matter. A reassertion of early Meiji goals was made in the so-called Boshin Rescript of 1908 (Meiji 41) and in Ministry of Education directives. The former reflected a belief that young people had come to believe that with victory in the Russo-Japanese War the tasks of the Meiji Restoration had been accomplished and they no longer felt the same national concerns earlier Meiji youth had felt. Given this assumption, the rescript proclaimed, "We hope that, with the cooperation of our loyal subjects, the noble work of the Restoration may be augmented and the benevolent virtue of Our Ancestors exalted."[25] Ministry of Education directives managed to make the point a bit less obscurely by declaring, "Especially after the war, the future expectations of the nation are more and more the responsibility of youth."[26]

This view of the problem ignored the evidence cited earlier that the nation had not been all that important to many educated youth long before the Russo-Japanese War. Moreover, even if it is assumed that some early Meiji youth closely identified their fate with that of the nation, such pronouncements ignored the changes that had taken place in the number of educated youth. It was much easier to identify your fate with that of the nation when there were only a few hundred or even a few thousand youth with a modern Western education than when there was an existing pool of several hundred thousand such youth. Given this logic of numbers, the repeating of slogans was of limited use in treating anguish, for this did not address the fundamental problem of too few opportunities for too many seekers. There was, however, a clear effort on the part of the government to deal with this imbalance, not by increasing opportunities, but by decreasing expectations, by making non-mobility seem more attractive, and by providing vicarious substitutes for conventional *risshin shusse*.

Shortly after the appearance of the anguished youth, Sawayanagi Masatarō, vice-minister of education during the 1902–1911 (Meiji 35–44) period and one of those involved in the compilation of ethics

---

25. The background to this rescript is discussed in Oka, "Nichiro sensō go," p. 368, and Sumiya, "Kokuminteki buijjon," pp. 14–22.
26. *Gakusei hachijū nen shi*, pp. 932–933, gives the text of a June 9, 1906, directive on this point.

texts (*shūshin kyōkasho*), wrote in *Seikō* and put himself on record in favor of changing the images of *risshin* being taught to Japanese schoolchildren. Claiming that youth were being given too high a set of expectations, he proposed that Japanese be educated more like their English counterparts who, in his opinion, knew that even university graduates could expect no more than a slow, limited rise. If students were "made to realize this," he felt they would "from the very beginning, without holding big expectations, realize that they must diligently apply themselves to their duty."[27] Youth so trained would not fall into anguish along the way.

The primary vehicle for conveying to youth a scaled-down set of expectations was the series of ethics texts used by elementary-school students. Because of a scandal in 1902 (Meiji 35) involving bribery of government officials by textbook firms seeking to get their products accepted, actual writing and editing of textbooks had passed into the hands of the government.[28] This change made the task of spreading a specific view of *risshin* easier than it had been during the middle years of the period, when textbooks were only approved, and much easier than early in the period, when there was no control and works such as *Saikoku risshi hen* and *Gakumon no susume* [An Encouragement of Learning] were used as ethics texts. Nevertheless, because of bureaucratic inertia, the first series of government-written ethics texts appeared in 1904 (Meiji 37) carrying an emphasis on *risshin* that reflected the attitude prevailing before the appearance of the anguished youth. *Risshin* was good and it ought to be encouraged. The second series of texts appeared, beginning in 1907 (Meiji 40), with much less emphasis on *risshin* and a changed framework in which it was to occur.[29]

27. "Nihon gakusei shōrai no hōshin," *Seikō* 9:6 (September 1, 1906): 13–15. Sawayanagi is more usually associated with a 1913 incident at Kyoto Imperial University where his high-handed firing of seven faculty members produced a strike and later his resignation.

28. Reproductions of these texts are found in Miyata Fumio, ed., *Dōtoku kyōiku shiryō shūsei* (Dai-ichi hōki shuppan, 1959), vol. 2. The bribery scandal is noted, ibid., pp. 4–5.

29. There were many changes in the texts other than *risshin* imagery, especially an increased emphasis on national mythology. These changes are discussed in Wilbur M. Fridell, "Government Ethics Textbooks in Late Meiji Japan," *Journal of Asian Studies* 29:4 (June 1970): 823–833; E. Patricia Tsurumi, "Meiji Primary School Language and Ethics Textbooks: Old Values for a New Society?" *Modern Asian Studies* 8:2 (1974): 247–261; and Harold J. Wray, "A Study in Contrasts: Japanese School Text-

The most blatant manipulation of lessons pertaining to advancement took place in the case of Toyotomi Hideyoshi. In the first series he had been offered as a model for *risshin* in a lesson which might be translated as "Let's Get Ahead" (*Mi o tateyo*). In this lesson he was described as a poor boy who had held from earliest childhood a desire to do something that would make him famous. He was depicted as always acting to realize his own goal.[30] In the second series, the lesson he appeared in was entitled "Let's Achieve a Lofty Ambition" (*Kokorozashi o tateyo*), and more emphasis was placed on his alleged contributions to the prosperity of the imperial household than on his own rise in rank and fame.[31] In the first series, the nature of his advancement was described with active constructions: he "rose in the world" (*risshin shite; mi o tatsuru*). In the second series, the phrase describing his rise was passive: he "was pulled up" (*hiki tateraremashita*). This made his career seem more like that of the diligent shop clerk who is eventually made assistant manager as a reward for his loyal service than like that of one who fought his way to the height of feudal power and rank. He was presented as Tōkichirō the sandal-taker rather than as Taikō the Imperial Advisor. Tōkichirō had been such a diligent servant that he put the sandals he cared for inside his kimono next to his body in order to warm them for his master Oda Nobunaga.[32] This was more than diligence, however, and in effect it said that the way to rise was to lick the boots (or sandals) of one's superior.

Despite the rewriting, the story of Toyotomi Hideyoshi was still about *risshin* and *shusse*. He rose in the world and left his native village (*shusse*) in order to pursue his quest. Although the textbook writers did not entirely deny this pattern, voices were being raised against the idea of *shusse*. Among those opposed was Yokoi Tokiyoshi (Jikei), an educator and agricultural specialist.[33] Yokoi noted in 1906 (Meiji 39) the popularity of the quest for "success" among rural

---

books of 1903 and 1941–45," *Monumenta Nipponica* 28:1 (1973): 69–86. These articles are all more or less dependent on the standard study in this field, Karasawa Tomitarō, *Kyōkasho no rekishi* (Sōbunkan, 1956).

30. Miyata, *Dōtoku kyōiku*, vol. 2, pp. 131–132.

31. Ibid., pp. 232–233.

32. The emphasis on Tōkichirō the diligent employee is pointed out in Mita, *Nihon no shinjō*, p. 192.

33. For a biography of Yokoi, see Tsunasawa Mitsuaki, *Nihon no nōhon shugi* (Kinokuniya shoten, 1971), chap. 4.

youth, claiming that rural people were even muttering the word in their sleep.[34] Although this was perhaps a testimonial to the influence of *Seikō*, it was not a compliment. Yokoi feared the impact of the desire for success on the rural order. He claimed that those who were successful and returned wealthy disrupted the existing order and stimulated extravagance. Those who failed often brought back socialism. Fearing the spread of this infection and the contamination of the peasants whom he saw as a counterrevolutionary mass preventing the whole nation from slipping into socialism, Yokoi became vehemently opposed to *risshin shusse* in any form. He called for less education rather than more, urged youth not to want to advance themselves, and passionately celebrated all aspects of the countryside, including the smell of urine and night soil.[35]

Yokoi's complete repudiation of *risshin shusse* did not become government policy, but the fears he expressed were part of the reason that ethics texts gave a model of *risshin* without *shusse* in the form of stories about Ninomiya Kinjirō (Sontoku).[36] The real Ninomiya (1787–1856) was a peasant reformer who had left behind a substantial rural movement based on his teachings. Although he had practiced within the context of the feudal order, he had not been a simple tool of the system. He had always demanded tax concessions for the villages he undertook to restore, and there was a strong current of bourgeois rationality in his thought in the form of careful analysis of costs and benefits. At the same time, this thrust was tempered by a concept of charity (*suijō*) that amounted to a type of mutual aid among equals (rather than benefices from a superior).

None of this appeared in the ethics textbooks, which presented only a very juvenile Ninomiya Kinjirō whose hard work was in the context of traditional family relationships, not profit-making or village reform.[37] He was pictured as the son of an impoverished family, working from morning to night to support two other children. On

34. Yokoi Tokiyoshi, *Tokai to inaka*, quoted in Sumiya, *Nihon teikoku*, p. 352.
35. See Yokoi Tokiyoshi, *Tokai to inaka*, in *Yokoi hakushi zenshū* (Dai-Nihon nōkai, 1925), vol. 4, pp. 545–547, and *Nōson kaizō ron*, *Yokoi zenshū*, vol. 4, pp. 266–270. For his celebration of the smells of night soil and urine, see *Nōson kaizō ron*, *Yokoi zenshū*, vol. 4, p. 190.
36. A good, concise summary of the background to Ninomiya's appearance in the texts is to be found in Takeuchi, *Nihonjin no shusse-kan*, pp. 93–98.
37. Concerning the manipulation of Ninomiya as a symbol, see Sumiya, "Kokuminteki *buijon*," pp. 22–23.

the side he made sandals in order to be of service to others, notwithstanding his own humble position. Placed with an uncle after his mother died, the young Kinjirō was a model worker. When scolded for studying on his uncle's time, he grew his own rape seed for oil so that he might study late at night without using his uncle's oil. Returning as an adult to his ancestral home, he found it dilapidated, and with his own hands he rebuilt it, all the time saving money, becoming in the end an "eminent man."[38] As used in the government texts, Ninomiya was something of a nonpolitical Lincoln who had never left the woods.

Although Ninomiya was not strictly a case of revision, since the first series carried essentially the same version of him, he was subject to more stress after the Russo-Japanese War. Statues of him depicted as a young man carrying a burden while reading a book were placed outside of elementary schools. The selective image of Ninomiya found in the textbooks was spread by his Hōtokusha (Repayment of Kindness Society) after it was largely co-opted into the government in 1906 (Meiji 39). A second group, the Teikoku Nōkai (Imperial Agricultural Association) founded in 1910 (Meiji 43), also emphasized a *risshin* without *shusse* of the type found in the textbook image of Ninomiya.[39] The journal of the Teikoku Nōkai criticized youth who thought they could not make a name for themselves as farmers and urged on rural youth a quest for fame as producers.[40] To encourage such youth and to give some meaning to this form of *risshin*, awards were made to honor productive youth, and they were given publicity in various journals.[41]

Seikō took up the idea of *risshin* without *shusse* after the Russo-Japanese War and gave its readers a heavy dose of articles celebrating the joys of the countryside. A typical item from this period had Yasuda Zenjirō, the parsimonious founder of the Yasuda (now Fuji) financial group, lamenting the depopulation of the countryside as youth flocked to the cities in search of *risshin*. He advised, "While it is good to select work suitable to yourself, continuing the work of

38. Miyata, *Dōtoku kyōiku*, vol. 2, pp. 211–212.
39. Concerning these groups, see Kinbara Samon, Sumiya Mikio, and Takami Junnosuke, "Kabu shidōsha no 'shisō' to seijiteki yakuwari," in *Shidōsha to taishū*, vol. 5 of *Kindai Nihon shisō shi kōza* (Chikuma shobō, 1960), pp. 125–138.
40. For an example, see ibid., p. 135.
41. Mita, *Nihon no shinjō*, p. 204.

your ancestors is easily the best."[42] This theme generated no more enthusiasm than did the celebration of expansionism, however, and letters from its readers remained overwhelmingly focused on the mechanics of acquiring nonelite secondary or higher education and petty urban *risshin*. The editor apparently recognized that to deny the *shusse* component of *risshin shusse* was to deny the chief attraction of the magazine: its information for provincial youth on urban opportunities. After 1911 (Meiji 44) it gave little attention to strictly rural *risshin*.

Toyotomi Hideyoshi in his ethics text manifestation was, however, compatible with urban *risshin* and the readership of *Jitsugyō no Nihon* and *Seikō*. The former could hold him up as a model employee, and the latter could fit him into its stress on humble origins, although at times it also used Hideyoshi to counsel contentment with low rank. For example, a *Seikō* story reported an alleged interview with a rubbish collector. In the interview he criticized youth "who cry about the difficulty of finding work and the problems of life while doing nothing," and at the end of the article he was reported to have said that being a rubbish collector was not so bad since "even the Great Taikō [Imperial Advisor] started as a sandal-taker."[43] Since the alleged interview did not portray the rubbish collector as advancing, the intended message was apparently contentment in low rank through vicarious association with Tōkichirō the sandal-taker who had become Imperial Advisor Toyotomi Hideyoshi.

Such extreme formulations were relatively rare in *Seikō*. More typical were its warnings against "rushing after success," a theme shared with *Chūgaku sekai*, and its emphasis on proceeding to success "step by step."[44] This idea was expressed by numerous *Seikō* contributors, including Shibusawa Eiichi, a semiretired entrepreneur whose words were a ubiquitous feature of youth magazines after the Russo-Japanese War. In a typical statement of the importance of proceeding "step by step," Shibusawa wrote, "Truly, in response to the environment, you must concentrate all your powers on your goal and, one pace at a time, one step at a time, take the

---

42. Yasuda Zenjirō, "Nōson no seinen ni ataeru sho," *Seikō* 20:2 (February 1911): 31.
43. "Kuzuya no mitaru shakai," *Seikō* 29:6 (September 1, 1915): 41–43.
44. "Seikō o isogunakare," *Seikō* 20:2 (February 1, 1911): 1.

path to advancement. If you have faith, the thing called *risshin shusse* will come before you know it."[45] This was essentially a very slippery formulation; the distinction between plodding and climbing was just about lost. If one did not consider where others were— and the reader was urged not to—this meant in effect that the reader should shuffle along until *risshin shusse* or death came, the latter being far more likely.

Jitsugyō no Nihon readers received a steady supply of advice with a similar slant from Nitobe Inazō, who had been headmaster at the First Higher School when the anguished youth appeared there. In 1909 (Meiji 42) he joined *Jitsugyō no Nihon* to become its resident (and only) "intellectual" for the next decade.[46] In explaining his extraordinary switch from his prestigious position at the First Higher School to *Jitsugyō no Nihon*, Nitobe declared that he wanted to use the mass circulation of the magazine (240,000 readers, he claimed) to minister to youth, to keep them from falling into anguish, becoming criminals, or worse yet, becoming socialists.[47] Whether this was in fact the sole reason for his shift is not clear. Nitobe was out of his intellectual depth as a headmaster for the First Higher School. In any event, whatever his actual reasons for joining *Jitsugyō no Nihon*, he did most definitely preach against both anguish and socialism.

Preach is the appropriate verb to use in his case because Nitobe was a Christian of sorts, specifically a professed Quaker, though this did not stop him from celebrating something he called "the way of the warrior" (*bushidō*) or from subsequently defending Japanese expansionism by military means. From Christianity he took such statements as "the poor are always with us" to argue against socialism and communism, and from time to time he drew on nominally

45. Shibusawa Eiichi, "Gakkō shusshinsha shosei shinzui," *Seikō* 10:6 (January 10, 1907): 1–4.
46. Nitobe stayed with *Jitsugyō no Nihon* until 1921 (Taishō 10), and was apparently financially dependent on Masuda Giichi in his later years. See Yamazaki Yasuo, *Dai-ni Chosha to shuppan-sha* (Gakufū shoin, 1955), pp. 139–143.
47. "Yo wa naze Jitsugyō no Nihon sha no henshū komon to naritaru ka." *Jitsugyō no Nihon* 12:1 (January 1, 1909): 5–11. Much writing on Nitobe has been hagiographic and either virtually ignores his work for *Jitsugyō no Nihon* and his dependency on Masuda or ignores the reactionary nature of his writing. See Sharlie C. Ushioda, "Man of Two Worlds: An Inquiry into the Value System of Inazo Nitobe," in *East Across the Pacific*, ed. Hilary Conroy and T. Scott Miyakawa (Clio Press, 1972), pp. 187–212, for an example of this type of treatment.

Christian examples to illustrate such virtues as perseverance and endurance.⁴⁸ Overall, Nitobe owed much more to the more conservative strains of Tokugawa thought than he did to Christianity. At many points he sounded rather like Kaibara Ekiken, a popular spokesman for the Tokugawa status quo. This was especially true in the case of what Nitobe called "cultivation" (*shūyō*), a subject that constituted the major portion of his writings for *Jitsugyō no Nihon*. As he himself explained, the purpose of cultivation was to make the discontented individual happy with the status quo.

> The rules of cultivation I am explaining here do not have as their goal the receiving of applause from the world nor the doing of difficult things nor the production of brave and heroic conduct. Wealth, honor, and fame ought not to be the goal of cultivation. Rather, instead, you ought to aim at being satisfied within your heart, no matter how poor you are. You ought to aim at being happy by yourself, no matter how much you are slandered. You ought to aim at feeling good fortune in the midst of adverse circumstances. You ought to aim at passing through the world with thanks, no matter what. These are the objects of the cultivation I am proposing.⁴⁹

Although it might be thought that such a negative message could not have been popular, quite the contrary is true. *Shūyō* went through some 140 printings between its appearance in 1911 (Meiji 44) and 1929 (Shōwa 4), suggesting sales of perhaps a quarter of a million!⁵⁰ Why this should be so is not entirely clear. Perhaps it was due to the unsophisticated nature of the *Jitsugyō no Nihon* audience. Nitobe wrote in an easy-to-read, semicolloquial style, which should have been easily understood by those with only the compulsory elementary education. Perhaps it was the similarity of his message to Tokugawa moralizing, and the familiarity appealed to readers. Perhaps, too, it was due to heavy promotion. The *Jitsugyō no Nihon* firm was one of the first Japanese publishers of the modern period to seek to "create demand" through heavy advertising and promotional activities. Advertisements for *Shūyō* touted it as the thing "for those who are confused, those who are in tears, those who are weak, those who are failing, those who are anguished,"⁵¹ but even without the

---

48. Nitobe Inazō, *Yowatari no michi*, in *Nitobe Inazō zenshū* (Kyōbunkan, 1970), p. 367. This work and others contained in volumes 8, 9, and 10 of his collected works were originally articles in *Jitsugyō no Nihon*.
49. Nitobe Inazō, *Shūyō* (Jitsugyō no Nihon sha, 1911), p. 16.
50. *Nitobe Inazō zenshū*, vol. 7, p. 691.
51. Copy from an advertisement in *Jitsugyō no Nihon* (August 15, 1911).

creation of a demand there were many such youth in late Meiji Japan. Most likely its appeal came from all of the elements cited plus the fact that the average reader of Nitobe could not realistically expect very much except continued adverse circumstances and that Nitobe not only seemed to offer a way of coping with these but made the endurance of what had to be endured into an elective virtue.

A second reason for a major shift in the content of writing on *risshin* after the Russo-Japanese War was a growing discovery of the need to socialize youth for employment rather than achievement of high rank. Until this period, those who directed their energies to guiding youth had given very little if any attention to the question of what would happen to young men after they had acquired an education. Beyond urging one career over another, mostly in rather broad terms such as "enterprise" over "politics," they did not provide vocational guidance. Indeed, few seem to have recognized that most educated youth would in fact be employed, that they would not be operating independently from society and the specific employment opportunities that it provided. Even when a writer recognized that most educated youth would become employees rather than independent scientists, inventors, or entrepreneurs, there was little recognition that the virtues demanded of an employee were not necessarily those virtues demanded of a schoolboy.

The short story "Hibon naru bonjin" [An Extraordinary Common Man] by Kunikida Doppo provides an interesting example of the limits of writing directed to youth before the Russo-Japanese War. Appearing in *Chūgaku sekai* (Middle-School World) in 1903 (Meiji 36), this story depicted the rise of one Katsura Shōsaku.[52] He was portrayed as the son of an impoverished samurai who had fallen on hard times with the Meiji Restoration. Since then his father had been concerned with various get-rich-quick schemes designed to raise the family name. In contrast to his speculating father, Shōsaku was a model of sobriety thanks to *Saikoku risshi hen*, which he read "like the Bible." Inspired by the stories in it, Shōsaku decided that he would "succeed in engineering." To accomplish this goal, he drew up a schedule for himself, which he followed explicitly. Although he was forced by poverty to work in a bank for a mere four or

---

52. Kunikida Doppo, "Hibon naru bonjin," in *Kunikida Doppo–Ishikawa Takuboku shū*, vol. 12 of *Nihon bungaku zenshū* (Shūei sha, 1967), pp. 181–190.

five yen a month, he kept working and saving toward his goal. After four years he quit the bank and went to Tokyo, where he studied intently, avoiding all the pitfalls of boardinghouse (*geshuku*) life. After a period of intense and isolated study, he graduated from a vocational school and immediately rose in the world by finding a job as a twelve-yen-a-month electrical technician.

According to the narrator of the story (Kunikida himself), Katsura Shōsaku was the sort of youth who would be prominent in the future.

> The more I knew that boy, the more I had to be impressed. It was different from being impressed by [Toyotomi] Hideyoshi, Napoleon, or some other genius. Such great men may or may not come in hundreds or thousands of years. An ordinary [*heibon na*] society is always producing men like Katsura Shōsaku, and such a society always has a demand for his type. The more men like Katsura it has, the greater its prosperity and fortune.[53]

Considering that by early Meiji standards, the *risshin* of Katsura Shōsaku was rather dwarfish, it might be thought that Kunikida was being critical of contemporary trends, that he was pointing out that the type of educated youth most in demand in a modern capitalistic society would be a mediocrity with a technical specialty, someone who was aware of nothing around him, who did not compare his lot with that of others, and who had no doubts about the value of what he was doing or the rewards the system provided in exchange for his sacrifices and labor. He would be a cog who by paying his way through school saved the state and his future employer the cost of polishing him for his intended usage.

Such an interpretation would be very far from the truth. Although Kunikida had bouts of self-doubt and was very much a romantic, he was at the same time a true believer in what he perceived to be Smilesean virtues. This story was a work not of cynicism but of idealism, one of several in this vein that Kunikida published in youth-oriented magazines.[54] Appearing as it did in *Chūgaku sekai*, "Hibon naru bonjin" was an attempt to give dignity to activities that would have been considered pedestrian by most readers of the magazine, who dreamed of bureaucratic wealth and honor following an elite

---

53. Ibid., p. 181.
54. His other major effort in this inspirational genre was "Hinode." It presented a specifically rural model. "Hinode," in *Kunikida Doppo shū*, vol. 18 of *Nihon gendai bungaku zenshū* (Kōdansha, 1962), pp. 160–167.

education. It is a commentary on Kunikida's intellectual sophistication and not on his sincerity that such a celebration of ordinary youth was at least ten years too late to be really progressive, since many youth now had no choice but to follow a path such as that of Katsura Shōsaku because of too few schools for too many aspirants.

Kunikida had been heavily influenced by Tokutomi Iichirō and his commonerism (*heimin shugi*). Katsura Shōsaku was the sort of model who would have appealed to Tokutomi. His career was a direct extension of what Minyūsha writers and journals such as *Shōnenen* [A Garden for Young People] had meant when they urged youth to go into more practical endeavors (*jitsugyō*) rather than into the bureaucracy or politics. It was an essentially scholastic conception of what constituted a practical endeavor. In leaving Katsura at the level of a twelve-yen-a-month electrical technician, Kunikida did, however, go further in adapting *risshin* to the reality of late Meiji society than did most other contemporary literature. At that time, *Seikō* had not yet begun to advise its readers to seek out second- or third-rate tracks to advancement. If it had published such a story, it doubtless would have had Katsura going on to become the Edison of Japan. Whether Kunikida was more sophisticated or had simply written all that had been asked of him is not clear. In any event, he shared the assumption of 1890s writers and of *Seikō*—which was in many respects a product of the 1890s—that Smilesean virtues would lead to employment.

Only a writer who knew business as an ideal and as an abstraction would make such an assumption. As Reinhard Bendix has noted, Smiles focused solely on the individual and "did not seem to envisage that the task required the cooperation of others."[55] His was an ethic appropriate to inventors and scientists and perhaps to artisans and craftsmen. It could be adapted to schoolboys because study is essentially a solitary process. Getting a job, however, involves human interaction. Keeping that job and rising in an organization requires still more attention to interpersonal relations on a daily basis. Kunikida did not recognize this, and his blind spot was shared by *Chūgaku sekai*, *Seikō*, and most of their contributors.

In marked contrast to the journals catering to students, *Jitsugyō no Nihon* was fully conscious of the fact that employment was the

---

55. Bendix, *Work and Authority*, p. 300.

probable present or future state of its readers and that the ethics and values associated with employment were rather different from those associated with schoolboys, scientists, and inventors. Along with its worship of wealth and businessmen, the magazine offered a steady stream of articles on what employers demanded from their employees, often basing these articles on interviews with businessmen. Three general variations from the pattern seen in the scholastic version of self-help may be observed in *Jitsugyō no Nihon*.

First, there was the application of Smilesean virtues to the workplace through shifting their beneficiary from the individual or his creative task to the employer. Hard work was not for the individual but for the employer. Frugality was not saving for study by struggle, for personal security, or for charitable activities: it was a matter of not wasting the time or supplies of the employer. Perseverance was not that which kept you going through the difficulties of study by struggle or trying again after each experiment failed: it was what kept you working hard even when your job was unpleasant or boring. Paying attention to the ordering or stabilization of society was not a matter of choosing the right school but a matter of following the chain of command and observing the formal hierarchies within a firm. Common sense was not the Smilesean virtue of the observant inventor but the instinct that allowed the employee to act in the interest of his employer even without specific instructions. The hallowed virtues of independence and autonomy, so stressed by those who followed the Nakamura Keiu interpretation of *Self-Help*, were not the basis of national independence or autonomy nor were they the virtues that led to personal economic independence. The youth with a firm sense of independence and autonomy was, according to *Jitsugyō no Nihon*, the person who was able to carry out his job to the profit of his employer without constant supervision.

The second feature of *Jitsugyō no Nihon* articles on virtues for the employee was that of putting emphasis on interpersonal relations. Readers were told in almost every issue that a proper facial expression was an essential virtue for the youth who would get ahead. A proper facial expression meant appearing appropriately interested and obliging (*shinsetsu*) to customers. It meant taking orders and doing unpleasant work in good grace and without complaining. The youth who would advance was told the importance of "amiability" (*aikyō*). It meant having good relations with other employees. "Harmony" (*wa*) meant avoiding arguments, giving in on small points even if you were correct. Knowing how to speak harmoniously (*onwa*) was a virtue said to be of particular importance for educated youth who tended to think that the argumentative style found in academia would succeed in business.

The third tendency of articles in *Jitsugyō no Nihon* was to belittle education beyond a certain point and to stress practical education over a liberal education. Middle-school graduates were regarded as singularly impractical and were repeatedly told that they should pay more attention to writing a good, clear hand and to developing speed and facility with the abacus (*soroban*). They were told that generally businessmen did not want overly educated youth with theoretical knowledge; they wanted practical, hardworking youth. In addition, the magazine explained that the youth who gained too much education was too old when he entered the job market. Employers preferred young men who were not yet set in their ways, who could be trained to the ways and manners of the firm. In general, this was probably sound advice. Relatively few enterprises in Japan were at a stage where they could use any number of students with nonspecialized secondary or higher education, and those that did employ such youth went to great pains to socialize them to the firm in a pattern based on traditional apprenticeship programs.[56]

In large measure this contrasting ethic developed in *Jitsugyō no Nihon* was based on values and ideas common among the Tokugawa merchant class. Many *Jitsugyō no Nihon* contributors and readers were the Meiji extension of that class. However traditional the expectations of employees were, there was little about them that was especially Japanese. Indeed, *Jisugyō no Nihon* seldom validated the virtues it proclaimed by recourse to Japanese traditions or models.

56. This description of employee virtues is a distillation of a number of articles in *Jitsugyō no Nihon*, including the following: "Jitsugyōka no seinen ni taisuru yōkyū," January 1, 1903, pp. 88–91; "Jitsugyōka no seinen ni taisuru yōkyū," February 1, 1903, pp. 64–66; "Yo wa ikanaru seinen o yōkyū suru," May 15, 1903, pp. 55–57; "Jitsugyō ni jūji sen to suru seinen no go-dai-jōken," April 1, 1904, pp. 16–18; "Jitsugyōteki seinen," October 1, 1904, pp. 26–29; "Risshin shosei ni hitsuyō naru dai-jū-jōken," November 15, 1904, pp. 30–40; "Jitsugyōkai wa ikanaru seinen o motomuru ka," June 1, 1905, pp. 17–18; "Jiko no shōkai ni chūi seyo," June 1, 1905, pp. 45–47; "Chitsujoteki seikatsu no jū-dai-kōtoku," June 1, 1905, pp. 40–41; and "Shūshoku yōketsu," October 10, 1905, pp. 70–73. Recruitment and preferences of higher-education graduates are discussed in Ozaki Moriteru, *Nihon shūshoku shi* (Bungei shunjū, 1967), pp. 17–22.

More often than not, it used late-nineteenth-century American writings, particularly those of Andrew Carnegie, to demonstrate the correctness of its advice and to assure its readers that applying such virtues to their lives as employees would indeed lead to advancement. It had been a translation of Carnegie's *Empire of Business* that had made *Jitsugyō no Nihon* into a successful firm, and the magazine let few issues after 1902 (Meiji 35) slip out without an article on Carnegie, his household, even his mother.

Advertising copy for his works promised even more benefits to the reader than those gained by the firm:

Andrew Carnegie, American multimillionaire who created one billion yen wealth with his bare hands and whose name Steel King thunders around the world, explains the secrets of wealth and success based on his own experience.[57]

These advertising claims were strikingly unrelated to the overall thrust of the original *Empire of Business*. As was the case with most of Carnegie's writing, he had more to say about contemporary economic problems and his concept of "the stewardship of wealth" than he did about getting ahead in the world.[58] In fact, *Jitsugyō no Nihon* translated only two chapters of *Empire of Business*: "The Road to Business Success" and "The Common Interest of Labor and Capital."[59] These were essentially the only portions of the book which dealt with personal advancement.

Carnegie was a self-proclaimed devotee of Samuel Smiles, but "The Road to Business Success" offered non-Smilesean advice to a non-Smilesean audience, students at a "commercial college." To

---

57. Advertisement for *Jitsugyō no Teikoku* [The Empire of Business] in *Seikō* 1:4 (January 1, 1903).

58. "The stewardship of wealth" covered the idea that the rich held their wealth in trust for the poor and ought to give it away before their deaths. The concept was developed most fully in his *Gospel of Wealth*. See Andrew Carnegie, *The Gospel of Wealth*, ed. Edward G. Kirkland (Harvard University Press, 1962). Although *Jitsugyō no Nihon* published a translation of this work, it gave little attention to philanthropy on the part of business. Christians and early socialists gave more emphasis to this aspect of Carnegie but not without criticizing him. For examples, see Sakai Kosen, "Kanegii no tomi no fukuin," *Yorozu* (March 12 and 13, 1903), in *Sakai zenshū*, vol. 1, pp. 254–258, and "Fugō Karunegii," *Rikugō zasshi*, no. 245 (May 15, 1901), pp. 8–12.

59. Andrew Carnegie, "The Road to Success," in *The Empire of Business* (Doubleday, Page, and Co., 1902), pp. 3–18, and Andrew Carnegie, "The Common Interest of Labor and Capital," ibid., pp. 71–94.

these young men, the Steel King gave a charge, "Do not rest content for a moment in your thoughts as head clerk, or foreman, or general manager in any concern, no matter how extensive." To go beyond these ranks, the aspirant should avoid speculation, drink only in moderation, and seek to maintain an untarnished credit rating. The last point could be achieved primarily through demonstrating the right character to those who would loan you money. This advice was, however, only the preface to the central theme of this speech, which was that the young man who would advance ought to be continually asking himself not "What must I do for my employer?" but "What can I do for my employer?" The aspiring youth should be continually looking for a chance to save his employer from disaster through his detailed knowledge of his own job. According to Carnegie, "You will never be a partner unless you know the business of your department better than the owners can."

The essential requisite for getting ahead was, in Carnegie's wording, a matter of being "noticed." This was an important shift from *Self-Help*, in which it was people of a special kind who noticed common things and utilized them, not the people themselves who were noticed and utilized. The only really Smilesean note Carnegie struck in this essay was his emphasis on youth of humble origin. He declared, "Look out for the boy who has to plunge into work direct from the common school and who begins by sweeping out the office. He is the dark horse you had better watch." The expectation that these boys would be heading upward to become chief clerks or partners was, nevertheless, one that belonged to a different order. Smiles had depicted most such youth as on their way to becoming inventors or scientists.

"The Common Interest of Labor and Capital" had a more Smilesean target audience, industrial workingmen, but little more emphasis on Smilesean virtues. Carnegie celebrated libraries and self-education, and he talked vaguely of inventive people in the past. He did not counsel workingmen to be reading and to invent in their spare time, as had many of the models in *Self-Help*. The library was, for Carnegie, the place where the craftsman and technician could become a better worker. Study at the library and "let no man know more of your specialty than you do yourself," he advised. The worker who did so would, in Carnegie's words, "be appreciated" by management and might rise to become foreman or even a partner in the company. This was advice for a much more structured world than that seen by Samuel Smiles and was a reflection of the dominance of large corporations in which workers were fitted into ever narrowing technical specialties.

Although the distinctly non-Smilesean value of being noticed or appreciated carried vague echoes of the virtues practiced by Honda Noboru in *Ukigumo*, it must be noted that Carnegie was not advocating any cynical manipulations. Writing from the standpoint of an employer, Carnegie did not want employees who merely gave the pretense of activity and concern; he wanted workers to believe that they would indeed be noticed and appreciated and from this hope be stimulated to extra effort. Nevertheless, there was ample room for the reader concerned with his own *risshin* to think that, since it was being noticed that counted, appearance was more important than actual effort. Unfortunately, *Jitsugyō no Nihon* seldom had contributions from readers, so there is no evidence to determine how youth responded to this advice. Moreover, even if the magazine had published compositions or questions, it is most unlikely that it would have published any essays that interpreted Carnegie in self-serving terms. The magazine very consciously spoke for the interests of employers.

Because Andrew Carnegie was a very wealthy man writing in a period during which a wide spectrum of youth and writers on advancement had come to value wealth most highly, it might be argued that the introduction of his works into Japan and their popularity were solely because of their association with his wealth, not because they represented a success ethic for the employee. Certainly his wealth added to the popularity of his writings, but there is evidence that his concern with the advancement of employees was a major factor in attracting readers. This is suggested by the fact that the other American author popular in Japan at this time had little personal wealth to recommend him, but he did offer an ethic that was even more specifically directed to modestly educated youth in petty clerical and sales positions than was the case with Carnegie.

This second popular writer was Orison Swett Marden, author of *Pushing to the Front* and publisher of the magazine *Success*. His career paralleled in some ways that of Samuel Smiles, with whom he shared the honor of being one of the most widely read foreign writers in Meiji Japan.[60] Born in Thornton, New Hampshire, he read *Self-Help* as a youth and declared later that it had led to his decision to "serve mankind." After graduation from the Hampton Institute in 1873 and Boston University in 1877, he studied medicine at Harvard and received his M.D. in 1882. Rather like Smiles, his means of working himself through school (catering and hotel management in Marden's case) distracted him from his professional career. Leaving college with not only his M.D. but twenty thousand dollars earned on the side, he invested in real estate off Newport, Rhode Island, making a substantial profit and earning the name "Lucky." In the so-called Nebraska boom, he overextended himself and went bankrupt. In 1894 (Meiji 27) he found a new career as a popular author when he published *Pushing to the Front*. It subsequently ran through 250 printings in the United States alone. This led to the founding of *Success*, a magazine that sold some 300,000 copies per issue at the height of its popularity and enjoyed the highest per page rate for advertising of any American journal of the time.[61] All told, his books sold more than three million volumes in the United States before 1925.[62]

No such comprehensive statistics exist for Japan, but Marden's biographer claimed sales of over one million copies of *Pushing to the Front* in Japan.[63] There is considerable secondary evidence of his popularity and influence. Japanese writing in the decades after the Russo-Japanese War abounds with fragments and clichés from his works, and many highly derivative books by Japanese were published.[64] Marden's books are more readily found in Japanese than in American libraries; the First Higher School library (now part of the

---

60. The basic biography of Marden is Margaret Connolly, *The Life Story of Orison Swett Marden* (Thomas Y. Crowell Co., 1925). A critical interpretation of his writing is found in Richard M. Huber, *The American Idea of Success* (McGraw-Hill, 1971), pp. 145 ff.
61. "Beikoku Seikō zasshi no rekishi," *Seikō* 3:5 (February 10, 1904), pp. 44–45.
62. Bendix, *Work and Authority*, p. 260.
63. Connolly, *Orison Swett Marden*, p. 206.
64. Nitobe Inazō drew upon Marden for sections of *Shūyō*, especially those parts pertaining to career selection. See Nitobe, *Shūyō*, pp. 65–98. Another previously cited work showing Marden's influence is Yanagiuchi, *Gakusei to risshi*, p. 85.

general education campus of Tokyo University) had a good collection.⁶⁵ Various translations and English-language editions of his works were published in Japan, some as late as the 1960s.⁶⁶ Many editions of Marden's works were annotated for use in teaching English in middle schools,⁶⁷ and his writings were a major source of material for both *Jitsugyō no Nihon* and *Seikō*; the latter was explicitly patterned on *Success*.

As was true of Andrew Carnegie, Marden saw himself as a Smilesean self-made man and as an advocate of Smilesean virtues; like Carnegie he actually taught a quite different ethic. *Pushing to the Front* was written in basically the same biographical and anecdotal format as *Self-Help*. Indeed, many portions were inspired by, one might say plagiarized from, *Self-Help*, a practice Marden was famous for. One critic observed, "Mr. Marden's labors, of the excerpting and arranging order, must have been something really appalling; and one is glad to reflect that this method was one which relieved him from the additional strain of severe and continuous thought."⁶⁸ Nevertheless, despite a large measure of inspiration and borrowing from works by Smiles and other writers of the character ethic, Marden had something rather different to say. In direct contrast to Smiles, who had been explicitly hostile to business, favoring instead inventors, scientists, and philanthropists, Marden gave considerable prominence to men such as Armour and Rockefeller, describing almost gleefully their stock market manipulations **and** rough and ready attitude toward the law.⁶⁹ Only after celebrating such men, whom Smiles would not have mentioned in the first place, did Marden get around to sounding a Smilesean note:

---

65. The National Diet Library had thirty-four volumes of his works, and the Tokyo University Library had an even dozen.

66. The card catalog of the National Diet Library listed three post–World War II translations of Marden, all published in Osaka. It was not clear which works were translated, but the Japanese titles suggest that they were items from later in his career when he was close to "New Thought."

67. Many of the items listed in the National Diet Library card catalog were of this type. The earliest listed was 1900 (Meiji 33); the last was 1924 (Taishō 13). Connolly, *Orison Swett Marden*, p. 206, indicates that there were a number of different editions of *Pushing to the Front* with Japanese notes.

68. Quoted in Wyllie, *Self-Made Man*, p. 128.

69. Despite the implications of the title *Pushing to the Front*, Marden does not use any significant amount of Social Darwinism in these descriptions.

These are illustrations of seizing opportunity for the purpose of making money. But fortunately there is a new generation of electricians, engineers, of scholars, of authors, and of poets who find opportunities, thick as thistles, for doing something nobler than merely becoming rich.[70]

Even at this, Marden did little more than give lip service to technologically and artistically creative careers. The opportunities that he claimed existed were those that would come to "the educated youth, to the office boy and to the clerk" (pp. 18–19).

Most of *Pushing to the Front* was given over to telling the young employee how he might rise in an organization *as an employee*, not how he might become something *other than an employee*. The basic thrust of the advice given by Marden was similar to that found in *Jitsugyō no Nihon*: do that which best serves your employer and you will prosper.

> Don't wait for a higher position or a larger salary. Enlarge the position you already occupy; put originality of method into it. Fill it as it never was filled before. Be more prompt, energetic, more thorough, more polite than your predecessor or fellow workmen. Study your business, devise new modes of operation, be able to give your employer points. (P. 93)

As a consequence of this stress, virtues that appear in *Self-Help* in the context of creativity and innovation appeared in *Pushing to the Front* in the context of white-collar employment. The "habit of attention," which in *Self-Help* was discussed in terms of scientific method, was illustrated in *Pushing to the Front* by reference to people with prodigious powers of memory (p. 111). When Marden spoke of precision, he was thinking not of those who worked with metal or scientific instruments, but of those who labored over ledgers and account books or legal documents.

> We must strive after accuracy as we would after wisdom, or hidden treasure, or anything we would attain. Determine to form exact business habits. Avoid slipshod financering [*sic*] as you would the plague. Careless and indifferent habits would soon ruin a millionaire. (P. 291)

The "accurate boy," Marden observed, "is always the favored one," but the accuracy he referred to was not the accuracy of the scientist or the engineer but the accuracy of the bookkeeper and the stock-

---

70. Orison Swett Marden, *Pushing to the Front or, Success Under Difficulties* (Thomas Y. Crowell, 1894), p. 15.

boy. Similarly, the sense of time and its saving found in *Pushing to the Front* was centered not on opportunity for personal cultivation but on profit. According to Marden, "One of the best things about school and college life is that the bell which strikes the hour for rising, for recitations, or for lectures, teaches habits of promptness." To the young man looking out for his own success, Marden advised, "Wear threadbare clothes if you must, but never carry an inaccurate watch" (pp. 130–131). This was a sense of time for the messenger boy, not the scientist or inventor.

As did *Jitsugyō no Nihon*, Marden celebrated virtues having to do with interpersonal relations, virtues that were hardly mentioned in *Self-Help* or that did not appear at all. In *Pushing to the Front*, there were whole chapters devoted to such subjects as "cheerfulness and longevity" (9), the potential profit in good manners (10), the importance of displaying enthusiasm (11), and others of this ilk. In these chapters little was said about ability or performance; the emphasis was on personality. According to Marden, "Every time we go into society, we must step on the scales of each person's opinion, and the loss or gain from our last weight is carefully noted" (p. 168). In such a situation, "A cheerful man is preeminently a useful man," and the youth aiming at success ought to have a winning smile (p. 134). One ought also to be polite, for the polite person could "get and do almost anything" (p. 156).

Tact and common sense were seen as useful, but Marden declared "genius" suspect lest it lead to becoming a "monstrosity."

> The world is full of theoretical, one-sided, impractical men, who have turned all their energies of their lives into one faculty until they have developed not a full-orbed, symmetrical man, but a monstrosity, while all their other faculties have atrophied and died. We often call these one-sided men geniuses. (P. 189)

In *Self-Help* the disparagement of genius was part of Smiles's argument that invention and creation could be accomplished by those with ordinary skills. Smiles had little concern with the question of whether the individual was "full-orbed" or not; he in fact celebrated those who put all their energies into one task even if it led to their being thought crazy by their less creative contemporaries. But Smiles was interested in and appreciative of creativity; Marden was interested in socializing youth to fit into slots set up by employers and large-scale organizations.

Marden's writings were explicitly used by *Jitsugyō no Nihon* because of the advice for employees they contained. A special 1903 (Meiji 36) issue entitled "Seikō taikan" [General View of Success] had a major section attributed to Marden in which the main topic was how advancement came to employees.[71] The magazine was taken by Marden's notion of "seizing opportunities," and it fitted neatly with the "discovery myth" put forward by Carnegie. The youth who was going to seize his opportunity had to be constantly studying in order to be ready to act when his opportunity came.[72] This was an attractive idea for a magazine that consciously spoke to the interests of employers, for it was a useful device to stimulate the employee to extra efforts. This is not to say that Marden's celebration of wealth went unnoticed by *Jitsugyō no Nihon*. A journal that could have feature articles on the smiles of businessmen would not let slip the opportunity to pick up on Marden's largely uncritical celebration of nineteenth-century American robber barons. Although they were not identified as such, it is probable that most of the biographies of American businessmen featured in *Jitsugyō no Nihon* were taken from *Success*.

Giving greater significance to the popularity of Marden and his works in Japan at this time was the use of his works for English-language instruction in middle schools and the appearance of passages from his works in the entrance examinations to the higher schools.[73] A cynical explanation for this usage, but one which cannot be ignored, can be found in the peculiar nature of Marden's English. At best, he was not a good writer. At worst, his prose was marked by breathless run-on sentences that strung together elliptical constructions studded with dubious word usages such as "financering." He dropped names with utter abandon, often without bothering to explain the relationship of the many obscurities he cited to the point he was trying to make. In other words, his writing was just the thing for late Meiji higher-school entrance examinations where the goal was not to test whether the student had a usable command

71. O. S. Marden, "Seinen to seikō," *Jitsugyō no Nihon* (May 12, 1903), pp. 191 ff.
72. O. S. Marden, "Seikō ni hitsuyō naru shikaku," *Jitsugyō no Nihon* February 1, 1903), pp. 56–57.
73. Yoshino Shinji tsuitōroku kankō-kai, *Yoshino Shinji* (Yoshino Shinji tsuitōroku kankō-kai, 1974), pp. 85–86. See also Miyake Setsurei (Yūjirō), *Meiji shisō shōshi*, in *Kuga Katsunan—Miyake Setsurei*, vol. 37 of *Nihon no Meicho*, ed. Kano Masanao (Chūō kōron sha, 1971), pp. 424–426.

of English but to cut down the surplus of applicants to the number of places. It is the type of English still used on university entrance exams in Japan today. Nevertheless, while Marden's prolix prose was the probable reason for the appearance of selections from *Pushing to the Front* on higher-school entrance examinations, his popularity can be directly traced to the declining situation of educated youth in which more middle-school graduates could not enter the higher schools and had to accept petty white-collar employment.

In writing *Pushing to the Front*, Marden declared that his purpose was to "encourage, inspire and stimulate boys and girls who long to be somebody and do something in the world, but who feel they have no chance in life."[74] As was seen in the discussion of anguish, there was good reason for Japanese youth from the 1900s on to believe that their chances were decreasing. This was explicitly a factor in the introduction of *Pushing to the Front* to Japan. The first Japanese rendering of it emphasized its appropriateness for youth "facing adverse circumstances," and this theme appeared regularly in advertising for it and Marden's other works.[75] There was, however, one problem with applying Marden's advice to Japan. The discouraged boys (and girls) he sought to inspire were not just any group anywhere, but American youth in the context of American society. Marden proclaimed:

With five chances on each hand and *one unwavering aim*, no boy, however poor, need despair. There is bread and success for every youth under the American flag, who has energy and ability to *seize his opportunity*. It matters not whether the boy is born in a log cabin or in a mansion; if he is dominated by a resolute purpose, and upholds himself, neither men nor demons can keep him down.[76]

In contrast to Smiles, Marden was extremely culture-bound. The opportunities he emphasized were specifically American opportunities for American youth. In theory this should have caused prob-

74. Marden, *Pushing to the Front*, preface.
75. Sumiya Kisaburō, *Risshin saku* (Kaitakusha, 1897). The cover blurb explained that this was a work for youth in adverse circumstances. This version was very much a paraphrase and deviated from the original text at many points. Since it was not particularly popular compared with *Saikoku risshi hen*, it has not been analyzed here. Moreover, Marden's works were probably better known in English than in Japanese. For examples of advertising of Marden's works see *Eigo sekai*, December 4, 1897; *Sekai no Nihon* 2:6 (October 15, 1898); *Rising Generation* 7:4 (June 17, 1902); *Rising Generation* 7:16 (July 7, 1902); *Seikō* 2:2 (May 10, 1903); *Seikō* 2:4 (July 10, 1903); *Seikō* 2:5 (August 10, 1903), *ABC zasshi* 1:1 (September 15, 1906).
76. Marden, *Pushing to the Front*, p. 53. Marden's emphasis.

lems of acceptance in Japan; in practice it did not. One early translation of *Pushing to the Front* simply deleted those portions of the work that implied there was something peculiar about the United States that made advancement easier to achieve there.[77] Candid analysis of the objective probabilities of advancement was never a conspicuous feature of writing on personal advancement, and ignoring the ratio of people to resources in the United States relative to Japan was a simple extension of the basic thrust of all writing on self-culture: that the individual created his own fate without regard to the environment.

Additional evidence for the proposition that the popularity of Marden came from the ethic he preached and not simply from the aura of wealth attached to America and American writers may be found in observing the changes in writing aimed at educated youth after the Russo-Japanese War. Although evidence for the declining position of youth was available after the Sino-Japanese War, youth-oriented publications tended to gloss over this change. Reading *Seikō* and *Jitsugyō no Nihon*, one would not have known about the 1902 (Meiji 35) depression. After the Russo-Japanese War, however, the situation for educated youth became openly recognized as less than bright. Articles on what contemporary journals called the "placement difficulty" (*shūshokunan*) began to appear, although youth-oriented publications strived to put the best possible construction on the situation. *Jitsugyō no Nihon*, for example, advised in 1906 (Meiji 39):

Recently, in our country there are many with a middle-school education who cannot enter banks or companies or who cannot enter higher school and are thus wandering without a goal. They ought to have a strong resolve to be independent and autonomous [*dokuritsu jiei*] and enter a shop or factory straight away. After piling up some experience they ought to try to develop their own fate. Stand up! The age of independence and autonomy comes![78]

Nevertheless, by dealing with the subject at all, the magazine was calling attention to the diminished education and employment opportunities facing youth.

77. Sumiya Kisaburō did this in *Risshin saku*.
78. "Okite yo dokuritsu jiei no jidai wa koreri," *Jitsugyō no Nihon* 9:1 (January 1, 1906):12–15.

With this open recognition, however circumscribed, of the changed circumstances faced by youth, there came greater emphasis in the literature on personality as the factor said to lead to success. The logic of this was quite simple. If there was only one youth with the required skills and education and ten who sought his services, it was extremely unlikely that a prospective employer could concern himself with the personality of the employee. If there was only one position demanding a given level of skill or education and ten would-be employees meeting the basic mechanical prerequisites, it was extremely probable that personality would enter into the selection process.

After the Russo-Japanese War some writers were speaking rather candidly on this subject. A *Jitsugyō no Nihon* editorial in 1906 (Meiji 39) counseled that "the most important step for getting work after graduation is to make calls on your seniors [senpai] and reveal to them your character and personality [jinkaku, seishitsu]."[79] A 1911 (Meiji 44) article explained the proper personality for employment by citing a university graduate who was now an employee of Furukawa Ichibei, owner of the notorious Ashio copper mine.[80] Among the keys to success the magazine ascribed to this youth were those of never appearing disagreeable and always following regulations to the letter. Previously, the magazine had offered this advice only to shop clerks and the like; now it was offering the advice in terms of university graduates. Given the market facing graduates from higher education in these years, it is probable that some were now reading *Jitsugyō no Nihon* and the works it published. Issues after the Russo-Japanese War give the impression that the educational level of its readers was increasing as the opportunities for educated youth declined.

Throughout the 1910s, writing emphasizing personality rather than performance became increasingly common. Much of it came from *Jitsugyō no Nihon* and its parent firm. A 1911 (Meiji 44) list of books published by the firm contained such items as *A Shining Personality* [Jinkaku no kōki], *Forging a Personality* (Jinkaku no tanren), *Cultivating Social Graces* [Kōsaijutsu shūyō], *Personality Cul-*

---

79. "Dokuritsu jiei to yūjin no kaitaku," *Jitsugyō no Nihon* 9:2 (February 1, 1906): 11–12.
80. Masuda Giichi, "Shin-sotsugyōsei ni kono yōi to kono kakugo nari ya," *Jitsugyō no Nihon* (August 1, 1911), pp. 17–20.

NEW ETHICS

tivation [Jinkaku shūyō], and others of apparently similar intent.[81] The basic thrust of these works may be understood from *Cultivating the Conversational Arts* [Danwajutsu shūyō] by Ashigawa Tadao, a frequent contributor to *Jitsugyō no Nihon*.[82] This book had sections on how to project warmth and evoke sympathy in hostile listeners, and a number of similar sections, all of which separated success from objective performance and which stressed the manipulation of interpersonal relations.

A certain amount of this other-directed ethic is perhaps to be traced to indigenous traditions, but two facts argue against assigning too much weight to Japanese traditions as a source or cause for the appearance of this literature. First, several of the titles offered by *Jitsugyō no Nihon* were translations from American works. The rise of bureaucratic capitalism in the United States was the source of much of the material. The only major difference to be noted between American and Japanese writing is that the Japanese writing was shifting to a consciously other-directed or personality ethic faster than its American counterpart. Ashigawa noted in his preface that while various American authors of the day were stressing the importance of personality, there was as yet none who had devoted a full-scale work to the subject. Thus, he had been forced to write his own book on the subject rather than simply translating. Indeed, the classic text of the personality ethic in the United States, *Public Speaking and Influencing Men in Business* by Dale Carnegie, did not appear until 1926 (Taishō 15).[83] Ashigawa anticipated by fifteen years the "personality salesmanship" that would be a major motif in later American writing. At most, it can be argued that the absence of "rugged individualism" in Japanese traditions meant that fewer Japanese than Americans would cling to the character ethic of advancement in a market situation where the personality ethic was called for.

A second reason for ascribing the appearance of this personality ethic of success to the dynamics of bureaucratic capitalism and to the relatively unfavorable market for educated youth is the appear-

81. These and other items were listed in the advertising pages included in Nitobe, *Shūyō*.
82. Ashigawa Tadao, *Danwajutsu shūyō* (Chiseidō shoten, 1910).
83. This work is better known under its later title, *How to Win Friends and Influence People*. The 1926 (Taishō 15) version was an official text for a number of large United States corporations. See Bendix, *Work and Authority*, pp. 302–303.

ance of this ethic in writing aimed at educated youth, not just in writing aimed at shop clerks employed in more or less traditional businesses. An interesting example of this is *Tōkyō gaku* [Tokyo Study] by Ishikawa Tengai, educator and textbook publisher.[84] Appearing in 1909 (Meiji 42), this curious work combined a bit of muckraking with advice on how to get ahead in Tokyo. It had some of the subjects that were to be found in earlier guides to Tokyo as far back as *Shōnenen*, such as warnings about bogus schools and the evils lurking in boardinghouses. What made *Tōkyō gaku* different was its emphasis on personality and the manipulation of social graces as keys to success. Sections of the book dealt with such topics as making people agree with you through persuasion, the techniques of calling on people, how to make use of introductions, how to select someone to introduce you, how to gauge a person's interests and respond to them for your own profit, how to create a sense of creditability and how to capitalize on this, how to fit into groups and use them for one's own advantage, and so on. Essentially, *Tōkyō gaku* dealt with the same topics as Dale Carnegie and other American authors of the personality-ethic genre of writing on advancement. The words of Sinclair Lewis, originally applied to Dale Carnegie, could just as well have been written about *Tōkyō gaku*, for it too taught you "how to smile and bob and pretend to be interested in people's hobbies precisely so that you may screw things out of them."[85] The only major difference was a strong background of resentment against this state of affairs in *Tōkyō gaku*. The author felt that the present competitive situation demanded that one screw his fellow man lest he himself be screwed, but this was not the way things should be.

Despite its inspiration derived from Marden and his magazine *Success*, *Seikō* was much slower to advocate other-directed virtues and never stressed them with the enthusiasm found in *Jitsugyō no Nihon* nor with the candor found in *Tōkyō gaku*. Initially, the editor seems to have seen Marden as simply an up-to-date Smiles, a view that was correct because Marden was a transitional figure standing between the character ethic of Smiles and the personality ethic of

---

84. Ishikawa Tengai, *Tōkyō gaku*, in *Meiji bunka shiryō sōsho*, ed. Meiji bunka shiryō sōsho kankō-kai (Kazama shobō, 1970), vol. 12, pp. 341–514.

85. Quoted in Huber, *American Idea*, p. 262.

Carnegie.[86] Only a few early articles recognized that its readers would become employees, and those articles having this recognition simply applied the usual list of Smilesean virtues to the workplace. After the Russo-Japanese War, the magazine did occasionally have a few articles by real businessmen and actual functionaries, but even then, most of the articles so attributed did not deviate much from scholasticized Smilesean virtue.

It was only late in the magazine's existence that it began to pay attention to the virtues suited to the employment situation. A 1913 (Taishō 2) article explained the "secrets of survival" for those looking to careers in the bureaucracy. Written by Nakakōji Kiyoshi, an official of the Agriculture and Commerce Ministry (Nōshōmushō), this piece noted that technical skill was not enough for success in government employment.[87] If the skilled person was too proud or had no sympathy for others because he was too utilitarian, he could not expect to maintain his position. What was demanded, said Nakakōji, was a "well-rounded personality," a person who "respects superiors, is close to equals, and loves subordinates." In essence this was exactly the situation described in the novel *Ukigumo* [Floating Clouds] where Utsumi Bunzō had found himself being fired because he merely did his job, while Honda Noboru got a raise by exploiting interpersonal relations.

The late entry of *Seikō* into the personality ethic is to be explained by the general academic coloring of the magazine and the residual of commonerism (*heimin shugi*) in the thought of its editor, Murakami Dakurō. *Seikō* held to a belief in the early Meiji formula that described the nation as a reflection of the people composing it. To have generally advocated the pattern put forth in *Jitsugyō no Nihon* and *Tōkyō gaku* would have amounted to virtual treason for *Seikō* writers. It would have required saying that the nation would be best served if it had large numbers of obsequious people. Even *Jitsugyō no Nihon*, which had no residual commonerism to overcome, felt obliged to explain that its advocacy of relying on contacts

---

86. *Self-Help* was still being produced and read, but advertisements for *Character* and *Duty* and translations of these works were more prominent. Significantly, both *Character* and *Duty* deal with the individual in social and employment situations to a greater degree than was true of *Self-Help*.

87. Nakakōji Kiyoshi, "Ikani seba kyōsō-jōri no yūsha to narubeki ka," *Seikō* 24:5 (February 1, 1913): 8–11.

did not amount to currying favor, although the distinction is lost on a contemporary reader.[88]

Seikō was saved from any intellectual dilemma by its concentration on students, especially those who would "study by struggle," for the inherent isolation of their quest did not usually raise issues of interpersonal relations. As long as it drew most of its outside editorial material from academics and intellectuals, all of whom belonged to the 1880s–1890s or earlier generations, the personality ethic of advancement was bound to be largely ignored. This was also true of *Chūgaku sekai*. In the last years of the Meiji era it did have a few articles on social graces written by Abe Isoo, one of the few early socialists who was still a true believer in *risshin* and self-help. Abe did not, however, approach *Jitsugyō no Nihon*, to say nothing of *Tōkyō gaku*, in his discussion of personality. His style was similar to *Character*, in which Smiles himself had given more attention to gentlemen as members of society, but it is likely that the proximate inspiration for Abe was Marden and not Smiles.[89]

88. Masuda, "Shin-sotsugyōsei," differentiated between making one's character known and currying favor (*ayu*).
89. Abe Isoo, "Fumanzoku no ten," *Chūgaku sekai* 10:8 (July 10, 1907): 182–189, and Abe Isoo, "Seinen shosei no michi," *Chūgaku sekai* 11:4 (March 10, 1908): 2–23.

Afterward: The Sarariiman (Salary Man) | 8

By the end of the Meiji era, indeed perhaps as early as the 1890s, the image of the student contained in the early Meiji ditty "Student Song" [Shosei bushi] was manifestly inappropriate to describe the future of *most* educated youth. True, generals, admirals, parliamentarians, and ministers of state *all began as students* (*shosei*). Nevertheless, in the early Meiji period the expectation had been that *all students would become* generals, admirals, parliamentarians, ministers of state, or would achieve comparably high rank. By the end of the period, even the most optimistic of contemporary observers could not help but note that only a fraction of all educated youth would achieve the statuses called for by "Student Song." Moreover, even those few who rose to the supreme heights of *risshin* would do so by following the systematic course: the right education obtained after passing through the examination barriers and perhaps the "placement difficulty" (*shūshokunan*) and then a period in low-ranked positions, proceeding step by step if at all.

Within the strict confines of the Meiji era itself, no poular ditty or term developed to describe the future of educated youth, to update "Student Song." With the knowledge conveyed by hindsight, it is possible to say that at least from the turn of the century, the majority of educated youth in late Meiji Japan were on their way to becoming what subsequent generations would know as the *sarariiman* (salary man), or white-collar worker engaged in menial tasks in government or business. The prototype for the *sarariiman* was the *ko-shiben*, or "lunch-bucket man," low-ranked civil servants who carried their lunches (*bentō*) in a container attached to a cord around their waists (*koshi*). They appeared in the background of a number of Meiji novels, including Ukigumo [Floating Clouds], which opened with a description of home-going government workers in Tokyo in 1887 (Meiji 20). First out of the gate were the higher-ranked and better-educated workers with their beards, moustaches, and Western suits. Behind them came the *koshiben*. "Their hair grey, their backs bent like a bow, they totter home feebly with their empty lunch boxes [*koshi-bentō*] dangling from their waists. Old and decrepit, they still somehow manage to hang on to a job, but so unimportant is their position, they are still allowed to work in Japanese dress."[1] As the references to age and traditional dress indicate, the *koshiben* were a carry-over from the ancien regime. The word and the custom were both known in the Tokugawa period when lower samurai who were engaged in clerical tasks were more likely to have a lunch box than a sword dangling from their waists.[2]

Eventually even the lowest ranked workers were required to dress in Western suits, and the distinction between high and low officials described in *Ukigumo* was lost. A 1909 (Meiji 42) ditty entitled "Scholar Song" [*Sukaraa songu*] satirized the early-morning procession of *koshiben* to be seen in the vicinity of the Kandabashi section of Tokyo. It described them trudging along in torn suits, with lunches dangling from their waists. As they shuffled along they looked with envy on gentlemen speeding by in automobiles and prayed to the gods and Buddha for similar favors. At home their wives were making buttons and their daughters were at work in cigarette factories. All they could be thankful for was the nine yen a month they received from the government.[3] With the change in dress came a new word for the *koshiben*.[4] They were styled *yōfuku-saimin*, or "pauper in a suit."

These late Meiji *koshiben* were not, however, the dying remnant of Tokugawa traditions dressed up in threadbare suits. If the *koshiben* are equated with the *yatoi*, the unclassified category of the civil

1. Futabatei Shimei, *Ukigumo*, in *Tsubouchi Shōyō—Futabatei Shimei*, vol. 1 of *Nihon bungaku zenshū* (Shūei sha, 1969), p. 256.
2. *Nihon kokugo dai-jiten*, vol. 8, p. 155.
3. Quoted in Matsunari Yoshie, Izutani Hajime, Tanuma Hajime, and Noda Masaho, *Nihon no sarariiman* (Aoki shoten, 1957), p. 37.
4. Ibid., p. 46.

THE SARARIIMAN (SALARY MAN)

service, who happened to have an average income of nine yen during much of the Meiji period, statistics show that they were a flourishing species. In 1887 (Meiji 20) there were 15,140 *yatoi*. In 1909 (Meiji 42) there were 100,558. Two decades later there were 356,574. Not only did the *koshiben* defined as *yatoi* increase absolutely, he increased more rapidly than the higher ranks of the civil service (*chokunin* and *sōnin*). In 1887 (Meiji 20) there were but 4.3 *yatoi* for each one of the more exalted officials. In 1909 (Meiji 42) the ratio was 12.3 to 1, and in 1929 (Shōwa 4), 21.7 to 1.[5]

The *koshiben* in government employ was, moreover, being joined by a private-sector equivalent known by such names as *shokuin* ("staff employee") or *gekkyū-tori* ("monthly salary receiver"). No comprehensive statistics on the corporate version of the *koshiben* exist prior to the 1920 (Taishō 9) census, but studies of individual companies show rapid increases in the clerical labor force in the last

---

5. These calculations are based on data for the indicated fiscal years as given in *Meiji Taishō kokusei sōran* (Tōyō keizai shinpō sha, 1975 [1927]), table 737, p. 664, and *Nihon teikoku tōkei nenkan*, no. 55 (1936), table 383, pp. 412–413. Unless otherwise stated, all subsequent references to the size of the national bureaucracy and its pay levels are from these two sources.

The equation of the *koshiben* and the *yatoi* made here is arbitrary. A good case (see below) may be made for equating the *koshiben* to the *hannin* ("clerk") and *yatoi* categories combined. If this alternative assumption is made, the number of *koshiben* in the national civil service becomes (ratios in parenthesis): 1887 (Meiji 20), 40,561 (11.4 : 1); 1909 (Meiji 42), 157,917 (19.4 : 1); 1929 (Shōwa 4), 455,863 (29.3 : 1)

Contemporary observers were aware of this changing ratio and saw it as indicative of declining opportunities for advancement (*risshin*). See Koike Shirō, *Hōkyū seikatsusha ron* (Seiunkaku 1929), pp. 34–39, and the sources cited in Matsunar_, *Nihon no sarariiman*, p. 32.

In interpreting the figures on civil service employment and compensation cited here and subsequently, several caveats must be kept in mind. (a) Only national civil servants (*bunkan*) are represented. The sources cited do not include most employees in governmental enterprises or quasi-governmental corporations (most notably Mantetsu). Local civil servants and teachers are not counted here. (b) Within the national civil service group, accounting categories are not entirely consistent. In 1922 (Taishō 11), nearly forty thousand individuals were switched from the *yatoi* to the *hannin* category. In 1927 (Shōwa 2) large numbers of provincial employees were added to the national totals. (c) Individual agencies appear to have not always furnished their employment totals in time for proper compilation in the *Tōkei nenkan*, with the result that the total for the previous year was used.

None of these *known* peculiarities of the data is believed to be of serious consequence here, but the reader is advised that while the direction of change derived from these sources is reasonably certain, statements of magnitude must be regarded as tentative.

THE SELF-MADE MAN IN MEIJI JAPANESE THOUGHT

years of the Meiji and the first years of the Taishō period.[6] With the 1920 (Taishō 9) census, it is possible to get a reasonably accurate sense of the size of the aggregate white-collar labor force. The census enumerated 1,514,511 people, or 5.5 percent of the gainfully employed population, as belonging to the category *shokuin*. The 1930 (Shōwa 5) census showed an increase to 2,055,444 people, or 6.9 percent of the gainfully employed population. While these proportions may seem small and thus inconsequential, it must be remembered that in prewar Japan roughly half the working population was agricultural. Further, the gainfully employed category included many proprietors. When the *shokuin* category is measured against nonagricultural labor, its relative importance appears far greater; 1 out of 5 nonagricultural male workers belonged to the *shokuin* category.[7]

Although the march of educated youth into the ranks of the *koshiben* had begun in the last years of the Meiji era, the direction of advance was not perfectly straight. One brief detour into prosperity during World War I served to delineate more clearly the overall decline of youthful fortunes. The fitful growth of the Japanese economy after the Russo-Japanese War was replaced by several years of rapid growth beginning in 1916 (Taishō 5) as Japan expanded into markets left vacant by a Europe and an America preoccupied with World War I. Fortunes were made overnight in a number of industries, particularly shipping. The exploits of the nouveau riche, es-

---

6. Matsunari, *Nihon no sarariiman*, pp. 31–32.
7. 1920 (Taishō 9) data from the summary census table given in Himuro Yoshihira, ed., *Kyūryō seikatsusha mondai* (Shakai rippō kyōkai, 1933), pp. 12–13; 1930 *shokuin* numbers from *Nihon rōdō nenkan*, no. 21 (1940), p. 74; and gainfully employed from *Asahi nenkan 1937*, p. 80. These figures should be regarded as approximations of the white-collar work force. The *Nihon rōdō nenkan* consistently stated that the census *shokuin* figure understated the size of the *hōkyū seikatsusha* (salaried employee) population. The lumping together of male and female workers, done in many discussions of employment patterns, also leads to an understatement of the relative size of the white-collar contingent as a proportion of all wage labor (outside of agriculture). For example, if the 1920 (Taishō 9) census data is adjusted to exclude agriculture workers and only males are considered, *shokuin* appear as 22.1 percent of the total nonagricultural work force. For other rearrangements of the census data, see Robert E. Cole and Ken'ichi Tominaga, "Japan's Changing Occupational Structure and Its Significance," pp. 53–95, in Hugh Patrick, ed., *Japanese Industrialization and Its Social Consequences* (University of California Press, 1976), esp. p. 66; and Kuroda Toshio, "Occupational Mobility," *Journal of Social and Political Ideas in Japan* 3:3 (December 1965): 36–44.

pecially the shipping parvenu (*fune narikin*), were given wide play in the press as they vied with one another in ostentatious consumption: building garish mansions, staging mammoth geisha parties, and lighting one-hundred-yen notes (about fifty dollars) to find their geta in the dark.[8]

Visions of fortunes to be made danced before the eyes of ordinary office workers, whose mood was expressed in a ditty, "Croquette" [Korokke], popular in 1917–1918 (Taishō 6–7).

> I take up my wallet around the last day of the month;
> When I open it and look, the money goes jingle, jingle.
> It goes jingle, jingle!
> Shall I buy stock or shall I buy land?
> I wake up in the middle of this thought.
> Ah, ha ha. Ah, ha ha. It's funny.[9]

Books on various get-rich-quick schemes, especially stock market speculation, enjoyed brisk sales in these years.[10]

The World War I boom years were good in terms of bureaucratic employment. The total number of national-government civil servants went from 224,883 in 1916 (Taishō 5) to 328,760 in 1921 (Taishō 10), an expansion of 46 percent. Compared with the golden years of the Meiji period, 1895–1900 (Meiji 28–33), when there had been a 98 percent increase, this expansion was not so impressive, but the absolute numbers were much greater. More important, the World War I boom was a sharp contrast with the immediately preceding period, 1910–1915 (Meiji 43–Taishō 4), during which the national bureaucracy had grown by only 19 percent. The 46 percent expansion was more than enough to buoy the spirits of those who looked to the government for their *risshin*, especially since there was included within this gross expansion a hefty increase in *sōnin*-level functionaries. This group, which represented the ideal for youth with higher education, expanded by 41 percent in the years 1916–1921 (Taishō 5–10). A good rate in and of itself, it was especially wel-

---

8. Nasu Yoshirō, "Dokusen shihon no kakuritsu to shakai seikatsu no henka," in *Seikatsu shi III*, vol. 17 of *Taikei Nihon shi sōsho*, ed. Morisue Yoshiaki, Hōgetsu Keigo, and Konishi Shirō (Yamakawa shuppan, 1969), pp. 229–230.

9. Quoted in Matsunari, *Nihon no sarariiman*, pp. 39–40.

10. "Shuppankai no keikō," *Chūō shinbun* (February 1, 1917), in *Shinbun shūroku Taishō shi*, ed. Watanabe Katsumasu (Taishō shuppan, 1978), vol. 5, p. 383. Hereafter abbreviated *SSTS*.

come, since the *sōnin* category had actually decreased by 1 percent during the period 1910–1915 (Meiji 43–Taishō 4).

The war boom and the expansion in the bureaucracy banished the term "placement difficulty" (*shūshokunan*) from the pages of youth-oriented publications and newspapers. The market for university graduates (for all practical purposes, Tokyo Imperial University students) improved sharply.[11] The proportion of all graduates not placed during their year of graduation fell from an average of 33 percent in 1912–1916 (Taishō 1–5) to 16 percent during the years 1917–1921 (Taishō 6–10). Not all this improvement was due to increased opportunities in the national bureaucracy, however, and the *risshin* orientation of Tokyo Imperial University graduates came increasingly to be directed at business.[12] In the period 1907–1916 (Meiji 40–Taishō 5) an average of 15 percent of Tōdai graduates had entered "companies and banks" (*kaisha, ginkō*); during the war boom years (1917–1921) more than a third did so. In the peak year of 1919 (Taishō 8), almost 40 percent went into the private sector.

The change is even more dramatic when only law students are considered, for they were nearly one-half of all Tōdai graduates in the early Taishō era and accounted for up to 80 percent of those recorded as not yet placed. In the period 1912–1916 (Taishō 1–5), 1 out of 2 law students was unplaced in their year of graduation. Between 1917 and 1921 (Taishō 6–10) the average was only 1 in 5 and in peak boom years such as 1918 and 1919 (Taishō 7 and 8), only 1 in 10 was not placed rapidly. Corporate employment claimed only 1 in 7 between 1912 and 1916 (Taishō 1–5) but 1 in 3 between 1917 and 1921 (Taishō 6–10) and in the peak year of 1919 (Taishō 8) more than 1 in

---

11. *Unless otherwise noted*, all subsequent discussions involving educational statistics are based on the *Monbushō nenpō*. One major peculiarity of Monbushō placement data for *imperial university* graduates should be noted here. Up through *Monbunshō nenpō*, no. 55 (1927), placement data is given for those who graduated in the fiscal year covered by the report. From *Monbushō nenpō*, no. 56 (1928), placement status was given for those graduating in the *prior* fiscal year. Because there was an extra year of job-seeking by graduates covered in the 1928 and subsequent reports, their placement rates were generally higher than before the change. Conversely, when the 1933 (Shōwa 8) edition of the *Monbushō nenpō* reported that 42 percent of the 1932 (Shōwa 7) graduates of the law faculty of Tōdai were not yet placed, it was indicating a much worse job market than when the 1917 (Taishō 6) edition had reported 40 percent in the same situation.

12. For a discussion of this shift, see Ozaki Moriteru, *Nihon shūshoku shi* (Bungei shunjū, 1967), pp. 32–37.

THE SARARIIMAN (SALARY MAN)

2. Since the civil service was also expanding vigorously, this shift to the corporate sector indicates that given sufficient promise of wealth alone, those young men from the institution and subject area most intimately associated with the traditional view of *risshin* as bureaucratic wealth *and* honor would opt for the material portion alone.[13] Their commitment to government service was relative, not absolute. At the less-elite institutions of higher education where the prejudice in favor of government affiliation was not as strong, companies found themselves forced to compete with one another to gain the favors of college and higher-commercial-school graduates. Starting wages were bid up, and students were courted with offers of special bonuses and promises of foreign study in the future.[14]

The war boom was not, however, an unmixed blessing to all elements of the white-collar labor force. Prices increased much faster than did wages in the public sector. During the first three years of the war boom, prices more than doubled while civil service wages were essentially constant. Stories and letters in newspapers reported near-starvation conditions among low-ranked urban functionaries. Police, elementary-school teachers, and civil servants of *hannin* and *yatoi* rank were especially hard hit; but even higher civil servants lost much of their real income.[15] White-collar workers in companies, in contrast, received a variety of special adjustments (*teate*) that kept their real incomes even with or ahead of inflation. Factory workers too enjoyed an extraordinary situation. Contemporary accounts indicated that highly skilled workers in the munitions industry could make up to 240 yen a month, a princely sum compared with the 35-yen average of *hannin* rank civil servants and

13. Contemporary accounts cite the relatively greater benefits being offered in the private sector as the reason for this change. "Kasumigaseki o mezashite," *Tōkyō Asahi shinbun* (October 18, 1922), in *SSTS* 10:387. Subsequently the proportion reported going into banks and companies fell, but this was not a shift back to government. Private business stopped hiring and the share not placed increased.
14. "Sotsugyōsei no mi no furikata," *Tōkyō Asahi shinbun* (December 6, 1920), in *SSTS* 8:405; "Subarashii sotsugyōsei no ureyuki," *Hōchi shinbun* (February 16, 1917), in *SSTS* 5:49–50; "Shigaku banzai no jōkeiki," *Yomiuri shinbun* (February 20, 1917), in *SSTS* 5:67; "Kōka no sotsugyōsei wa shohō kara hippari dako," *Miyako shinbun*, in *SSTS* 5:111–112.
15. Matsunari, *Nihon no sarariiman*, pp. 44–49; Takahashi Shōkuma, "Kyōikusha no seikatsunan," *Shakai seisaku jihō*, no. 1 (September, 1920), pp. 115–130; Aoki Kensaku, "Shiritsu chūtō gakkō no byōhei," *Shakai seisaku jihō*, no. 15 (November 1921), pp. 320–344; *The Japan Year Book 1920–1921*, p. 298.

nearly double the 125-yen average for *sōnin*.[16] The ditty "Croquette" became applicable only to workers in the private sector; government workers on fixed wages could not consider speculation when they could not pay for daily necessities. Organized protest and the fear that radical thought would spread among discontented government employees led in 1920 (Taishō 9) to a restructuring of the pay scale. Average compensation jumped more than 80 percent, but as critical articles noted, the adjustment was considerably less than the toll taken by inflation.[17]

The war boom did not last long. The speculative bubble burst in 1920 (Taishō 9). To the general slackening of demand was added the impact of reductions called for by the 1921 disarmament agreements.[18] The Gross National Product contracted, and prices began to move downward. Functionaries with jobs found that the same inertia that worked to prevent raises during inflation worked to prevent cuts during deflation. Company employees, in contrast, found themselves faced with a loss of their wartime bonuses and adjustments. Organized opposition to these reductions flourished briefly in 1920–1921 (Taishō 9–10), then disappeared as company employees were faced with a far more threatening problem: mass firings of clerical and managerial personnel. Many large firms cut hundreds of employees from their white-collar payrolls.[19]

In place of those discharged, companies hired a much smaller number of new employees with higher education. These firings and subsequent hirings were not, however, simply a matter of firms' "rationalizing" by replacing older, less-educated workers with better-

16. "Shokkōren no zensei jidai," *Tōkyō Asahi shinbun* (August 16, 1917), in *SSTS* 5:284. Even if this account was exaggerated, conventional series of blue-collar wages show them to have been above *hannin* levels. For example, in 1919 (Taishō 8) the average construction-worker wage was 48.0 yen (assuming a 25-day month). Average *hannin* compensation was 37.2 yen. Blue-collar data from Ohkawa Kazushi, Shinohara Miyohei, Umemura Mataji, ed. *Prices*, vol. 8 of *Estimates of Long-Term Economic Statistics of Japan Since 1868* (Tōyō keizai shinpō sha, 1967), table 25, pp. 244–245.

17. The average increase was calculated by using the average wage for all government employees in fiscal 1919 (Taishō 8) and 1921 (Taishō 10). A detailed discussion and criticism of the new pay scale is found in Ogawa Gōtaro, "Zōhō no kenkyū," *Keizai ronsō* 12:6 (June 1921): 878–903.

18. *Industrial Labour in Japan*, International Labour Office Studies and Reports Series A (Industrial Relations), no. 37 (ILO, 1933), pp. 289–290.

19. *Nihon rōdō nenkan*, no. 2 (1921), pp. 331–333, and Ozaki, *Shūshoku*, pp. 95–97.

educated younger workers who were presumably more productive. Contemporary accounts indicate that firms broke their agreements with students who had yet to enter the company and discharged employees with higher education who had entered only a few years earlier. These workers were then replaced with new employees of a similar educational level who could be obtained at much lower wages thanks to the depression.[20] Adding to the pressure on educated graduates was a fall in government hiring. The proportion of unplaced Tokyo Imperial University graduates climbed to 40 percent for the years 1922–1926 (Taishō 11–15) and for law graduates to 84 percent, with 100 percent unplaced in 1926 (Taishō 15). Only in 1924 (Taishō 13) was there a break in this pattern when company hiring from the rebuilding boom following the Great Kantō Earthquake took a modest number of graduates.

Beginning in 1923–1924 (Taishō 12–13), national government employees came to share the experience of their brethren in private industry. Under the name of "administrative retrenchment" (*gyōsei seiri*), some twenty-two thousand government workers were fired or moved to less attractive positions.[21] A striking feature of this administrative retrenchment was that it, unlike many earlier ventures,

---

20. Ozaki, *Shūshoku*, pp. 122–124, and contemporary accounts, including "Teidaide no kaishain ni," *Yorozu chōhō* (August 17, 1920), in *SSTS* 8:305; "Kumon no Furukawa," *Tōkyō Nichi nichi shinbun* (August 14, 1920), in *SSTS* 8:302; and "Hayaku ga zokuzoku kuru sotsugyōsei no shūshoku," *Tōkyō Asahi shinbun* (June 12, 1920), in *SSTS* 8:214–215.

21. Descriptions of the magnitude of firings at this time vary widely. Matsunari, *Nihon no sarariiman*, p. 57, mentions dismissal of approximately 5,000 civil and military officials in 1922 (Taishō 11), and Ozaki, *Sarariiman*, p. 105, claims 60,000 for the later years. Contemporary newspaper accounts cite figures ranging from 18,000 to 40,000. "Hyaku-nijū-yo-man no shitsugyōsha," *Kokumin shinbun* (October 18, 1924), in *SSTS* 12:396–397, and "Tobu kubi ichi-man-hassen," *Yomiuri shinbun* (October 21, 1924), in *SSTS* 12:398–399, I have relied on the estimate in *Nihon rōdō nenkan*, no. 7 (1926), p. 44. This figure is, however, at odds with government reports on the size of bureaucratic employment. Gross employment levels (from the sources cited in note 5) indicate a change between 1923 (Taishō 12) and 1924 (Taishō 13) of only 9,820. Apparently a portion of the 20,563 (14.6%) decrease in the *hannin* category was made up through increases in the *yatoi* category of 12,656 (7.6%). It is not clear whether the discharged *hannin* became *yatoi* at lower wages and benefits or the *yatoi* increase was new hiring.

An additional, and perhaps more important, factor in explaining the divergent accounts and data is the failure of contemporary reports to observe the legalistic distinctions between the many categories of government employees. The data sources cited

saw many *sōnin* rank civil servants being terminated. Contemporary accounts reported imperial university graduates and former civil servants up to the 200-yen bracket (average *sōnin* pay was 207–228 yen in these years) appearing at employment exchanges along with ordinary laborers.[22] This crisis sparked the first formal attempt to gather comprehensive unemployment statistics. The first survey done in October 1925 (Taishō 14) covered twenty-four industrial centers and put the unemployment rate for salaried workers at 3.15 percent and that for blue-collar workers at 3.02 percent.[23] Unemployment and not just placement difficulties were now recognized facts of white-collar life.

The boom generated by rebuilding after the Great Kantō Earthquake came to an end in 1927–1928 (Shōwa 2–3) with a round of bank failures which in turn brought down affiliated and dependent enterprises.[24] Government employment actually increased in the same period.[25] This odd situation did not last long, however, and in 1929 (Shōwa 4) government employees, first at the local level and then at the national level, once again experienced a round of dismissals. Although the net effect was to cut the civilian bureaucracy a mere 0.7 percent (on a base of nearly half a million people), the personal impact on those dismissed was devastating because of the generally depressed state of the economy and absence of other em-

---

here are for classified civil servants (*bunkan*), but as was observed in note 5, there were large numbers of other civilian government employees not covered by this category. Moreover, American experience would suggest that *announced* government cutbacks are usually considerably greater than *realized* reductions, and this phenomenon may have existed in Japan at this time. Of course, unrealized threats produce no less anxiety than those completely carried out, and this should be kept in mind in evaluating the apparently small reductions that take place subsequently.

22. "Ichi-man nin no chishiki kaikyū," *Yomiuri shinbun* (October 28, 1925), in *SSTS* 13:419–420; "Chūtō kyōin no shitsugyōsha sanzen nin," *Miyako shinbun* (July 7, 1925), in *SSTS* 12:284; and "Sattō shita gakushiren," *Jiji shinpō* (March 11, 1926), in *SSTS* 14:93.

23. Harada Shūichi, *Labor Conditions in Japan* (Columbia University Press, 1928), pp. 133–134. Among those reported unemployed were 5,469 civil servants, 6,652 commercial employees, and 6,837 from industry and transportation. See also *Nihon rōdō nenkan*, no. 7 (1926), pp. 44, 92–93. The survey cited by Harada and those done subsequently were widely criticized for seriously understating the level of unemployment. For a discussion of this, see Jack D. Downard, "Tokyo: The Depression Years, 1927–1933," (Ph.D. dissertation, Indiana University, 1976), pp. 117–125.

24. Matsunari, *Sarariiman*, p. 63; Nasu, "Dokusen shihon," p. 273; *Nihon rōdō nenkan*, no. 9 (1928), p. 52, and no. 10 (1929), p. 62.

25. *Nihon rōdō nenkan*, no. 10 (1929), pp. 58–59.

ployment opportunities.[26] Moreover, even as the internal dynamics of the Japanese economy were generating unemployment, the effects of the stock market crash and depression in the United States began to be felt in Japan. Official statistics—which probably much understated the actual situation—reported 63,410 unemployed salary receivers (hōkyū seikatsusha) in December, 1929 (Shōwa 4), representing 3.86 percent of the 1,643,873 survey base. In October, 1932 (Shōwa 7), white-collar unemployment peaked at a reported 88,668 people, who were 5.26 percent of the 1,686,243 survey population.[27] One out of five unemployed persons was classified as a (would-be) salary receiver, and if day laborers (who usually had high unemployment) are excluded, one out of three was so classified.

The uncertainty of the period was compounded in the public sector by government proposals for pay cuts for those still employed. The first such proposal, in 1929 (Shōwa 4), was defeated, and the second, in 1931 (Shōwa 6), was so modified in response to a general and widespread opposition movement that it had relatively little impact on most government employees. Nevertheless, the threat of more comprehensive cuts in pay and positions continued to exist in the next few years, adding to the generally uncertain future of white-collar workers in the government.[28] Local officials and teachers were in an even more unstable position because they were subject to the vagaries of local-government finances and direct community pressure. Teachers experienced arbitrary pay cuts, defaults, and firings

---

26. *Nihon rōdō nenkan*, no. 11 (1930), p. 70. Like earlier dismissal rounds, this one seems to have involved actual firing and shifts within categories which may be summarized as follows:

	hannin		yatoi		total	
1929–1930	−7698	−6.5%	+12,057	+3.6%	+4,221	+0.9%
1930–1931	+7361	+6.6%	−10,657	−3.1%	−3,115	−0.7%
1931–1932	−3710	−3.1%	+16,836	+5.0%	+13,287	+2.8%

27. 1929 (Shōwa 4) data from *Nihon rōdō nenkan*, no. 11 (1930), p. 69, and 1932 (Shōwa 7) data from *Nihon rōdō nenkan*, no. 14 (1933), p. 81.

28. Concerning these attempts to cut civil service pay and the resulting opposition movement, see Robert M. Spaulding, "The Bureaucracy as a Political Force, 1920–45," in James W. Morley, ed., *Dilemmas of Growth in Prewar Japan* (Princeton University Press, 1971), pp. 52–56; Tanabe Tadao, "Genpō mondai to kanri no danketsu," *Shakai seisaku jihō*, no. 130 (July 1931), pp. 87–95; Sagara Toshimitsu, "Sarariiman no tetsugaku," *Kaizō* 13:7 (July 1931): 120–133; and Matsunari, *Nihon no sarariiman*, pp. 81–84. The impact of the cuts was as follows: *yatoi*, 2.2%; *hannin*, 1.2%; *sōnin*, 9.6%; and *chokunin*, 11.4%. These results are based on comparison of fiscal 1930 (Shōwa 5) and fiscal 1932 (Shōwa 7) average compensation levels.

as local governments cut their wage bills by replacing older teachers with younger and less-expensive graduates.[29]

These firings by companies and government agencies marked what some contemporary observers regarded as the proletarianization of educated workers, who were now forced to beat the pavement and to make the rounds of the labor exchanges in a quest that was familiar to blue-collar workers. In some respects white-collar workers were in an even worse position than their blue-collar comrades. Contemporary accounts note that labor exchanges had much less success placing unemployed white-collar job seekers than they had with regular blue-collar workers or day laborers. The unemployed would-be white-collar worker was likely to remain out of work longer than his blue-collar counterpart, and if he was over thirty, his prospects of finding a position comparable to what he had enjoyed before dismissal were minimal.[30]

Dismissals in the private sector and in government enterprises (as distinguished from the civil service) continued until 1933 (Shōwa 8), when *The Japan Labor Year Book* [Nihon rōdō nenkan] was able to report that for the first time since the end of the World War I boom the employment situation of white-collar workers was beginning to improve. The source of this change was increased exports and military procurements, especially the latter.[31] Progress was slow, however, even as the military budget soared 922 percent between 1930 (Shōwa 5) and 1939 (Shōwa 14) and total government expenditure increased 158 percent in the same period. Officially estimated white-collar unemployment declined from the previously noted peak of 88,668 people, or 5.26 percent of the 1,686,243 survey base in October 1932 (Shōwa 7), to 47,652 people, or 2.5 percent of the 1,867,115

29. "Shōgaku kyōin genpō," *Kokumin shinbun* (March 5, 1930), in *Shinbun shūsei Shōwa hennenshi* (Taishō Shōwa hennenshi kankō-kai, 1968), vol. 5, p. 151 (hereafter abbreviated, *SSS*); "Shōgakkō no sensei no shoninkyū," *Tōkyō Nichi nichi* (March 18, 1930), in *SSS* 5:180–181; "Shōgaku kyōin no genpō," *Tōykō Jiji shinpō* (March 20, 1930) in *SSS* 5:185–186; "Shōgaku kyōin no taishokusha," *Hōchi shinbun* (April 9, 1930), in *SSS* 5:226; "Kyōin no hōkyū junan," *Tōkyō Asahi shinbun*, in *SSS* 5:603; and Karasawa Tomitarō, *Kyōshi no rekishi* (Sōbun sha, 1955), pp. 155–158.

30. Sakisaka Toshirō, *Chishiki kaikyū ron* (Kaizō sha, 1935), pp. 327–331, Shūshoku mondai kenkyū-kai, *Gakusei to shūshoku no jissai* (Tōkyō jitsugyō sha, 1934), pp. 150–159, and Abe Isoo, *Shitsugyō mondai* (Nihon hyōron sha, 1929), p. 198, for data on the performance of the exchanges.

31. *Nihon rōdō nenkan*, no. 15 (1934), p. 82; no. 16 (1935), p. 106; and no. 17 (1936), p. 103.

survey base in January 1939 (Shōwa 14). Even with this decline the white-collar unemployment rate was higher than that of blue-collar workers (estimated at 1.5 percent). Further rapid decreases in 1939 (Shōwa 14) cut the white-collar figure to 28,449, or 1.5 percent of the 1,936,140 survey base, but this left their rate above that for blue-collar workers. As a result, at the end of 1939 (Shōwa 14 , one out of five unemployed persons was classified as a would-be salary receiver, and if day laborers are excluded, two out of five were so designated.[32]

It was in these years of crisis for white-collar workers that the term *koshiben* was replaced by *sarariiman* (salary man). Precisely when and how the word was introduced or created is not clear.[33] When *koshiben* first organized in 1919 (Taishō 8) to demand inflation adjustments, their organizations were styled in the press and in *The Japan Labor Year Book* as S.M.U., or salary men's union.[34] The term *sarariiman* itself was not, however, commonly used at this time, and when the abbreviation S.M.U. appeared in newspapers it was given as an equivalent for expressions such as "union of those who live on salary" (*hōkyū seikatsusha kumiai*).[35] A likely source for popularizing the word *sarariiman*, if not actually introducing it, was Kitazawa Rakuten, an extremely popular cartoonist of the Taishō and Shōwa eras. His series of cartoons describing *sarariiman* heaven and *sarariiman* hell (*sarariiman no tengoku; sarariiman no jigoku*) explicitly used the term and may have appeared as early as 1916 (Taishō 5).[36]

32. 1932 (Shōwa 7) data from *Nihon rōdō nenkan*, no. 14 (1933), p. 81, and 1939 (Shōwa 14) data from *Nihon rōdō nenkan*, no. 21 (1940), p. 120.
33. Standard dictionaries are little help in this context. The earliest literary example of the term given in the *Nihon kokugo dai-jiten* is from the mid-1930s. "Sarariiman," *Nihon kokugo dai-jiten*, vol. 9, p. 160. The *Kadokawa gairaigo jiten* (Kadokawa, 1967), p. 497, gives examples from the 1920s, but my own research turned up earlier examples. In a personal communication, Professor Takeuchi Yō suggests that the first usage of a similar term may have been *sarariimensu yunion* (salary men's union) in *Rōdō shinbun*, no. 13 (1919).
34. *Nihon rōdō nenkan*, no. 1 (1920), pp. 513–514.
35. "Kyōin kumiai naru," *Tōkyō Asahi shinbun* (April 18, 1920), in *SETS* 8:139–140.
36. These cartoons are reproduced in Kitazawa Rakuten kenshō-kai, *Rakuten manga shū taisei—Taishō hen* (Gurafuikku sha, 1973), p. 125. Neither the source nor the date is given, but the context suggests that they appeared before the Kantō Earthquake (1923, Taishō 12) in *Jiji gahō*. Among the constituents of the *sarariiman* heaven were quitting time, the absence of the boss, two-day weekends owing to national holidays coming on a Monday, and so forth. Included in the *sarariiman* hell

THE SELF-MADE MAN IN MEIJI JAPANESE THOUGHT

Not until the twenties, however, did the word become common with the publication of two well-known but very different works on the subject. One was an essay that appeared in *Chūō kōron* [Central Review] under the striking title "An Age of Terror for the *Sarariiman* and His Liberation from It" [Sarariiman no kyōfu jidai to sono kaihō].[37] The second was an anecdotal and essentially apolitical work by Maeda Hajime, who later went on to become an official in Nikkeiren (Japan Federation of Employers). In 1928 (Shōwa 3) he published the first volume of his *Tale of the Sarariiman* [Sarariiman monogatari], which combined a measure of journalistic scholarship with tips on *risshin*. This work proved so popular that a second volume was issued in short order.[38]

Nevertheless, despite the popularity of *Sarariiman monogatari* and its sequel, there was hostility to the term. Ōya Sōichi recalled that in the late twenties he wrote for a magazine called *Sarariiman*, which encountered hostility because of its title. Readers regarded *sarariiman* as a synonym for *koshiben* or *yōfuku-saimin* and did not like to be reminded of their status.[39] A similar prejudice was evident in journals such as *Chūō kōron* and *Kaizō* [The Reconstruction], perhaps the two most important magazines serving the interwar intelligentsia. With rare exceptions before 1929 (Shōwa 4), the magazines used terms such as "the new middle class" (*shin-chūsan kaikyū; shin-chūtō kaikyū;* or *shin-chūkan kaikyū*), "those who live on a salary" (*hōkyū seikatsusha*) or "intellectual laborers" (*chishiki rōdōsha*), rather than *sarariiman*. Such terminology was in part demanded by the Marxist formulas and leftist politics into

---

were rush hours, guests who came after the middle of the month, working overtime on accounts, and being slandered by fellow workers. For another series of cartoons concerning the *sarariiman*, see Suyama Teiichi, "Manga ni yoru sarariiman no hyaku-nen shi," in *Bessatsu Chūō kōron keiei mondai* 4:2 (June 1965): 135–142.

37. Aono Suekichi, "Sarariiman no kyōfu jidai to sono kaihō," *Chūō kōron* 44:12 (December 1929): 65–79. This was later incorporated into a book, *Sarariiman kyōfu jidai* (Senshin sha, 1930).

38. Maeda Hajime, *Sarariiman monogatari* (Tōyō keizai, 1928), and *Zoku-Sarariiman monogatari* (Tōyō keizai, 1928). These two books are very useful sources on *sarariiman* life and company employment practices and payment schemes in the 1920s.

39. Ōkōchi Kazuo, Ōya Sōichi, Odaka Kunio, Kōshi Kōhei, and Maeda Hajime, "*Bijinesuman* no hyaku-nen o kaiko suru," *Bessatsu Chūō kōron keiei mondai* 4:2 (June 1965): 145. For another expression of hostility to the term *sarariiman*, see Nii Itaru, "Sarariiman ron," *Chūō kōron* 43:12 (December 1928): 39–40.

which writers for these journals sought to plug the sarariiman, but it is not hard to detect an element of snobbishness in their choice of terminology, especially in "intellectual laborers."[40] Resistance to the word was destined, however, to be a losing battle, and after 1930 (Shōwa 5) it became general even in these journals.

Economic fluctuation was the principal agent for drawing a large number of already employed intellectual laborers into the quasi-proletarian status of the koshiben or sarariiman. In the case of educated youth emerging into the marketplace, there was a compounding factor, a vast increase in their numbers relative to the growth in demand for their services. This might not have happened. During the last five years of the Meiji era (1907–1911, Meiji 40–44) the yearly output of graduates from colleges (senmon gakkō) and universities (daigaku) fluctuated within narrow limits, showing if anything a trend to decreasing production. Budget considerations in the national sector and a generally depressed economy in the private sector limited the growth of facilities. Knowledge of the placement difficulty faced by graduates and the problems of paying for higher education worked to restrict enrollments.

Had nothing happened to alter student and parental preferences or had nothing been done to make more facilities available, there might well have been an improvement or at least a stabilization of the market position of youth possessing higher education, the depressed state of the economy notwithstanding. As the economy began to pick up in the first years of the Taishō, the decline in enrollments was reversed, and as the World War I boom developed, demands were made for an increase in higher educational facilities. Students and their parents wanted more education. Business and industry wanted more graduates. In 1918 (Taishō 7) orders were issued which paved the way for a modest expansion in facilities and which

---

40. Overall, the sarariiman received relatively little attention in Japanese Marxian analysis, and according to one commentator, it was not until 1960 that scholars began to come to grips with the fact that the middle class in general and white-collar workers in particular were not going to disappear! Okada Yuzuru, "Notes by the Editor," Journal of Social and Political Ideas in Japan 1:2 (August 1963): 74–75. For examples of prewar efforts to deal with the ambiguities of the sarariiman, see Kawazu Noboru, "Hōkyū seikatsusha no chii narabi ni undō," Chūō kōron 36:1 (January 1921): 84–94; Morimoto Kōichi, "Chishiki kaikyū dōmei ron," Chūō kōron 36:4 (April 1921): 25–39; and Sakisaka Toshirō, Chishiki kaikyū ron (Kaizō sha, 1935).

encouraged a continued increase in higher-education enrollments.[41]

Like all the developments that may be associated with these years of so-called Taishō democracy, there was much that was ambiguous about this alleged "reform" of higher education. Especially in the first years after the order was issued, much of the expansion was a paper phenomenon involving little more than the transfer of schools from one accounting category to another. Private colleges (*senmon gakkō*) were simply allowed to legally claim university status, in effect recognizing what many had been doing for years. Little financial aid was extended to the private sector, and private universities had only meager resources to draw upon.[42] In 1928 (Shōwa 5) they spent on average only one-fifth as much per pupil as did the national universities, had higher student/teacher ratios, and utilized large numbers of part-time faculty.[43] The cost to the student in the private sector was not necessarily lower, meaning that in large measure the reform extended the opportunity to get a generally inferior higher education under the label "university" to more who could pay, not more who had only ability.[44]

The 1918 (Taishō 7) reform did not bring about parity in the employment prospects of private- and national-sector graduates. Grad-

---

41. For a discussion of the various orders issued at this time, see Ogata Hiroyasu, *Nihon kyōiku tsūshi* (Waseda daigaku shuppanbu, 1970), pp. 249–254. In English see Asō Makoto and Amano Ikuo, *Education and Japan's Modernization* (Ministry of Foreign Affairs, 1972), pp. 46–47. Background is given in Ozaki, *Shūshoku*, pp. 27–31.

42. Not only did they get little aid, they were required to deposit a security bond of 100,000 yen per college with the government for the privilege of calling themselves universities. *The Japan Year Book 1920–1921*, pp. 243–244. Some have seen this requirement as a final government attempt to strike down private universities and maintain imperial-university privileges. Takenaka Teruo, "Teidai hōka tokken ronkō," *Momoyama gakuin daigaku jinbun kagaku kenkyū* 13:1 (1977): 59–87, esp. 83–86.

43. Amano Ikuo, "Continuity and Change in the Structure of Higher Education," in *Changes in the Japanese University: A Comparative Perspective*, ed. William K. Cummings, Amano Ikuo, and Kitamura Kazuyuki (Praeger, 1979), pp. 27–29.

44. For some unfortunately rather fragmentary data on costs, see Ōuchi Hyōe, "Todai gakusei seikatsu no ichi danmen," *Kaizō* 17:8 (August 1935): 1–17; "Senjika gakusei seikatsu chōsa," *Nihon hyōron* 14:5 (May 1939): 339–382; and "Shōgakkō kara daigaku sotsugyō made gakuhi yaku ichiman," *Fukuoka Nichi nichi* (October 31, 1936), in *SSS* 11:678–679. In practice the important difference between private and public universities was not in school fees but in the costs of gaining admission. Little or no cramming was necessary for private-university admission, and there were few *rōnin* in the private sector.

uates of the various imperial universities enjoyed preferential treatment and higher pay if they entered government service at the national level. This discrimination explains in part why two out of five private university graduates reported as entering government service (other than education) were listed as becoming local or provincial officials (*kōri*). No such category was included in the data for imperial universities, for provincial and local government affiliation was not part of the bureaucratic wealth-and-honor formula held by elite students who expected to become *kanri* or national government officials. The primary market for private-university graduates who found employment within a year of graduation was private business including family enterprises. In the ten-year period 1927 to 1936 (Shōwa 2 to Shōwa 11) three out of four private university graduates went into the private sector. The comparable figure for Tokyo Imperial University graduates was one out of two.[45]

Not all the expansion in higher-education facilities and graduates after 1918 (Taishō 7) was the product of juggled accounting categories. There was enough real expansion to seriously aggravate the latent problem of an excess of educated youth relative to the demand for their services.[46] Between 1919 (Taishō 8) and 1929 (Shōwa 4) the number of male graduates from national universities, private universities, and private colleges tripled, so that instead of the approximately six thousand who sought placement during the height of the World War I boom, there were more than seventeen thousand seeking placement as the economy plunged into the most severe portion

45. Those reported as having entered the military have been excluded from the calculations as have those graduating in medicine or pharmacy. It is probable that a larger fraction of the private university graduates listed as "placement unknown or not yet determined" (32 percent) eventually entered the private sector than was the case for comparable Tōdai graduates (18 percent).

46. Calculation of just how much of the expansion was due to "reform" and how much was due to continuation of past growth patterns is beyond the scope of this study. Simple "trend line analysis" using 1916–1921 (Taishō 5–10) patterns to predict later numbers tends to suggest that no more than 20 percent of the subsequent increases were anything other than a continuation of past growth. Enrollment in higher education had really begun to pick up in 1912 (Taishō 1) after the doldrums of the late Meiji well before the reform. The only conspicuous increase in facilities (as contrasted with accounting changes) was in the higher schools. My thanks to Professor Henry D. Smith for calling my attention to the statistical juggling that made it appear that there had been an enormous increase in enrollment and graduates because of the 1918 (Taishō 7) "reform."

of the generally depressed interwar years.[47] This average annual growth rate in excess of 11 percent was several times the growth rate of the economy and was soon reflected in the placement rates of graduates. The percentage of university and college graduates reported as having found work soon after graduation declined from approximately 80 percent in 1923 (Taishō 12) to 50 percent in 1929 (Shōwa 4) and to a bare 36 percent in 1931 (Shōwa 6).[48]

Behind these aggregates were sharp variations by school and field of study. The worst areas were those contained within the faculty of letters and what contemporary accounts referred to as "flunky learning" (*koshiben-gakumon*): law and economics.[49] The placement rate for college and university students in these areas declined from 72 percent in 1923 (Taishō 12) to 38 percent in 1929 (Shōwa 4). By way of contrast, graduates in the sciences and engineering suffered a decline in their placement rate of 88 to 76 percent in the same period, leaving them better off during the depression than those in liberal studies were during their best years. Other specialties largely immune to the depression and glut of graduates included medicine, pharmacy, engineering, and business (but not economics). There was somewhat more volatility in engineering and business than in the medical specialties, but overall they enjoyed high placement rates.[50]

47. The three categories of higher educational institutions grouped here represent the primary producers of potential *sarariiman*. National- and public-college (*senmon gakkō*) graduates are not included, because of their concentration in professional fields, especially medicine and engineering, which had very different demand schedules compared with the liberal studies. A complete readjustment (to eliminate strictly professional course graduates from imperial university totals, for example) of Monbushō accounting categories is, however, beyond the scope of the present study.

48. Data from Sakisaka, *Chishiki kaikyū*, p. 322. The series Sakisaka gives is *apparently* based on surveys of placement status in the year of graduation and is more useful than Monbushō data for the reason explained in note 11 above.

49. What I have translated here as "faculty of letters" refers to the Japanese *bungakubu*, which included, in the case of Tōdai, such subjects as education, art, linguistics, history, philosophy, sociology. Data were given by faculties that in some cases, such as economics and law, were equivalent to what Americans would call a major; but in other cases faculties included many majors. "Flunky" is a status translation of *koshiben*, not a literal rendering. For use of the term *koshiben gakumon*, see "Fukeiki o hanei suru sotsugyōsei no junan jidai," *Asahi shinbun* (January 17, 1928), in *Nihon no ayumi* 1:80.

50. Data from Abe, *Shitsugyō mondai*, p. 195, and Obama Toshinari, "Sarariiman no shoninkyū shirabe," *Chūō kōron* 45:7 (July 1930), in *Shōwa shonen*, vol. 1 of *Dokyumento Shōwa shi*, ed. Hayashi Shigeru (Heibonsha, 1975), p. 21. For other con-

THE SARARIIMAN (SALARY MAN)

The problem was that most of the post–World War I graduates were concentrated, either by preference of by lack of facilities, in the areas of study with poor employment prospects. In 1930 (Shōwa 5) only 11 percent of all private-university graduates were in the fields of medicine, science, or engineering. The rest were concerned in the "flunky specialties" with their soft employment prospects. The imperial universities as a whole had a third of their 1930 (Shōwa 5) graduates in the three fields with hard employment prospects, but this still left the majority in those fields with soft or volatile prospects. For the same soft specialties, there was only marginal difference in the gross placement rates of imperial and private universities, although there were sharp qualitative differences.[51]

Graduates in soft specialties from lower-level institutions generally found placement easier than did graduates in the same fields who came from universities, public or private.[52] Those schools which might properly be called post-secondary rather than higher-education—vocational colleges (*jitsugyō senmon gakkō*), normal schools (*shihan gakkō*), and type A vocational schools (*kōshu jitsugyō gakkō*)—had good placement rates and only minor and sporadic unemployment among their graduates, thanks to their specific occupational preparation.[53]

Thus, one of the catch phrases of the day commonly used to describe the situation of educated youth, "although I graduated from a university . . ." (*daigaku o deta keredo . . .*), needs modification and qualification.[54] Even at the height of the depression, not all univer-

---

temporary observations on the relative attractiveness of various fields, see *Gakusei to shūshoku*, pp. 14–15; "Hanbun wa shūshoku senu," *Kokumin shinbun* (January 8, 1926), in SSTS 14:9–10; "Kōtō yūmin ni wa hōkade ga ōi," *Yorozu chōhō* (February 17, 1926), in SSTS 14:61; "Kaku daigaku shūshoku sensen," *Asahi shinbun* (March 2, 1931), in *Nihon no ayumi* 2:9; "Gakushi-sama demo kuchi ga areba jōjō," *Hōchi shinbun* (March 12, 1930) in SSS 5:168; "Shinshi no tamago," *Yorozu chōhō* (February 6, 1925), in SSTS 13:62; and "Wakai gakushi-san," *Tōkyō Nichi nichi* (January 31, 1926), in SSTS 14:37.

51. See Kawai Eijirō, *Gakusei shisō mondai* in *Kawai Eijirō zenshū* (Shakai shisō sha, 1969), vol. 19, p. 72, table "Gakkō shubetsu shūshoku jōkyō hyō."

52. *Gakusei to shūshoku*, pp. 21–23; Karasawa, *Gakusei*, p. 212; and Kawai, *Gakusei shisō*, pp. 72–73.

53. Maeda, *Sarariiman*, p. 11; Obama, "Shoninkyū," p. 21; Abe, *Shitsugyō mondai*, p. 196; Kawai, *Gakusei shisō*, p. 74; and "Shūshoku sensen meian no wakare michi," *Kokumin shinbun* (March 3, 1930), in SSS 5:144.

54. This was the title of a 1929 (Shōwa 4) film directed by Ozu Yasujirō. Unfortunately the film no longer exists. For a description of this and other films Ozu made

sity (and college) graduates were in trouble. Those with an economically productive specialty were largely untroubled by the depression. The slogan only had meaning for those who had persisted, despite changed market conditions and an industrializing economy, in pursuing those liberal studies that had been appropriate to those seeking wealth and honor through bureaucratic affiliation. Moreover, educated youth in general were not touched as harshly as might be thought if one looks only at college and university students. Though certainly affected by the depression, those youth with only a secondary or post-secondary education, those youth who could aspire only to the low or middle managerial and bureaucratic ranks or to narrowly defined technical positions, were *relatively* less harmed by the depression than the would-be elites. The depression was less a crisis for what Japanese are wont to call the *puchi-buru* (petty bourgeoisie) than it was for those who sought to become something more.

Youth faced with the conditions described above had before them a number of options, including shifting to fields with better job prospects. Karasawa Tomitarō has called attention to an interesting relation between economic conditions and the numbers of students seeking entrance to normal, technical, or commercial schools.[55] During the boom period around World War I, competition rates for normal schools declined steadily as students turned to other areas offering greater rewards. Large numbers of teachers quit and went into companies.[56] Business and technical schools, by way of contrast, enjoyed unprecedented numbers of applicants and high competition rates. With the end of the war boom, competition rates for business and industrial schools fell, and normal-school rates climbed as youth rediscovered the relative attractiveness of modest but stable incomes in a period of economic contraction and deflation. The increase was especially notable in the case of the higher normal schools. Their graduates could become middle-school teachers and receive pay and

---

about the *sarariiman* and university students, see Donald Richie, *Ozu* (University of California Press, 1974), pp. 206–215.

55. Karasawa, *Gakusei*, pp. 200–203, and Karasawa Tomitarō, *Kyōshi no rekishi* (Sōbun sha, 1955), pp. 265–285.

56. "Kyōin shibō," *Jiji shinpō* (August 17, 1920), in *SSTS* 8:305, and "Kotoshi mo kyōin busoku," *Yorozu chōhō* (January 29, 1920), in *SSTS* 8:44.

perquisites similar to lower-ranking *sōnin* civil servants, along with considerable local prestige. In the war boom years there had been "only" three or four applicants for each seat in the higher normal schools; during the depression years there were ten to twelve. With recovery after the Great Depression, enthusiasm for becoming a teacher cooled, and business schools became the center of student attention. In 1932 (Shōwa 7), 4.6 students sought each seat at Tokyo University of Business (Tōkyō Shōka Daigaku) (now Hitotsubashi University); in 1939 (Shōwa 14), after military involvement in China was affecting the job market, there were 8.4 applicants for each seat. In the same period, normal-school rates were approximately half those of the business school, and higher-normal competition rates were moving rapidly downward.

University students also made adjustments to market conditions. Applications to the faculty of letters (*bungakubu*) of Tokyo Imperial University were stagnant from the mid-twenties even as total applications increased by more than 50 percent. Applicants to the law and economics faculties grew substantially but with sharp year-to-year variations of up to 40 percent, reflecting student doubt about employment prospects. The clearest indication of adaptation and changing preference was, however, in application numbers and competition rates for students wishing to study engineering at Tokyo Imperial University. In 1920 (Taishō 9) there were 242 applicants and all were admitted; in 1935 (Shōwa 10) there were 930 applicants of whom only 35 percent were admitted.

Adjustments in the private-university sector took a number of forms. Applications to the universities themselves grew steadily from their recognition under the 1918 (Taishō 7) reform and then stagnated in the mid-thirties. Applications to their preparatory courses (*yoka*), the private-university equivalent of the higher schools, peaked in 1929 (Shōwa 4) and then declined by almost one-third. Dropout rates for both university and preparatory courses increased notably in the early thirties.

Medical studies in particular attracted students, as the field was considered both highly profitable and largely resistant to depressions. Competition ratios for government schools climbed.[57] Some

---

57. In 1920 (Taishō 7) the ratio for the medical faculty at Tōdai was 1.9 to 1, and in 1930 (Shōwa 5), 3.2 to 1. Law, by way of contrast, moved from a ratio of 1.1 to 1 up to 1.8 to 1 in the same years. These ratios are, of course, above and beyond the selection

private-sector schools moved to take advantage of student desires by offering admission in exchange for contributions said to have ranged up to 3,000 yen.[58] The potential for enrollment expansion and financing by such means was of course limited. A contribution of 3,000 yen represented more than the average yearly salary of even a *sōnin* class higher civil servant and could readily be paid only by a wealthy parent concerned to see that his offspring carried on the family medical practice. Other areas having good job prospects (primarily engineering) did not have constituencies that could afford comparable "donations," and in the absence of other major funding sources, private universities expanded primarily in the *koshiben* fields.

As a consequence of the limited places, fields with good job prospects, and the existence of a core of students who would stick to the soft fields and the private universities even with their well-known and documented employment record, the placement difficulty for these students continued long after those in the hard-subject areas were being snapped up in the industrial and governmental expansion resulting from the war in Manchuria and China and the successful export drive of the late thirties. By 1934 (Shōwa 9) graduates from Waseda University in technical or engineering specialties were enjoying a nearly 100 percent placement rate. By 1937 (Shōwa 12) articles began to appear in business magazines explaining how companies could compete for engineering graduates. Not until 1939 (Shōwa 14) did the placement rates for those in "flunky specialties" hit 70 percent, the rate characteristic of these fields in the best of times, indicating that their difficulties were more or less over.[59]

---

exercised through the higher-school entrance exams. The ratio for national medical schools (*kanritsu ika daigaku*) went from 1.2 to 1 in 1925 (Taishō 14) to 1.8 to 1 in 1930 (Shōwa 5).

58. Concerning this type of admission to private medical schools, see "Shiritsu isen no kanemōke," *Yomiuri shinbun* (April 7, 1930), in *SSS* 5:222, and Nagai Toshiaki, "Gakkō kigyō no uraomote," *Chūō kōron* 47:6 (June 1932): 322–328. Nihon Daigaku, cited in the Nagai article, was involved in a similar scandal as recently as 1979. This type of activity, it should be noted, can become a scandal only when there is a general public expectation that even private-school admission must be based solely on tested performance and where such American institutions as "alumni preference" and "wild card" admissions are not accepted.

59. The effect of military expansion on placement rates is noted in Ozaki, *Shūshoku*, pp. 243–247. Monbushō data also show this impact. In the eight-year period 1927–1934 (Shōwa 2 to Shōwa 9), an average of 38 percent of all private-university

The limited adjustment that took place in overall university enrollments and between areas of study is not to be explained solely in terms of limitations on certain preferred facilities. The socioeconomic background of the constituencies for each type of postsecondary education, the expectations of those constituencies with respect to higher education, and the peculiarities of the system itself explain the *relative* stability in the university sector compared with the shifts that took place elsewhere. More volatility is to be noted in the post-secondary areas (normal, business, and other vocationally oriented schools) because there was less lead time between choice of track and graduation than in higher education. These schools had courses only three or four years long, and the decision to compete for entry to one of them was made relatively close to ultimate graduation and the job market. These schools were less expensive than the universities (either public or private), both in terms of actual fees and in terms of the number of years of income that students had to forego while in school or while preparing for entrance examinations. They attracted more students who had to consider immediate job prospects than did the universities.

University education was, by virtue of its length, inherently somewhat separated from year-to-year fluctuations in the job market. This was especially true for the imperial universities. Youth had to make a commitment to preparation for the examination of a specific higher school in either its arts and letters or its sciences division, depending on their intended area of university study. By this fact alone, their future was circumscribed six or seven years before ultimate graduation. Because the 1918 (Taishō 7) reform had resulted in a substantial increase in higher schools, there had come to be more graduates than could be accommodated by Tokyo Imperial University and a spread in the quality of those graduates because of variations in the higher schools.[60] Students from the less-effective

---

graduates were still not placed one year after graduation. In the next four years, 1935–1938 (Shōwa 10 to Shōwa 13), the rate dropped to 17 percent. For Tōdai law graduates, the respective rates were 34 and 15 percent.

60. Until the early 1920s the imperial universities had admission rates of 90 to 100 percent; screening took place at the higher-school entrance examinations. This situation changed in 1922 (Taishō 11) when the overall admission rate for Tōdai dropped to 75 percent. This forced a number of students to consider other imperial universities. "Ushio no gotoki kōkō sotsugyōsei," *Miyako shinbun* (March 26, 1926), in *SSTS* 14:113. This trend continued, and in 1935 (Shōwa 10) the overall admission rate was

schools who were unsuccessful in gaining admission to Tōdai or one of the other highly desired imperial universities found themselves members of what *Chūgaku sekai* [Middle-School World] called the "stay-behind gang" (*inokori-gumi*).[61] These were higher-school students who had actually graduated or could graduate but who remained in school an extra year or two to better their chances of getting into the more desirable of the imperial universities, usually Tokyo, which was at once the most prestigious and the largest.[62]

The difference in the proportion of graduates from each higher school gaining entry to the most desired of the imperial universities meant higher competition rates for the schools with the most successful graduates.[63] This in turn meant a concern with finding and entering those middle schools that got you into the most effective higher schools. Such middle schools had competition rates of 11 or 12 to 1, nearly as high as for entry to the best higher schools. Newspaper accounts indicate that the pecking order had, moreover, extended downward to the elementary-school level in the mid-twenties, and concern was being expressed about the disruptive effects of examination preparation on elementary-school students.[64] Individual entrepreneurs and even such establishments as Waseda Univer-

---

only 52 percent, with some faculties considerably lower. For comment on this new "examination hell," see Hugh Keenleyside and A. F. Thomas, *History of Japanese Education and Present Education System* (Hokuseido Press, 1937), p. 214; "Nageki no kōtō gakusei," *Tōkyō Asahi shinbun* (February 28, 1936), in *SSS* 11:146–147. In 1930 (Shōwa 5) competition for university entry had spilled over to Kyoto Imperial University, and its law faculty began entrance examinations. "Kyōdai hōgakubu hajimete nyūgaku shiken," *Ōsaka Mainichi* (February 27, 1930), in *SSS* 5:132.

61. This term is used and explained in "Zenkoku kōkō sotsugyōsei no daigaku nyūgaku kyōsōritsu," *Chūgaku sekai* 30:11 (September 1927): 162–169. See also, "Kōtō yūmin sanzen nin chikaku," *Yomiuri shinbun* (January 26, 1930), in *SSS* 5:50.

62. Accounts bewailing (or celebrating) the dominance of Tōdai graduates seldom correct for the relative size of the school. For example, in 1916 (Taishō 5), when it was already sharing its place with other imperial universities, graduates from Tōdai were 70 percent of the imperial-university total, and still 26 percent if private colleges are included. Even in 1930 (Shōwa 5) Tōdai graduates constituted 11 percent of all graduates from the primary *sarariiman*-producing institutions (as defined in n. 47).

63. The proportion of graduates from each higher school advancing to Tōdai varied widely. In general the older "number schools" did well, but so did some of the newer schools. Urawa Higher School (now Saitama Uniyersity) had nearly 90 percent of its graduates advance to Tōdai and Kyōdai, and its competition rates exceeded those of the First Higher School.

64. "Jūdai na shakai mondai," *Yomiuri shinbun* (April 29, 1924), in *SSTS* 12:172; "Nyūgaku junbi no inokori yoshū," *Yomiuri shinbun* (January 12, 1925), in *SSTS*

sity capitalized on the situation by offering cram courses for those facing the various entrance examinations.[65] Successful applicants occasionally turned their abilities into cash by hiring themselves out as substitutes (*kaedama*) to take the examinations for students with more money than brains or application.[66]

More volatility (in terms of application and dropout rates) was inherent in the private sector because only the best schools (for all practical purposes Keiō and Waseda) had competition rates approaching those of the national higher schools and few required anything of their would-be entrants other than a middle-school diploma and the ability to pay school fees.[67] Dropping out did not mean giving up a struggle that may have extended back to elementary school. In contrast, entrance to the imperial universities, especially Tokyo Imperial University, was the product of fundamental decisions and a struggle begun up to twelve or more years before ultimate graduation, a situation hardly conducive to snap changes in course to follow the job market.

13:20; "Shōgaku jidō no ichi-dai-nankan," *Hōchi shinbun* (February 3, 1920), in *SSTS* 8:51; *Asahi nenkan* (1925), p. 253; and "Junbi kyōiku o genkin," *Yomiuri shinbun* (February 11, 1930), in *SSS* 5:96–97.

65. Advertisement "Tokubetsu sōgō jukenka," *Asahi shinbun* (January 10, 1932), in *Nihon no ayumi* 2:105. Waseda was also in the mail-order middle-school business in these years. See its advertisements in *Asahi shinbun* (April 13, 1928), p. 5.

66. For an early example of an article on this type of cheating, see "Shiken no kaedama ga nennen ōku naru," *Hōchi shinbun* (March 20, 1917), in *SSTS* 5:108. In school, cheating, called *kanningu* ("cunning"), was a popular subject in examination preparation magazines such as *Chūgaku sekai*. The treatment of the subject was somewhat ambiguous, combining how-to guidance with rather thin moralizing. "Seitokan no *kanningu* seisai bokumetsu saku," *Chūgaku sekai* (April 1924), pp. 15–21, and subsequent issues. Corruption on the part of schools was also a common subject, especially middle schools (private) that would sell diplomas to students seeking entry to private colleges (*senmon gakkō*). "Kane de uru sotsugyō shōsho," *Jiji shinpō* (January 10, 1936), in *SSS* 11:14; and "Tōkyō tōkai shōgyō no inchiki," *Hōchi shinbun* (February 1, 1936), in *SSS* 11:67.

67. Private universities were essentially replicating the higher-school-to-imperial-university pattern of the Meiji era. Entry to their preparatory courses (*yoka*) was tantamount to admission to their university section. Of the private universities, only Keiō and Waseda had, to borrow a phrase from *Chūgaku sekai*, "entrance examinations that are anything to worry about." "Shōwa saisho no jukenka no taisei o hōzu," *Chūgaku sekai* 30:7 (May 1927): 2–10 for a general discussion of the public- and private-university selection process. According to *Monbushō nenpō* data, Keiō competition rates (*yoka*) averaged 3.8:1 for 1926–1935 (Shōwa 1–10) while those of Waseda were 4.6:1. None of the other private schools approached these levels except in medicine. *Monbushō nenpō*, no. 63 (1935), pp. 302–305 and no. 58 (1930), pp. 309–310.

Then again, it may be wondered whether those who looked to the imperial universities really considered the job market until they faced it directly. It would seem that they were more concerned with where they studied rather than with what they studied. They expected to advance after graduation on the aura attached to their school and not on their own specific marginal contribution to society or the economy. They were the extension into the twentieth century of the *Eisai shinshi* [Talent Forum] youth and of Ishizaka Masatsugu, who had not concerned themselves with the particular content of the study that so dominated their dreams. A large portion of private-university enrollment would appear to have been accounted for by the second string of those holding this attitude, those who for reasons of intelligence or finances were unable to go to the imperial universities but who were nevertheless so committed to a traditional version of *risshin* that they were willing to take their chances with the private universities. Because private-university graduates would go on to a *risshin* sufficient to justify the cost of their education in smaller proportions than was true of national-university graduates, investment in such an education was a more speculative proposition. In prosperous times families were doubtless more willing to gamble, but in less than prosperous times they were less willing (and able) to pay for an education that might very well turn out to be consumption and not investment.[68] This would have added to the volatility of private-university enrollments.

Under these circumstances, literature on *risshin shusse* or *seikō* flourished, although writers aiming at those with or hopeful of acquiring higher education seldom used these particular terms. This was probably a consequence of the conceits developed among the anguished youth of the Meiji era.[69] Nevertheless, the genre, if not

68. It is possible that parents of private-university students were as a group harder hit than those in the national sector or that private-university students were more dependent on their own earnings. Available data do not permit testing these issues. The economic rationality of higher education as an investment was, however, questioned in this period, as is discussed below.

69. *Risshin shusse* and *seikō* seem to have appeared more in advertising for mail-order middle schools and in advertisements for Kōdansha publications. For examples, see the following advertisements: "Dai-Nihon chūgakkai," *Asahi shinbun* (April 3, 1928), p. 1; and "Kingu," *Asahi shinbun* (April 3, 1928), p. 6; and "Waseda daigaku kōgiroku," *Asahi shinbun* (April 13, 1928), p. 5.

the terms, was much in evidence. The twenties and thirties saw the founding of a substantial number of new periodicals devoted to helping students prepare for entrance examinations. Some were general, in the pattern of *Chūgaku sekai* [Middle-School World] and *Shōnenen* [A Garden for Young People] before it. Others were geared to specific subjects, most commonly English and mathematics, used to cut down the surplus of applicants.[70] This literature was, however, essentially a linear development of Meiji patterns; there was simply more of it in these years.

What was new and conspicuous in the period between the two world wars was the appearance of a large volume of literature on the subject of placement (*shūshoku*) for university (*daigaku*) and college (*senmon gakkō*) graduates. The depressed conditions of the late twenties and early thirties made certain that the authors of works such as *Placement Tactics* [Shūshoku no senjutsu], *The Placement Battle Line* [Shūshoku no sensen], and *Placement Secrets* [Shūshoku no hiketsu] prospered even if educated youth did not.[71] An examination of the issues and strategies in one such work, *Students and the Realities of Placement* [Gakusei to shūshoku no jissai], published in 1934 (Shōwa 9), provides a vivid picture of what it meant to be a university or college graduate seeking work during the thirties.[72]

Compared with any Meiji writing aimed at students with higher education, this work was remarkably concrete and without the tendency of earlier writing to gloss over actual market conditions. Indeed, the guide began by declaring that the opportunities presented by the early Meiji era were now a historical curiosity. The student should not hold any grand dreams and should realize that he was facing a most unfavorable market for finding work let alone achieving any great rank or wealth. Detailed statistical tables describing

---

70. *Chūgaku sekai* did not survive the Shōwa depression, because of financial difficulties in the parent firm. At least eight other magazines specializing in examination preparation were founded in the 1930s. Some of these are described in Arase Yutaka, "Mass Communications Between the Two World Wars," *Developing Economies* 5:4 (December 1967): 748–766. The author's statement that these magazines were a "new genre" (pp. 755–756) is, of course, an error.

71. Titles from Ozaki, *Shūshoku*, p. 210, and Karasawa, *Gakusei*, pp. 210–211.

72. Shūshoku mondai kenkyū-kai, *Gakusei to shūshoku no jissai* (Tōkyō jitsugyō sha, 1934). The choice of this guide was fortuitous: it turned up at a book fair in Kanda. Subsequent examination of other placement guides confirmed that the advice in *Gakusei to shūshoku* was typical of the genre and the period.

the grim reality of the 1930s labor market drove this point home with a concreteness and a precision never seen in Meiji works.[73] Warned that he could expect "fifty, a hundred, or even five hundred applicants for each two or three positions" the student was advised that he must begin his preparations for placement while yet in school, the earlier the better. His task was twofold and partially contradictory: he had to become a well-rounded (*enman*) member of society (*shakaijin*), and at the same time he was urged to develop some characteristics that would set him apart from the rest of the hoard seeking work. Achieving distinction in sports was suggested as one of the best ways for setting himself apart.[74] This was good advice, for other accounts suggest that companies did indeed favor those who had achieved some fame in sports.[75] Though the guide did not explain why athletes should be favored, two factors counted most heavily. First, athletes were a cheap form of corporate advertising. Second, athletes were less likely to be infected by deviant ideas, especially left-wing thought. To achieve the goal of becoming well rounded, the aspirant was advised to join many clubs, cultivate hobbies, and read popular newspapers and magazines. Study was not given much weight as an activity leading to employment.

Once well rounded and cultivated with or without athletic distinction, the aspirant had to make himself known and to learn about job openings. The guide explained that there were many methods for achieving these related tasks, but the best was to be recommended by your school. The problem was that schools could only recommend their best students according to grade standing. Achieving high grades was not necessarily compatible with the other activities necessary to becoming an attractive candidate.[76] Moreover, formal placement activities by schools were a relatively new endeavor. Waseda University did not have a placement office until 1925 (Taishō 14), although as Tokyo College it had been a major producer of graduates for years.[77] The effectiveness of the school as an agency of placement

---

73. *Gakusei to shūshoku*, pp. 13–29.
74. Ibid., pp. 80–81.
75. Ozaki, *Shūshoku*, pp. 139–141; "Gakusei—kinō kyō," *Asahi shinbun* (October 23, 1930), in *Nihon no ayumi* 1:256; and "Yakyū senshuren," *Asahi shinbun* (January 27, 1930), in *Nihon no ayumi* 1:216.
76. *Gakusei to shūshoku*, p. 98.
77. Ozaki, *Shūshoku*, pp. 163–164.

depended on the reputation of the school and the positions occupied by its graduates. Waseda, despite its formal placement facilities and a good reputation, had 35 percent of its graduates unplaced in 1935 (Shōwa 10). Keiō Gijuku, the academy founded by Fukuzawa Yukichi, had only 7 percent unplaced, a figure that was probably the minimum for any school in even the best of times.

The difference was to be accounted for by Keiō's having a very strong "old boy" network with graduates well-placed in big business, and a large number of students who were never in the job market in the first place because they stood to inherit a family firm.[78] Waseda was the one private school offering a quality education to even relatively poor students. Indeed, the school advertised itself as such. Poor boys did not inherit family businesses and they did not have contacts, however, and Waseda did not have an especially good placement record. It did do better for its graduates than most private colleges, some of which had up to 75 percent unplaced in some years because of their low quality *or* because they concentrated on law and other "flunky specialties."[79]

Because of the limitations on formal placement operations, the guide emphasized finding work through the cultivation of individual contacts. Techniques for approaching those who might be useful to the aspirant were discussed, and the job-seeker was furnished with a short course in the art of calling (*hōmon*). Here, such vital topics—the guide styled them a "matter of life or death" (*shikatsu mondai*)[80]—as how to sit properly, to eat cakes, and to drink tea during a visit were carefully explained, as was the importance of dressing properly. A last-minute shoeshine was recommended, and specifications were given for a clean and properly displayed handkerchief. The language of deference and respect was reviewed, and the aspirant was counseled to avoid difficult words in order to properly display his character. Throughout the interview the young man was advised to "keep smiling," something one would imagine to be most difficult under the circumstances. In this context, perseverance (*nintai*), one of the most cherished values of early Meiji writers on

78. Ibid., pp. 176–179, for a discussion of Keiō placement.
79. Hōsei University is a good example of such a school. Less than one-third of its graduates were rapidly placed in the 1930s.
80. *Gakusei to shūshoku*, p. 106. Interviewing in general is discussed on pp. 106–120.

self-advancement, took on a new meaning. According to the guide, perseverance was that virtue which allowed you to maintain self-control when you did finally gain an appointment and were kept waiting beyond the scheduled time. It brought you back again if you did not succeed in gaining an interview.[81] This was a striking contrast to perseverance as it had appeared in the Nakamura Keiu translation of *Self-Help*, but then early Shōwa Japan was a most un-Smilesean world.

The aspirant who failed to get a job through his school or through his contacts was left with two alternatives: employment agencies (labor exchanges) and advertisements. The guide indicated that the aspirants disliked the exchanges because of their popular association with day laborers and apprentices. This was a mistaken image, it asserted, for there were now employment agencies specializing in white-collar occupations, and the agencies were under the authority of the minister of the interior (*naimu daijin*).[82] Nevertheless, as a practical matter, the student could not expect much from the exchanges, simply because there were so many aspirants and so few openings.[83] Finally, there were newspaper advertisements. These offered the possibility of finding work without the entanglements and obligations that resulted from using connections. The problem was that many newspaper advertisements directed at college and university graduates were fraudulent. At best, the guide advised, the non-fraudulent advertisements offered jobs more suitable to those with middle-school education or its equivalent.

Those who did not find placement through any of the channels described above were faced with competing for publicly advertised positions in governmental agencies and business. Here the applicant would find himself facing competition ratios vastly exceeding those for access to higher education. According to the guide, the Ministry of Railroads (Tetsudōshō) had recently received over 30,000 applications for a total of 1,200 positions. The Tokyo Municipal Government (Tōkyō Shiyakusho) had more than 7,000 graduates competing for 200 places. These ratios of 25 to 1 and 35 to 1 were, however, exceeded by the *Tōkyō Asahi shinbun*. It had recently been forced to select from among 800 applicants to fill four positions, a ratio of 200

---

81. Ibid., p. 108.   82. Ibid., pp. 103–104.
83. Use and performance of the exchanges is discussed, ibid., pp. 150–164. See also Abe, *Shitsugyō mondai*, pp. 197–201, and Sakisaka, *Chishiki kaikyū*, pp. 327–328.

to 1.[84] Generally the ratio of applicants to hires was greatest for university graduates and least for those with vocational educations. University graduates had fewer prospects and had to compete more aggressively for the available jobs.[85]

One answer to this situation was to turn to positions not normally sought by graduates with higher education. Suggestions offered by the guide ranged from emigrating to Brazil to going to work in a factory. As proof of the utility of the latter alternative, the guide related the story of a higher-technical-school (*kōtō kōgyō gakkō*) graduate with bad grades who had hid his background and gone to work in a factory. Although he had been a poor student, he was by virtue of his education superior to everyone else in the factory. Soon he came to the attention of the owner, married his daughter, and achieved *risshin shusse*.[86] Contemporary newspaper accounts record the relatively unprecedented phenomenon of university and college graduates seeking to become policemen, railroad firemen, elementary-school substitute teachers, petty clerks in municipal governments, and even janitors.[87] Such jobs were regarded, however, not as a clever *risshin* strategy, but as a stop-gap measure until something better came along.

A much more attractive alternative and one to which the guide devoted a whole chapter was to seek work with one of the firms or agencies involved in the exploitation of Manshūkoku, the Japanese-dominated state in Manchuria. The chapter began with the apparently mandatory references to Japan's special position in Manchuria, the half-century struggle for it, and the standard clichés about the expenditure of "four billion yen in national treasure" and "the

---

84. *Gakusei to shūshoku*, pp. 184–186.
85. According to data given in Abe, *Shitsugyō mondai*, p. 196, in the period 1927–1929 (Shōwa 2–4), 12.0 percent of the university and 30.4 percent of the type A vocational graduates who applied to companies were hired. For those applying to banks, the respective ratios were 22.7 percent and 45.2 percent. Competition rates for those wishing to become higher civil servants (*kōtōkan*) ranged from 3.1:1 to 44.2:1 in 1930 (Shōwa 5). Obama, "Shoninkyū," pp. 22–23.
86. *Gakusei to shūshoku*, pp. 169–175. Story on p. 173.
87. Examples include "Gakushi junsha ga hyaku-yo nin," *Yomiuri shinbun* (August 2, 1930), in *SSS* 5:486; "Toto taru hōgakushi ga shōgakkō no kozukai-san," *Fukuoka Nichi nichi* (September 7, 1930), in *SSS* 5:548–549; "Shūshokunan ichi danmen gakushi-san no daiyō kyōin," *Tōkyō Nichi nichi* (March 8, 1936), *SSS* 11:167–168; "Daigaku wa deta keredomo jū nin hitori no ukiyo," *Ōsaka Jiji shinpō* (April 5, 1936), in *SSS* 11:233; and "Gakushi da totemo," *Ōsaka Mainichi shinbun* (February 1, 1930), in *SSS* 5:69.

lifeblood of two hundred thousand Japanese dyeing the wide fields crimson." This out of the way, the guide turned quickly to the meaning of Manchuria for its readers: jobs. Already there were more than 210,000 Japanese in Manchuria, and more than 70 percent of them were "salary receivers" (*gekkyū-tori*), the guide observed. Still more important, new graduates were being employed in quantity (*tairyō*). Companies were "competing with one another to employ superior talent for their Manchurian operations." Declaring that the "small number of graduates" would not meet the demand, the guide predicted that the development of Manchuria would bring about an increasingly fortunate (*takō naru*) future for educated job seekers.[88]

When the guide was published in 1934 (Shōwa 9), those with technical training and *sarariiman* employed in certain favored firms and industries were already benefiting from military adventurism on the continent. The optimistic prediction of the guide that demand would exceed supply did not come about through Manchuria alone. It required the triumph of national megalomania, military involvement in China proper, and a full-scale arms buildup.[89] Until the late 1930s most higher-education graduates continued to be faced with the now familiar placement difficulty.

From the perspective of employers, the placement difficulty was a selection difficulty, or more correctly a rejection difficulty. Unlike the early years of the twentieth century when companies had first tried and usually failed to recruit and hold university graduates, the 1920s and 1930s saw them with the problem of selecting a few college and university graduates from the hordes who would turn up for any possible opening. For this purpose many companies had turned to examinations of one kind or another, and by 1934 (Shōwa 9), when the placement guide *Gakusei to shūshoku no jissai* was written, it was "almost impossible to get a job without going through an examination."[90] Although the primary placement agency may have

88. *Gakusei to shūshoku*, chap. 16, pp. 297–310. Clichés, p. 297.
89. For examples of contemporary reporting on the effect of the Manchurian and armaments boom on *sarariiman*, see "Gōsei na bōnasu saikō ni nen bun," *Ōsaka Asahi shinbun* (June 16, 1936), in *SSS* 11:390; Kobayashi Ichizō, "Shin-sarariiman ni ataeru," *Kaizō* 21:4 (April 1939): 62–65; and Ōyama Chiyotake, "*Bōnasu* no 'yūetsu' to 'hiai,'" *Kaizō* 22:12 (July 1940): 272–277. For additional sources concerning the effect on graduate placement, see Ōuchi Hyōe, "Tōdai gakusei seikatsu no ichi danmen," *Kaizō* 17:8 (August 1935): 1–17, and Keenleyside, *Education*, p. 274.
90. *Gakusei to shūshoku*, p. 126.

been one's connections, and the examinations merely an excuse to reject surplus applicants, as was suggested by some contemporary observers,[91] examining the content of these tests and the advice on taking them does tell much about what was sought (or not sought) in employees with higher education.

The advice given by the guide with respect to preparing for the written portion of employment examinations was quite conventional: pay attention to the clock and write clearly so the examiners would be appreciative.[92] Far more striking than the advice on technique was the material presented in a separate chapter devoted to reporting the contents of recent examinations. Few of the sample questions bore any obvious relation to the business or the activity of the agency or company using them. The Ministry of Railroads had called for responses on the merits and demerits of party politics, arms reduction, Chinese ethics, bicameral legislative systems, amnesties (*onsha*), Marconi, Hindenburg, and "coup d'etat." The Tokyo Municipal Government had wanted its applicants to discourse on such topics as benevolent government, cosmopolitanism, and nonsense (*nansensu*). Morinaga Confectionary had asked its applicants to write on symphonic jazz, Picasso, and the NRA, among other subjects. The Central Bank of Manchukuo (Manshū Chūō Ginkō) asked for a critique of the sentences handed out to the military and civilian participants in the abortive coup d'etat known as the May 15th Incident.[93]

Assuming the guide was accurate in reporting these and other similar combinations of employers and examination subjects, the reader must wonder what employers were attempting with these questions and what sort of responses they wished to elicit. It is quite clear that they were not trying to measure mechanical competency or knowledge in their field of activity. Conformity, not competence, was being tested. With varying degrees of subtlety, the questions aimed at making sure the aspirant was politically safe, specifically that he was not infected with communism, socialism, or overly liberal ideas, and that he was not too caught up in such suspect contemporary fads as the so-called *ero-guro nansensu* (erotic-grotesque nonsense). The guide warned that any extremes in thought, right or

---

91. Ozaki, *Shūshoku*, p. 211.
92. *Gakusei to shūshoku*, p. 128.
93. Ibid., pp. 195, 202, 227, and 209.

left, were to be avoided. Deviation to the left was, however, given more attention. The guide described adherence to left-wing thought as "like being drugged with opium."[94] This concern with orthodoxy and stability was further suggested by the requirement of most companies and agencies that the applicant write essays on his interests (*shumi*) and his family. As one critic has observed, the companies did not expect to buy just your labor; they expected to purchase your soul as well.[95] The depression and the surplus of applicants gave them the leverage to enforce such requirements.

The applicant who passed through the essay and written part of the exam then moved to another barrier, what the guide called the "oral examination" (*kōtō shiken*). With respect to this portion of the placement process, the guide explicitly indicated the importance of personality and orthodoxy rather than mechanical competence. Much of the advice was similar to that in the section on making calls and contacts: the applicant should not overdress lest he look like a movie star, should avoid slamming the door of the interview room, use proper respect-language, and avoid overly difficult words, and so on.[96] The real meat of this section was in the discussion of the type of person most likely to find favor with an employer. As explained by the guide, this was the person who had a personality suitable for the group he was trying to enter. Each employer had somewhat different desires, but in broad terms the candidate had to be temperate (*onwasei*) and smooth (*enmansei*). He should be orderly, attentive, responsible, dutiful, positive, optimistic, interesting (*shumi yutaka*), bright, receptive, and polite. Bright, it must be noted, referred not to intelligence but to a personality of the kind that would allow the aspirant to laugh off discontents. Academic performance came dead last on the list.[97]

This emphasis on personality and appearance rather than acquired knowledge and academic performance was not a peculiarity of this guide. According to Ozaki Moriteru, in the early 1920s a number of firms, including those belonging to the Mitsui and Mitsubishi

94. Ibid., pp. 138–139.
95. Takami Jun quoted in Nasu, "Dokusen shihon," p. 258.
96. *Gakusei to shūshoku*, pp. 129–132. Ozaki reports that some schools conducted mock interviews so that their students could practice and develop a proper interview style. *Shūshoku*, p. 184.
97. For the list of virtues, *Gakusei to shūshoku*, pp. 136–139.

groups, had shifted to a policy of "personality first" (*jinkaku dai-ichi shugi*) in recruiting. *Jitsugyō no Nihon* [Business Japan] and other journals carried stories to the effect that the ideal applicant was the person with middling grades (*chūryū no seiseki*) and a malleable personality suited to business. Those with high grades were regarded as lacking in stability, given to argumentation, and prone to boredom in the company environment.[98] Similar statements appeared in the 1930s.[99]

The more extreme statements to the effect that companies really preferred mediocrities cannot, however, be taken at face value, especially when they appeared in *Jitsugyō no Nihon*. Given the history, audience, and style of this magazine, it must be assumed that it was trying to reassure its readers and keep their dreams of *risshin* alive. So too for the guide *Gakusei to shūshoku no jissai*: after all, it was aimed at those who were still unemployed. If it is assumed, as some contemporary reports indicated, that grades were used by companies to make a first cut in the hordes of applicants, then there would have been more students with poor grades in the unemployed audience for the guide than among those already employed.[100]

Given that unemployment was essentially a problem only for those with nonspecialized educations, there was no reason to give too much weight to grades as an indicator of acquired knowledge, for what the students had studied and how well they had learned it did not directly say anything about their ability to carry out the tasks of a future employer. This was in effect stated by the guide, for even while playing down the importance of grades, it did say that those with high grades were prime candidates for employment—because outstanding academic performance demonstrated that the aspirant was "an extremely industrious person" (*hijō no doryokuka*) or that he possessed an "analytical mind" (*zunō no meiseki*).[101] In other words, grades gave an indication of personal attributes, what the individual *might* do, not what he knew that was of use to the employer. Essentially the literature that was aimed at un-

98. Ozaki, *Shūshoku*, pp. 136–137.
99. "Shūshoku sensen no shin-keikō shūsaikei wa dame," *Jiji shinpō* (April 21, 1936), in *SSS* 11:263, and Ōuchi, "Gakusei seikatsu," p. 10, citing a *Tōkyō Nichi nichi* article.
100. Sagara Toshimitsu, "Sarariiman shūshoku tetsugaku," *Kaizō* 14:3 (March 1932): 2.
101. *Gakusei to shūshoku*, p. 139.

employed graduates of higher education stressed the importance of personality because most of those who were unemployed could offer neither good grades nor mastery of a utilitarian specialty. Personality was their only competitive attribute.

Some of the blue-chip employers whose preferences were reported in the placement guide did in fact put grades or performance high on their lists despite the ordering in the guide's commentary.[102] Government employment, especially the higher civil service, was to a large degree determined by performance as measured through the higher civil service examinations. Nevertheless, this does not allow the conclusion that the well-rounded conformist personality was sought only by second- and third-rate employers or only for relatively menial positions in first-rate agencies. Even with its rigid examination system for entry into managerial (as contrasted with technical) positions, the government had ample opportunity to enforce demands with respect to personality. Passing the written examinations was an exercise in conformity, for they did not test problem-solving ability or seek innovative responses. According to Spaulding, the most common advice for higher civil service examination preparation was to repetitively read texts by known examiners, and some aspirants were said to have read the same text up to sixteen times.[103] Those who passed the written test were then subjected to an oral examination, which most examiners (and candidates) thought was intended to test "character" (*jinbutsu*), a euphemism for the orthodox and personable individual.[104] Finally, not all those who had passed both examinations had to be appointed, and not all were. Thus the apparently objective higher civil service examinations allowed substantial discretion for eliminating those who had only ability and lacked the properly conformist attitudes and personality.[105]

102. Among those mentioning grades were Mitsubishi, *Ōsaka Asahi*, and the Bank of Japan (Nihon Ginkō). Ibid., pp. 141–143 and 147.
103. Spaulding, *Higher Civil Service*, p. 286.
104. Ibid., pp. 217–218. *Gakusei to shūshoku*, pp. 194–195, reported that the Home Ministry (Naimushō) asked those who had passed the higher civil service examinations questions about their families, their choice of schools, their interests and hobbies (*shumi*), and where other graduates from their schools were active.
105. "Ability" is used here with reservation. Popular mythology credits the higher civil service with attracting the brightest students, who were further screened by objective, competitive examinations. A more reasonable view would be that the higher civil service was staffed by people who had first of all the ability to pass a certain type of test. Whether those tests were effective in selecting those best suited to govern (as

THE SARARIIMAN (SALARY MAN)

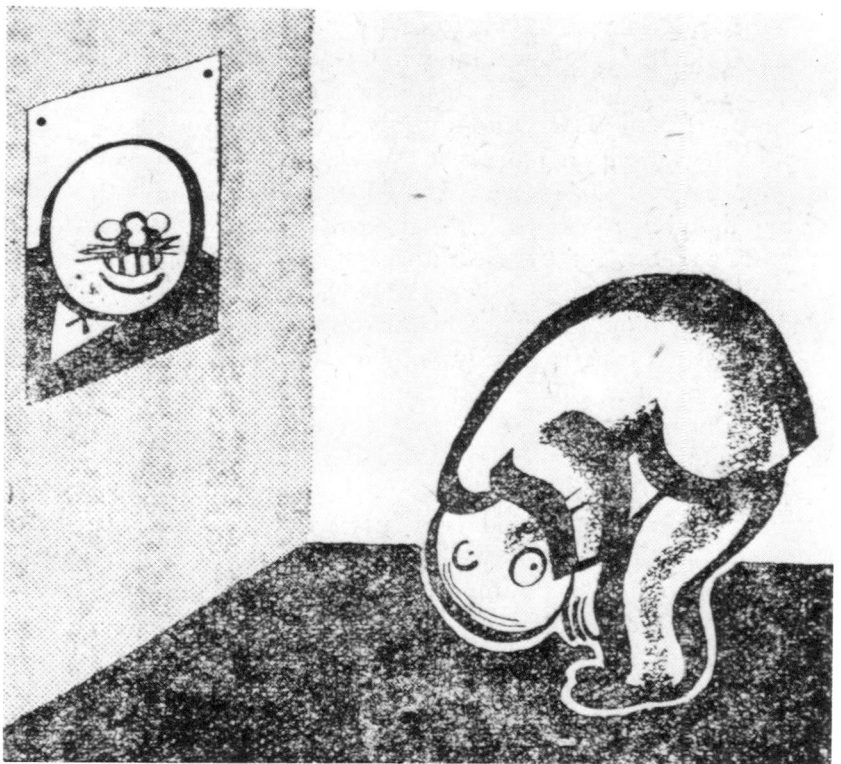

Cartoon from a 1934 (Shōwa 9) article in Chūō kōron [Central Review], "The Philosophy of Placement" [Shūshoku no tetsugaku]. The original caption explains that the young man is practicing the technique for dealing with an arrogant boss (gōman naru shachō). Other cartoons in this group all stressed the weak position of graduates in higher education vis-à-vis employers and their desperate efforts to find jobs.

Companies were even less formally committed to objective criteria, and while some blue-chip employers cited by the guide listed academic performance or ability, others did not. Again, this does not mean that those who did not mention ability sought out mediocrities. It is more probable that this was an unstated assumption, for first-class employers were in a position to demand both ability and group-oriented character. Their very attractiveness in terms of stability and long-run opportunities assured them of large numbers of applicants, even in high-demand fields. The more attractive the employer the more leverage it had with respect to applicants.

Given the competitive environment and market conditions for educated youth in this period, companies could afford to employ higher-education graduates in even the most trivial tasks, such as coupon and newspaper clipping. Maeda Hajima described the corporate life of probationers (*minarai*) in his *Sarariiman monogatari*. During the probation period, popularly known as "kindergarten for university graduates" (*daigakude no yōchien*), the newly entered graduate spent his days stamping documents until his hands turned purple, practiced his *soroban* technique, and learned to bow so that his muscles moved without any conscious thought on his part. Most of all, he learned not to complain lest he be replaced by a more compliant candidate.[106] In such a situation, intelligence and curiosity were distinct handicaps, if not for long-run *risshin* at least for short-run survival.

The graduate who was able to find a purchaser for his soul under these circumstances found that it was worth precious little in absolute terms in the short run and relatively little more than that of a blue-collar worker without an expensive and hard-to-get education, and if he was an imperial-university graduate, very much less than it had been worth in the middle years of the Meiji era. According to data given in *Sarariiman monogatari*, the 1927 (Shōwa 2) graduate of an imperial university could expect to start at seventy to ninety yen

---

contrasted with those best suited to fit into the bureaucratic structure) is arguable. Considering the performance of the civilian government from World War I onward, it must be wondered whether the examination system gave Japan better leadership than had the ad hoc mechanisms that brought the Meiji oligarchs to power.

106. Maeda, *Sarariiman monogatari*, pp. 59–66. See also Ozaki, *Shūshoku*, pp. 215–216.

a month, depending on field and school of graduation. If 1889 (Meiji 20) starting salaries for the graduates of the Imperial University are used as a reference, then the soul of the early Shōwa graduate was, after correction for inflation, worth at least 50 percent less.[107]

Comparisons for private-university graduates over the same period are more difficult, since they came into being in a strict sense only after the 1918 (Taishō 7) reforms. Nevertheless, since the private universities were the lineal descendants of the early Meiji colleges (senmon gakkō), comparisons may be made on this basis. The 1927 (Shōwa 2) starting pay of private-university graduates (forty-five to seventy-five yen, depending on school and company) was from 35 to 70 percent more than was typical of private-college graduates in the late 1880s and early 1890s.[108] Private higher education had clearly advanced relative to state-controlled higher education. Indeed, some companies, including the numerically significant Mitsubishi and Mitsui conglomerates, went so far as to largely abandon pay distinctions between the graduates of imperial and private universities.[109] Government agencies did, however, continue to discriminate and gave premiums of up to 80 percent to imperial-university graduates.[110]

With or without discrimination by sector, it was characteristic of the employment situation faced by educated youth that their employers made little effort to evaluate them as individuals. Either all university graduates or all graduates of a particular university category were started at the same salary. They were treated as a homogeneous commodity with all brands being of the same value, or they were treated as a partially differentiated commodity with some

---

107. Meiji salary data from Spaulding, *Higher Civil Service*, p. 91; Shōwa data from Maeda, *Sarariiman monogatari*, pp. 71–99; and consumer price index from Ohkawa, *Prices*, p. 135, col. 3. Because the base period for the consumer price index used was 1934–1936 (Shōwa 9–11), it reflects Shōwa rather than Meiji consumption patterns.

108. Mid-Meiji sources often suggested that a college education was worth one-fourth of an Imperial University education. Data from Spaulding were adjusted accordingly and used as the base for these calculations.

109. Concerning Mitsubishi policy, see Obama, "Shoninkyū," pp. 24 and 30. On discrimination schemes in general, Ozaki, *Shūshoku*, pp. 223–224.

110. Obama, "Shoninkyū," p. 23, gives starting salaries for private- and imperial-university graduates in various government agencies. The Ministry of Railroads (Tetsudōshō) was the worst, and only the Ministry of Justice (Shihōshō) did not discriminate.

brands being worth more than others, but in either case, they were treated as a commodity, not as individuals.

In the latter part of the Meiji era, *starting* wages for some (Tokyo) Imperial University graduates had approached blue-collar levels. In the early Shōwa period *starting* wages for all university graduates were near blue-collar levels and for a large portion even below. In 1927 (Shōwa 2) the average daily wage of factory workers would yield a monthly income of fifty-two yen. For all workers in construction, the average was seventy-six yen.[111] This meant that the youth who spent at least eight years in school beyond what was typical of the best-educated blue-collar workers found himself earning only slightly more than such workers *during his first few years* and then only if he had graduated from one of the educational tracks that required the greatest investment in preparation. If he graduated from any less prestigious and difficult-to-enter institution, he began and remained for some time below blue-collar levels. The *top* wage for private-university graduates, seventy-five yen, was slightly under the average wage of construction workers. Average compensation for civil servants shows a similar pattern. In 1889 (Meiji 22) *sōnin* class civil servants had enjoyed average pay that was twelve times that of construction workers. In 1927 (Shōwa 2) the relative differential had fallen to three times. This put them in the same relation as *hannin* had been to construction workers in 1889 (Meiji 22). Inertia in bureaucratic compensation as the depression worsened would produce an increase in these ratios, but by any monetary measurement the relative rewards to the years spent pursuing higher education were much lower in the 1930s than in the 1880s.

Direct wages were not, of course, the only measure of income. The *sarariiman* did receive a number of allowances above his basic wage, and there were bonuses from time to time. But, along with his extra compensation, he had extra expenses, especially those suits which were a mark of his status, such as it was, and a major item in his budget.[112] He had to seek to maintain a certain level of nominal middle-class respectability even if this meant that an excessive frac-

---

111. Data from Ohkawa, *Prices*, table 25, p. 245. "Construction workers" refers here to craftsmen, not common laborers. It is curious that this series gives no data on white-collar wages.

112. For the lore of suits, see Maeda, *Sarariiman monogatari*, pp. 37–45.

tion of his income was spent on rent. His education socialized him to a higher level of consumption, and his comrades spurred him into competitive spending.[113]

The blue-collar worker needed neither the suits nor the correct address, and writers contemporary with the *sarariiman* suggested, perhaps self-servingly, that ordinary workers had more real disposable income than did many *sarariiman*.[114] According to *Sarariiman monogatari*, it was only the bonuses and extra allowances that allowed the white-collar worker to get out of his yearly cycle of debt and to maintain a marginal and threadbare middle-class living standard.[115] Observing this situation, some contemporary writers wondered whether nonvocational higher education was an economically rational investment.[116] Since no calculations on rate of return have been made for this period, the question of rationality cannot be answered definitively. It might be suggested, however, that investing money in higher education was rather like putting money into a savings account coupled to a lottery, a type of account that has been available in Japan. In exchange for a chance to receive a large prize, the investor accepts a lower rate of return than is available in conventional accounts. Essentially, this would seem to have been the situation in prewar Japan as it has been shown to be the situation currently.[117]

Concerned as it was with placement, a guide such as *Gakusei to shūshoku no jissai* had relatively little to say about post-employment life; there was a large specialized literature to which the employee could turn. Nevertheless, its brief notes were indicative of the general thrust of the more specialized literature on how the few might reap something more than a modest return on their investment in higher education.[118] The guide began with an attempt to re-

113. Ozaki, *Sarariiman*, pp. 128–129.
114. Sakisaka, "Chishiki kaikyū," p. 292.
115. Maeda, *Sarariiman monogatari*, pp. 122–133, describes bonus systems and their role in *sarariiman* life.
116. Sakisaka, "Chishiki kaikyū," p. 295; Koike, "Hōkyū seikatsusha," pp. 40–41; and *Gakusei to shūshoku*, pp. 166–167.
117. Kozo Yamamura and Susan B. Hanley, "*Ichi hime, ni Tarō*: Educational Aspirations and the Decline in Fertility in Postwar Japan," *Journal of Japanese Studies* 2:1 (Autumn 1975): 95–96.
118. This section is based on *Gakusei to shūshoku*, pp. 175–181.

store faith in the possibilities of *risshin*, something that was most necessary after the grim picture painted in the rest of the work. It noted that youth typically became frustrated as they progressed through school and the placement difficulty, losing along the way their dreams of becoming executives (*jūyaku*) or ministers of state. The student should not, however, allow himself to become indifferent, the guide warned. All executives and ministers of state had started as poor flunkies (*binbō koshiben*). If you became indifferent, you could expect to spend the rest of your life in indifferent ranks. To avoid this you should look at the biographies of men of lofty ambitions (*risshin restsuden*) and see how great men in the past had sweated blood to get ahead. Contemporary youth should expect to do nothing less.

To get ahead in the company, the aspirant should learn his position so well that executives would say, "If it's not that fellow, it just won't do." This did not mean broad initiative or creativity; the aspirant was warned against spreading himself too thinly. He should concentrate only on what was assigned to him. He should accept the fact that as a new employee he would be stamping papers, delivering messages, answering the phone, and serving tea. He should banish completely any thoughts that such work was inappropriate to one with higher education, and he should absolutely avoid complaints about his situation. Such diligence was the norm. To get ahead one had to be noticed. The best way to be discovered was to arrive early and leave late. By so doing the aspirant increased the chances that he would be noticed by executives coming into the office at odd times on their way to or from outside appointments. Since this happened only two or three times a month and without advance notice, the aspirant had to arrive early and leave late every day in order to maximize his chances of being noticed. This was, of course, a clear use of the discovery myth to get extra work from an employee, and the guide displayed its pro-management bias by emphasizing that the aspirant to *risshin* should not be cynical or calculating in his display of diligence. It had to come from the heart, and he should resolve that he would not move to another firm. The aspirant should work as though he expected that his efforts would lead to his being called away by another firm, but because of his extra display, he would usually find himself recognized by his own employer.

Hard work above and beyond official duty was not enough. The guide noted that some people thought it sufficient simply to work quietly and hard without joining in corporate life (*dantai seikatsu*). This was not enough, it warned, and when the time came to trim employees (*jin'in seiri*), such a quiet person would not be missed by his fellows as he was severed from corporate life. Joining in this life was a prerequisite for maintaining one's position, but at the same time it was necessary to strike a balance. Too much socializing, especially if it cut into one's work performance, was to be avoided. In indicating that an otherwise dutifully working employee might well find himself eliminated, the guide was expressing a concern that was to be found throughout the literature of this period. Although large firms may have been moving in the direction of the so-called lifetime employment (*shūshin koyō*) that is so conspicuous in post–World War II Japan, works such as the guide assumed that firing was possible and a likely fate unless one strove above and beyond official duties and properly fitted into corporate life. Similarly, it was not assumed that the *sarariiman* would spend his whole life at one firm even if he was not fired. The guide took pains, as was noted above, to fit thoughts of changing employers into increased striving for the current employer. If anything, the prime limitation on changing employers would appear to have been the absolute scarcity of jobs in this period, not any institutional or ideological barriers.[119]

119. There is an ever-growing body of literature on the subject of the so-called "Japanese employment system," especially the issue of "lifetime" commitment and employment. For a bibliography of this literature, see W. Mark Fruin, "The Japanese Company Controversy: Ideology and Organization in a Historical Perspective," *Journal of Japanese Studies* 4:2 (Summer 1978): 262–271, notes 1 and 6. As Fruin points out, this controversy has been fought largely without data or research. His own study of the personnel records of a food-processing firm is a major step forward. Another could be made by examining journals such as *Jitsugyō no Nihon*, *Daiyamondo*, and *Sarariiman*, to determine precisely when the different elements of the "Japanese employment system" first figured in advice to employees and would-be employees. Because this chapter was written and researched in the United States without access to these sources, this failure cannot be corrected here. The sources available do suggest that only a few elements of the "Japanese employment system" existed at this time—seniority pay, bonuses, salary supplements—but that lifetime or permanent employment did not exist even on the ideological level. On this last point it may be noted that a 1936–1937 (Shōwa 11–12) survey of Osaka company *sarariiman* asking them their greatest fear reported that 48 percent listed "getting fired" (*kakushu*). Illness was second at 22 percent. As for what they most wanted from the government, the first-place reply was "unemployment insurance." See Hoshino Shūichirō, "Hōkyū seikatsusha no mitaru hōkyū seikatsu," *Shakai seisaku jihō*, no. 196 (January 1937), p. 101.

THE SELF-MADE MAN IN MEIJI JAPANESE THOUGHT

Essentially the same assumptions and advice were to be found in *Sarariiman monogatari* by Maeda Hajime and in the numerous writings of Noma Seiji, whose publishing firm, Kōdansha, produced nearly two-thirds (by circulation) of all periodical literature consumed by Japanese in the Shōwa era.[120] Although dealing with *risshin shusse* and occasionally using the word itself, most literature on post-employment life was perhaps best characterized by two words that occurred frequently in it: *yowatari*, or "getting along with the world," and *shosei*, or "conduct of life."[121] The stress in this literature was on interpersonal relations rather than on objective performance.[122] It advised the aspirant to be properly polite to superiors and subordinates, always amiable and concerned with preserving harmony. All difficulties were to be greeted with a smile, and complaining was absolutely forbidden. One was thankful for everything and properly thankful to everyone. Morality was declared relative, and direct confrontations were to be avoided even when you were certain of your own correctness. Readers were taught to say yes when they really meant no and schooled in the art of making enemies into allies. What little was said about learning, intelligence, or creativity in this writing was usually negative. "Sincerity" (*seijitsu*) and "diligence" (*kinben*) were, however, positively evaluated.

The literature used models who were essentially Smilesean, including men such as Edison, Lincoln, and (Samuel) Johnson, but they were fitted into a discovery-myth pattern most often illustrated by Toyotomi Hideyoshi. As in the case of late Meiji ethics texts, the emphasis was not on the cunning and ambitious Toyotomi, who had clawed and back-stabbed his way to the pinnacle of feudal power, but on the diligent Kinoshita Tōkichirō, whose efforts

---

120. Advice on advancement within the company is given in Maeda, *Sarariiman monogatari*, chap. 8. Concerning Noma Seiji and Kōdansha, see Noma Seiji, *Noma of Japan: The Nine Magazines of Kodansha* (Vanguard, 1934), and Kuwahara Takeo, Katō Hidetoshi, and Yamada Minoru, "Jyaanarizumu no shisōteki yakuwari," in *Shidōsha to taishū*, vol. 5 of *Kindai Nihon shisō shi kōza* (Chikuma shobō, 1960), pp. 141–184.

121. Although these essentially synonymous words do carry some connotation of "getting ahead" (*shusse*), the dominant feeling they convey is that of "getting by." *Shosei* might be better rendered as "coping with life."

122. The generalizations below are based on examination including but not limited to the following: Noma Seiji, *Taiken o kataru* (Dai-Nihon yūbenkai kōdansha, 1930); *Shusse no ishizue* (Dai-Nihon yūbenkai kōdansha, 1931): *Shosei no michi* (Dai-Nihon yūbenkai kōdansha, 1930); and Nitobe Inazō, *Yowatari no michi* (Jitsugyō no Nihon sha, 1912), in *Nitobe Inazō zenshū* (Kyōbunkan, 1970), vol. 8, pp. 5–384.

as a sandal-taker had eventually earned him the notice of Oda Nobunaga. Even when the older Toyotomi was presented, he was treated as an organization man. A best-selling Shōwa biography of Hideyoshi described his military organization in the terminology of the modern corporation and equated superior subordinate relations within it to the relations between company executives and employees.[123] In sum, the advice offered by this literature was to keep a low profile, be diligent, and you might be rewarded. Even if you were not, be happy because you could be much worse off. It was an ethic for a society in which there was a surplus of candidates for any one position, a situation which allowed any deviant to be replaced by an almost unlimited number of alternates who would do their utmost to be conformist and, as the contemporary phrase went, "usable people" (tsukawareru hito).

There was little to distinguish these works from late Meiji articles in *Jitsugyō no Nihon* [Business Japan]. Indeed, one of the best sellers in the Taishō and Shōwa periods, *Yowatari no michi* [Ways of Getting through the World] by Nitobe Inazō, was in fact compiled from *Jitsugyō no Nihon* articles published during the last years of the Meiji period.[124] What was new in the Taishō and Shōwa eras was the specific application of this ethic to youth with higher education. *Jitsugyō no Nihon* had aimed largely at elementary-, higher-elementary-, or at most middle-school graduates. Works such as *Sarariiman monogatari* and *Gakusei to shūshoku no jissai* were specifically directed at university and college graduates. Just as there had been a moving together of the white- and blue-collar pay, there had been a moving together of the ethos and behavior of shop clerks and youth with higher education. Perhaps this is best illustrated by the readership of *Kingu* [King], the most famous of the Kōdansha publications. This monument to mediocrity and middlebrow taste was edited to contain "the kind of matter which any member of the household could read aloud without embarrassment in the presence of any other member, whether child or grandmother, widow or spinster."[125] In it

---

123. Yada Sōun, *Taikō-ki*, as described in Senuma Shigeki, *Hon no hyaku-nen shi* (Shuppan nyūsu, 1965), p. 266.

124. *Yowatari no michi* was based on articles appearing in *Jitsugyō no Nihon* after the Russo-Japanese War. It was first published in book form in 1912 (Meiji 45). By 1926 (Taishō 15) it had been reprinted 72 times, and by 1929 (Shōwa 4), 86 times. *Nitobe Inazō zenshū*, vol. 8, p. 591.

125. Noma, *Noma of Japan*, p. 243.

were stories of petty *risshin* and volumes of advice on the conduct of life and how to get along in the world. It was popular with better-educated members of the working class, the lower middle class, and according to surveys, even students at Tokyo Imperial University.[126]

The popularity of *Kingu* among such a diverse readership indicates the degree to which the expansion of higher education after World War I had resulted, not in the elevation of aspirations and culture, but in the generalization of a lowest-common-denominator value system evolved from a mix of the shop clerk and *koshiben* mentalities subsumed under the new word *sarariiman*. This impression is further strengthened by the appearance of articles stressing petty strategies in a popular intellectual journal such as *Kaizō*. A 1932 (Shōwa 7) article gave advice on job interviews that included a discussion of how to avoid letting negative elements in your background come out and how to divert attention if they did. The aspirant was warned to avoid mentioning any dead siblings lest the interviewer think illness ran in the family. The self-supporting student (*kugakusei*) was told to hide his background because companies thought such students too independent. If his hobbies included literature, he was advised to answer Japanese chess (*shōgi*) when questioned. A detailed section covered other issues, such as whether he should admit to ever having visited a cafe and how to state his capacity for alcohol.[127] A 1931 (Shōwa 6) article for would-be functionaries dealt with the use of regulations as a shield and the question of building up a sphere of influence (*nawabari*).[128] Although the tone of this article was slightly apologetic, that it could appear in a journal such as *Kaizō* indicates the degeneration brought about by the surplus of graduates.

It is difficult to say with any accuracy what aspirants to *risshin* rather than those who wrote to them thought about the techniques of getting ahead, but a very interesting and possibly unique bit of survey research done in 1936–1937 (Shōwa 9–10) does provide some clues.[129] Published in the prestigious *Shakai seisaku jihō* [Social

---

126. "Senjika gakusei seikatsu chōsa," *Nihon hyōron* 14:5 (May 1939): 363, describing 1934 (Shōwa 9) preferences. *Kingu* was the third most often cited magazine among Tōdai students.

127. Sagara Toshimitsu, "Sarariiman shūshoku tetsugaku," *Kaizō* 14:3 (March 1932): 8–10.

128. Suehiro Gentarō, "Yakunin-gaku sansoku," *Kaizō* 13:8 (August 1931): 73–78.

129. Hoshino Shūichirō, "Hōkyū seikatsusha no mitaru hōkyū seikatsu," *Shakai seisaku jihō*, no. 196 (January 1937), pp. 99–112, esp. p. 107.

THE SARARIIMAN (SALARY MAN)

Policy Report], this study questioned some five hundred Osaka area company *sarariiman* about a number of issues, including the ways to *shusse*, or get ahead in corporate life. First and second place went to what the author of the study called "meritocratic" (*jitsuryokuteki*) responses, such as sincerity, honesty, diligence, hard work. Almost as many gave what he called "artful" (*gikōteki*) strategies, such as flattery, patronage, fancy maneuvering (*kōtō seisaku*). Many stressed the art of looking busy when you had nothing to do. Perseverance (*nintai*) was cited, but it was not the early Meiji variety; in this context it meant not voicing discontent. Another popular response was the suggestion that, to *shusse*, one ought to stick close to the boss and spend heavily on entertainment. Some respondents indicated considerable cynicism, suggesting "get rid of your conscience" or "become a grand fool." Under the circumstances it is perhaps less surprising that so many gave "artful" responses as it is that a slight majority clung to the "meritocratic" formulas.

Under the conditions prevailing in the market for educated youth in the Taishō and Shōwa eras, there existed a number of youth who would have been called "anguished youth" (*hanmon seinen*) or "decadent youth" (*tandeki seinen*) during the Meiji era. The post–World War I equivalent of decadence was known as "erotic-grotesque nonsense" (*ero-guro nansensu*) and was explicitly seen by contemporary observers as an outlet for frustrated *sarariiman* and educated youth.[130] Anguish had entered the popular language and was used as a generic term for discontent and frustration, but the specific type of romantic youth noted in the late Meiji period was clearly in evidence in the interwar period.[131] Indeed, it might be said that the late Meiji style of anguish was institutionalized during the Taishō and Shōwa years.

Iwanami Shigeo, one of the original anguished youth at the First Higher School, founded the publishing firm that bears his name, and it initially concentrated on "philosophy" (*tetsugaku*) where that term is understood broadly to include not just formal, academic philosophy but also "meaning of life" (*jinseikan*) works. One of the

130. The linkage between late Meiji currents such as "naturalism" (*shizen shugi*) and Taishō-Shōwa "decadence" (*dekadansu*) was made by Aono, "Sarariiman no kyōfu," pp. 70–73. See also Maeda, *Sarariiman monogatari*, pp. 140–149, for a description of early Shōwa cafe society.
131. Sugimoto Chiyono, "Japanese Students," *Trans-Pacific* 17:6 (June 1929).

most successful publications of the Iwanami firm was *Santarō nikki* [The Diary of Santaro]. The author of this work was Abe Jirō, another of the original anguished youth. His adolescent confession of romantic egoism was almost a composite of "On the Aesthetic Life" [Biteki seikatsu o ronzu] by Takayama Rinjirō (Chogyū) and *Whither* [Doko e] by Masamune Hakuchō.[132] Despite its overall lack of originality and its general vacuity, it became must reading for higher-school students through the twenties and thirties.[133]

It fit into that one position of the life cycle of educated youth when they were between entrance-examination cramming and job seeking, when they had time to consider whether there was meaning to their existence, and when the cloistered environment of the higher schools allowed them to play at being egotistical without fear of harming their careers. This was but a passing phase of their lives, however, and surveys show that when they went to the imperial universities, their interests shifted from *Santarō nikki* and other philosophical works to more practical reading matter such as *Ekonomisto* [Economist], *Bungei shunjū*, and even *Kingu*.

A certain measure of political activity was a conspicuous feature of student life in the twenties and thirties, but it is highly questionable whether this was a product of the declining situation faced by educated youth. Political activity first appeared in the boom years around World War I, not during the depression years. It may have been in part a reaction to the overall decline of status experienced by educated youth,[134] but the proximate cause appears to have been youth's finding inspiration in the burgeoning labor movement, the rice riots of 1918 (Taishō 7), romantic Russian populism, and other developments of the late teens and early twenties.[135] If anything, activism seems to have declined as the conditions for educated youth worsened in the late twenties and early thirties, although it is difficult to isolate the impact of the market because police repression was also increasing in these years.

132. This is my own view of *Santarō nikki* from Abe Jirō, *Santarō nikki*, in *Abe Jirō—Kurata Hyakuzō*, vol. 46 of *Gendai Nihon bungaku zenshū* (Chikuma shobō, 1969), pp. 5–58.

133. Concerning its popularity, see Senuma, *Hon no hyaku-nen shi*, p. 131; *Ningen sanka*, vol. 11 of *Nihon bungaku no rekishi* (Kadokawa shoten, 1968), pp. 103–105; and "Senjika gakusei," p. 363.

134. Henry Dewitt Smith, II, *Japan's First Student Radicals* (Harvard University Press, 1972), p. 34, suggests this.

135. Ibid., chaps. 2 and 3 for a discussion of other factors.

THE SARARIIMAN (SALARY MAN)

Contemporary observers did see activism decreasing with the depression, and studies of the student movement indicate that much of the apparent activism of the late twenties and early thirties was in fact an extension of traditional "school disturbances" (*gakkō sōdō*) known since the Meiji era.[136] These appeared political in this period only because a tiny minority of left-wing activists capitalized on these events and gave them a nominally political coloring.[137] If there was any relation between worsening job prospects and student activism, it was for students to take advantage of their cloistered or protected positions to vent their frustrations by tilting with school administrations over such weighty issues as the distribution of tickets for the annual Waseda-Keiō baseball game and whether Waseda should erect a statue of the founder's wife.[138] In this sense there was an essential continuity between late Meiji and Taishō-Shōwa youth, although the latter appear at first glance to have been more politically active than the former. Most students were essentially inner directed and concerned primarily with their own world and not with society at large.

136. Ibid., pp. 21–26.
137. Ibid., pp. 215–219.
138. Ibid., pp. 218 and 25.

Conclusion: The Self-Made Man and the Japanese Sense of Self

A narrative of the development of the *sarariiman* is important in and of itself. It tells how and when the most desired career pattern in contemporary Japan evolved. It dates the appearance of the so-called "new middle class" and the institutions in which it lives and works. As early as the turn of the century, most features of the *sarariiman* pattern were fully developed. Aspirants to white-collar status struggled to acquire education by institution and not by specialty. They were faced with high rates of competition and had to supplement their education by attendance at cram and preparatory schools in order to crack the examination barrier. Once in the school track that would carry them to a given white-collar status, they had to do little to assure their eventual graduation.

From at least the turn of the century, their hard-won education gave them little more income *at graduation* than factory workers and skilled craftsmen received with much less investment in formal schooling. Their rewards were in the distant future, received in exchange for conformity to the group life (*dantai seikatsu*) of the bureaucratic organization, governmental, business, and academic, that employed them. Most of the changes following the Meiji era involved the generalization and involvement of an increasing proportion of the working population in this basic pattern, not sharp qualitative change.

Although a distinct *sarariiman* ethic was not articulated by name until the late 1920s, *Pushing to the Front* represented a shift in the

CONCLUSION

direction of an ethic centered on personality rather than performance during the Meiji period itself. Prototypes for this emphasis were much older, however, and most elements had appeared in writing directed at samurai beginning at least in the early eighteenth century if not before. Kaibara Ekiken had advised diligence above and beyond official duties, careful attention to the etiquette of rank and status, avoidance of displays of intelligence, abiding concern for human relations, and concessions to group opinion. Writers who sought to guide the samurai had maintained this emphasis throughout the Tokugawa period.

The writings of Yoshida Shōin on the ideas of Yamaga Sokō had amounted to a description of the complete and well-rounded functionary. If such an ethos was to be found even in the writing of a moralistic radical activist such as Yoshida, it must have existed in larger measure and with more cynicism in the samurai population at large.[1] The frequent complaints of late-Tokugawa-era writers about samurai "yes men" seeking advancement through obsequiousness suggests that this ethos was well known with or without an explicit literature to support it. The model of Honda Noboru in *Ukigumo* [Floating Clouds] and the criticism of Tokutomi Iichirō directed at youth who were trying to gain *risshin* by kowtowing indicate that this spirit was flourishing during the early Meiji period, long before *Pushing to the Front* was required reading for educated youth.

Despite the similarity in samurai and *sarariiman* ethics for advancement, there was no direct line from the former to the latter. With a few rare exceptions, most notably the writing of Fukuzawa Yukichi, the period from the Meiji Restoration through the Russo-Japanese War saw little said about personality and human relations as the way to advancement. Even in the first decades of the twentieth century, the personality ethic was somewhat suspect and had to be defended when it was advanced. It may be argued that earlier youth did not need to be told about the importance of personality

1. Standard moralistic works for samurai touch on *risshin* with varying degrees of explicitness. Whether there was a self-conscious genre of literature on self-advancement for samurai comparable to that known to exist for townsmen and peasants is not clear. No work has been done on concepts of *risshin* held by samurai during the Tokugawa era. Such a study would seem of vital significance because of the common thesis that discontent among "lower samurai" was a factor in the Meiji Restoration.

327

and etiquette, because they were recruited from a narrow stratum already socialized to this ethos, whereas later youth were more diverse in origin and needed such advice. This type of change doubtless had some role in bringing about the shift in ethics, but other factors appear to have been more important.

The *sarariiman* ethos was explicitly one of obsequiousness. As long as it was generally believed that the nation was a reflection of the individuals composing it, it was intellectually difficult, indeed almost treasonous, to advocate the personality ethic. Intellectuals and journalists held to the Smilesean equation more strongly than did businessmen. When the literature of self-advancement came to draw on businessmen or their spokesmen, the earlier ethic was bound to recede. Nevertheless, the appearance of the personality ethic among writers who were intellectuals and who had previously championed the Smilesean character ethic demonstrates that more than a change in authorship brought about the change in values and ethics.

The most important factor in the shift from performance to personality was the change in the market for educated youth. Early Meiji youth could expect to become leaders while still young, and writing aimed at them reflected this expectation. Late Meiji youth could expect to become leaders only when they were well along in years and then only if they had conformed to the social demands of the agency that employed them. Indeed, they could not expect to find or maintain employment if they did not conform, because purchasers of their services were able to pick and choose from among a large supply of qualified and even overqualified youth.

In this sense the situation of educated youth from the turn of the century onward was very similar to that of the Tokugawa samurai. At 5 or 6 percent of the population, there had been more samurai than the Tokugawa order needed to staff its offices. Those who would maintain their position or even rise a bit did so by competing in rule-following diligence, personality, and bribery. Once graduated, the educated youth was in a similar position to the samurai who had been differentiated from the masses by birth. His education performed the same function, but unfortunately there were more of his kind than the Meiji order (carried over into the Taishō-Shōwa years) needed. Like the samurai *koshiben* of the Tokugawa and early

Meiji periods, the late Meiji, Taishō, and Shōwa youth maintained his position and perhaps advanced a bit as a *sarariiman*, not by brilliance, but by diligence for his employer and by the relations he cultivated with his superiors. He was in this sense a modern-day samurai.

However interesting the rise of the *sarariiman* may be, it is in the realm of intellectual history that this study produces some of its most important results. The writing on *risshin* raises serious questions about prevailing interpretations of early Meiji thought. Judged by his writing on self-advancement, Fukuzawa Yukichi appears as a most conservative, even reactionary, samurai ideologue.[2] Rather than representing the influence of Western liberal thought, his writing represented a continuation of Tokugawa conceptions of the proper social order. Rather than being a critic of the Meiji government and of carry-overs from the ancien regime, Fukuzawa worked to support the Meiji government by discouraging resistance. He accepted the basic social hierarchy of the Tokugawa system and was more concerned with explaining to samurai how they could maintain their dominance in the face of social and economic change than he was with bringing about reform. His concept of advancement was, through and through, a samurai-functionary model.

With this aspect of Fukuzawa's thought documented, it may be suggested that historians, both Japanese and non-Japanese, have been misplacing their efforts when they have sought a liberal, antigovernment, and antibureaucratic tradition in the founder of Keiō Gijuku. Although Nakamura Keiu was explicitly Confucian and as close to orthodoxy as it was possible to come under the Tokugawa system, direct comparison of his writing on self-advancement with that of Fukuzawa shows that Nakamura was closer to nineteenth-century British liberalism and humanitarianism than was Fukuzawa. The respect for manual labor, for women, and for elements of parliamentary politics that runs through his writings suggests that much needs to be done to come to grips with the potential and limits of Confucianism in Japan. More weight must be given to the

2. I have developed this theme at greater length in Earl H. Kinmonth, "Fukuzawa Reconsidered: *Gakumon no susume* and Its Audience," *Journal of Asian Studies* 37:4 (August 1978): 677–696.

opinions of contemporary commentators who credited Nakamura Keiu with at least as much or more influence than Fukuzawa.³ Those who would write intellectual history must recognize that there are important thinkers not represented by countless *denki* ("biographies") and massive *zenshū* ("collected works").

The role played by *Saikoku risshi hen* in early Meiji Japan demonstrates certain methodological problems in the history of thought in Japan. Japanese historians have ignored *Saikoku risshi hen*, except at the level of passing notice, because they have assumed that it was part of popular culture or was read only by merchants. It became part of Japanese popular culture, but initially *Saikoku risshi hen* was the property of the intellectual and political elite. Supercilious prejudices should not be allowed to determine what is the proper province for the history of thought. Works that the Japanese of the Meiji period considered valuable or important must be taken as their readers took them, not according to contemporary prejudices.

The role of translation in determining what a given Western work said to its early Meiji audience must be explored carefully, with due attention to both the original and the translation. Japanese histories abound with lists of translated works, a number of which are credited with being very influential in Meiji Japan. The changes in nuance between *Self-Help* and *Saikoku risshi hen* show that until proven otherwise, early "translations" must be assumed to have been something rather different from the original work.

Even if the meaning of a Western work was not changed through deliberate distortion or simple incompetence (both evident in the translations of British political novels), there was the possibility that readers would find something in a work that neither the author nor the translator intended. The case of *Saikoku risshi hen* demonstrates that without some determination of the matrix through which readers accepted a given popular work, the analysis of a text in isolation is an exercise in futility. It is the reader and not the au-

---

3. Appreciations of Nakamura Keiu (and criticisms of Fukuzawa Yukichi) are common throughout the Meiji period. See Kitamura Tōkoku, "Meiji bungaku kanken," in *Kitamura Tōkoku—Yamaji Aizan*, vol. 6 of *Gendai Nihon bungaku taikei* (Chikuma shobō, 1969), p. 135; Tokutomi Iichirō, "Kunshikoku no shin-kunshi Nakamura Keiu-kō," *Kokumin no tomo*, no. 122 (June 23, 1891), pp. 1–6; and Abe Isoo, "Nakamura Keiu sensei," *Chūgaku sekai* 15:5 (April 1, 1912): 8–18. These three examples are only a small subset of such appraisals.

thor who makes a work historically significant. The use to which the Risshisha (Society of Lofty Ambition) put *Saikoku risshi hen* and the selectivity of *Eisai shinshi* [Talent Forum] composition writers could hardly be predicted from a knowledge of the content of the book, no matter how thorough that knowledge might be.

In terms of intellectual history, the greatest influence of the literature on self-advancement was its contribution to Japanese concepts of the self and the development of individualism as an idea and a mode of behavior.[4] Individualism, defined as the combination of individuated behavior plus an ideological support for such behavior, first appeared in Japan among the "anguished youth." Although few of them would have acknowledged such a relation, the tradition of writing on self-advancement (*risshin*) had taught Meiji youth to think about themselves and provided the base for subsequent discussion of individualism in more elevated and philosophical terms.

---

4. Writing on Japan abounds with references to the weakness or even absence of individualism in the thought and behavior of Japanese. Those who make this type of judgment seldom bother to define individualism, apparently assuming that it is a well-understood and defined concept. Like all "ism" words, it has been used with an enormous range of meanings such that one study of the concept in Western writing has concluded that no coherent definition exists. See Stephen Lukes, *Individualism* (Harper & Row, 1973), p. 42. Such an amorphous concept might better be abandoned or recognized primarily as a polemical term and reserved for editorials. It can be made somewhat more precise, however, by considering its constituents. Ronald Dore has done this in terms of behavior in describing the "individuated person." According to Dore, such a person seeks and wants gratification for himself or those he chooses, rather than for some group. He tries to realize his desires through his own efforts, knowledge, and skills rather than through collective activity. His beliefs, opinions, moral standards, and goals are determined according to strongly held and internalized principles of right and wrong, rather than being determined by contemporary social demands. Responsibility is his alone and is measured against the dictates of individual conscience rather than against group standards. See Ronald P. Dore, *City Life in Japan* (University of California Press, 1958), p. 387. Such behavior by itself does not constitute "individual-ism," however, and must be backed by some ideological justification. At a minimum there should be a recognition or a justification for the following: the idea that each individual human being is possessed of a supreme and intrinsic value or dignity; the idea that each individual ought to be autonomous or self-directing in terms of his own thought; the idea that the individual should have an area of "privacy" where he can pursue his own good in his own way; and the idea that he should pursue self-development, seeking to realize the maximum of his own potentialities. These constituent elements are discussed in Lukes, *Individualism*, pp. 45 ff. The elements enumerated here are the ones I believe to be essential. Others given by Lukes, such as "political individualism" and "ethical individualism," follow from the others. It is this combination of behavior and ideas that constitutes "individual-ism."

THE SELF-MADE MAN IN MEIJI JAPANESE THOUGHT

This relationship appears from an analysis of the developments in writing on *risshin* itself, but it was also noted by at least one observer of the Meiji intellectual scene. At the beginning of the twentieth century, Miyake Yūjirō (Setsurei), a trained philosopher, declared that Japanese conceptions of the self had come out of the indigenous tradition of striving for self-advancement (*risshin shusse*) bolstered by Western thought, specifically the writings of Samuel Smiles, Orison Swett Marden, and Theodore Roosevelt, whom he ranked along with Nietzsche in terms of contributing to Japanese individualism.[5] Although the linkage of Smiles, Marden, and TR to Nietzsche may seem absurd, Miyake knew Japanese youth well. Evidence developed in this study supports his assertion.

Until the discovery of European romantics in the late 1890s, the only body of literature and thought in Japan that dealt with the individual as a *positive* concept was that belonging to the *risshin* genre. Both Confucianism and Buddhism had a concept of the self and gave much attention to the subject, but they did so in the context of suppressing or negating the self. Confucianism was used most often to link the individual to social or political entities and to encourage contentment with the status quo. It denied the intrinsic worth of all individuals, an essential element for individualism, and called instead for recognition of differential worth according to age, sex, rank, or relationship. It did not suggest, except to a limited degree in the somewhat dissident Wang Yang-ming tradition, that each individual ought to be autonomous or self-directing in his own thought. It generally did not recognize a sphere of privacy in which the individual was free to pursue his own way.

Prior to the Meiji Restoration there was little basis for challenging the self-denying thrust of Confucianism. Japan had had no Renaissance and no Reformation. There was no concept of one man in a unique relationship with one god that would provide a rationale for transcending contemporary social conventions. The development of the idea that service to a national or an imperial imperative justified breaking with contemporary society did, however, provide a context in which certain constituents of individualism came to be stressed and accepted. Notions of intrinsic worth were extended on the basis

---

5. Miyake Setsurei (Yūjirō), *Meiji shisō shōshi*, in *Kuga Katsunan—Miyake Setsurei*, ed. Kano Masanao, vol. 37 of *Nihon no meicho* (Chūō kōron sha, 1971), pp. 424–426.

of performance and knowledge, not hereditary status or birth order.

This thrust was continued and institutionalized after the Meiji Restoration. Youth were encouraged to seek self-fulfillment defined as advancement (*risshin, mi o tateru*) to the maximum of their abilities. They were encouraged to become something other than what they were by birth. The 1872 (Meiji 5) proclamation on educational control, *Saikoku risshi hen*, and *Gakumon no susume* [An Encouragement of Learning] all focused on the individual. They encouraged each young man to think about his particular abilities and what he could do with them. Even the *Eisai shinshi* [Talent Forum] youth who were striving to raise the family name were forced by circumstances to be dependent on their own efforts, to seek to become something other than what their fathers had been.

The goal of this writing was not, however, to encourage individualism. Early Meiji writers were all more or less concerned with liberating the individual from traditional restraints on his development so that he could be a more effective participant in collective goals, unbound by anachronistic limits that might prevent some vital element of talent from failing to make its way into a position of maximum utility to the state. That the response of youth to this charge to advance themselves was dependent on a pool of ambitious young men does not alter the fact that the justification proceeded from the state or society, not from the individual.

In their social and national orientation, early Meiji writers were little different from men such as Smiles or Mill. While major Anglo-American writers came to celebrate the individual as such, Japanese did not. Those styled "the new generation in Meiji Japan" did not differ fundamentally from earlier writers on the issue of individualism. They did not advocate it and could not understand it Writers of this "generation" celebrated certain constituents of individualism—individual performance, responsibility, respect, and fulfillment (defined as *risshin*)—but they always subordinated the individual and his ethics to state and social goals. As Tokutomi so clearly stated—"Rich country! Strong army! What are these if they are not the result of commoner morality?"—the issue dividing his group from earlier writers was one not of generation or of goals but of class.

The Minyūsha writers and Tokutomi in particular held to a view in which commoners, specifically rural gentry, were the locus of all virtue in Japan. This was rooted in his own experience, and every virtue he celebrated—such as frugality, hard work, study, invention—had a more bourgeois cast than the exposition of the same virtues in Fukuzawa Yukichi or the *Eisai shinshi* [Talent Forum] writers. It is significant that the most complete endorsements of Samuel Smiles and his writings came from Nakamura Keiu and Tokutomi Iichirō, both of whom were closely tied to the more bourgeois elements of the peasantry.

This distinction must not, however, be pushed too far or extended into other areas. The wealthy peasants and rural samurai were not a bourgeoisie in sharp conflict with an aristocracy. They had had access to samurai rank before the Meiji Restoration, and after it they had access to elected and bureaucratic office by way of education. This reduced possible tension at the same time that the wealthy peasants and rural samurai needed the central government to protect their privileges as landowners.

The more bourgeois concept of advancement found in specifically rural samurai or wealthy peasant interpretations of *Saikoku risshi hen* did not by itself mean that they could function as a source of grass-roots democracy or as an alternative to bureaucratic centralism. The case of Ishizaka Masatsugu illustrates the degree to which wealthy peasants were attracted by the bureaucracy and did not represent a really viable alternative to samurai concepts of the social order and advancement within it. Wealthy peasant or rural samurai background did not lead individuals to a greater acceptance of individualism. The only complete formulation of individualism advanced before the Sino-Japanese War came from Kitamura Tōkoku, a youth of explicitly samurai background.

The basic dividing line between generations in Meiji Japan came not in the late 1880s but between the Sino-Japanese and Russo-Japanese wars when the anguished youth first appeared and the literature of success first flourished. Tokutomi Iichirō noted this, as did other commentators belonging to his age group. When he observed Japanese youth in 1904 (Meiji 37), Tokutomi was struck by what he called an "awakening to the self" (*kojinteki jikaku*) that had two distinctly different forms:

According to my vantage point, the ones awakened to self in a material sense turn to the worship of money. Among the comparatively healthy of these are the so-called success-fevered types of today. Those who are awakened to self in a spiritual sense are the ones who are defeated, despairing, dissolute, tired of the world. The relatively healthy of these are the ones searching for the meaning of existence [*jinsei*].

According to Tokutomi, it was this awakening that set late Meiji youth off from those who had gone before. Those who had brought about the Meiji Restoration had thought of themselves not as individuals but as property of the state. Some had acted selfishly (*wagamama*), but they had looked to the interests of the state. So too for those who had participated in the people's rights movement. It had emphasized the individual, but for the sake of the nation. It was only an extension of the movement to revere the emperor and overthrow the Tokugawa. Contemporary youth, in contrast, thought only of themselves and their own private interests.[6]

The literature of *risshin* supports this basic division of Japanese youth in the Meiji period, but it cannot be taken without qualification, as some Japanese scholars have done. It exaggerates the difference between early and late Meiji youth with respect to their interest in wealth. One of the most frequently appearing characters in student compositions before the Sino-Japanese War was wealth (*tomi*). That it usually but not always was associated with honor (*tōtoi*) does not alter the fact that long before the success literature appeared Meiji youth had been lusting after wealth. Nor was failure to pay much attention to the state new. Tokutomi himself had complained about this in 1887 (Meiji 20). Early *Eisai shinshi* [Talent Forum] writers seldom had spontaneously mentioned either the nation or the imperial household, and neither was prominent in compositions about advancement within the stabilized social order of the 1890s.

It does not seem that the failure to make the linkage between individual aspirations and state benefit came because this connection was known to all and too obvious to bear repeating. Repeating the obvious and stringing together clichés was the basic mode by which early Meiji youth put together the compositions they offered to journals. The essayists linked individual *risshin* to national prosperity in only two cases: when the issue was being raised editorially and they thought they could get their names in print by feeding a maga-

6. Tokutomi Iichirō, "Seinen no kifū," *Kokumin shinbun* (September 25, 1904), in *Sohō bunsen*, pp. 785–791.

zine what it wanted, and when it appeared—as it did during the movement for liberty and people's rights—that activities in the name of the nation would bring *risshin*. In other words, concern for the nation was not an independent variable. Interest fluctuated according to *risshin* expectations.

When this paucity of concern for the nation before the Sino-Japanese War is recognized, much of the alleged difference between early and late Meiji youth disappears. Nevertheless, Tokutomi and other contemporary observers (as well as postwar historians) did see a difference. This came in part from a desire to make an editorial point, but it also had a base in social reality. The attitudes of youth had not changed so much as had the group called "youth." When Meiji observers spoke of "youth" (*seinen*) they referred to those with at least a secondary education. The mass of youth defined solely by age did not enter into their consciousness. In the early Meiji period, youth so defined numbered in the thousands. By the turn of the century, they numbered in the hundreds of thousands.

In terms of the opportunities and structures for advancement, youth before and after the Sino-Japanese War belonged to different worlds. Those who were in their twenties around the turn of the century had grown up entirely within the stabilized social order postulated by *Shōnenen*. They graduated into a world where even the services of the most highly educated were not particularly in demand. Those who were in their twenties in the late 1880s were part of a small elite who were on their way up before the *risshin* ladder had been stabilized. They may not have been able to cash in on the extreme disruption of the immediate post-Restoration period, but they could still do things undreamed of by later youth. Tokutomi, for example, while yet in his teens had been able to found his own profitable private academy and attract students. Twenty years later, his own scattered education would not have qualified him for a proper teaching post in a government school, and his private academy would not have attracted students, because it had no place in the stabilized social order and its ladder to *risshin*.

Early Meiji youth could appear to be serving the state, even if they themselves did not make this identification, simply because there were so few of them. Almost anything an early Meiji youth did short of committing himself full time to the brothel quarters appeared to serve the nation because almost anything new, different, or vaguely

Western appeared to be useful to the state and society. Similarly, the early Meiji youth had more incentive to identify his future with that of the nation because the demand for his skills and knowledge was such that he soon acquired a position of leadership. The late Meiji youth who spent twenty years acquiring an education (in the case of imperial-university graduates) and then graduated into a world where he became a clerical flunky or a middle-school teacher at approximately the same pay as a carpenter had no great reason to be concerned with the nation or the contribution he could make to society.

The elemental constituents of individualism, both conceptual and behavioral, did not acquire individualistic connotations until the 1900s, largely because the relative ease of obtaining advancement kept *risshin* linked to social goals and smoothed over any contradictions between individual and social goals. An early Meiji youth who defied parental injunctions and went off to Tokyo to study or to plunge into politics had a relatively good chance of reaching his goals because of the disorganization of society and the relative demand for educated youth. Coming back home wearing brocade (the early Meiji symbol of affluence) would in most cases make the individual into a community and family hero, whatever the circumstances of his departure. The late Meiji youth who did the same thing had a demonstrably lower chance of gaining *risshin* sufficient to validate his deviancy, and thus he would appear selfish and individualistic even though his actions might not have differed one bit.

The individualism seen in the late Meiji period was not, however, simply an optical illusion. The anguished youth had discovered individualism in the fullest sense of the word. They advocated and to a degree practiced individuated behavior. They most definitely asserted the primacy of the individual, his self-direction, and his self-fulfillment. They really were a new generation in the manner described by Mannheim: "those who work up the material of their common experiences in different specific ways."[7] One can imagine a dialogue between Tokutomi and any late Tokugawa figure, including those who became the Meiji oligarchs. They were concerned about the same social and national issues. One cannot imagine a dialogue between Takayama Chogyū or Masamune Hakuchō and any

7. Mannheim, *Sociology of Knowledge*, p. 304.

early Meiji or late Tokugawa thinker. The meaning of existence that so troubled the anguished youth was simply not part of the consciousness of late Tokugawa and early Meiji figures; it could not be, for nothing had happened to challenge their fundamental beliefs.

While the individualism that appeared between the Sino-Japanese and Russo-Japanese wars among the anguished youth was absolute and total in formulation, it was at the same time limited and self-destructing. Miyake Yūjirō (Setsurei) observed the precarious balance between arrogance and despair in those who had discovered individualism. Defining individualism solely as the absolute reliance on the self left the anguished youth without support in times of crisis. The deathbed retreat of Takayama into the conventional Nichiren Buddhism of his childhood was hardly an impressive showing for someone who had been celebrating the *Übermensch*. The individualists of the early twentieth century traded on the toleration the state extended to them provided they remained apolitical and relatively inconspicuous, even though the Meiji state was founded on a denial of individualism and was ever extending its control over the individual.

Because it was so narrowly defined in terms of an ultrasuperior elite, the individualism of the anguished youth had no appeal in society at large. The same elite base meant that it continually suffered defections. As long as the elite who had discovered themselves did not succumb completely to temporary passion and throw themselves over Kegon Falls or jump in to Mount Aso, the system came through for them. With the exception of Fujimura Misao, the original anguished youth ended up as part of the Taishō-Shōwa establishments: government, academic, and even business.

As a practical matter, late Meiji individualism was poorly argued and justified. It lacked almost any supportive argument other than Takayama's claim that the thought of Nietzsche was the wave of the future. Subsequent authors were unable to go much beyond this. No argument linking individualism to social utility was tried, and perhaps none was possible, because such had already been taken by the advocates of conventional *risshin*. Indigenous religious traditions did not provide a transcendent justification for individualism, and Christianity was too foreign to provide much practical support.

The greatest limitation on individualism in Japan was its relation to capitalism. Meiji individualism could not link itself to business, since Japanese capitalism had not found such arguments congenial. Business ideologues in Japan denied individualism. Typical were the words of Shibusawa Eiichi when he declared, "I believe that in order to get along in society and serve the State, we must by all means abandon this idea of independence and self-reliance and reject egoism completely."[8] Even without a traditional aversion on the part of Japanese businessmen to a rhetoric of individualism, the late Meiji proponents of it could find no comfort in the future development of capitalism. It was their misfortune to discover the self just as business shifted into the phase of large-scale bureaucratic development. As John D. Rockefeller observed of the late nineteenth-century American scene, so too of Japan: "The day of combination is here to stay. Individualism has gone, never to return."[9] Bureaucratic capitalism did not justify itself with a rhetoric of individualism, and it certainly did not want individualistic employees.

In the long run it was the employment situation faced by educated youth that kept individualism from being more than a curious phase in their life cycle. The market conditions faced by educated youth beginning at about the turn of the century were not conducive to deviancy. Certainly by the twenties, corporations and government agencies had so many educated youth to choose from at any level of secondary and higher education that any deviancy from social, corporate, or agency norms required a choice between individualism and unemployment. Indeed, as the guide *Gakusei to shūshoku no jissai* [Students and the Reality of Placement] advised, it was not enough to passively conform and do your job. It was necessary to conform aggressively and consciously unless you wanted to be unemployed.

It was this pressure that explains why individualism and the readership of works associated with it, such as *Santarō nikki* [The Diary of Santarō], became institutionalized as a higher-school phenomenon. The higher-school years were the one time in the life cycle of an educated Japanese when he was not directly under parental pressure or cramming for examinations and the one time when he was

8. Quoted in Marshall, *Capitalism and Nationalism*, p. 35.
9. Quoted in Richard Weiss, *The American Myth of Success* (Basic Books, 1969), p. 9.

not worried about finding or keeping a job. Higher school was the one moment in his existence when he could indulge his ego without worrying about what it would do to his chances for *risshin*.

Though the comparison must of necessity be subjective and impressionistic, to be tested by future research and events, it may be suggested that the pressures for conformity in Japan were greater than in other modern nations, not because of the more conservative and elitist features of the Meiji state but because of its more progressive and equalitarian reforms. Japanese traditions without doubt discouraged individualism, but the greatest pressure faced by youth was that inherent in the bureaucratic environment and in their market situation. To the degree that Japan was a late developer and bureaucratic capitalism was relatively more important than entrepreneurial capitalism at an earlier period, there was more pressure for conformity than in early developing nations. The pressure for conformity was increased further by the ratio of people to resources and opportunities. Compared with a frontier nation such as the United States or to an old colonial power such as Britain, Japan had an inherently high ratio of people to possibilities.

This unfavorable ratio was further increased in Japan because the ratio of aspirants to places was not controlled by the ascriptive factors so prominent in Anglo-American culture. Aside from sex, which was a discriminatory factor in all countries, *potential* competitors for elite positions in Japan came close to being the whole male population. Compared with Germany and even England, aristocratic privilege was nonexistent in Japan. Compared with the United States—where race, religion, ethnic background, and regional origin all eliminated large segments of the American population from contention for the governmental, managerial, and academic positions constituting *risshin*—Japan was an extremely equalitarian society, not in structure but in potential for advancement. Through no virtue of its own, Japan lacked many of the factors that kept competition for elite status under control in the United States. Unless it can be shown that the costs of education were *much more* important as a screening device in Japan than in the United States, it must be assumed that the "log cabin myth" was closer to reality in Japan than in the United States, where only whites from New England and the Midwest having parents of northern European origin and belonging to major Protestant sects could compete for those careers which by Japanese standards constituted *risshin shusse*. By itself the relatively open recruitment of elites that existed in Japan would be praiseworthy and an apparently liberal and progressive ideal worthy of emulation. Nevertheless, it can be suggested that this openness contributed to the rise of illiberal and reactionary politics in the 1930s and 1940s and contributed to the apparently muddled civilian leadership that led Japan into war.

Writing shortly after World War II and observing a number of former military and political leaders on trial for their alleged war crimes, historian Maruyama Masao was puzzled by the behavior of the accused during the trial and by what was being revealed about their behavior during the years leading up to the war.[10] He found it difficult to understand how the Japanese wartime leaders, men whom he characterized as "prize students," could have become "pathetic robots, manipulated by outlaws . . . on whom they looked down from the height of their positions." These men appeared "dwarfish" and passive, submitting to faits accomplis, taking refuge in jurisdictional or specialty limits, and shirking responsibility.

Contrary to what Maruyama thought, there was nothing especially Japanese about the patterns on display at the trials. They are endemic in the bureaucratic situation, military or civilian. In the American army, the ethos on display at the trials is exemplified in the pithy advice "Cover your ass!" and in the American navy by the formula "Not on my watch!"[11] What was perhaps peculiar to Japan was the pressure for this kind of behavior. Those willing to assume responsibility for unpopular decisions or who are willing to stand up for what they believe right when it means going against popular views are rare enough in any society whether or not it has a tradition of individualism and an internalized morality. Martyrs are always in short supply. Those with less commitment can, however, be expected to take responsibility and to assert their own opinions when to do so does not involve sacrifice of their present position or future career or when their skills and knowledge are in such great demand

---

10. Maruyama Masao, "Thought and Behavior Patterns of Japan's Wartime Leaders," trans. Ivan Morris, in *Thought and Behavior in Modern Japanese Politics*, ed. Ivan Morris (Oxford University Press, 1969), pp. 84–134.

11. For a description of this mentality at work in the United States, see Stuart H. Loory, *Defeated: Inside America's Military Machine* (Random House, 1973), esp. part 2, "A Generation of Yes Men," pp. 27–119.

that they can sacrifice current position to principle and continue without major loss elsewhere. To the degree that the Japanese system was relatively open and continually plagued by a surplus of would-be elites, fewer of the wartime leaders possessed these supports for independent conduct. They were not a natural elite who would maintain their status no matter what action they took. They were an artificial elite made up of nonspecialized components that could be replaced from a large stock of ready and eager standbys. Even that elite of elites, the Tokyo Imperial University law graduate, was available in greater numbers than either government or business could use.

Rather than looking upon the men on trial as "prize students," it might be more appropriate to look upon them as "survivors." Their average year of birth was roughly 1883 (Meiji 16) and most were born in the 1880s. This meant that at least half and perhaps two-thirds or so belonged explicitly to the first group of Meiji youth to begin their climb to *risshin* in the "stabilized social order" postulated by *Shōnenen* [A Garden for Youth]. Many were just of the right age to have been reading and writing compositions such as "Systematic Study." They would have entered the higher schools just as the competitive pressures of other would-be students were changing the entrance examinations from tests of qualification to devices for rejection. They would have memorized trivia and studied third-rate English prose, including Orison Swett Marden, in order to get on the track to *risshin*.

Some would have been passing through the Imperial University while Lafcadio Hearn was there and may have been among those who prompted him to comment on the conformist personality of the students he encountered. They were "bound by custom" and "would never dream of yielding to any impulses at variance with order, however generous or sensible such impulses may be." Even without the advice of the personality-ethic literature that appeared after World War I, they already knew that a single misplaced word might ruin their career chances and believed that "by silent submission and tireless observance of duty" they might rise quickly in the world.[12]

12. Lafcadio Hearn, "Official Education," in *Japan: An Attempt at Interpretation* (Tuttle, 1955), pp. 427–428. This work was originally published in 1904 (Meiji 37).

CONCLUSION

Whatever their expectations, the youth Hearn observed and those who became the leaders in the 1930s and 1940s had the dubious distinction of being the first group to graduate into the placement difficulty that existed (with the exception of the World War I boom) from the Russo-Japanese War onward. This they did after studying for and passing the higher civil service examinations by careful attention to the task of feeding back to the examiners precisely what they wanted to read and by presenting the proper demeanor expected of would-be functionaries at the oral examinations. They began their bureaucratic careers during the doldrums preceding the World War I boom, and they were among those who experienced the threat of dismissal and the reality of declining real income that marked the 1920s and 1930s. The men Maruyama saw on trial were survivors, perhaps because of their ability, but it is at least as probable that they were survivors because they had cultivated the proper contacts, because they had made sure that their relations with superiors were most cordial and ingratiating, and because they had committed no infractions of the rules and permitted themselves no deviation that could be used against them by competitors.[13]

By the time these young men reached positions of nominal leadership, they were thoroughly steeped in the art of surviving, of keeping themselves in position and keeping other equally qualified and interchangeable contenders out. Nowhere were they trained to exercise dynamic leadership, to take strong stands even if they had to put their careers on the line for principle. If they were dwarfed, that came about by the pressures of surviving in a society where racial, ethnic, and religious factors did not control the competition for elite status. They were dwarfed by the most attractive aspect of Japanese society, its lack of discrimination on ascriptive grounds, and by the system for selecting elites from the horde of applicants, a system that is usually described as modern and rational. Or, to explain this in the terms used by Japanese, it may be said that the wartime leadership was dwarfed not by the *hōkenteki* ("feudal," "premodern") aspects of Japanese society but by the *kindaiteki* ("modern").

---

13. The discussion here is phrased in terms of those who followed the civilian bureaucratic route to positions of leadership, but many of the same pressures, including examinations and periods of low growth or retrenchment, apply to military careers as well.

THE SELF-MADE MAN IN MEIJI JAPANESE THOUGHT

Had the Meiji reforms not been so successful in opening recruitment and then spreading the desire for *risshin* to an ever increasing portion of all Japanese youth, there might have been a more responsible and confident elite in the Taishō and Shōwa eras, one more willing to take stands on issues and less concerned with maintaining individual positions. As it was, the success of the Meiji system contributed to Shōwa failure. It demonstrated that objective and apparently rational bureaucratic selection of leadership in the absence of democratic restraints but in the presence of a vast surplus of aspirants could produce a system that was not rational as a whole. Each individual was more concerned with maximizing his security and opportunities through ducking responsibility and demonstrating enthusiastic conformity.

In lieu of a real democratic revolution, modern Japan might well have been better served by a system that more sharply restricted the pool from which it recruited aspirants to elite status. Such a system would not necessarily have produced an elite that made better decisions, but by contributing to a greater sense of individual responsibility, decision-making, and possibly even opposition, it might have resulted in critical decisions being made somewhat more often by responsible debate rather than by default. There might have been more coherent if not always better responses to the issues facing Japan in the 1930s and 1940s. It is hard to imagine any worse decision-making coming from a more restricted system, and at the very least, Japanese society might have gained something from the talent and energy of those freed from examination preparation.

After World War II several factors worked to reduce the dysfunctional products of the Japanese system. Agreement by consensus is easiest to reach if all participants share the same view of the problems that occur and if the range of issues and options is rather limited. Defeat and the Supreme Commander for the Allied Powers effectively produced these favorable conditions. The military was removed from contention for political and economic power, and Japanese foreign policy was essentially reduced to seconding that of the United States. These changes left the power elite more homogeneous than before the war and free (or forced) to concentrate on a rather limited range of options within the domestic sphere, largely in economics. At the same time, purges and the demonstrated failings of the older leaders disrupted at least temporarily the climb by seniority to top positions, allowing (relatively) young men into positions of responsibility where they had more opportunity to act on their abilities rather than on their aggressively conformist personalities. In effect, defeat and the occupation provided something of that second Restoration that Japanese had been looking for since the beginning of the stabilized social order in the early 1890s.[14]

All this does not mean, however, that the disabilities arising from a surplus of would-be elites has been forever banished from Japan. The system may appear to be functioning very well at the moment, but apparent success can arise in two distinct ways. Brilliant performance in the face of severe and complex obstacles is one way to achieve success, but mediocre performance in the absence of serious challenges and diversions can produce the same result. Until the current Japanese system is tested against a problem or two having the complexity and divisive potential of those arising in the 1930s and 1940s, it is premature to celebrate contemporary Japan as some sort of superstate that has solved all the problems endemic to modern industrial nations.

If there is any lesson for the United States in Japanese experience, it may be in the data provided on the relation between expanding educational opportunity, the job market for college and university students, and the appearance of political opposition among educated youth. In interpreting the developments leading up to World War II, or as some prefer to call it, the Pacific War, Japanese historians such as Maruyama Masao and Ienaga Saburō have been faced with the task of explaining the response of Japanese intellectuals to militarism and expansionism.[15] Unable to find any general opposition to these currents, they have sought to excuse intellectual complicity by asserting that even if intellectuals did not resist, they were not enthusiastic, and the real responsibility and support for militarism and expansionism lay with "pseudo-intellectuals" or "sub-leaders." As various American scholars have pointed out, first-rank intellectuals were in fact much more involved in positive efforts to support militarism and expansionism than has been admitted in the writ-

14. This still partially speculative discussion grew out of exchanges with Professor Takeuchi Yō.
15. Ienaga Saburō, *The Pacific War, 1931–1945* (Pantheon, 1978), chap. 6 (esp. pp. 116–128) and chap. 10 (pp. 203–228), and Maruyama Masao, "Ideology and Dynamics of Japanese Fascism," pp. 25–83 in *Thought and Behavior*, esp. pp. 57–65.

ings of Maruyama and Ienaga; but even if they are granted their rather transparent attempt to shift responsibility, the question of acquiescence remains.[16] Perhaps the answer is to be found in the literature of *risshin shusse* and the job market for educated youth.

By any measure the position of "university-educated salaried employees," the prewar intelligentsia as defined by Maruyama, was steadily declining in the decade before the so-called Manchurian Incident. The worst of the placement difficulty and the peak in salary-receiver (*hōkyū seikatsusha*) unemployment came in 1931–1932 (Shōwa 6–7). Although the establishment of Manchukuo was in part justified in terms of bringing about a solution to the crisis in Japanese agriculture, the chief beneficiaries of radicalism and adventurism in the army appear to have been the higher-education graduates and already-employed *sarariiman* (salary men). Even though Manchukuo did not live up to the most extreme expectations for it, foreign and domestic observers alike credited it with ending the placement difficulty of the 1930s and substantially benefiting salary receivers.

Educated youth and the *sarariiman* intelligentsia, moreover, paid little, at least initially, for the benefits they received from Manchukuo and militarism.[17] Throughout the 1930s and into the 1940s, students in schools of at least middle-school status received draft deferments. The university student could avoid the conscription examination until his late twenties, and because of the lax and protective grading policies of even the best universities, he faced no fear of flunking out into the army. By the time he graduated, there was a good possibility that he had developed a physical ailment or other condition that would result in total exemption. Even if he was not so fortunate, the university graduate—like all those with middle-school educations and above—served for only one year. He could

16. Ienaga is somewhat more critical of intellectuals than Maruyama, who seems to take extraordinary pains to shift responsibility. For recent American work on the activities of intellectuals, see Donald Keene, "The Barren Years: Japanese War Literature," *Monumenta Nipponica* 33:1 (1978): 67–112; Miles Fletcher, "Intellectuals and Fascism in Early Shōwa Japan," *Journal of Asian Studies* 39:1 (November 1979): 39–64; and James B. Crowley, "Intellectuals as Visionaries of the New Asian Order," pp. 319–374 in *Dilemmas of Growth in Prewar Japan*, ed. James W. Morley (Princeton University Press, 1971).

17. Details of the 1930s conscription system may be found in *The Japan Year Book 1939–1940*, pp. 225–228, and *The Japan Year Book 1940–1941*, pp. 213–215.

CONCLUSION

also gain easy promotion to officer status, a privilege that in any army makes the experience much more tolerable.

Thus, there appears an interesting contrast between educated youth in Japan of the 1930s and those of the United States in the 1960s with respect to the impact of war on their quest for advancement. Vietnam came on top of a relatively good job market for college and university graduates. It brought little or no direct economic benefit, certainly nothing comparable to what Manchukuo and militarism did for Japanese students and *sarariiman* in the 1930s. Even more important, it was potentially very costly. American students were continually faced with the threat expressed in the formula "A, B, C, D, or Vietnam." Deferment ended at an earlier age in the United States, and some exemptions, such as those for household heads, were not available at all. The college or university graduate who was drafted during the Vietnam War received little if any special treatment and served a regular tour of duty. If he was fortunate and able to manipulate the system, the American draftee found his pursuit of *risshin* and education interrupted during a period when the army was not an economically attractive employer in either absolute or relative terms. If he was unfortunate and unable to work out a soft assignment, the American draftee ran a fairly high risk of getting killed or being maimed.

This difference in costs and benefits rather than any more subtle questions of culture and morality may well constitute the primary explanation of why the intelligentsia in the United States resisted and that of Japan did not. Differences in the legal framework for dissent and the degree of police repression may have been factors, but an examination of the timing of repressive legislation and arrests under it in Japan suggests that most was largely precautionary, designed to handle opposition that never materialized. Moreover, even if it is allowed for the sake of argument that there was more repression in Japan, the lack of even passive dissent remains to be explained. Perhaps there were university graduates who refused a good job offer from the South Manchurian Railway Company or from Nissan because they were engaged in the imperialistic exploitation of Manchuria. Perhaps there were some who refused because of their antiwar principles to take employment with Mitsubishi because the group was involved in arms manufacture. But, if there

347

were any significant number of such young men, they have escaped notice so far. Until they are discovered, the impression gained from all commentaries written during the 1930s must be that the intelligentsia in general and college and university graduates in particular made no effort whatsoever to reject the opportunities or profits that came out of Manchukuo and militarism. There appears to be little or no evidence of any significant number of youth sacrificing their *risshin* to principle even if that could be done without risking imprisonment. The reservations and criticisms voiced by the intelligentsia developed only after they, as well as the peasant conscripts, had been charged the costs of militarism and expansionism.

Only future events will show whether the widespread opposition among the postwar Japanese intelligentsia to things military is a permanent change or simply the product of a shift in the relative *risshin* possibilities offered by the civilian and military approaches to expansion. If Japan can weather some future prolonged period of placement difficulty and unemployment for highly educated youth without having the intelligentsia become more enthusiastic (or acquiesce) with respect to nationalism and militarism, then perhaps the change in attitudes after World War II can be declared permanent and fundamental. So too for the United States. The permanence of the counterculture of the 1960s and the depth of the lesson allegedly taught by Vietnam will be proven only if opposition to American overseas military adventures rises once again, especially in a situation where educated youth are facing a poor job market such that they will benefit directly from conflict and where they need not personally pay the costs of militarism through involuntary service.

Finally, at the risk of ending this book on such a note of pessimism that the aversion to the subject of *risshin* found in Japanese writers seems totally justified, it must be noted that there is no logical or empirical basis for crediting the educated youth discussed here with any great positive contribution to the economic growth of Japan, regardless of whatever may be said in speculation about the political costs of their numbers. As Ronald Dore has argued, there are serious logical and methodological flaws, to say nothing of contradictory results, in those studies that have sought to relate increasing levels of education to economic growth. Beyond a certain minimal level, education may not be the cause of growth and development but instead may be simply a form of consumption coming with increasing affluence. Indeed, an increase in the general level of education may act as a brake on economic development by diverting scarce resources from more productive activities.[18]

Japan may well be the best example of what can be called "the Cadillac phenomenon."[19] Surveys of automobile ownership will generally show that as income levels rise the proportion of people owning Cadillacs increases. Just as it would be ridiculous to argue that most wealthy people got that way by owning Cadillacs, so too is it unreasonable to argue that Japan prospered because of its supply of highly educated would-be functionaries. Until proved otherwise, it is perhaps best to regard the increasing number of highly educated youth in Japan during the period discussed here as a drain on growth or as a form of consumption brought about by increasing income levels and to credit—as did companies prewar and postwar—the minimally educated rural youth with making the greatest marginal contribution to real output. Even without considering the possible political consequences of having too many youth with secondary and higher education, there is little basis for finding good in the prewar Japanese system of higher education and elite recruitment.[20] Until proven otherwise, it is perhaps best to assume that Japan grew *in spite* of and not because of its elites and would-be elites. Those who stayed out of the competition described here (or who were kept out) deserve more credit than they usually receive.

These tentative conclusions about the relation between the desire for advancement and the mechanisms used for selection of elites in prewar Japan (and possibly also for postwar Japan, for which the final results are not yet in) should not, of course, be taken as a brief for controlling the pool of would-be elites in any country by such ascriptive factors as race, religion, or ethnic origin. The relationship suggested here does, however, give some indication of what should

18. Ronald Dore, *The Diploma Disease: Education, Qualification and Development* (University of California Press, 1976), esp. chap. 7 (pp. 84–97).

19. This phenomenon is noted in ibid., p. 88.

20. It is perhaps worth noting that the negative picture of prewar Japanese elites given here is *not* dependent on a rejection of (or reaction to) Japanese goals of the 1930s and 1940s. It is possible to accept the various goals and claims put forward during the 1930s and 1940s and still come to the conclusion that Japanese leadership, both military and civilian, was not especially competent.

be avoided in making any system of elite recruitment and selection open to all aspirants without undesirable side effects.[21]

If schooling—the putting in of time at institutions, rather than education (which can come from formal and informal sources), what Samuel Smiles called "wisdom"—is used to select and sort aspirants for elite and near-elite status, then there will be continual pressure to expand the institutions offering each type of schooling, with a resultant devaluation of both the contents and the graduates. At the same time, the number of aspirants who must be sorted by other means will increase. If the selection mechanism depends on examinations, there exists the danger that these will become elimination contests and not tests of qualification for the ultimate role to be assumed by those who pass.

This danger is especially great with examinations that test for a "stock of knowledge" rather than evaluating performance in real-life situations. The only way such examinations can be adjusted to deal with a surplus of applicants, all or most of whom are at least minimally qualified, is to add detail and complexity for their own sake. The person who spends his or her life learning how to prepare for and pass such examinations is not necessarily the person best prepared to assume leadership, especially during crises. A dynamic environment seldom presents problems that can be answered solely from memorized information.

Perhaps such a system can work reasonably well (as it seems to be doing in contemporary Japan) as a kind of intelligence test distributed over time,[22] but such a system may work well in spite of itself. Perhaps enough people who have *both* leadership ability and test-passing skills get through the system so that the resultant elite is not populated solely by adept test-takers. Economic expansion, moreover, aids the functioning of such a system. It provides consolation for those who fail to enter the most elite track and reduces for all the incentive to look for adventuristic or totalitarian schemes to increase opportunities. More important, expansion reduces the relative weight in the overall power structure of those selected from the most elite track and gives a relatively greater role to those who are innovators rather than survivors.

21. Dore discusses a number of alternative methods for elite recruitment and selection in *Diploma Disease*, part 3, esp. chaps. 12, 13, and 15.
22. This is how Dore interprets the present Japanese system. Ibid., chap. 3, esp. pp. 47–50.

CONCLUSION

The real test of any system or mechanism takes place in a hostile and adverse environment, not in a controlled situation and favorable surroundings. I emphasize this point in order to caution readers to be alert for the facile and often spurious associations that seem to plague writing on Japan. When Japan is "on our side" and functioning well according to American criteria, each and every element of Japanese society is seen as good. When the system is not performing well or Japan is "not on our side," each and every element of Japanese society is seen as evil. The extreme of this kind of association was of course reached during and shortly after World War II when everything from Japan's feudal heritage to the alleged toilet-training habits of Japanese mothers was seen as contributing to militarism and aggression. Just as many elements cited by scholars in the 1930s, 1940s, and early 1950s as contributing to an aggressive and militaristic Japan most probably had no causal relation to those trends whatsoever, so too may many contemporary elements be unrelated to the apparent success of Japan. Rather than serving as a model for imitation, Japan perhaps best serves as an experimental model forcing foreign observers to test their own intellectual constructs and conceits to see their own societies in a new light, somewhat in the manner in which the early Meiji reception of *Self-Help* revealed thought currents in Anglo-American history commonly obscured by familiarity and "common sense" interpretations.

Appendix: *Eisai shinshi* Contributors and Contributions

To confirm subjective impressions of the nature of *Eisai shinshi* contributors and contributions, a count was made of the various ideas appearing in essays dealing with personal advancement. Yoshiko Kinmonth assisted in this survey.

Issues examined:	147		
Period covered:	March 10, 1877, to December 27, 1879		
Compositions analyzed:	202		
Sex Distribution:	SEX	NUMBER	PERCENTAGE
	Male	149	74
	Female	31	15
	Unknown	22	11
Age Distribution:	AGE	NUMBER	PERCENTAGE
	7	3	2
	8	6	3
	9	3	2
	10	10	5
	11	31	16
	12	45	24
	13	52	28
	14	23	12
	15	9	5
	16	3	2
	17	3	2
	18	1	1

APPENDIX

Regional Distribution:	AREA	NUMBER	PERCENTAGE
	Tokyo	54	28
	Kumamoto	16	8
	Chiba	12	6
	Kyoto	10	5
	Nagasaki	10	5
	Shizuoka	9	5
	Aomori	8	4
	Kanagawa	7	4
	Nagano	7	4
	Fukushima	6	3
	Akita	5	3
	Osaka	5	3
	Mie	5	3
	Hiroshima	4	2
	Kagoshima	4	2
	Miyagi	4	2
	Aichi	3	2
	Ishikawa	3	2
	Yamanashi	3	2
	Other	15	8

Class Distribution: Samurai, 11%   Commoner, 7%   Not specified, 88%

Themes by Class:		SAMURAI	COMMONER	ALL
	Wealth and honor	4	2	65
	Wisemen and fools	2	6	38
	Study	4	10	123
	Learning	8	4	96
	Perseverance	2	7	43
	For the country	3	1	39
	For the household	1	0	20

EISAI SHINSHI CONTRIBUTORS AND CONTRIBUTIONS

	THEME	NUMBER	PERCENTAGE
Overall Summary of Themes:	Warning of laziness. Encouraging study and/or hard work (*benkyō, taida*)	123	61
	Calling for education and learning (*kyōiku, gakumon*)	96	48
	Indicating wealth and honor, a life of ease, or prosperity as a goal (*fūki, kōfuku, anraku*)	65	32
	Warning against the waste of time	44	22
	Encouraging perseverance (*nintai*)	43	21
	Indicating fame or renown (*kōmyō*) as goal	41	20
	Indicating the country would benefit	39	19
	Seeing mankind divided into fools and wisemen (*kengu*)	38	19
	Hoping to undertake a great task (*daigyō*)	29	14
	Having or accomplishing a great purpose (*risshi*)	24	12
	Specific mention of benefits to the household (*ie*)	20	10
	Planning a heroic deed or life (*eiyū*)	13	6
	Polishing character (*hinkō*)	10	5
	Calling for exercise and clean living (*kenkō*)	8	4
	Calling for filial piety	6	3
	Shame (*haji*) as the result of failure	6	3
	Frugality	5	2

Note: A number of themes appeared less than 5 times. In particular the emperor was noted but 3 times. Only 1 mention of the "community" was made.

Bibliography

The number and type of sources in this book precludes the presentation of a complete, conventional bibliography. Three lists of sources have been provided: (1) Youth-oriented Periodicals in alphabetical order by title; (2) Source and Article Collections, in alphabetical order by title; and (3) Articles and Monographs, in alphabetical order by author or editor. The third of these lists is not meant to be exhaustive; journalistic pieces have generally been excluded, as have many scholarly works not central to the arguments of this study.

Unless otherwise specified, all Japanese-language sources were published in Tokyo and all English-language sources in New York City. Where possible, names have been romanized according to P. G. O'Neill, *Japanese Names* (Tokyo: John Weatherhill, Inc., 1972).

Youth-oriented Periodicals
Listed here are the principal periodicals directed at youth (young men seeking or possessing secondary or higher education) which were found to be useful for this study. The approximate dates given represent the period for which the magazine was used. In most cases this corresponds to the period for which the magazine was published or for which the Meiji bunko has reasonably complete holdings. There is little scholarship on youth-oriented periodicals in Japanese, but the reader wishing to know more about the items cited in the text or the larger universe of such magazines should consult the following: Ishii Kendō (Tamaji), "Meiji shoki no shōnen zasshi," *Taiyō* 33:8 (June 1927): 406–414; Kimura Shōshū, *Meiji shōnen*

BIBLIOGRAPHY

bunka shi (Dōwa shunjū sha, 1949); Kimura Shōshū, *Shōnen bungaku shi Meiji hen* (Dōwa shunjū sha, 1949); Masuda Yoshihiko, *Jitsugyō no Nihon sha nanajū nen shi* (Jitsugyō no Nihon sha, 1967); and Yamazaki Yasuo, *Chosha to shuppansha* (Gakufū shoin, 1954) and *Dai-ni Chosha to shuppansha* (Gakufū shoin, 1955).

Aichi gakugei zasshi [Aichi Arts and Sciences Magazine]. Late 1880s–1890s.
Akita shōnen zasshi [Akita Magazine for Young People]. Mid-1890s.
Bunko [Library]. Late 1890s–1900s.
Chūgaku bundan [Middle-School Literary Circle]. 1900s.
Chūgaku sekai [Middle-School World]. Late 1890s–late 1920s.
Eibun shinshi (The Student) [English Essay Forum]. Mid-1900s.
Eigo seinen (The Rising Generation) [English (for) Youth]. Early 1900s.
Eisai shinshi [Talent Forum]. Late 1870s–late 1890s.
Fukoku seinen [Youth of a Rich Country]. Mid-1900s.
Gakusei hissenjō [Battlefield of Student Writing Brushes]. Mid-1890s.
Gakusei no shiyū [Friend of the Student]. Late 1880s.
Gakutei shūhōroku [School Record]. Late 1870s.
Jitsugyō no Nihon [Business Japan]. Late 1890s–1910s.
Jitsugyō shōnen [Business Youth]. Late 1900s.
Kokumin no tomo [Friend of the People]. Late 1880s–1890s.
Kugakukai [Struggling-Student World]. 1902.
Manabi no tomo [Friend of Learning]. Early 1890s.
Manabi no tomoshibi [Light of Learning]. Late 1890s.
Meiyo gakutei shinshi [Honor School Forum]. Early 1880s.
Nihonjin [The Japanese]. Late 1880s–early 1900s.
Nihon no shōnen [Young People of Japan]. Late 1880s–mid-1900s.
Ōbun gakusei gakujutsu zasshi [Foreign-Language Student Magazine]. Mid-1880s.
Seikō [Success]. Early 1900s–mid-1910s.
Shōgaku sakubun shinshi [Elementary-School Composition Forum]. Late 1870s.
Shōgaku seito no tomo [Friend of the Elementary-School Student]. Early 1890s.
Shōkokumin [Little Citizen]. Late 1880s–1890s.
Shōnenen [A Garden for Young People]. Late 1880s–1890s.
Shōnen bunko [A Library for Young People]. Late 1880s–1890s.
Shōnen sekai [World of Young People]. Mid-1890s–mid-1900s.
To-Bei zasshi [Going to America Magazine]. Mid-1900s.
Yōnen zasshi [Magazine for Children]. Mid-1890s.

Source and Article Collections

Abe Jirō—Kurata Hyakuzō. Vol. 46 of *Gendai Nihon bungaku zenshū*, Chikuma shobō, 1956.
Asahi nenkan. Ōsaka Asahi shinbun sha.

BIBLIOGRAPHY

Asahi shinbun ni miru Nihon no ayumi. Edited by Tsunoda Hideo. Asahi shinbun, 1974.
"Bijinesuman no seikatsu hyaku-nen." *Bessatsu Chūō kōron keiei mondai* 4:2 (June 1965): 143–398.
Bushidō sōsho. Edited by Inoue Tetsujirō. Hakubunkan, 1905.
Dōtoku kyōiku shiryō shūsei. Edited by Miyata Fumio. Dai-ichi hōki shuppan, 1959.
Fujita Tōko—Aizawa Seishisai—Fujita Yūkoku. Edited by Hashikawa Bunsō. Vol. 29 of *Nihon no meicho.* Chūō kōron sha, 1974.
Fukuzawa Yukichi zenshū. Edited by Tomita Masafumi and Tsuchibayashi Shunichi. Iwanami shoten, 1959.
The Japan Year Book. Foreign Affairs Association of Japan.
Kaibara Ekiken. Vol. 14 of *Nihon no meicho.* Edited by Matsuda Michio. Chūō kōron sha, 1969.
Kawai Eijirō zenshū. Shakai shisō sha, 1968.
Kikuchi Kan—Kume Masao shū. Vol. 57 of *Nihon gendai bungaku zenshū.* Kōdansha, 1967.
Kindai Nihon seiji shisō shi I. Vol. 3 of *Kindai Nihon shisō shi taikei.* Yūhikaku, 1971.
Kindai Nihon shakai shisō shi I. Vol. 1 of *Kindai Nihon shisō shi taikei.* Yūhikaku, 1968.
Kitamura Tōkoku. Edited by Nihon bungaku kenkyū shiryō kankō-kai. Yūseidō shuppan, 1972.
Kitamura Tōkoku—Yamaji Aizan. Vol. 6 of *Gendai Nihon bungaku taikei.* Chikuma shobō, 1969.
Kōtoku Shūsui [Denjirō] zenshū. Meiji bunken, 1968.
Kuga Katsunan—Miyake Setsurei. Edited by Kano Masanao. Vol. 37 of *Nihon no meicho.* Chūō kōron sha, 1971
Kunikida Doppo—Ishikawa Takuboku shū. Vol. 12 of *Nihon bungaku zenshū.* Shūei sha, 1967.
Kunikida Doppo shū. Vol. 18 of *Nihon gendai bungaku zenshū.* Kōdansha, 1962.
Kuroiwa Ruikō shū. Vol. 47 of *Meiji bungaku zenshū.* Chikuma shobō, 1971.
Kyōjun. Vol. 5 of *Nihon kyōkasho taikei.* Edited by Ishikawa Ken. Kōdansha, 1969.
Masamune Hakuchō shū. Vol. 11 of *Nihon bungaku zenshū.* Shūei sha, 1969.
Meiji bunka shiryō sōsho. Edited by Meiji bunka shiryō sōsho kankō-kai. Kazama shobō, 1970.
Meiji honyaku bungaku shū. Vol. 7 of *Meiji bungaku zenshū.* Chikuma shobō, 1972.
Meiji kaikaki bungaku shū II. Vol. 2 of *Meiji bungaku zenshū.* Chikuma shobō, 1967.
Meiji keimō shisō shū. Vol. 3 of *Meiji bungaku zenshū.* Chikuma shobō, 1967.

BIBLIOGRAPHY

Meiji no shūen. Vol. 8 of *Nihonjin no hyaku-nen.* Sekai bunka sha, 1972.
Meiji seiji shōsetsu shū I. Vol. 5 of *Meiji bungaku zenshū.* Chikuma shobō, 1966.
Meiji seiji shōsetsu shū II. Vol. 6 of *Meiji bungaku zenshū.* Chikuma shobō, 1967.
Meiji shisōka shū. Vol. 13 of *Nihon gendai bungaku zenshū.* Kōdansha, 1968.
Meiji shōnen bungaku shū. Vol. 95 of *Meiji bungaku zenshū.* Chikuma shobō, 1970.
Miyake Setsurei [Yūjirō] shū. Vol. 33 of *Meiji bungaku zenshū.* Chikuma shobō, 1967.
Nihon kokugo dai-jiten. Shōgakkan, 1974.
Nihon kyōkasho taikei kindai hen. Kōdansha, 1961.
Nihon no gakusei no rekishi. Kōdansha, 1970.
Nihon rōdō nenkan. Ōhara shakai mondai kenkyūjo.
Nihon teikoku Monbushō nenpō. Monbushō.
Nihon teikoku tōkei nenkan. Naikaku tōkei kakari.
Nitobe Inazō zenshū. Kyōbunkan, 1970.
Ogyū Sorai. Edited by Bitō Masahide. Vol. 16 of *Nihon no meicho.* Chūō kōron sha, 1974.
[Ōmachi] Keigetsu zenshū. Kyōbun sha, 1926.
"Risshin shusse." *Gendai no esupuri.* No. 118 (May 1977).
Sakai Toshihiko [Kosen] zenshū. Hōritsu bunka sha, 1971.
Seikatsu shi III. Vol. 17 of *Taikei Nihon shi sōsho.* Yamakawa shuppan-sha, 1969.
Shidōsha to taishū. Vol. 5 of *Kindai Nihon shisō shi kōza.* Chikuma shobō, 1960.
Shinbun ga kataru Meiji shi. Edited by Araki Masayasu. Hara shobō, 1976.
Shinbun shūroku Taishō shi (SSTS). Edited by Watanabe Katsumasa. Taishō shuppan, 1978.
Shinbun shūsei Shōwa hennenshi (SSS). Taishō Shōwa hennenshi kankō-kai, 1968.
Sohō bunsen. Minyūsha, 1915.
Sources of Japanese Tradition. Edited by Ryusaku Tsunoda, Wm. Theodore de Bary, and Donald Keene. Columbia University Press, 1964.
Takayama Chogyū [Rinjirō]—Anesaki Chōfū [Masaharu]—Sasakawa Rinpū. Vol. 13 of *Gendai Nihon bungaku zenshū.* Kaizō sha, 1928.
Taoka Reiun zenshū. Hōsei daigaku shuppan-kai, 1969.
Tokutomi Sohō [Iichirō] shū. Vol. 34 of *Meiji bungaku zenshū.* Chikuma shobō, 1974.
Tokutomi Sohō—Yamaji Aizan. Edited by Sumiya Mikio. Vol. 40 of *Nihon no meicho.* Chūō kōron sha, 1971.
Uchimura Kanzō zenshū. Iwanami shoten, 1933.
Yokoi [Tokiyoshi, Jikei] hakushi zenshū. Dai-Nihon nōkai, 1925.
Yoshida Shōin. Edited by Matsumoto Sannosuke. Vol. 31 of *Nihon no meicho.* Chūō kōron sha, 1973.

Articles and Monographs

Abe Isoo. *Shitsugyō mondai.* Nihon hyōron sha, 1929.
Abe Yoshishige. *Waga oitachi.* Iwanami shoten, 1966.
Abegglen, James C. *The Japanese Factory.* Free Press, 1958.
Abegglen, James C., and Mannari, Hiroshi. "Leaders of Modern Japan: Social Origins and Mobility." *Economic Development and Cultural Change* 9 (October 1960): 109–134.
Amano Ikuo. "Continuity and Change in the Structure of Higher Education." In *Changes in the Japanese University: A Comparative Perspective.* Edited by William Cummings, Amano Ikuo, and Kitamura Kazuyuki. Praeger, 1979. Pp. 10–38.
Aono Suekichi. *Sarariiman kyōfu jidai.* Senshin sha, 1930.
———. "Sarariiman no kyōfu jidai to sono kaihō." *Chūō kōron* 44:12 (December 1929): 65–79.
Arase Yutaka. "Mass Communications Between the Two World Wars." *Developing Economies* 5:4 (December 1967): 748–766.
Arima Tatsuo. *The Failure of Freedom.* Cambridge: Harvard University Press, 1969.
Ashigawa Tadao. *Danwajutsu shūyō.* Chiseidō shoten, 1910.
Asō Makoto. *Daigaku to jinzai yōsei.* Chūō kōron sha, 1960.
Asō Makoto and Amano Ikuo. *Education and Japan's Modernization.* Tokyo: Ministry of Foreign Affairs, 1972.
Asukai Masamichi. "Keimō shugi minken ron nashonarizumu." In *Kindai Nihon shakai shisō shi I,* vol. 1 of *Kindai Nihon shisō shi taikei.* Yūhikaku, 1968. Pp. 107–143.
Azumi Koya. *Higher Education and Business Recruitment in Japan.* Teacher's College Press, 1969.
Beasley, W. G. *The Meiji Restoration.* Stanford: Stanford University Press, 1972.
Bellah, Robert N. *Tokugawa Religion: The Values of Pre-Industrial Japan.* The Free Press, 1957.
Bendix, Reinhard. *Work and Authority in Industry.* Harper Torch Books, 1963.
Bernstein, Gail Lee. *Japanese Marxist: A Portrait of Kawakami Hajime 1879–1946.* Cambridge: Harvard University Press, 1976.
Briggs, Asa. *Victorian People.* London: Penguin Books, 1965.
Brunschwig, Henri. *Enlightenment and Romanticism in Eighteenth Century Prussia.* Chicago: University of Chicago Press, 1974.
Carlyle, Thomas. *On Heroes, Hero-Worship, and the Heroic in History.* London: Cassel & Company, 1891.
Carnegie, Andrew. *The Empire of Business.* Doubleday, Page & Co., 1902.
———. *The Gospel of Wealth (And Other Timely Essays).* Edited by Edward C. Kirkland. Cambridge: Harvard University Press, 1962.
Cawelti, John G. *Apostles of the Self-Made Man.* Chicago: University of Chicago Press, 1965.

BIBLIOGRAPHY

Connolly, Margaret. *The Life Story of Orison Swett Marden.* Thomas Y. Crowell Co., 1925.
Crowley, James B. "Intellectuals as Visionaries of the New Asian Order." In *Dilemmas of Growth in Prewar Japan*, edited by James W. Morley. Princeton University Press, 1971. Pp. 319–374.
Dore, Ronald P. *City Life in Japan.* Berkeley & Los Angeles: University of California Press, 1958.
———. *The Diploma Disease: Education, Qualification and Development.* Berkeley & Los Angeles: University of California Press, 1976.
———. *Education in Tokugawa Japan.* London: Routledge and Kegan Paul, 1965.
———. "The Legacy of Tokugawa Education." In *Changing Japanese Attitudes Toward Modernization*, edited by Marius B. Jansen. Princeton: Princeton University Press. Pp. 99–132.
———. "Mobility, Equality, and Individuation in Modern Japan." In *Aspects of Social Change in Modern Japan*, edited by Ronald P. Dore. Princeton: Princeton University Press, 1967. Pp. 113–150.
Dower, John W. "E. H. Norman and the Uses of History." In E. Herbert Norman, *Origins of the Modern Japanese State*, edited by John W. Dower. Pantheon, 1975.
Duus, Peter. "Whig History, Japanese Style: The Minyūsha Historians and the Meiji Restoration." *Journal of Asian Studies* 33:3 (May 1974): 415–436.
Feldman, Horace. "The Growth of the Meiji Novel." Ph.D. dissertation, Columbia University, 1952.
Fletcher, Miles. "Intellectuals and Fascism in Early Showa Japan." *Journal of Asian Studies* 29:1 (November 1979): 39–64.
Fridell, Wilbur M. "Government Ethics Textbooks in Meiji Japan." *Journal of Asian Studies* 29:4 (August 1970): 823–833.
Frietzsche, Arthur H. *The Monstrous Clever Young Man—The Novelist Disraeli and His Heroes.* Salt Lake City: Utah State University Press, 1959.
Fruin, W. Mark. "The Japanese Company Controversy: Ideology and Organization in a Historical Perspective." *Journal of Japanese Studies* 4:2 (Summer 1978): 267–300.
Fujiwara Kiyozō. *Kyōiku shisō gakusetsu jinbutsu shi.* Tōa seikyō sha, 1943.
Fukaya Masashi. *Gakureki shugi no keifu.* Reimei shobō, 1969.
Fukuchi Shigetaka. *Shizoku to shizoku ishiki.* Shunjū sha, 1956.
Fukuzawa Yukichi. *The Autobiography of Yukichi Fukuzawa.* Translated by Eiichi Kiyooka. Schocken, 1972 [1899].
———. *An Encouragement of Learning* [Gakumon no susume]. Translated by David A. Dilworth and Umeyo Hirano. Tokyo: Sophia University Press, 1969.
———. "The Kyūhanjō of Fukuzawa Yukichi." Translated by Carmen Blacker, *Monumenta Nipponica* 9:1–2 (1953): 304–329.
———. *Gakumon no susume.* Iwasaki shoten, 1950.

Futabatei Shimei. *Mediocrity* [Heibon]. Translated by Glenn W. Shaw. Tokyo: Hokuseidō Press, 1927.

———. *Ukigumo* [Floating Clouds]. In Marleigh Grayer Ryan, *Japan's First Modern Novel: Ukigumo of Futabatei Shimei.* Columbia University Press, 1967. Pp. 197–356.

Gluck, Carol. "The People in History: Recent Trends in Japanese Historiography." *Journal of Asian Studies* 38:1 (November 1978): 25–50.

Gotō Yasushi. *Jiyū minken.* Chūō kōron sha, 1972.

———. "Ueki Emori cho Risshisha shimatsu kiyō." *Shigaku zasshi* 65:1 (January 1956): 59–76.

Harada Shūichi. *Labor Conditions in Japan.* Columbia University Press, 1928.

Harry D. Harootunian. "*Jinsei, jinzai,* and *jitsugaku*: Social Values and Leadership in Late Tokugawa Thought." In *Modern Japanese Leadership: Transition and Change,* edited by Bernard S. Silberman and Harry D. Harootunian. Tucson: University of Arizona Press, 1966. Pp. 83–120.

———. *Toward Restoration.* Berkeley and Los Angeles: University of California Press, 1970.

Hearn, Lafcadio. *Japan: An Attempt at Interpretation.* Rutland, Vt.: Tuttle, 1955 [1904].

Hikida Masahiro. "Jiyū minken." In *Meiji kyōiku seron no kenkyū,* edited by Motoyama Yukihiko. Fukumura shuppan, 1972. Vol. 2, pp. 143–210.

Himuro Yoshihira, ed. *Kyūryō seikatsusha mondai.* Shakai rippō kyōkai, 1933.

Hiraoka Toshio. "Meiji yonjū nendai bungaku ni okeru seinen-zō." *Bungaku* 37:6 (June 1969): 18–36.

Hirota Masaki. *Fukuzawa Yukichi kenkyū.* Tōkyō daigaku shuppan-kai, 1976.

Hirschmeier, Johannes. *The Origins of Entrepreneurship in Meiji Japan.* Cambridge: Harvard University Press, 1964.

Hofstadter, Richard. *Anti-intellectualism in American Life.* Knopf, 1963.

Hoshino Shūichirō. "Hōkyū seikatsusha no mitaru hōyū seikatsu." *Shakai seisaku jihō,* no. 196 (January 1937): 99–112.

Huber, Richard M. *The American Idea of Success.* McGraw-Hill, 1971.

Ienaga Saburō. "Kokumin no tomo." *Bungaku* 23:1 (January 1955): 38–44.

———. *Nihon dōtoku shisō shi.* Iwanami shoten, 1955.

———. *The Pacific War, 1931–1945 [Taiheiyō sensō].* Translated by Frank Baldwin. Pantheon, 1978 [1968].

Ike, Nobutaka. *The Beginnings of Political Democracy in Japan.* Baltimore: Johns Hopkins Press, 1950.

Irokawa Daikichi. *Kindai kokka no shuppatsu.* Vol. 21 of *Nihon no rekishi.* Chūō kōron sha, 1966.

———. "Meiji nijū nendai no bunka." In *Iwanami kōza Nihon rekishi.* Iwanami shoten, 1968. Vol. 17, pp. 269–315.

———. *Meiji no bunka.* Iwanami shoten, 1970.

———. *Meiji no seishin.* Chikuma shobō, 1968.

———. *Meiji seishin shi*. Ōga shobō, 1964.
———. *Shinpen Meiji seishin shi*. Chūō kōron sha, 1973.
———. "Shin Tōkoku-zō no shutsugen." *Shisō*, no. 522 (November 1967), pp. 30–44.
Ishii Kendō (Tamaji). "Meiji shoki no shōnen zasshi." *Taiyō* 33:8 (June 1927): 406–414.
———. *Nakamura Masanao den*. Seikō zasshi sha, 1907.
Ishikawa Tengai. *Tōkyō gaku* [1909]. In *Meiji bunka shiryō sōsho*, edited by Meiji bunka shiryō sōsho kankō-kai. Kazama shobō, 1970. Vol. 12, pp. 341–514.
Itō Hideo. *Kuroiwa Ruikō den*. Kokubun sha, 1975.
Itō Sei. *Nihon bundan shi*. Kōdansha, 1964.
Jansen, Marius B., ed. *Changing Japanese Attitudes Toward Modernization*. Princeton: Princeton University Press, 1965.
Japanese National Commission for UNESCO. *The Role of Education in the Social and Economic Development of Japan*. Tokyo: Ministry of Education, 1966.
Kamishima Jirō. *Kindai Nihon no seishin kōzō*. Iwanami shoten, 1961.
———. "Meiji no shūen." In *Kindai Nihon seiji shisō shi I*, vol. 3 of *Kindai Nihon shisō shi taikei*. Yūhikaku, 1971. Pp. 381–424.
Kano Masanao. "Ichi minken shijuku no kiseki." *Shisō*, no. 536 (February 1969), pp. 54–75.
———. "'Inaka shinshitachi' no ronri." *Rekishigaku kenkyū*, no. 249 (1961), pp. 5–15, 60.
———. "Kokka shugi no taitō." In *Kindai Nihon seiji shisō shi I*, vol. 3 in *Kindai Nihon shisō shi taikei* (Yūhikaku, 1971). Pp. 287–305.
———. "Kokusui shugi ni okeru shihon shugi taisei no kōsō." *Nihon shi kenkyū*, no. 52 (1961), pp. 23–44.
———. *Nihon kindai shisō no kaisei*. *Shin-hyōron sha*, 1957.
———. "Sengo keiei to nōson kyōiku." *Shisō*, no. 521 (November 1967), pp. 42–62.
———. *Shihon shugi keiseiki no chitsujo ishiki*. Chikuma shobō, 1969.
———. "Taiyō." *Shisō*, no. 450 (December 1961), pp. 135–147.
Karasawa Tomitarō. *Gakusei no rekishi*. Sōbun sha, 1955.
———. *Kyōshi no rekishi*. Sōbun sha, 1955.
———. *Meiji hyaku-nen no jidō shi*. Kōdansha, 1968.
Katayama Sen. *Gakusei To-Bei annai*. Rōdō shinbun sha, 1901.
———. *Shin-To-Bei*. Shuppan kyōkai, 1904.
———. *To-Bei annai*. To-Bei kyōkai, 1901.
———. *To-Bei no hiketsu*. To-Bei kyōkai, 1906.
Kaufman, Walter. *Nietzsche: Philosopher, Psychologist, Antichrist*. Princeton: Princeton University Press, 1968.
Kawashima Takeyoshi. *Nihon no shakai to seikatsu ishiki*. Gakusei sha, 1955.
Keene, Donald. "The Barren Years: Japanese War Literature." *Monumenta Nipponica* 33:1 (1978): 67–112.

———. "The Sino-Japanese War of 1894–95 and Its Cultural Effects in Japan." In *Tradition and Modernization in Japanese Culture*, edited by Donald Shively. Princeton: Princeton University Press, 1971. Pp. 121–180.
Kikuchi Dairoku. *Japanese Education*. London: John Murray, 1909.
Kikutei Kōsui (Satō Kuratarō). *Seiro nikki*. In *Meiji kaikaki bungaku shū II*, vol. 2 of *Meiji bungaku zenshū*. Chikuma shobō, 1967 [1884]. Pp. 354–398.
Kimura Ki. "Meiji tennō no shin-teiōgaku—*Saikoku risshi hen* denrai hyaku-nen o kinen shite." In *Meiji bunka kenkyū*, edited by Meiji bunka kenkyū-kai. Nihon hyōron sha, 1968. Vol. 2, pp. 83–100.
Kimura Shōshū. *Meiji shōnen bunka shiwa*. Dōwa shunjū sha, 1949.
———. *Shōnen bungaku shi Meiji hen*. Dōwa Shunjū sha, 1949.
Kinbara Samon, Sumiya Mikio, Takami Junnosuke. "Kabu shidōsha no 'shisō' to seijiteki yakuwari." In *Shidōsha to taishū*, vol. 5 of *Kindai Nihon shisō shi kōza*. Chikuma shobō, 1960. Pp. 104–140.
Kinmonth, Earl H. "The Self-Made Man in Meiji Japanese Thought." Ph.D. dissertation, University of Wisconsin, Madison, 1974.
———. "Fukuzawa Reconsidered: *Gakumon no susume* and Its Audience." *Journal of Asian Studies* 37:4 (August 1978): 677–696.
Kinoshita Naoe. *Pillar of Fire* [Hi no hashira]. Translated by Kenneth Strong. London: George Allen & Unwin, 1972.
Kirby, R. J. "Dazai Jun [Shundai] on *Bubi* or Preparation for War." *Transactions of the Asiatic Society of Japan*. First series, 32 (May 1905): 24–47.
Kitazawa Rakuten kenshō-kai. *Rakuten manga shū taisei—Taishō hen* (Gurafuikku sha, 1973).
Koike Shirō. *Hōkyū seikatsusha ron*. Seiunkaku shobō, 1929.
Kōsaka Masaaki. *Japanese Thought in the Meiji Era*. Translated by David Abosch. Tokyo: Pan-Pacific Press, 1958.
Kurita Kakuya. *Shuppanjin no ibun*. Kurita shoten, 1968.
Kuwahara Takeo, Katō Hidetoshi, Yamada Minoru. "*Jyaanarizumu* no shisōteki yakuwari." In *Shidōsha to taishū*, vol. 5 of *Kindai Nihon shisō shi kōza* (Chikuma shobō, 1960). Pp. 141–184.
Lehman, Jean Pierre. *The Image of Japan*. London: Allen and Unwin, 1978.
Lukes, Stephen. *Individualism*. Harper and Row, 1973.
Lytton, Sir Edward Bulwer. *Ernest Multravers*. Philadelphia: J. B. Lippincott: 1889 [1837].
Maeda Ai. "Meiji risshin shusse shugi no keifu." *Bungaku* 33:4 (April 1965): 10–21.
———. "Nakamura Keiu." *Bungaku* 33:10 (October 1965): 61–71.
Maeda Hajime. *Sarariiman monogatari*. Tōyō keizai shuppanbu, 1928.
———. *Zoku-Sarariiman monogatari*. Tōyō keizai shuppanbu, 1928.
Makibayashi Kōji. "Kitamura Tōkoku to Tokutomi Sohō." In *Kitamura Tōkoku*, edited by Nihon bungaku kenkyū shiryō kankō-kai. Yūseidō shuppan, 1972. Pp. 140–151.
Mannari Hiroshi. *The Japanese Business Leaders*. Tokyo: University of Tokyo Press, 1974.

Mannheim, Karl. *Essays on the Sociology of Knowledge.* Edited by Paul Kecskemeti. London: Routledge and Kegan Paul, 1952.
Marden, Orison Swett. *Pushing to the Front or, Success Under Difficulties.* Thomas Y. Crowell, 1894.
Marshall, Byron K. *Capitalism and Nationalism in Prewar Japan.* Stanford: Stanford University Press, 1967.
Maruyama Masao. "Patterns of Individuation and the Case of Japan: A Conceptual Scheme." In *Changing Japanese Attitudes Toward Modernization,* edited by Marius B. Jansen. Princeton: Princeton University Press, 1965. Pp. 489–532.
———. *Thought and Behavior in Modern Japanese Politics.* Expanded edition. Edited by Ivan Morris. Oxford University Press, 1969.
Masuda Yoshihiko. *Jitsugyō no Nihon sha nanajū nen shi.* Jitsugyō no Nihon sha, 1967.
Masumi Junnosuke. *Nihon seiji shi ron.* Tōkyō daigaku shuppan-kai, 1966.
Matsunari Yoshie, Izutani Hajime, Tanuma Hajime, Noda Masaho. *Nihon no sarariiman.* Aoki shoten, 1957.
Mayer, Arno J. "The Lower Middle Class as a Historical Problem." *Journal of Modern History* 47:3 (1975): 409–436.
Metzger, Thomas A. *Escape from Predicament.* Columbia University Press, 1977.
Mihashi Takeo. *Meiji zenki shisō shi bunken.* Meijidō shoten, 1976.
Mill, John Stuart. *On Liberty.* Edited by David Spitz. Norton, 1975 [1859].
Minami Hiroshi. *Psychology of the Japanese People.* Translated by Albert R. Ikoma. Tokyo: University of Tokyo Press, 1971.
———. *Taishō bunka.* Keisō shoin, 1965.
Minamoto Ryōen. *Tokugawa gōri shisō no keifu.* Chūō kōron sha, 1972.
———. *Tokugawa shisō shōshi.* Chūō kōron sha, 1973.
Mita Munesuke. *Gendai Nihon no shinjō to ronri.* Chikuma shobō, 1971.
Monbushō. *Gakusei hachijū nen shi.* Monbushō, 1954.
Moore, Ray Avril. "Adoption and Samurai Mobility in Tokugawa Japan." *Journal of Asian Studies* 29:3 (May 1970): 617–632.
———. "Samurai Discontent and Social Mobility in the Late Tokugawa Period." *Monumenta Nipponica* 24:1–2 (1969): 79–92.
Mori Ōgai. *Maihime.* Ōbunsha bunko, 1969 [1890].
Motoyama Yukihiko, ed. *Meiji kyōiku seron no kenkyū.* Fukumura shuppan, 1972.
Nagai Michio. "Chishikijin no seisan *ruuto.*" In *Chishikijin no seisei to yakuwari,* vol. 4 of *Kindai Nihon shisō shi kōza.* Chikuma shobō, 1959. Pp. 197–234.
———. "Westernization and Japanization: The Early Meiji Transformation of Education." In *Tradition and Modernization in Japanese Culture,* edited by Donald Shively. Princeton: Princeton University Press, 1971. Pp. 37–76.
Nakaizumi Tetsutoshi. *Nihon kinsei kyōiku shisō no kenkyū.* Yoshikawa kōbunkan, 1966.

Nakamura Keiu (Masanao). *Jiyū no ri* [J. S. Mill, *On Liberty*]. In *Jiyū minken hen*, vol. 2 of *Meiji bunka zenshū*. Nihon hyōron sha, 1969 [1872]. Pp. 1–84.

———. *Saikoku risshi hen (SKRH)* [Samuel Smiles, *Self-Help*]. Nomura Genjirō, 1888 [1871].

———. *Saikoku risshi hen.* In vol. 1 of *Nihon kyōkasho taikei kindai hen*, edited by Ishikawa Ken. Kōdansha, 1961. Pp. 7–77.

Nakane Chie. *Kinship and Economic Organization in Rural Japan.* London: University of London Press, 1967.

Nasu Yoshirō. "Dokusen shihon no kakuritsu to shakai seikatsu no senka." In *Seikatsu shi III*, vol. 17 of *Taikei Nihon shi sōsho*. Yamakawa shuppan, 1969. Pp. 217–388.

Natsume Sōseki. *Mon.* Translated by Francis Mathy. Tokyo: Tuttle, 1972 [1910].

———. *Sore kara.* Ōbunsha bunko, 1966 [1909].

Nihon shoseki shuppan kyōkai. *Nihon shuppan hyaku-nen shi nenpyō.* Nihon shoseki shuppan kyōkai, 1968.

Nitobe Inazō. *Shūyō.* Jitsugyō no Nihon sha, 1911.

Niwa Jun'ichirō. *Karyū shunwa* [Edward Lytton. *Ernest Multravers*]. In *Meiji honyaku bungaku shū*, vol. 7 of *Meiji bungaku zenshū*. Chikuma shobō, 1972 [1878]. Pp. 3–109.

Noda Masaho. "Fukyō ni aegu sarariiman." *Bessatsu Chūō kōron keiei mondai* 4:2 (June 1965): 230–235.

———. "Sarariiman kaisō no keisei." *Bessatsu Chūō kōron keiei mondai* 4:2 (June 1965): 201–205.

Noma Seiji. *Noma of Japan: The Nine Magazines of Kōdansha.* Vanguard, 1934.

———. *Shosei no michi.* Dai-Nihon yūbenkai kōdansha, 1930.

———. *Shusse no ishizue.* Dai-Nihon yūbenkai kōdansha, 1931.

———. *Taiken o kataru.* Dai-Nihon yūbenkai kōdansha, 1930.

———. *Watakushi no hansei.* Chikura shobō, 1936.

Obama Toshinari. "Sarariiman no shoninkyū shirabe." *Chūō kōron* 45:7 (July 1930). In *Shōwa shonen*, vol. 1 of *Dokyumento Shōwa shi*, edited by Hayashi Shigeru. Heibonsha, 1975. Pp. 20–30.

Ogata Hiroyasu. *Nihon kyōiku tsūshi.* Waseda daigaku shuppanbu, 1970.

Ogawa Tarō. *Risshin shusse shugi no kyōiku.* Reimei shobō, 1968.

Oguri Fūyō. *Seishun.* Shunyōdō, 1906.

Ohkawa Kazushi, ed. *Prices*, vol. 8 of *Estimates of Long Term Economic Statistics of Japan.* Tokyo: Tōyō keizai shinpō sha, 1967.

Oka Yoshitake. "Nichiro sensō go ni okeru atarashii sedai no seichō." *Shisō*, no. 512 (1967), pp. 1–13 [137–149], and no. 513 (1967), pp. 89–104 [361–376].

Okawada Tsunetada. "Meiji seinen no seiji ishiki." In *Kindai Nihon seiji shisō shi I*, vol. 3 of *Kindai Nihon shisō shi taikei.* Yūhikaku, 1971. Pp. 360–380.

———. "Seinen ron to sedai ron." *Shisō*, no. 514 (April 1964), pp. 37–57.

Ōkōchi Kazuo, Ōya Sōichi, Odaka Kunio, Kōshi Kōhei, and Maeda Hajime. "*Bijinesuman* no hyaku-nen o kaiko suru." *Bessatsu Chūō kōron keiei mondai* 4:2 (June 1965): 143–156.
Ōkubo Toshiaki. "Nakamura Keiu no shoki yōgaku shisō to 'Saikoku risshi hen' no yakujutsu oyobi kankō." *Shien* 26:2–3 (January 1966): 67–92.
Ōkuma Shigenobu. *Fifty Years of New Japan*. Dutton, 1909.
O'Neill, P. G. *Japanese Names*. Tokyo: John Weatherhill, Inc., 1972.
Ono Hideo. *Meiji wadai jiten*. Tōkyōdō shuppan, 1968.
Ossowski, Stanislaw. *Class Structure in the Social Consciousness*. London: Routledge & Kegan Paul, 1963.
Ōwatari Junji. "Sarariiman no senji seikatsu." *Kaizō* 21:8 (August 1939). In *Bessatsu Chūō kōron keiei mondai* 4:2 (June 1965): 303–312.
Ozaki Moriteru. *Nihon shūshoku shi*. Bungei shunjū, 1967.
———. *Sarariiman hyaku-nen*. Nihon keizai shinbun sha, 1968.
Ozaki Tokutarō (Kōyō). *Konjiki yasha*. Shunyōdō, 1915.
Ozawa Saburō. *Uchimura Kanzō fukei jiken*. Shinkyō shuppan-sha, 1961.
Passin, Herbert. *Society and Education in Japan*. Columbia University Press, 1965.
Pierson, John D. "The Early Liberal Thought of Tokutomi Sohō." *Monumenta Nipponica* 29:2 (1974): 199–224.
———. "The Journalist Tokutomi Sohō: Problems of Westernization and Modernization in Meiji Japan." Ph.D. dissertation, Princeton University, 1972.
Pyle, Kenneth B. *The New Generation in Meiji Japan*. Stanford: Stanford University Press, 1969.
Ranis, Gustav. "The Community Centered Entrepreneur in Japanese Development." *Explorations in Entrepreneurial History* 8:2 (December 1955): 80–98.
Rohlen, Thomas P. *For Harmony and Strength: Japanese White-Collar Organization in Anthropological Perspective*. Berkeley and Los Angeles: University of California Press, 1974.
Rubin, Jay. "Kunikida Doppo." Ph.D. dissertation, University of Chicago, 1970.
Ryan, Marleigh Grayer. *Japan's First Modern Novel: Ukigumo of Futabatei Shimei*. Columbia University Press, 1967.
———. *The Development of Realism in the Fiction of Tsubouchi Shōyō*. Seattle: University of Washington Press, 1975.
Sakai, Tadao. "Confucianism and Popular Educational Works." In *Self and Society in Ming Thought*, edited by William Theodore de Bary. Columbia University Press, 1970. Pp. 331–366.
Sakisaka Toshirō. *Chishiki kaikyū ron*. Kaizō sha, 1935.
Sakurai Mamoru. *Chūgaku kyōiku shikō*. Rinsen shoten, 1975 [1942].
Sakurai Shōtarō. *Meiyo to chijoku*. Hōsei daigaku, 1971.
Sangu Makoto. "'Saikoku risshi hen' oyobi sono ruisho ni tsuite." *Gakutō* 43:2 (February 1939): 20–25, and 43:3 (March 1939): 15–16.
Sansom, George B. *The Western World and Japan*. Knopf, 1951.

Sasama Yoshihiko. *Ashigaru no seikatsu.* Yūzankaku, 1969.
Schwartz, Benjamin. *In Search of Wealth and Power.* Cambridge: Harvard University Press, 1964.
Senuma Shigeki. *Hon no hyaku-nen shi.* Shuppan nyūsu, 1965.
Shimazaki Tōson. *Haru.* Iwanami bunko, 1970 [1908].
———. *Sakura no mi no juku-suru toki.* Iwanami bunko, 1972 [1919].
Shinji Yoshimoto. *Edo jidai no buke no seikatsu.* Shinbundō, 1961.
Shively, Donald H. "The Japanization of Middle Meiji." In *Tradition and Modernization in Japanese Culture*, edited by Donald H. Shively. Princeton: Princeton University Press, 1971. Pp. 77–120.
———. "Nishimura Shigeki: A Confucian View of Modernization." In *Changing Japanese Attitudes Toward Modernization*, edited by Marius B. Jansen. Princeton: Princeton University Press, 1965. Pp. 193–242.
Shively, Donald, ed. *Tradition and Modernization in Japanese Culture.* Princeton: Princeton University Press, 1971.
Shōwa joshi daigaku kindai bungaku kenkyū-shitsu. "Nakamura Keiu." In *Kindai bungaku sōsho.* Shōwa joshi daigaku kōyō-kai, 1956. Vol. 1, pp. 406–458.
Shūshoku mondai kenkyū-kai. *Gakusei to shūshoku no jissai.* Tōkyō jitsugyō sha, 1934.
Smiles, Aileen. *Samuel Smiles and His Surroundings.* London. R. Hale, 1956.
Smiles, Samuel. *The Autobiography of Samuel Smiles, LL.D.* Edited by Thomas Mackay. London: Dutton, 1905.
———. *Character.* London: John Murray, 1913 [1871].
———. *Self-Help; with Illustrations of Conduct and Perseverance* (SH). London: John Murray, 1876 [1867].
———. *Self-Help; with Illustrations of Conduct and Perseverance.* Tōkyō: Kaishindō, 1889 [1867].
Smith, Henry DeWitt, II. *Japan's First Student Radicals.* Cambridge: Harvard University Press, 1972.
Smith, Thomas C. "Landlords' Sons in the Business Elite." *Economic Development and Cultural Change* 9:1 (October 1960): 93–108.
———. "'Merit' as Ideology in Tokugawa Japan." In *Aspects of Social Change in Modern Japan*, edited by Ronald P. Dore. Princeton: Princeton University Press, 1967. Pp. 71–90.
Spaulding, Robert M. "The Bureaucracy as a Political Force, 1920–45." In *Dilemmas of Growth in Prewar Japan*, edited by James W. Morley. Princeton: Princeton University Press, 1971. Pp. 33–80.
———. *Imperial Japan's Higher Civil Service Examinations.* Princeton: Princeton University Press, 1967.
Strong, Kenneth. "Tanaka Shōzō: Meiji Hero and Pioneer Against Pollution." *Bulletin of the Japan Society* 67:10 (June 1972): 6–11.
Sugai Yoshinobu. "Shakai shugi." In *Meiji kyōiku seron no kenkyū*, edited by Motoyama Yukihiko. Fukumura shuppan, 1972. Vol. 2, pp. 211–260.
Sumiya Kisaburō. *Risshin saku* [O. S. Marden. *Pushing to the Front*]. Kaitaku sha, 1897.

Sumiya Mikio. *Dai-Nihon teikoku no shiren*. Vol. 22 of *Nihon no rekishi*. Chūō kōron sha, 1966.

———. *Katayama Sen*. Tōkyō daigaku shuppan-kai, 1960.

———. "Kokuminteki buijon no tōgō to bunkai." In *Shidōsha to taishū*, vol. 5 of *Kindai Nihon shisō shi kōza*, Chikuma shobō, 1960. Pp. 9–42.

———. *Nihon chinrōdō no shiteki kenkyū*. Ocha no mizu shobō, 1976.

———. *Nihon no shakai shisō*. Tōkyō daigaku shuppan-kai, 1968.

———. *Nihon rōdō undō shi*. Yūshindō, 1966.

Suyama Teiichi. "Manga ni yoru sarariiman no hyaku-nen shi." *Bessatsu Chūō kōron keiei mondai* 4:2 (June 1965): 135–142.

Suzuki Yasuzō. *Jiyū minken kenpō happu*. Vol. 3 of *Kindai Nihon rekishi kōza*. Hakujō sha, 1939.

Swift, Thomas D. "Yamakawa Hitoshi and the Dawn of Japanese Socialism." Ph.D. dissertation, University of California, Berkeley, 1970.

Takahashi Masao. *Nakamura Keiu*. Yoshikawa kōbunkan, 1966.

Takeuchi Yō. *Nihonjin no shusse-kan*. Gakubun sha, 1978.

———. "Risshin shusse shugi no keifu to ronri." *Kansai daigaku shakai gakubu kiyō* 7:1 (November 1975): 33–49.

———. "Risshin shusse shugi no ronri to kinō." *Kyōiku shakaigaku kenkyū* 31 (1976): 119–129.

Takichi Yoshio. *Meiji bunken mokuroku okuzuke*. Nihon hyōron sha, 1932.

Tamaki Motoi. *Nihon gakusei shi*. Sanichi shobō, 1961.

Tokutomi Iichirō [Sohō]. *Taishō seinen to teikoku no zento*. Minyūsha, 1916.

Tokutomi Kenjirō (Roka). *Footprints in the Snow* [Omoide no ki]. Translated by Kenneth Strong. Tokyo: Tuttle, 1971.

Torii Miwako. *Meiji ikō kyōkasho sōgō mokuroku I shōgakkō hen*. Komiya shoten, 1967.

Tōyama Shigeki. *Fukuzawa Yukichi*. Tōkyō daigaku shuppan-kai, 1970.

———. "Ishin no henkaku to kindaiteki chishikijin no tanjō." In *Chishikijin no seisei to yakuwari*, vol. 4 of *Kindai Nihon shisō shi kōza*. Chikuma shobō, 1959. Pp. 155–196.

———. "Nihon kindaika to Tōkoku no kokumin bungaku ron." *Bungaku* (May 1952). In *Kitamura Tōkoku*, edited by Nihon bungaku kenkyū shiryō kankō-kai. Yūshindō, 1972. Pp. 40–47.

Tōyō keizai shinpō. *Meiji Taishō kokusei sōran*. Tōyō keizai shinpō sha, 1975 [1927].

Travers, Timothy H. E. "Samuel Smiles and the Victorian Work Ethic." Ph.D. dissertation, Yale University, 1970.

Tsubouchi Yūzō [Shōyō]. *Tōsei shosei katagi*. In *Tsubouchi Yūzō*, vol. 3 of *Meiji Taishō bungaku zenshū*. Shunyōdō, 1928 [1886].

Tsuboya Zenshirō. *Hakubunkan gojū nen shi*. Hakubunkan, 1937.

Tsunasawa Mitsuaki. *Nihon no nōhon shugi*. Kinokuniya shoten, 1971.

Tsunoda, Ryusaku; de Bary, William Theodore; and Keene, Donald. *Sources of Japanese Tradition*. Text edition. Columbia University Press, 1964.

Tsurumi, E. Patricia. "Meiji 'Primary School Language and Ethics Text-

books: Old Values for a New Society?" *Modern Asian Studies* 8:2 (1974): 247–261.
Uchida Roan. "Meiji jū nen zengo no shōgakkō." *Taiyō* 33:8 (June 1927): 415–420.
Uchida Yoshihiko. *Nihon shihon shugi no shisō zō.* Iwanami shoten, 1967.
Uchida Yoshihiko and Shioda Shōbee. "Chishiki seinen no shoruikei." In *Chishikijin no seisei to yakuwari*, vol. 4 of *Kindai Nihon shisō shi kōza.* Chikuma shobō, 1959. Pp. 235–282.
Uete Michiari. "'Kokumin no tomo' to 'Nihonjin.'" *Shisō*, no. 453 (March 1962), pp. 112–122.
Ukita Kazutami. "Educationalists of the Past and Their Share in the Modernization of Japan." In *Fifty Years of New Japan*, edited by Ōkuma Shigenobu. Dutton, 1909. Vol. 2, pp. 134–160.
Waley, Arthur. The *Analects of Confucius.* London: George Allen & Unwin, 1938.
Wray, Harold J. "A Study in Contrasts: Japanese School Textbooks of 1903 and 1941–1945." *Monumenta Nipponica* 28:1 (1973): 69–86.
Wyllie, Irwin G. *The Self-Made Man in America: The Myth of Rags to Riches.* New Brunswick: Rutgers University Press, 1954.
Yamamoto Akira. "Kyōyō to ikigai." In *Nihonjin no seikatsu*, vol. 4 of *Kōza-hikaku bunka.* Kōdansha, 1976. Pp. 183–210.
Yamamura, Kozo, and Hanley, Susan B. "*Ichi hime, ni Tarō*: Educational Aspirations and the Decline of Fertility in Postwar Japan." *Journal of Japanese Studies* 2:1 (Autumn 1975): 83–126.
Yamamura, Kozo. *A Study of Samurai Income and Entrepreneurship.* Cambridge: Harvard University Press, 1974.
Yamazaki Yasuo. *Chosha to shuppansha.* Gakufū shoin, 1954.
———. *Dai-ni Chosha to shuppansha.* Gakufū shoin, 1955.
———. *Iwanami Shigeo.* Jiji tsūshin sha, 1961.
Yanagida Izumi. *Meiji shoki honyaku bungaku no kenkyū.* Vol. 5 of *Meiji bungaku kenkyū.* Shunjū sha, 1961.
———. *Meiji shoki no bungaku shisō I.* Vol. 4 of *Meiji bungaku kenkyū.* Shunjū sha, 1965.
———. *Seiji shōsetsu kenkyū.* Shunjū sha, 1967–1968.
Yanagiuchi Yoshinosuke. *Gakusei to risshi.* Shinsei sha, 1902.
———. *Nijūsseiki no gakusei.* Shinsei sha, 1902.
———. *Tōto to gakusei.* Shinsei sha, 1901.
Yasuda Saburō. *Shakai idō no kenkyū.* Tōkyō daigaku shuppan-kai, 1971.
Yasukawa Junnosuke. *Nihon kindai kyōiku no shisō kōzō.* Shin-hyōron sha, 1970.
Yoshida Seiichi and Shimomura Fujio. *Wakon yōsai.* Vol. 10 of *Nihon bungaku no rekishi.* Kadokawa shoten, 1968.
Yoshino Shinji tsuitōroku kankō-kai, *Yoshino Shinji.* Yoshino Shinji tsuitōroku kankō-kai, 1974.

Index

Abe Isoo, 247, 276
Abe Jirō, 211, 324
Abe Yoshishige, 211, 215, 248
ability. *See* genius
accuracy, 267
achievement ethos: Anglo-American, 4–5, 11–13, 11–12n, 160–161, 273, 340–341, 351; Japanese scholarship on, 6–8, 34n, 55–56, 58n, 163, 166n, 194–195n, 212, 220, 220–221n, 228, 240n, 329–331
Aichi gakugei zasshi (Aichi Arts and Sciences Magazine), 120, 128
Alger, Horatio, 11, 11–12n, 13, 95, 120
amiability, 260, 268
Analects, 38
Anesaki Masaharu (Chōfū), 214–215, 220
anguished youth (*hanmon seinen*), 206–240, 241–257, 337–340; mentioned, 323–324, 331
anshin ritsumeikan (spiritual tranquility), 246
Ashigawa Tadao, 273
Ashio (copper mine), 230, 272
attention, 13, 73, 260, 267
autonomy. *See* independence

Barclay, David, 39
Bendix, Reinhard, 6, 259
benkyō, 71–73, 71n. *See also* study
biography: mentioned, 164, 246, 269, 318, 330; and Samuel Smiles, 14–15, 15–16; as source, 2, 7, 8, 320
Bismarck, 86
"Biteki seikatsu o ronzu" (On the Aesthetic Life), 233–234, 324
blue-collar workers: compensation for, 131, 223, 223n, 283–284, 284n, 316; and unemployment, 286, 287, 288, 289
bonuses, 284, 316
Boshin Rescript (1908), 249
Briggs, Asa, 13
Bright, John, 99, 107
brocade, 76, 79
Buddhism: and anguished youth, 210, 238, 245–246; mentioned, 30–31, 57–58, 332, 338
bungaku seinen (literary youth), 82n, 150. *See also* anguished youth
Bungei shunjū, 324
bureaucracy. *See* civil service
bushi (warriors). *See* samurai
bushidō (way of the warrior), 160, 255, 256
business: and "Japanese employment system," 319n; mentioned, 130–131, 150, 162; placement and compensation in, 85n, 133, 284–285, 294–296, 296–298, 303–314, 315, 339; popularity of, 111–112, 157–158, 217, 282–283, 296–297; and samurai, 35, 39–40,

373

INDEX

52, 54; and Sino-Japanese War, 154, 157–160, 162; small (*chūshō kigyō*), 5; in student compositions, 68–69, 111–112, 135; and Tokutomi Iichirō, 100, 101, 101n, 109–111, virtues for employment in, 257–276, 317–323, 319n, 339. *See also* businessmen; *Jitsugyō no Nihon*; education, vocational

businessmen, 39, 226. *See also* entrepreneurs

Byron, 211, 231

"Cadillac phenomenon," 349
California, 115, 192
Calvinism, 31n
Carlyle, Thomas, 150, 151–152; mentioned, 102, 202, 211, 231, 245; and Samuel Smiles, 29n; and Takayama Chogyū, 236n
Carnegie, Andrew: his *Empire of Business*, analyzed, 262–264; and *Jitsugyō no Nihon*, 158–159; mentioned, 160, 197; and "stewardship of wealth," 103–104, 262n; and Tokutomi Iichirō, 103–104
Carnegie, Dale, 273, 274
Cawelti, John G., 6
Character, 10, 14, 23, 73, 86n, 102, 105, 111, 275, 275n, 276
character, 28, 312
character ethic, 12–14. *See also* achievement ethos, Anglo-American; personality ethic
charity (*suijō*), 252
Charter Oath, 9, 32, 154
cheating, 301, 301n
Chichibu Incident, 115
Chishiki (Knowledge), 120–121
chishiki rōdōsha (intellectual laborers), 290
chokunin (imperially appointed civil servant), 279
Christianity: and anguished youth, 210, 231, 239, 245–246, 338; and Kitamura Tōkoku, 149, 150; and *kugaku* (study by struggle), 180–181; mentioned, 146, 174, 175, 248, 255, 256, 262n; and Nakamura Keiu, 23–24; and Samuel Smiles, 30–31, 31n

Chūgaku bundan (Middle-School Literary Circle), 213–214

Chūgaku sekai (Middle-School World): and anguished youth, 242–243; described, 164, 175, 198, 303n; mentioned, 116, 154, 158, 226, 228, 276, 300, 303

Chūō kōron (Central Review), 159, 159n, 226, 290

civil service: compensation in, 131, 222–223, 223n, 279, 279n, 283–284, 284n, 287, 314–315; examinations, 132n, 215n, 307n, 312, 312–313n, 343; mentioned, 71, 80, 101, 115–116, 131, 144, 145–146, 161, 293, 334; and personality ethic, 75, 312, 312–313n; placement in, 184, 187, 226–227, 227n, 278–279, 279n, 281–282, 285–288, 285–286n, 287n, 306–307; and samurai, 40, 79–80, 118; and *senmon gakkō* (colleges), 132n, 293

class. *See* social class
Cobden, Richard, 99, 107
Cold War, and American scholarship, 3–4
colleges. *See senmon gakkō*
commerce. *See* business
commoners: and education, 68–69, 128; and *Eisai shinshi*, 64–65, 68–69; and Fukuzawa Yukichi, 49; mentioned, 97, 333; in samurai writing, 38n; and Tokutomi Iichirō, 97–98, 109
communism, 309
community-centered entrepreneurs, 3–5, 4n, 76
competition rates. *See* entrance examinations
conformity. *See* individualism
Confucianism: and individualism, 27–29, 332; mentioned, 74, 75, 84, 89, 102, 248, 329; and Nakamura Keiu, 21–22, 27–28, 31, 38, 41, 51; and *risshin shusse*, 56–57; and samurai, 38–39, 50–51, 79
Coningsby, 89

connections, 144, 305
correspondence courses. *See* education, by correspondence

Dai-Ichi Kōtō Gakkō. *See* First Higher School
dantai seikatsu (corporate life), 319
Dazai Shundai (Jun), 38, 50
decadent youth (*tandeki seinen*), 206, 239, 323. *See also* anguished youth
Demosthenes, 84
denki. *See* biography
diligence, 13, 70
"discovery myth," 263, 269, 318
Disraeli, 88, 89, 91, 92, 93, 95, 97, 136
Doko e (Whither), 238–240, 243, 324
Dore, Ronald P., 30, 39, 42, 51, 204n, 331n, 348
Dōshisha University, 175
draft, 132, 346–347
Dumas, Alexandre, 88
Duty, 14, 275n

Ebina Danjō, 175
eccentricity, 28, 53, 234
economics, study of, 133, 195, 294, 297
Edison, Thomas A., 199, 259, 320
education: and anguished youth, 214–220, 237, 333; by correspondence, 183–184, 187; corruption in, 126; costs of, 126–127, 292, 292n, 340; early Meiji system of, 55–56, 59–62; and economic growth, 348–349; and emigration, 188, 191, 193; and family, 79, 217, 219; late Meiji system of, 180, 183–184, 187, 194–197; mentioned, 128, 261, 268; mid-Meiji system of, 124–126, 124n; and social class, 60, 61–62, 68–69, 128; statistics of, 194–195, 195n, 282n; Taishō-Shōwa system of, 291–302, 292n, 293n, 294n, 297n, 298n, 299n, 300n, 301n, 302n; and teaching, 131, 239, 296–297; value of, 41, 131–132, 211–227, 295–296, 317. *See also Gakumon no susume*; higher schools; imperial universities; placement in job market; *senmon gakkō*; study; Dōshisha University; Kyoto Imperial University; Tokyo Imperial University; Waseda University
—vocational: placement and compensation for graduates in, 295, 307, 307n; mentioned, 215, 261; popularity of, 112, 157–158, 194–195, 196–198, 196n, 296–297, 299
"Education of the Working Classes," 13–14
Eisai shinshi (Talent Forum), 62–75, 64n, 64–65n, 65n, 81–88; mentioned, 97, 102, 103–104, 111–112, 117, 123, 126, 136, 142, 148, 154, 163, 178, 228, 240, 302, 331, 333, 335
Emerson, Ralph Waldo, 175
emigration, 188, 191–193, 307
employment. *See* placement in job market
employment agencies, 306
Endymion, 91, 93
engineering, 130, 295, 297, 298
England, 22, 43, 90, 98–100, 106–107, 199
English language, 139–140, 269–270, 303
enseikan (world weariness), 209
enterprise. *See* business
entrance examinations: and anguished youth, 214–220; cheating on, 301, 301n; early Meiji, 60–61; and elite selection, 342, 350; late Meiji, 157–158, 187, 194–197, 215–220, 218n, 244, 269–270; magazines related to, 123, 198, 303, 303n; mentioned, 137; mid-Meiji, 125, 127, 127n, 132, 301; scholarship on, 7; Taishō-Shōwa, 299–301, 299–300n, 300n, 301n, 303n. *See also Chūgaku sekai*; higher schools; middle schools; *senmon gakkō*; *Shōnenen*; Tokyo Imperial University; education, vocational
entrepreneurs, community-centered, 3–5, 4n, 76. *See also* businessmen
Ernest Multravers, 88, 89–90, 91, 92, 93
ero-guro nansensu (erotic-grotesque nonsense), 309, 323

375

INDEX

essays. *See* compositions
ethics texts (*shūshin kyōkasho*): late Meiji, 249–253; and *Self-Help*, 11, 33, 73, 102; Tokugawa era, 49, 53–54, 56–57, 72. *See also* Kaibara Ekiken
evolution: in *Tenjin ron*, 248. *See also* social Darwinism
examinations. *See* civil service, examinations; entrance examinations

factory workers. *See* blue-collar workers
fame. *See* name
family system (*ie*): and advancement, 77–80, 77n; and anguished youth, 214, 238; and education, 79, 182–183, 217; in *Eisai shinshi*, 72, 75–79; mentioned, 31, 52, 114, 118, 127–128, 142–143, 147, 187, 192, 238, 239, 252–253, 310, 312
filial piety, 130, 135, 233. *See also* Confucianism
First Higher Middle School. *See* First Higher School
First Higher School (Dai-Ichi Kōtō Gakkō): and anguished youth, 207, 208, 211, 212, 214, 215, 220; entrance examinations, 124, 127, 157, 187, 218, 219; mentioned, 243, 265–266, 323
fortune. *See* wealth
Franklin, Benjamin, 29, 40, 176, 231
Freeland, H. U., 22
frugality, 40, 73, 104, 112, 260
Fujimura Misao, 207–209, 212, 233, 248, 252, 338
Fujita Denzaburō, 110, 111
Fujita Tōko, 213
Fujiwara Tadashi, 211
Fukaya Masashi, 194–195n
fūki hinsen (wealthy and honored, impoverished and despised). *See* wealth and honor
Fukoku seinen (Youth of a Rich Country), 222
Fukuzawa Yukichi, 45–54, 74, 329–330; mentioned, 67, 106, 153, 199, 305, 327, 334. *See also Gakumon no susume*

fune narikin (shipping parvenu), 281
Furukawa Ichibei, 272
Futabatei Shimei, 85, 137, 143, 216. *See also Ukigumo*

gakkō sōdō (school disturbances), 103, 325
gakumon (learning). *See Gakumon no susume*; study; wealth and honor
Gakumon no susume (An Encouragement of Learning), 45–54, 74; mentioned, 12, 56, 65, 73, 163, 250, 333. *See also* Fukuzawa Yukichi
gakusei (educational control). *See* education, early Meiji system of
Gakusei hissenjō (Battle Field of Student Writing Brushes), 134, 139
Gakusei no shiyū (Student Friend and Teacher), 123
Gakusei to shūshoku no jissai (Students and the Realities of Placement), 303–314, 317–319, 321
Gakusei to-Bei annai (Student Guide for Going to America), 188
Gantō no kan (Thoughts Upon the Precipice), 207, 209
gekkyū-tori (monthly salary receiver), 279, 308
genius, 16, 70, 268, 312
Gentlemen's Agreement, 193
Genyūsha, 64–65n
geshuku (boarding house), 129, 147, 219, 258
Gladstone, 86, 107
Goethe, 211, 235
gōnō (wealthy peasants): and education, 60, 61–62, 68–69, 119, 128; as Japan's middle class, 105, 105–106n, 109–111, 333; mentioned, 34–35, 81
gōshi (rural samurai), 77–78, 81, 105, 128. *See also gōnō*
gōshō (wealthy merchants), 34–35, 34n, 52, 62
Gould, Jay, 160, 176
government service. *See* civil service
grades, 215–216, 311
Great Britain. *See* England
group orientation. *See* individualism; personality ethic

376

gyōsei seiri (administrative retrenchment), 144, 285–286. *See also* unemployment

hanmon seinen. See anguished youth
hannin (petty government officials; clerks), 184, 187, 222, 279n, 283–284, 316
harmony, 3, 260–261
heaven, 31, 31n, 46, 100
Heimin shinbun (Commoner Newspaper), 200, 244
heimin shugi (commonerism), 161, 275
heroes: and Thomas Carlyle, 151–152; in student compositions, 83–86, 136, 151–152; mentioned, 30, 151n, 202; in political novels, 92–97, 93n; and Sino-Japanese War, 154, 228; and Takayama Chogyū, 236n; and Tokutomi Iichirō, 101–102
"Hibon naru bonjin" (An Extraordinary Common Man), 257–259
higher schools: degrees granted at, 226n; entrance examinations for, 187, 194–197, 195n, 196n, 216–220, 269–270, 299–300n; and imperial universities, 300n; and *Santarō Nikki*, 324, 339
hōkenteki (feudal), 343
hōkyū seikatsusha (those who live on salary), 290
hōkyū seikatsusha kumiai (union of those who live on salary), 289
honor and wealth. *See* wealth and honor
Horiuchi Shinsen, 172n, 240n
Hōtokusha (Repayment of Kindness Society), 253
Huber, Richard M., 6
humble origins, 16–17, 38–39, 43, 51–52, 73, 263

Ienaga Saburō, 345
imperialism, 153–154, 202, 204–205. *See also* militarism; nationalism
Imperial Rescript on Education, 135, 146n
imperial universities: degrees granted at, 226n; entrance to, 215n, 299–300, 299–300n; placement and compensation for graduates from, 226–227, 282–283, 282n, 293. *See also* Kyoto Imperial University; *senmon gakkō*; Tokyo Imperial University
Imperial University. *See* Tokyo Imperial University
independence, 27–28, 35, 53, 53n, 260
individualism: and anguished youth, 234, 243; and Confucianism, 27–29, 31–32, 332; defined, 32n, 331, 331n; and Fukuzawa Yukichi, 53, 333; limitations on, 140–145, 340–345; and Meiji education, 56–57; mentioned, 28, 75, 145, 243, 273, 332, 333, 334, 339; and J. S. Mill, 28, 29, 32; and Nietzsche, 236–238, 338; and *risshin shusse*, 331–339; in *Saikoku risshi hen*, 27–32, 333; and Samuel Smiles, 29, 31; and samurai ethos, 29–30; and Tokutomi Iichirō, 333–335
inflation. *See* prices
inokori gumi (stay-behind gang), 300
Inoue Enryō, 175
Inoue Tetsujirō, 175, 242–243
intelligentsia, 1–2, 244–245, 345–348
Ishii Kendō (Tamaji), 166, 166n, 171, 176
Ishikawa Takuboku, 220, 220–221, 238, 245
Ishikawa Tengai, 274
Ishizaka Masatsugu, 114–115, 117, 230, 240, 302, 334
Iwakura Tomomi, 153
Iwamoto Zenji, 174
Iwanami Shigeo, 211, 232, 323
Iwasaki Yatarō, 153, 161

"Japanese employment system," 319n
Jefferson, Thomas, 151, 175
jin'in seiri (retrenchment), 319
jinseikan (outlook on life), 246, 323
jitsugaku (practical studies), 41
Jitsugokyō genkai (Practical Words for Instruction), 45–45n, 53–54
jitsugyō (practical endeavors; enterprise), 111, 259
Jitsugyō no Nihon (Business Japan),

377

158–159, 164–166, 255–257, 259–261; and anguished youth, 213, 245–247, 255–257; on education, 188, 217; mentioned, 175, 199, 200, 254, 266, 267, 269, 271–272, 275, 311, 321
Jitsugyō no Teikoku (Empire of Business). See Carnegie, Andrew
Jitsugyō shōnen (Business Youth), 165
jiyū minken undō (movement for liberty and people's rights), 23, 81–82, 101–102
Jiyū no ri (*On Liberty* by J. S. Mill), 23, 28
job market. See placement in job market
jōkyō (going up to Tokyo), 117
"Jukensei no shuki" (Diary of an Examination Taker), 218–219

Kaibara Ekiken, 57n, 59, 74, 256, 327
Kaizō (The Reconstruction), 290, 322
kanson minpi ("honor the official and despise the people"), 101
Karasawa Tomitarō, 296
Karyū shunwa (A Spring Tale of Flowers and Willows), 89–90. See also *Ernest Multravers*
Katayama Sen, 96, 172, 188, 191–193
Katō Hiroyuki, 32–33, 100n, 153, 175
Kegon Falls, 207, 338
Keikoku bidan (Beautiful Tales of Managing a Country), 96
Keiō Gijuku: entrance to, 301, 301n; and *Gakumon no susume*, 45; placement and compensation for graduates of, 304–305; mentioned, 325, 329; and Waseda University, 199
Kido Kōichi, 153
Kikuchi Kan, 215n
Kikutei Kōsui (Satō Kuratarō), 94
Kimura Ki, 89
Kimura Shōshū, 64n
kindaiteki (modern), 343
Kingu (King), 321, 324
Kinoshita Naoe, 180, 224
Kinoshita Tōkichirō, 251, 320. See also Toyotomi Hideyoshi
Kipling, Rudyard, 174

Kitamura Tōkoku, 147–151; mentioned, 79–80, 210, 212, 231, 232, 234, 334
Kitazawa Rakuten, 289
Kōda Rohan, 171n, 174
Kōdansha, 320
Koike Seiichi, 158
Kokumin no tomo (Friend of the People), 103, 108, 134, 154, 221. See also Tokutomi Iichirō
Konjiki yasha (The Miser), 161–162
"Korokke" (Croquette), 281
koshiben (lunch-bucket man; flunky), 277–278, 289, 290, 294n, 322, 328
koshiben-gakumon (law and economics; flunky learning), 294
Kōtoku Denjirō (Shūsui), 172, 174, 181–182, 220, 230
Kozuka Kuya, 174
Krupp, 160
kugaku (study by struggle), 127, 178, 180–183, 276, 322
Kugaku no hanryo (Comrade of the Struggling Student), 181
Kugakukai (Struggling Student World), 178. See also *kugaku*
Kume Masao, 218–219
Kunikida Doppo: as anguished youth, 230–232; his "Hibon naru bonjin" (An Extraordinary Common Man), 257–259
Kuroiwa Ruikō, 180, 181, 224, 226, 247–248
Kusunoki Masashige, 233
Kyōiku jiron (Education Review), 194, 196
kyōkun (instruction), 245
Kyōto Imperial University, 215n, 299–300n

labor. See work
laissez faire, 4, 17
law, study of: placement and compensation for graduates in, 133, 227, 282–283, 294; popularity of, 115–116, 132–133n, 195, 297, 297n
learning (*gakumon*). See study
Lewis, Sinclair, 274
"lifetime employment" (*shūshin koyō*), 319, 319n

INDEX

Lincoln, Abraham, 86, 176, 253, 320
literacy, 34–35, 34n, 45n
literature: as *risshin* substitute, 150–151, 228–230, 245
Lives of the Engineers, 16
"log cabin myth," 340
Longfellow, 108
Looking Out for No. 1, 11
love (*renai*), 147–148, 244. See also *Maihime*; *Tōsei shosei katagi*; *Ukigumo*
lower middle class. See middle class
loyalty, 233
Lu Hsun, 6
Lukes, Stephen, 331n
Lytton, Sir Edward Bulwer. See *Ernest Multravers*

Macaulay, T. B., 86, 106
Maeda Ai, 70, 72, 73
Maeda Hajime, 290, 314, 320
Maihime (Dancing Girl), 142–143, 148
Makino Nobuaki, 243
manabi (learning), 123. See also *benkyō*; study
Manabi no teguruma (Wheelbarrow of Learning), 123
Manabi no tomo (Friend of Learning), 123
Manchuria, 298, 298–299n, 307–308, 346
Mannheim, Karl, 162–163, 337
manufacturers. See businessmen
Marden, Orison Swett, 264–271; mentioned, 3, 202, 231, 274, 276, 332, 342. See also *Pushing to the Front*
Marshall, Byron, 164, 164n
Marumaru chinbum, 62, 62n
Maruyama Masao, 6–7, 163n, 341, 345
Marxism, 6–7, 8, 290–291, 291n
Masamune Hakuchō, 238, 324
materialism. See wealth; wealth and honor
Matsumura Kaiseki, 175
medicine, study of, 295, 297–298, 297–298n, 298n
Meiji Emperor, 32, 76, 175
Meiji Restoration: and anguished youth, 220, 249; and Fukuzawa Yukichi, 48; mentioned, 240, 345;
and samurai, 9–10, 67; "second," 99, 108, 153, 229; and "stabilized social order," 123–124, 136
Mencius, 33–34
merchant class, 34, 165, 261. See also *gōshō*
"merchants of death," 6
Metzger, Thomas A., 31–32
middle class, 7, 7n, 105–106, 109–111, 291n. See also new middle class
middle school: correspondence courses for, 183–184, 187; costs of, 180; examinations in, 216; placement and compensation for graduates of, 131–132, 137, 184, 187, 187n, 194–197, 194–195n, 195n, 196n, 216–218, 271–272; mentioned, 261, 346; scandals, 301n; students, 180, 219
militarism and military: mentioned, 79–80, 100, 184; and Nakamura Keiu, 20–21; and placement, 288, 298, 308, 343n, 345–348
Mill, J. S., 23, 27–28
Ministry of Education (Monbushō), 210, 217, 249
Minyūsha (Friends of the People), 97, 103, 108, 161, 175, 259, 333. See also Tokutomi Iichirō
Mitsubishi, 315, 347
Mitsui, 315
Miyake Yujirō (Setsurei), 332, 338
modernization, 4n
Monbushō. See Ministry of Education
Monbushō nenpō (Ministry of Education Annual Report), 194–195n, 282n
Mori Arinori, 224
Mori Ōgai, 123, 142, 240n
Murakami Senjō, 174
Murakami Shunzō (Dakurō), 166, 166n, 171, 176, 201, 275. See also *Seikō*

Nakakōji Kiyoshi, 275
Nakamura Fusetsu, 178, 223, 226
Nakamura Keiu, 20–24; and Fukuzawa Yukichi, 48, 51, 53, 329–330; mentioned, 10, 44, 71, 72, 73, 89, 123, 171, 260, 306; and

379

INDEX

Tokutomi Iichirō, 102, 104. See also *Saikoku risshi hen*
Nakane Chie, 77
Nakatsu, 45, 47, 48
name, 78, 80, 86, 114, 229
Napoleon, 21, 39, 80, 86, 104, 151, 258
naikin. See *fune narikin*
nationalism: and anguished youth, 214, 228, 232, 232n, 238, 249, 335–337; and individualism, 28, 53, 333; mentioned, 30, 35; and Nakamura Keiu, 23–24, 26–27, 33, 43; and personality ethic, 75, 275–276; and placement, 337; in political novels, 90–91, 95, 96, 97; in *Seikō*, 171, 199, 202–205; and Samuel Smiles, 20–21, 26–27; in student compositions, 76, 82–83, 135; and Takayama Chogyū, 234, 235; and Tokutomi Iichirō, 104, 333–335
Natsume Sōseki, 166, 240n
Neo-Confucianism. See Confucianism
new middle class (*shin-chūtō kaikyū*; *shin-chūsan kaikyū*; *shin-chūkan kaikyū*), 2, 290, 326
Newton, 70
Nichiren, 238, 338
Nietzsche, 211, 212, 214, 236n, 236–239, 247, 332, 338
Nihon no shōnen (Young People of Japan), 133, 134, 139, 221
Nihon Rōdō Nenkan (Japan Labor Yearbook), 288, 289
Nihonjin (The Japanese), 98n, 133, 221–222
Nikkō, 161, 207
Ninomiya Kinjirō (Sontoku), 252–253
nintai. See perseverance
Nishikawa Kōjirō, 172, 244
Nishimura Shigeki, 33, 73, 75
Nissan, 347
Nitobe Inazō, 255–257, 255n, 321
Niwa Jun'ichirō, 88, 89, 90
Noma Seiji, 320
normal schools (*shihan gakkō*). See education, and teaching
"number schools," 124, 300n. See also higher schools

Obata Tokujirō, 45
Oda Nobunaga, 251, 321
Ogawa Tarō, 60
Ogyū Sorai, 38, 43, 50, 52
Oka Yoshitake, 163n
Okada Takeshi, 246
Ōkubo Toshimichi, 153
Ōkuma Shigenobu, 88, 113
Ōkura Kihachirō, 34, 34n, 110
Ōmachi Keigetsu, 64–65n, 242–243
Omoide no ki (A Record of Remembrances), 77–78, 105–106, 110, 214n
Osaka, 5, 47, 94, 117
Ossowski, Stanislaw, 67
Ōsugi Sakae, 245
Ōya Sōichi, 290
Ozaki Kōyō, 161–162
Ozu Yasujirō, 295, 295n

Pacific War, 345. See also World War II
Palissy, Bernard, 16
parliament: in *Eisai shinshi*, 82–83, 86–88; mentioned, 116, 117, 329; and Nakamura Keiu, 27, 329; and political novels, 93, 96; and Tokutomi Iichirō, 98–99, 108–109; and youth, 108–109, 115–116, 117, 130, 229. See also politics; *seiji seinen*
patriotism. See nationalism
Peale, Norman Vincent, 11
peasants. See *gōnō*
perseverance (*nintai*): mentioned, 94, 104, 248; for *sarariiman*, 305, 323; and Samuel Smiles, 13, 15–16; in student compositions, 69–71, 112, 134
personality ethic: in Anglo-American writing, 13, 268, 273; in early Meiji writing, 73–75; in late Meiji writing, 260–261, 272–273, 274–276; mentioned, 74, 107–108, 144, 275; in Taishō-Shōwa writing, 304, 311–314, 317–323; in Tokugawa era writing, 74, 326–327
philosophy, 210, 245, 323
placement in job market: "difficulty" of (*shūshokunan*), 277, 282, 343; in

early Meiji, 75; examinations for, 308–312; guides to, 302–314, 303n, 317–323, 319n; in late Meiji, 184, 187, 187n, 197–198, 215n, 222, 244; mentioned, 328, 339; in mid-Meiji, 131–133, 132n, 221, 224; in Taishō-Shōwa, 278–279, 279n, 280n, 281–289, 282n, 283n, 284n, 285n, 285–286n, 287n, 291–296, 293n, 298, 298–299n, 302–317, 307n, 312n, 312–314n. See also civil service; education, vocational; Gakusei to shūshoku no jissai; middle school; private universities; senmon gakkō; Tokyo Imperial University; unemployment
political novels (seiji shōsetsu): genre analyzed, 88–97; mentioned, 117, 240
political youth. See seiji seinen
politics: and anguished youth, 230, 238, 243–245, 324–325; mentioned, 3–4, 19, 36, 49–50, 68, 309–310; opposition, 345–349; and youth, 81–88, 114–116, 129–130, 324–325. See also political novels; seiji seinen
popular culture, 5, 330
poverty, 17. See also wealth; wealth and honor
Power of Positive Thinking, 11
prices, 222, 283–284
private universities: entrance to, 292n, 297–298, 298n, 301, 301n, 302, 302n; formation of, 291–292, 292n; placement and compensation for graduates of, 292–293, 293n, 298, 302n, 315–316. See also *senmon gakkō*
Protestantism, 31n
Public Speaking and Influencing Men in Business, 273
puchi-buru (petty bourgeoisie), 296
punctuality, 41, 69, 268
Puritanism, 31n
Pushing to the Front, 265–271; mentioned, 3, 231, 326

Rangaku (Dutch Learning), 47

religion. See Buddhism; Christianity
renai. See love
Ringer, Robert J., 11
risshi (lofty ambition), 33–34, 69
risshin shusse (rise in the world): and individualism, 331–339; mentioned, 90, 107–108, 149, 211; usage of the term, 55–58 58n, 162–163, 302n
Risshisha (Society of Lofty Ambition): mentioned, 81, 117, 331; and *Saikoku risshi hen* 35–36, 44
Rockefeller, John D., 191, 339
Rōdō sekai (Labor World), 171–172, 174
Rohlen, Thomas R., 11–12n
romanticism, 237
rōnin (masterless samurai), 196, 196n, 218–220, 218n, 221, 223. See also entrance examinations
Roosevelt, Theodore, 246–247, 332
Russo-Japanese War, 212, 271–272
Ryan, Marleigh, 11–12n

Saigō Takamori, 136, 153
Saikoku risshi hen (*Self-Help* by Samuel Smiles), 20–23 24–43; mentioned, 10, 10n, 44, 45–46n, 54, 65, 69, 71, 88, 94, 95, 96, 175, 231, 250, 257, 330, 331, 333. See also Nakamura Keiu; *Self-Help*; Smiles, Samuel
Sakai Kosen (Toshihiko): on anguished youth, 220, 230, 244; and *Eisai shinshi*, 64–65n; on *kugaku* (study by struggle), 180, 182; on success, 159, 163, 172, 200
Sakura no mi no juku suru toki (Cherry Ripening Time), 91
Salvation Army, 239
samurai: aspirations, 2n, 7, 7–8n, 35, 39, 40, 43, 57–58, 59, 78, 79–80, 118, 327n; defined, 9n, 35; and education, 58–62, 128; ethos, 30, 38n, 42, 66, 72–73, 105; and family system, 77n, 78; and Fukuzawa Yukichi, 48, 52–53; instructions for, 56–57, 57n, 59, 74, 120, 326–327; as *koshiben* (flunkies),

381

INDEX

278, 328–329; mentioned, 1, 57, 64–65, 120, 143, 149, 164, 238, 239, 334; and politics, 35–36, 81, 92, 96–97; and *Saikoku risshi hen*, 10n, 33–43, 34n; and *sarariiman*, 326–329; and Tokutomi Iichirō, 100–102, 103, 105–107, 109; and wealth and honor, 38n, 54, 66–68, 160–161

sangō zasshi (three-number magazine), 123

Santarō Nikki (The Diary of Santarō), 324, 339

sarariiman (white-collar worker; salary man), 277–325, 326–329; advice for, 317–323; compensation of, 314–317; and education, 282–283, 282n, 291–296, 293n, 294n, 296–302; mentioned, 1; numbers of, 278–280, 279n, 280n; placement guides for, 303–312, 314; and samurai, 328–329; scholarship on, 7–8, 291n; origin of term, 289–290, 289n; and unemployment, 284–290, 285–286n, 286n; and World War I boom, 280–284

Sarariiman monogatari (Tale of the Salary Man), 290, 314, 320, 321

sarariiman no jigoku (sarariiman hell), 289, 289–290n

"Sarariiman no kyōfu jidai to sono kaihō" (An Age of Terror for the Sarariiman and His Liberation from It), 290

sarariiman no tengoku (sarariiman heaven), 289, 289–290n

Satō Kuratarō (Kikutei Kōsui), 94. See also *Seirō nikki*

Sawayanagi Masatarō, 249–250

Schwartz, Benjamin, 11–12n

science, study of, 15, 73, 267, 295

secrets of success. See *seikō*

seiji seinen (political youth), 81–116, 82n, 129–130

Seikō (Success), 165–166, 171–172, 174–178, 182–183, 197–205, 274–276; mentioned, 198, 213–214, 217, 245–246, 247, 251–252, 253–254, 259, 266, 271

seikō (success), 162–163. See also

risshin shusse, usage of the term

Seikyōsha (Politics, Education Society), 98n, 161, 175

seinen. See youth

Seirō nikki (Diary of Life), 94–95, 117

Seiyō hinkō ron (*Character* by Samuel Smiles), 23

Seiyō setsuyō ron (*Thrift* by Samuel Smiles), 23

seiza (quiet sitting), 246

Self-Help, 10–20, 42–43; mentioned, 1, 22, 44, 53, 72, 73, 89, 91, 94, 95, 102, 105, 111, 130, 163, 176, 250, 260, 306, 330, 351. See also *Pushing to the Front*; *Saikoku risshi hen*

self-help, 29, 29n

senmon gakkō (college): defined, 132–133, 226n; entrance to, 195n; placement and compensation for graduates of, 221–222, 227, 291; and imperial universities, 132n; popularity of, 133, 195–197, 217; raised to universities, 292, 292n

Setchūbai (Plum Blossoms in the Snow), 93–94, 95

sex, 129, 147, 233

Shakai seisaku jihō (Social Policy Report), 322–323

Shakai shugi (Socialism), 224

Shakespeare, 88

Shelley, 211

Shibusawa Eiichi, 153, 161, 254–255, 339

Shiga Shigetaka, 123, 175

shiken jigoku (examination hell), 1, 124–125, 299–300n. See also entrance examinations

Shimazaki Tōson, 91

Shinkōron (New Review), 242

Shin-Nihon no seinen (Youth of the New Japan), 107–108, 107n, 171

Shirakami Genjirō, 154

shishi (men of lofty ambition), 34, 86, 118

shizen shugi (naturalism), 232

Shōgaku sakubun shinshi (Elementary-School Composition Magazine), 76

Shōheikō (School of Prosperous Peace), 21, 41
shokkaku (eating guest), 181, 187
shokuin (staff employee), 279–280, 280n
Shōnen bunko (A Library for Young People), 123, 128, 139
Shōnen sekai (World of Young People), 140, 153–154, 228, 229
Shōnenen (A Garden for Young People), 123–131; mentioned, 135, 164, 216, 219, 259, 303, 336, 342
Shōrai no Nihon (Future Japan), 99–102, 108
"Shosei bushi" (Song of the Student), 115, 229, 277
shosei (coping with life), 320
shosei (student), 118
shūshin koyō (lifetime employment). See "Japanese employment system"
shūshokunan. See placement in job market, difficulty of
shusse (*yo o deru*; *yo ni deru*). See *risshin shusse*
Shūyō (Cultivation), 256–257
shūyō (cultivation), 256
Sino-Japanese War, 153–154, 157
Smiles, Samuel, 11–20, 266–268; and Andrew Carnegie, 262–264; and Orison Swett Marden, 265, 266–268, 274; mentioned, 1, 3, 10, 39, 70, 91, 95, 102, 123, 127, 130, 140, 201, 332; and political novels, 94–95. See also *Saikoku risshi hen*; *Self-Help*
Smith, Adam, 30, 104
Smith, Henry D., 293, 293n
Smith, Thomas C., 39
S.M.U. (salary men's union), 289
social class. See *gōnō*; *gōshi*; *gōshō*; humble origins; merchant class; middle class; new middle class; samurai; sarariiman
Social Darwinism: in student compositions, 111–112, 134, 137–139; and Fukuzawa Yukichi, 52–53; mentioned, 130, 134, 202, 244; and Tokutomi Iichirō, 100, 100n, 111–112

socialism: and anguished youth, 243–245; and *kugaku* (study by struggle), 180; and Nitobe Inazō, 255; and placement, 309; and *Seikō*, 172, 174, 199–202; and Tokutomi Iichirō, 103; and Yokoi Tokiyoshi, 252
sodomy, 219
sōnin (imperially approved civil servant), 279, 281–282, 284, 298
sōshi (stalwart youth; political bullies), 87–88, 98–99, 102, 129–130, 150
South Manchurian Railway Company, 347
Spaulding, Robert, 312
speech making, 84–85, 92
Spencer, Herbert: and Samuel Smiles, 11–12n; and Tokutomi Iichirō, 100, 100n. See also Social Darwinism
"stabilized social order" (*chitsujo tadashiku naritsuru*): in student compositions, 136, 137–139; defined, 123–124; mentioned, 193, 216, 336, 342. See also *Shōnenen*
"step by step," 254
Stephenson, George, 69, 70
"strenuous life," 246–247
study: in *Eisai shinshi*, 68, 70, 71–73, 112; in *Gakumon no susume*, 46–47; mentioned, 248; and placement, 304, 310; in *Seikō*, 176; "systematic," 137–139. See also wealth and honor
Success, 202, 265. See also Marden, Orison Swett; *Seikō*
success. See achievement ethos, Anglo-American; *seikō*
suicide, 151, 207, 209
suits, 278, 316
"Sukaraa songu" (Scholar song), 278
Sumiya Mikio, 193
"Systematic Study," 137–139, 140, 148–149, 229, 342

Taiyō (The Sun), 159, 226, 232, 235
Takayama Chogyū (Rinjirō), 232–238, 247, 324, 337, 338
Takiguchi Nyūdō, 235
talent. See genius

INDEX

Tanabashi Ichirō, 161
Tanaka Shōzō, 34n
tandeki seinen (decadent youth), 206, 206n, 239
Taoka Reiun, 85, 228–229, 238, 245
Tayama Katai, 240n
teachers. *See* education, and teaching
teate (adjustments), 283. *See also* bonuses
Teikoku Nōkai (Imperial Agricultural Association), 253
Tenjin ron (On Heaven and Man), 247–248
terakoya (common schools), 59
Thrift, 14, 23
time. *See* punctuality
To-Bei (Going to America), 193
Tōdai. *See* Tokyo Imperial University
tokoroten ("pass 'em out"), 215. *See also* entrance examinations
Tokutomi Iichirō (Sohō), 97–113, 115n, 145–148, 234, 242–243, 333–335; and anguished youth, 210; mentioned, 35, 123, 128, 129n, 136, 161, 171, 174–175, 202, 206n, 220, 229, 234, 275, 327
Tokutomi Kenjirō (Roka), 77, 213, 214n, 240n
Tokyo: guides to, 125, 126, 128–129, 219, 274; mentioned, 5, 76, 117, 182, 337; and *Tōsei shosei katagi*, 118–120
Tokyo College (Tōkyō senmon gakkō). *See* Waseda University
Tōkyō gaku (Tokyo Study), 274
Tokyo Imperial University: entrance to, 124–126, 297, 299–300, 299–300n, 300n, 301; placement and compensation for graduates of, 131, 132–133n, 222–223, 223n, 224, 227, 282–283, 286, 293, 300n, 315, 316, 342; mentioned, 61, 116, 118, 120, 131, 158, 215n, 294n, 322
Tōkyō Kōtō Shōgyō Gakkō (Tokyo Higher Business School), 157, 158
Tōkyō Shōka Daigaku (Tokyo University of Business), 297. *See also* education, vocational
Tosa, 35, 81

Tōsei shosei katagi (Character of Present Day Students), 118–120, 141–142
Toyotomi Hideyoshi (Kinoshita Tōkichirō): in *Eisai shinshi* compositions, 86, 136; in ethics texts, 251; mentioned, 151, 160, 236, 254, 258; and personality ethic, 320–321
Travers, Timothy H. E., 11–12n, 26–27
Triple Intervention, 153
Tsubouchi Yūzō (Shōyō), 118, 123, 141. *See also Tōsei shosei katagi*
Tsunajima Ryōsen, 210

Uchida Roan, 64–65n
Uchimura Kanzō, 146, 157, 180, 181
Ukigumo (Floating Clouds), 143–145, 278; mentioned, 162, 229, 264, 275, 327
unemployment: late Meiji, 224, 226–227; Taishō-Shōwa, 284–289, 285–286n, 286n. *See also* placement in job market
universities. *See* education; imperial universities; *senmon gakkō*

Vanderbilt, 159, 160
Vietnam, 347

wages. *See* compensation
Wang Yang-ming, 332
Waseda University: entrance to, 301, 301n; and examination preparation, 300–301; placement and compensation for graduates of, 298, 304–305; and Keiō Gijuku, 199; mentioned, 184, 325; and *Seikō*, 198–199
Washington, George, 86, 236
Watt, James, 69, 70
wealth: in Anglo-American writing, 3–5, 17–18, 19, 44, 91, 103–104, 160–161, 262, 262n, 267; in *Saikoku risshi hen*, 37–38, 44; in late Meiji success literature, 103–104, 157, 159–162, 164–165, 176, 191, 192. *See also* wealth and honor
wealth and honor: in *Eisai shinshi*,

INDEX

65–66, 68, 70, 71–72, 73, 81; in *Gakumon no susume*, 46, 53–54; and Meiji education, 58–59, 75; mentioned, 73, 116, 117, 134, 149, 161, 211, 217, 223, 234, 283; samurai concepts of, 37–38, 38n, 53–54, 54, 66–68, 78, 97; in Tokugawa thought, 50–51
Wellington, 39
Whitman, Walt, 175
women, 24, 44, 92, 93, 329
Wordsworth, 231
work (labor): as *benkyō* (study), 71–73; and Fukuzawa Yukichi, 51, 329; mentioned, 91, 127, 191, 248, 260; and Nakamura Keiu, 42, 329; and samurai, 42, 66; in *Self-Help*, 13, 19–20; and Tokutomi Iichirō, 102–103, 243
World War I: impact of, on *sarariiman*, 280–284; and *Seikō*, 204
World War II: leadership in, 341–345
Wyllie, Irwin G., 6

Yamada Bimyō, 123
Yamada Kyūsaku, 83–85, 93
Yamaga Sokō, 40, 327
Yamagata Teisaburō, 123
Yamaji Aizan, 224, 231
Yamakawa Hitoshi, 34n

Yasuda Zenjirō, 253–254
yatoi (common civil service employee), 278–279, 283–284
Yen Fu, 11–12n
yo ni deru. See *risshin shusse*
yo o deru. See *risshin shusse*
yōfuku-saimin (pauper in a suit), 278, 290
Yokoi Tokiyoshi (Jikei), 251–252
Yokoyama Gennosuke, 178
Yōnen zasshi (Magazine for Children), 139, 140
Yorozu chōhō (Complete Morning News), 180, 181, 182, 226, 247
Yoshida Shōin, 30, 40, 327
youth (*seinen*): defined, 5, 336; Japanese scholarship on, 240n; and Tokutomi Iichirō, 107–108, 112–113, 334–336. *See also* anguished youth; *bungaku seinen*; *seiji seinen*
yowatari (getting along with the world), 320, 320n
Yowatari no michi (Ways of Getting Through the World), 321

Zen, 57–58
zenshū (collected works), 8, 320
Zola, 245

385

Designer:	Sandy Drooker
Compositor:	G & S Typesetters, Inc.
Printer:	Thomson-Shore, Inc.
Binder:	John H. Dekker & Sons, Inc.
Text:	VIP Trump Medieval
Display:	VIP Trump Medieval

Capital University Library
MAIN 301.411 K622
Kinmonth, Earl H.,
The self-made man in Meiji Japanese thou

3 5269 00028302 8

301.411
K622
  Kinmonth, E. H.
    The self-made man in Meiji Japanese
  thought.

301.411
K622

AUTHOR Kinmonth, E. H.

TITLE The self-made man in Meiji Japanese thought.

BORROWER'S NAME

DATE DUE

CAPITAL UNIVERSITY LIBRARY
2199 EAST MAIN STREET
COLUMBUS, OHIO 43209